THE NEOCONSERVATIVE VISION

From the Cold War to the Culture Wars

Mark Gerson

MADISON BOOKS
Lanham • New York • Oxford

Originally printed in hardcover in 1996 by Madison Books.

Published by Madison Books
4720 Boston Way
Lanham, Maryland 20706

12 Hid's Copse Road
Cummor Hill, Oxford OX2 9JJ, England

Distributed by National Book Network

The Library of Congress has cataloged the hardcover edition as follows:

Gerson, Mark.
The neoconservative vision : from the Cold War to the culture wards /
Mark Gerson.
p. cm.
Includes bibliographical references and index.
1. Conservatism—United States. I. Title.
JC573.2.U6G47 1996
320.5'2'0973—dc20 *95-31521*
CIP

ISBN 1-56883-054-5 (cloth: alk. paper)
ISBN 1-56833-100-2 (pbk. : alk. paper)

™ *The paper used in this publication meets the minimum requirements of American National Standard for Information Sciences—Permanence of Paper for Printed Library Materials, ANSI Z39.48–1984.*
Manufactured in the United States of America.

To my mother and father
With love, gratitude, and devotion

Contents

Acknowledgments

My first contact with neoconservative thought came during my freshman year in college, thanks to a great friend, Jon Fielder. Jon gave me my first issue of every journal and magazine discussed in this book and introduced me to the work of almost every thinker discussed in the following pages. Without this start and Jon's constant intellectual companionship, it is safe to say this book would never have been conceived, let alone completed.

The same can be said for Williams College Professor Jeff Weintraub, my teacher and mentor. Because Jeff is something of a cross between an oracle and an encyclopedia, a conversation with him might go from warrior aristocracies to Smithian economics to the latest essay by Gertrude Himmelfarb—all the while illuminating, simplifying, and explaining the topic at hand. In so doing, he shows the common links in disparate ideas and events, making the incomprehensible coherent and the intellectual enterprise a great pleasure. Generous with his genius, Jeff spent countless hours of discussion and hundreds of letters helping me to refine, develop, or challenge each argument or idea I considered including in this book. His stunning brilliance, truly great teaching, warm kindness, and endless patience have affected me in more ways than I will perhaps ever know. I am blessed to be his student and his friend.

I would also like to thank the rest of the Williams College Political Science Department, especially Gary J. Jacobsohn. Though almost every member of the department is significantly to the left of the neoconservatives and of me, they could not have been more encouraging of my efforts. Because I do not want anybody to get in trouble, I will not publish how many regulations they lifted, rules they bent, or grants they gave so that I would be able to pursue the study of neoconservatism to the best of my ability. These professors are a living manifestation of what liberalism was, and provide a vivid example of what it once again can be.

I would like to acknowledge several friends, colleagues, and teachers who have helped this project through their close reading and trenchant criticism of various drafts along the way. Special thanks go to Paige Baty, James McGregor Burns, Don Carlson, Kristin Daley, Brian Duchin, Susan Dunn, Sam Fleischacker, Dan Greenberg, Daniel Greene, Mike Hennessy, Laurence Herman, Neil Horne, David Kensinger, Joe Ketchum, Jon Kowallis, George Marcus, Ben Morehead, Rebecca Olshin, Jorge Pedraza, Jason Poling, Shawn Raymond, David Ruder, Julie Burnham Ruder, Jim Rutherford, Joseph Sadighi, Adam Scheer, Matt Scott, Wendy Shalit, Tim Watson, Jay Webber and Alan Wolfe.

Many thanks are also extended to several other people who, through their knowledge, experience, and insight have helped immeasurably at numerous stages throughout the book: Matthew Berke, Tucker Carlson, Dan Mahoney, Adam Meyerson, John Renna, and Noah Pickus. I also extend my gratitude to my brother, Rick, who showed an early manuscript to his professor, Rabbi David Novak, who in turn had me send it to Madison Books. At Madison Books, I am indebted to Jon Sisk and Julie Kirsch for their great help and to Lynn Gemmell for her meticulous editing.

I would also like to thank the people who gave of their time to be interviewed for this book: Elliott Abrams, William Bennett, William F. Buckley Jr., Midge Decter, Edwin Feulner, Carl Gershman, Gertrude Himmelfarb, Irving Kristol, William Kristol, Joshua Muravchik, Richard John Neuhaus, Michael Novak, Martin Peretz, Norman Podhoretz, Jude Wanniski, George Weigel, and James Q. Wilson.

Finally, a debt of eternal gratitude is due my parents, Susan and Michael Gerson. Words like gratitude, support, even love, all sound woefully inadequate here; suffice it to say that if I knew what to say, I would be a Nobel Prize-winning poet.

1

Introduction to Neoconservative Thought

For me, then, "neo-conservatism" was an experience of moral, intellectual, and spiritual liberation. I no longer had to pretend to believe—what in my heart I could no longer believe—that liberals were wrong because they subscribe to this or that erroneous opinion on this or that topic. No—liberals were wrong, liberals are wrong, because they are liberals. What is wrong with liberals is liberalism—a metaphyics and a mythology that is woefully blind to human and political reality. Becoming a neo-conservative, then, was the high point in my cold war.—Irving Kristol, 1993.

Ideological labels are a reality without a constituency. Politicians consider them too restrictive; having a label attached to one's beliefs alienates people who, for whatever reason, eschew the label. Intellectuals think labels are too inclusive: how, the intellectual asks, can I be a liberal or a conservative or a radical when that enemy of all right reason, Jones, is? William F. Buckley, a forthright American conservative, put it best when he wrote,

> One is never entirely satisfied, for reasons of vanity, with any label that presumes to describe one's own political philosophy. Somehow, one's own position, so delicately sculpted, so majestic in its implications, is . . . impoverished . . . by such labels as are appropriate to describe the positions of one's cruder associates.[1]

The endurance of labels in light of their lack of popularity is a triumph of necessity over vanity. A person's ideas, positions, prejudices, party affiliation, way of approaching social questions—in short, his *Weltanschauung*—do not develop in a vacuum; they are not born of themselves. Even the most nuanced and sophisticated thinkers are attached to specific tradition of thought and develop from studying with others in that same tradition or, more crudely but no less accurately put, those covered by the same label.

It should come as no surprise that intellectual development is a social process that, almost like an invisible hand, guides people of like minds together to the point where they are considered by others to be a group worthy of a unifying label. This is not to say that all people covered by such a label think alike; of course there are differences, even significant differences among individuals in any group. This is so in any field of human endeavor, and certainly does not exclude the intellectual life. But this difference does not necessarily work against unity or even cohesion. Jazz fans may vigorously dispute whether Louis Armstrong or Frank Sinatra is the greater vocalist, but such fans will likely close ranks against partisans of rock or rap. Thought can be considered similarly; differences of opinion, outlook, and emphasis within a particular intellectual school or movement often help to develop and nurture—not alienate—others with the same affiliation. Groups of thinkers who remain unchallenged grow sterile; conflict and argument are the bare necessities of a healthy intellectual life.

Nonetheless, Americans, perhaps more than any other people, object to political labels with a curious ferocity. Does this attitude derive from the frontier individualism embedded in the American character—that sustained sense of autonomy and uniqueness? Probably to some extent. There is also a rather high-brow argument sometimes advanced against labels—that labels on this side of the Atlantic are meaningless when put in historical perspective. And there is a point to this. It is almost a cliché to say that there is no real conservatism in the United States because there is no feudal heritage of order, hierarchy, and social position. But, as James Burnham wrote in *Suicide of the West*, "I have great respect . . . for many of the old clichés. The plain, platitudinous, commonsense opinion is very often the true opinion, stripped down to essentials."[2] That is the case here. America was born out of the distinctly nonconservative act of revolution and never had much use for the more traditional mores of the Old World. Allegiance to monarchy or aristocracy, ties to rank and station, even respect based on position rather than character—all of these attributes of medieval European conservatism were dumped into the Boston waters along with the tea, if not long before.

This does not obviate the use of labels; actually, it makes them more important because they are less self-evident. While Peter

Berger is correct in maintaining that "The contemporary American ideology of conservatism is deeply and unmistakably liberal in inspiration,"[3] the idea of American conservatism—even a deeply and unmistakably liberal conception of it—is perfectly legitimate. Is this contradictory, perhaps a little confusing? Maybe. But it does not really matter; labels are not revelations of truth, they are products of convenience. A label merely serves the purpose of separating schools of thought and providing a general rubric under which individuals can develop intellectually and align politically.

Because labels do not signify metaphysical truth, trying to define them with exacting precision is not usually necessary or possible. Even William Buckley, who has spent a considerable part of his distinguished career defining the basis for the word "conservatism" through his writings and his status as a cultural icon, concedes that even he cannot easily define his own label. "I could not give you a definition of Christianity in one sentence, but that does not mean that Christianity is undefinable," he replies by analogy. Nonetheless, we can recognize whether an individual is a conservative or a liberal in the course of a simple discussion. Buckley attests to this.

> I feel I know, if not what conservatism is, at least who a conservative is. I . . . know who is a liberal. Blindfold me, spin me like a top, and I will walk up to the single liberal in the room without zig or zag and find him even if he is hiding behind the flower pot.[4]

As Buckley suggests, it is not difficult to distinguish between liberals and conservatives in American politics, though many of each contend that their politics are too sophisticated to be compartmentalized with the label. Labels, even applied to people who repudiate them, are often meaningful—as is proven by the fact that people react to them, almost instinctually and sometimes viscerally. If a liberal comes into a room and starts talking like a liberal, no doubt a panoply of assumptions, prejudices, arguments, and ideas—positive or negative—will rush to the head of almost any listener. This identical reaction would probably be produced if the same individual entered a room and simply declared, "I am a liberal," saying nothing else. In short, despite the difficulty of readily defining them, the labels of liberal and conservative remain useful—even indispensable—for understanding much of American political thought. They point to genuine realities even if these realities are messy and complex.

There is one label in American political discourse that evades simple characterization and often invites inaccuracy when it is characterized. This is the term "neoconservative," which has been applied broadly to a prominent group of largely Jewish intellectuals who, once *considered* to be on the left, are now on the right. The central figure of neoconservatism (often called the godfather) is Irving Kristol. He is joined in varying degrees by a host of other intellectuals, all of whom will be discussed in this book. Included in this consideration are Gertrude Himmelfarb, Midge Decter, Norman Podhoretz, George Weigel, Jeane Kirkpatrick, Michael Novak, Richard John Neuhaus, James Q. Wilson, Joshua Muravchik, Daniel Patrick Moynihan, Nathan Glazer, Daniel Bell, Ruth Wisse, Arnold Beichman, Walter Lacquer, Milton Himmelfarb, Elliot Abrams, Peter Berger, William Bennett, Thomas Sowell, Ben Wattenberg, Sidney Hook, Brigette Berger, Aaron Wildavsky, George Gilder, Samuel Lipman, Saul Bellow, Roger Kimball, Joseph Epstein, Hilton Kramer, Seymour Martin Lipset, Paul Johnson, Murray Friedman, Leon Kass, James Nuechterlein, Carl Gershman, Penn Kemble, and Martin Peretz. Others who are closely aligned with the neoconservatives but are, for different reasons, more properly labeled conservative (without a prefix) are William Kristol, Hadley Arkes, Robert Nisbet, George Will, Mary Ann Glendon, and David Novak. A sister group, the Straussians, includes Harvey Mansfield, Allan Bloom, Walter Berns, and Werner Dannhauser.

How is the list of neoconservatives determined? Admittedly, not very scientifically. No one has ever been able to give sufficient definition of the term neoconservative, but this is no shame considering Buckley's luck with an easier term. Some neoconservatives edit journals, some teach in universities, some work in think tanks and several hold chairs at the American Enterprise Institute. But lots of people who are not neoconservative do those things. As a preliminary guideline, suffice it to say that if an intellectual writes regularly for *Commentary* or *The Public Interest*, he is a neoconservative. If he writes for *Policy Review, The New Criterion, First Things, Crisis, The American Spectator, Forbes, Fortune, The American Scholar, The American Enterprise, The National Interest, National Review, Public Opinion, Society, Foreign Affairs, The Washington Quarterly,* he might be—better cross-reference him with *Commentary* and *The Public Interest.*

What about books? Yes, the neoconservatives have written books—including several seminal books—but as the first serious analyst of neoconservatism, Peter Steinfels, noted, "the geography of the intellectuals' world is a geography of journals."[5] Irving Kristol, for instance, has never written a full-length book—his four books are collections of essays. And, almost always, neoconservatives' books are based on essays they have previously published in their magazines.

The magazines of neoconservatism have—and always have had—low circulations. The circulations of the main neoconservative journals are all under 30,000. The neoconservatives readily admit that their enterprise is an elitist one; they have no intention of reaching the vast majority of people directly. They want engaged readers, especially those who have intellectual and political influence. Richard John Neuhaus, editor in chief of *First Things,* maintains,

> I'd edit *First Things* for five hundred readers, if I could pick the five hundred readers. But obviously I can't; I need 30,000 so that I can have the five hundred that I want. Now that sounds frightfully elitist. And of course it is. The intellectual life is an elitist enterprise. And intellectuals who are embarrassed by that or attempt to deny it are simply being foolish.[6]

The five hundred that Neuhaus—and his writers and colleagues—want are the opinion makers and the policy makers. It is through these people that the ideas in the journals are disseminated to millions of Americans. The ultimate odyssey of an article is as follows. While this example is hypothetical, similar paths have been followed numerous times.

John Doe writes an article on welfare reform and single mothers for *The Public Interest.* William Raspberry of the *Washington Post* devotes a column to it, and a *Wall Street Journal* editorial questions Raspberry's interpretation two days later. George Will is intrigued by the article, devotes a *Newsweek* column to it, and invites Doe to appear on *This Week With David Brinkley*, where Doe is questioned by Will, Brinkley, and Sam Donaldson before a national audience. *The New York Times* condenses the article into an op-ed, and runs it the next Sunday. Pretty soon, Doe receives speaking engagements from around the nation, and is able to explain his insight to thousands of people directly. Public officials from both parties call him for advice, and Doe is invited to testify before Congress. If the timing is right, Doe may receive a phone call from the president of the United States offering a high appointment. After all this, maybe only 10,000 people may have read Doe's article—but his main idea is conveyed in one form or another to millions of others.

Philosophical Roots and Intellectual Ties

What is the theoretical and ideological orientation that ties this group of intellectuals together? A number of serious commentators have denied that any such a unifying orientation exists. For example, the distinguished political sociologist Seymour Martin Lipset has written,

> Neoconservatism, both as an ideological term and as political grouping, is one of the most misunderstood concepts in the political lexicon. The reason is simple. The word has never referred to a set of doctrines to which a given group of adherents subscribed. Rather, it was invented as an invidious label to undermine political opponents, most of whom have been unhappy with being so described.[7]

Though Lipset speaks with unusual authority on these matters, I would argue that this statement is only partially correct. While it may not refer to a set of doctrines, the term neoconservative does in fact capture a genuine political grouping with a coherent and distinctive ideological orientation. Lipset is correct in saying both that neoconservatism is grossly misunderstood and that it was originally conceived as an insult; the socialist Michael Harrington first used it as a criticism in a 1973 *Dissent* article. However, a lot of labels throughout history have originated in scorn; for instance, the artistic category "impressionist" was coined by a disgruntled critic who thought the Impressionists were undisciplined dilettantes. Thinkers have often made the decision to accept labels derived in insult and to define it for themselves: for instance, Irving Kristol and the term "neoconservative." Kristol explains, "It usually makes no sense—and this, by the way, the left has always known—to argue over nomenclature. If you can, you take what people call you and run with it."[8]

As Kristol suggests, the genesis of a label is usually unimportant for the integrity of the group to which it refers. Instead, the significant question is, "Does the group being labeled have a coherent and distinct intellectual framework?" This intellectual framework is not always easily appreciated or even understood. But that does not matter, for popularity is hardly a test of truth. A coherent and distinctive intellectual framework can be mangled, caricatured, misinterpreted, or denied by people on all sides of the political spectrum—and remain as coherent and distinctive as ever. Neoconservatism is the perfect example of this.

Lipset is also correct in stating that discussion of neoconservatism tends to be invidious as well as perplexed. The left considers neoconservatism with a curiosity that easily transfers into animosity; there is something about neoconservatism that often drives otherwise intelligent liberals into a frenzy. The left does not know quite what to make of the neoconservatives; the left perceives the neoconservatives as an undeniably intelligent and influential group of thinkers who speak their language, cite their sources—in short, understand them perfectly—but almost always come down on the wrong side.

The right, too, traditionally had a difficult time understanding the neoconservatives. While there is now a broad conservative consensus on most issues, the neoconservatives continue to accept the welfare state, though not in its present incarnation. This is troubling to many conservatives, who have long regarded the infringement of government into the economy as a negation of freedom and the first step in what Friederich von Hayek called the road to serfdom. Nonetheless, most on the right have come to realize that the neoconservatives are extraordinarily effective in challenging the left and, at a minimum, have come to appreciate the power of neoconservative social science in illustrating the failure of sweeping government programs.

And the neoconservatives themselves? In 1979, when neoconservatives were the most discussed group of American intellectuals in the postwar period, Irving Kristol wrote, "I myself have accepted the term [neoconservative], perhaps because, having been named Irving, I am relatively indifferent to baptismal caprice. But I may be the only living and self-confessed neoconservative, at large or in captivity."[9] As Kristol suggests, the other neoconservatives for a long time wanted nothing to do with the label. They had never viewed themselves as conservatives; they did not know anyone who called himself a conservative and probably—with the exceptions of Gertrude Himmelfarb and Irving Kristol—would have been as surprised to meet one as they would have been to meet a Martian. In the past fifteen years, many of the neoconservatives have embraced the label, but a few (notably Daniel Bell) are lifelong deniers. And while the neoconservatives always realized that they formed a distinctive school of thought, they never named it, and thus never had to clarify or defend it. As Nathan Glazer has written, "There is hardly one of us who has written an article explaining what neoconservatism is."[10] And they could not speak about a label whose existence they largely did not recognize.

Aside from the fact that the neoconservatives have never offered a comprehensive defense of neoconservatism per se, there are several reasons why neoconservatism has been so widely misunderstood. Most of them have to do not so much with neoconservatism itself, but with the limitations of the categories most used in contemporary American political discourse—liberalism and conservatism. Whereas neoconservatism rejects the liberal notion that a society of atomized individuals pursuing their interests and following their desires will somehow lead to the common good, neoconservatism insists on the liberal idea that involuntary characteristics such as race, rank, and station should never restrain an individual. Likewise, while neoconservatism rejects the traditional conservative emphasis on the authority of tradition and glorification of the past, it shares conservative concerns with order, continuity, and community.

Does this mean that neoconservatism simply picks and chooses what it wants from liberalism and conservatism? No; many of these apparently disparate themes derive from a distinctive and important current of social and political thought which is not reducible to either liberalism or conservatism but is a part of the republican virtue tradition.[11] The republican virtue tradition has always stressed that political liberty requires the moral foundation of a virtuous citizenry; that political virtue includes both the capacity for association and an active concern for the common good; and that these virtues are, in turn, nurtured by participation in a free community. While this mode of thinking about society and politics may now seem unfamiliar to many, it is one on which the Founding Fathers drew quite naturally, and its greatest expositor is Alexis de Tocqueville. It is a striking fact that practically every important neoconservative argument is anticipated at some level by Tocqueville. The difficulties democracies have in combating totalitarian threats, the indispensability of religious morality for both social order and political liberty, the significance of mores, the importance of mediating structures, and other major neoconservative arguments are all essential themes in *Democracy in America*.[12]

Many of the key organizing themes of neoconservative thought, which I will attempt to elucidate in later chapters, cease to appear inchoate, opportunistic, or merely eclectic when they are placed in the historical context of the republican virtue tradition. In particular, an emphasis on individual liberty is not peculiar to liberalism, nor are community and virtue exclusively conservative ideas; rather their essential interdependence has always been emphasized within the republican virtue tradition. This fundamental relationship is captured in what the sociologist Jeff Weintraub has termed its distinctive conception of "willed community."[13]

Freedom and community are sometimes posited in both liberal and conservative thought as opposing forces that have to be compromised and reconciled in order for society to exist. The republican virtue tradition rejects this notion; it maintains that individual freedom is nourished and exercised in communities, which are created and maintained by the voluntary commitments of individuals. Accordingly, there is nothing inherently repressive about shared values and common goals and nothing inherently decadent in diversity and pluralism. This powerful combination of freedom and virtue is gracefully encapsulated in Weintraub's phrase, "the creative potential of collective action."[14] As this book will demonstrate, all the antagonists of neoconservatism have negated this vision by either stressing freedom at the expense of community or stressing community at the expense of freedom. Likewise, several of the most interesting and influential neoconservative arguments speak directly to the creative potential of molding freedom and community; prominent examples include the discussions of capitalism (covered in Chapter 5) and mediating structures (Chapter 6).[15]

I believe that much of the misunderstanding about which Lipset writes derives at some level from the lack of informed awareness that the republican virtue tradition is given in current political discourse. The ideas—and the labels—of liberalism and conservatism are so ingrained in the American political psyche that even our most distinguished thinkers have confused key concepts by missing the ways these concepts are rooted in the republican virtue tradition. This point is inadvertently brought out in a critical essay on neoconservatism by the distinguished leftist political philosopher Michael Walzer in 1979. Walzer raises the following criticism in a discussion of Daniel Bell:

> "The foundation of any liberal society," Bell has written, "is the willingness of all groups to compromise private ends for the public interest." Surely that is wrong; at least, it is not what leading liberal theorists have told us. The root conviction of liberal thought is that the uninhibited private pursuit of private ends . . . will produce the greatest good for the greatest number. . . . From this maximizing game, however, large numbers of men and women . . . were once excluded. They were too poor, too weak, too frightened. It is in this exclusion, I suspect, which figures in neoconservative writing as the moderation and civility of times gone by.[16]

While Walzer is correct to criticize Bell's attribution of concern for the common good to the liberal tradition, he does not clearly specify the alternative. Thus, Walzer seems to suggest, unfairly, that Bell's uneasiness about a general free-for-all of conflicting interests must imply a preference for a society in which some groups are unable to press their interests in the public arena. Working implicitly with only the categories of liberalism and conservatism, Walzer reduces the neoconservative outlook to an anxious and incomplete liberalism that seeks to shore up the instability of the shaking edifice of changing desires, passions, and interests. The very title of Walzer's review essay, "Nervous Liberals," reveals his reading of neoconservatism.

But the neoconservatives are neither nervous nor liberal. There is nothing incoherent about simultaneously recognizing the legitimacy of particular interests and arguing that they need to be moderated by an overarching concern for the common good. This combination is, in fact, the hallmark of any serious conception of civic virtue. What Bell's formulation makes clear, in effect, is the extent to which neoconservatism is a quintessential embodiment of the republican virtue tradition. The idea of groups voluntarily sacrificing legitimate private ends to serve the public interest is precisely what is implied in the conception of the "willed community."

The idea of willed community in the republican virtue tradition elucidates many aspects of neoconservatism which have been called by its critics contradictory, paradoxical, or hypocritical. Throughout the past half-century, neoconservatives have been asked questions such as: How can you support pride in ethnicity and oppose affirmative action? How can you support free market capitalism and accept a welfare state? How can you be for religious orthodoxy and religious pluralism? How can you be for democratic freedom and want to criminalize the Communist Party? How can you be for free speech and want to censor pornography? By redefining notions of liberal and conservative and reinterpreting notions of the parochial and the universal, the neoconservatives have demonstrated how to do so, consistently and with principle.

Neoconservatism represents a coherent theoretical and ideological perspective; the question that logically follows is: "What kind of interpretative approach can best capture and clarify that coherence?" According to the sociologist Karl Mannheim, there are two ways to write about social and political thought.[17] The first, which he calls the "narrative" method, focuses on individual thinkers, demonstrating how ideas pass from one thinker to the next within a particular group or label. The other method, the analysis of "styles of thought," analyzes how ideas "develop, fuse and disappear,"[18] over time and through experience. The study of styles of thought is launched from the premise that people think in patterns which they do not develop by themselves. These patterns are fairly malleable; individuals working within them will, almost by definition, work to adapt and transform them. The adaptation of ideas within a tradition is integral to the nature of thought. This notion of creative thinking within a broader pattern of thought is posited against the narrative method, which does not place primacy on the social and intellectual milieu from which thinkers derive.

In the past fifteen years, there has been a flood of material about neoconservatives, almost all of it written in the narrative method. Nearly every major magazine, every intellectual journal, and several books have published material profiling a particular neoconservative or discussing the neoconservatives as a group. While many of these works are interesting to read and provide useful information, there is something missing from all of them—and this is not necessarily the fault of the research, writing, or even analysis of the author. It is the fault of the narrative method the author utilizes; the neoconservatives he discusses usually emerge as interesting and influential thinkers, but only loosely aligned to a larger movement, broader tradition, and comprehensive style.

It is tempting to analyze neoconservatism using the narrative method because the neoconservatives are extraordinary eclectic. Michael Novak, for instance, has written major books on economics, religion, sports, welfare policy, and moral philosophy. One could easily devote a college course or a dissertation to Novak's thought. However, much will be lost in an analysis of Novak's work without a consideration of Irving Kristol's role at the American Enterprise Institute, Joseph Schumpeter's discussion of intellectuals, Richard John Neuhaus's book, *The Naked Public Square*, Nathan Glazer's work on ethnicity, Reinhold Niebuhr's conception of original sin, and George Weigel's writings on Catholicism. Can all of this be accomplished in a chapter on Novak specifically? Maybe a very long chapter, but it would quickly cease to be about just Novak when all these surrounding influences are adequately explored. It would be about a style of thought, neoconservatism.

Neoconservatism lends itself very well to a study using Mannheim's style of thought method. Most neoconservatives consider themselves as part of an intellectual pattern, and view the ideas of the other neoconservatives as integral to their work. No neoconservative I interviewed discussed his or her work without extensive reference to Irving Kristol. This is no coincidence. Neoconservatives know that they are part of a unique movement, building off a base of distinct principle, with Kristol a few years in front of the rest in his thinking.[19] Neoconservatives, of course, have pride and confidence in their own work, but they see themselves as inseparable members of an intellectual community. Part of the unwritten code of this community is that there is to be no competition between neoconservative journals, which cater to similar though not identical audiences. Neoconservatives want to articulate the ideas they develop together and do not especially care how it is done or who receives the credit. George Weigel says,

> There is a kind of Henry V quality about all this. "We few, we happy few, we band of brothers." I mean, that really is true. [We are] people who have been together in a great moral cause. . . . It just forms very lasting bonds of affection. The other thing is that this is just a lot of friends. There are some very intense friendships here. I don't think there is any great mystery about that. These are all very interesting people, it seems to me. We're shmoozers.[20]

Instead of focusing on neoconservatives, this book purports to demonstrate the ideas, developments, and style of neoconservatism. That is as much by necessity as by choice. Irving Kristol once wrote that the American Founders were a very unusual group of revolutionaries, at least in one sense: "The men who made the revolution were the men who went on to create the new political order, who then held the highest elected positions in this order, and who all died in bed. Not very romantic, perhaps. Indeed positively prosaic."[21] Something similar can be said about the neoconservatives. Surely, one of the best parts of intellectual histories concerns the sexual and personal politics among the various players. Mary McCarthy slept with how many truck drivers before she married Edmund Wilson and then left him for Philip Rahv? For better or for worse, there is none of that here. Unlike most other groups of intellectuals (any number of schools in Paris, the New York intellectuals), the neoconservatives have lived remarkably unscandalous personal lives. They have generally married young, had children, stayed married, and maintained close nuclear and extended families. In that sense, it is not surprising that they began to explore and celebrate the bourgeois virtues with such ease in the final stage of neoconservatism. All they had to do was to examine their own lives, with which they seem to be pretty satisfied.

Neoconservatism is a unique and interesting school of thought because it is primarily a philosophical movement that has political relevance. The neoconservatives came to politics through moral ideas, not the other way around. That helps to explain why neoconservatism can change without sacrificing intellectual integrity, and elucidates the concerns of critics of neoconservative political positions.

Many labels in America apply specifically to certain political or cultural positions. Hear the term "conservative" and one automatically thinks of low taxes, high military spending, strict interpretation of the Constitution, and traditional values. Remove any one of those pillars, and the label "conservative" no longer applies. Or take an even broader term, "liberal." What comes to mind? An activist central government, expansive personal autonomy, a broad reading of the Constitution, and a hesitancy toward overseas military involvement. Take away one of those pillars and the appellation "liberal" loses much of its significance.

Now, select any number of issues. Does a person believe in the unrestricted right to an abortion? He's a liberal. Does someone want to abolish the National Endowment for the Arts? He's a conservative. Does someone want to purge Christmas displays from Town Hall? He's a liberal. Does someone believe that high schools should distribute condoms? He's a liberal, too. How about someone who favors extensive privatization of government services? He is a conservative. This list could—and does—go on indefinitely.

But try doing it with the term neoconservative. On second thought, don't, because it cannot be done. There is not one political position that can be considered distinctly neoconservative. There are modes of thought, styles of reasoning, and ways of analyzing the social world, but no distinctive political positions. As James Q. Wilson has said,

> There is no such thing as a neoconservative manifesto, credo, religion, flag, anthem, or secret handshake. As a tendency, it is shot through with inner tensions. The magazines to which I contribute are edited and written by people who in most cases are aware of these tensions and usually find easy answers hard to come by. This often leads to the statement that neoconservatives never favor anything. That's untrue. But they are rarely in favor of things that can be stated simply. Neoconservatism is a mood, not an ideology. . . .[22]

Neoconservatism has political implications because the major neoconservative editors—Irving Kristol, Norman Podhoretz, Hilton Kramer, Joseph Epstein, and Richard John Neuhaus—select people to write for their journals who extrapolate political ideas from certain philosophical premises. In his analysis of conservative philosophical thought, Mannheim (unwittingly, of course) described the relationship between neoconservative philosophy and politics perhaps better than anyone who has tried directly.

> There is no means of knowing in advance what form a "conservative" action in the political sense will take . . . . How a conservative will react can only be determined approximately if we know a good deal about the conservative movement in the period and in the country under discussion. . . . Acting along conservative lines . . . involves more than automatic responses of a certain type; it means that the individual is consciously or unconsciously guided by a way of thinking and acting which has its own history behind it, before it comes into contact with the individual. . . . No *a priori* deductions can be made from the "principles" of conservatism.[23]

Principles and Ancestors

The neoconservative style of thought upon which its politics is based derives from four fundamental principles, three of which can be linked to a specific intellectual ancestor. This not to say that the principles go straight from the ancestor to the neoconservative, in the mode of, say, God and Moses. But ideas never work so directly; as Lord Acton wrote, "Ideas have a radiation and development, an ancestry and posterity of their own, in which men play the part of godfathers and godmothers more than that of legitimate parents."[24] The principles of neoconservatism have been discussed for thousands of years, and have had many great interpreters who have influenced the neoconservatives. It is the application of the idea to the intellectual, social, and political life of modern America that is derived from the ancestor. The ancestors made these principles vivid to the neoconservatives by coordinating the principles within the context of American social and political life. In essence, the ancestors provided the neoconservatives with an interpretative framework with which to understand and utilize venerated principles. Each principle yields at least two major derivations, which are listed below the principles.

(1) *Life is infinitely complex.* This idea and its implications were promulgated by Lionel Trilling, perhaps America's greatest literary critic. Trilling, the mentor to Norman Podhoretz and a friend and inspiration to Midge Decter, Irving Kristol, and Gertrude Himmelfarb, taught that the human predicament must be analyzed with a critical eye and a humble mind. Because man knows so little about the world, his ability to change it is limited.

(a) This appreciation of complexity has always led the neoconservatives to be very suspicious of sweeping policy programs. Because the intricacies of human action cannot be understood even by the actors themselves, there is no way that social engineering from a central source can ever work.

(b) Likewise, the neoconservatives warn that people should beware of plans or blueprints to remake society. Such strategies will inherently be blunt and external, whereas human problems are nuanced and usually derive from internal sources.

(c) While social institutions may not seem rational to the human eye, they embody inherited wisdom garnered as a result of their longevity. As a result, man should approach social institutions with reverence, knowing that they serve mankind in ways that are often more essential than they are obvious. This derivation comes directly out of *Reflections on the Revolution in France* by Edmund Burke. Many neoconservative ideas are significantly influenced by European conservatives, especially Burke, Tocqueville, Acton, and Michael Oakeshott.

(2) *Man can be good, but man can also be evil.* This idea was forcefully enunciated by Reinhold Niebuhr, the great theologian of the Cold War. A tremendous influence on Irving Kristol and Michael Novak especially, Niebuhr's significance is articulated in Novak's 1972 *Commentary* article, "Needing Niebuhr Again." The core of this concept is epitomized in a line from Niebuhr's seminal work, *The Children of Light and the Children of Darkness*. "It is man's capacity for justice that makes democracy possible, but it is his tendency to injustice that makes it necessary."[25]

(a) Good and evil do not operate on equal terms. Children of light, always searching for the generous qualities in others and possessing a faith in human intentions, are often no match for children of darkness, who prey on the naiveté of their often soft-headed opponents.

(b) The children of light must overcome their natural tendency to see only the good in others. Not everyone has the same intentions, and the examination of intentions is necessary, though sometimes messy. This is crucial because the failure to correctly identify destructive forces is the first step to being conquered, or at least infiltrated, by the children of darkness. Furthermore, the children of the light must do more than just identify their enemies; they must sometimes be willing to confront them with the only language understood by the children of darkness—physical force.

(3) *Man is a social animal.* This idea, derived especially from the post-World War II American rediscovery of Tocqueville, has influenced the neoconservative conception of the importance of community consecrated by shared values and mores. This understanding was augmented by the great teacher and philosopher at

the University of Chicago in the mid-century, Leo Strauss, who argued that man is, in the Aristotelian sense, a political animal. In defending classical philosophy against what he considered to be the ravages of modernity, Strauss stressed the indispensability of virtue for any political community. Social institutions are meaningful, but nothing can take the place of individuals with moral characters striving to work together to create a community of virtue.

(a) Communities make claims on the autonomy of man. Freedom is an essential good, but it must serve the larger end of societal virtue. Freedom is not an end in itself; it is a means to serve virtue, which is nurtured and developed through communities.

(b) Social institutions must work to inculcate virtue and prepare man to live the good life both in private and as a citizen in the public sphere. This is the crucial component of civilization; correspondingly, whatever institutions best serve this purpose should be encouraged and aided in every possible way.

(c) Politics and economics are functions of culture. Any system or set of ideas that purports to replace the workings of culture (mores, traditions, systems of authority, relationships) with anything political or economic is bound to fail. The failure will not be incidental: either it will take the form of mass human suffering or it will leave man in a state of spiritual torpor. And when man is not spiritually satisfied, he will be prone to turn to forces that, despite preaching a message of human fulfillment through community, will deliver mass human suffering.

(4) *Ideas rule the world.* Marxists and libertarians are economic determinists, the current academic left is gender, race, or sexual determinist, and the neoconservatives are, if anything, ideological determinists. This is the most important principle of neoconservatism because it determines how a society is going to understand and act upon the other three. This emphasis on the crucial importance of ideas and intellectuals—for good or for ill—cannot be traced to a single source, though it is best articulated in Tocqueville's *The Old Regime and the French Revolution.*

(a) If a society does not take seriously the ideas of complexity, evil, and community, it will flounder. A society that does not have the self-confidence to defend its principles will fall prey to the forces intent on subverting or altering those principles.

(b) Words have meaning. Words signify ideas, and ideas determine reality. A democratic society must not allow the key signifiers of its civil religion—words like democracy, freedom, liberty, virtue—to be misappropriated. Those who want to drastically change a society will often do so by expropriating its language; this possibility must be watched vigilantly at all times.

The power of these principles, especially when integrated into a coherent worldview, is truly remarkable. Specific issues that neoconservatives have addressed in depth—Communism, public television, the poverty rate, affirmative action, capitalism, government employees, footnotes, Central America, deviance, Pat Buchanan, liberty, mediating structures, Horatio Alger, Alger Hiss, multiculturalism, modern literature, religion in the public square, intermarriage, smoking, the United Nations, abortion, homosexual writers, the defense budget, the National Council of Churches, radical students, intellectuals, ethnicity, Israel, the family, McCarthyism, libertarians, lawyers, feminism, businessmen, conformity, the Third World, school choice, riots, race, judicial activism, Pope John Paul II, the Vietnam War, Social Security, pornography, anti-Semitism, environmentalism—seem too diverse to comprise a coherent structure. But this is not the case. By applying the four principles, the neoconservatives have been able to weave a consistent style of thought through a diverse intellectual panoply.

Before studying these positions, it is important to understand the context in which they arose. And for that—as for so much else—Mannheim provides a useful interpretative guide. "Conservatism . . . arises as a counter-movement in conscious opposition to the highly organized, coherent and systematic 'progressive' movement."[26] From Edmund Burke to the present, systematic conservative theory tends to find much of its motivating impulse, perhaps paradoxically, in critique. True to Mannheim's characterization, neoconservatism has always formulated its political positions in opposition to others. Positing no a priori conception of political results, neoconservative political positions have above all been the product of their principles applied to issues generated by the left.

Yes, the left—for the neoconservatives have almost always considered their opponents on the right to be nonopponents. Because the neoconservatives assumed without question the need for a minimal welfare state, the legitimacy of labor unions, and the justice of civil rights, they never felt the need to argue with those who doubted these things. Talk from conservative politicians, writers, and publicists of the welfare state as the beginning of the road to serfdom, the inviolable right to contract, and "states rights" more or less bored the neoconservatives from the start. So, too, did the conservative intellectuals from the 1940s through the early 1960s, some of whom harbored an almost theocratic opposition to economic progress and the democratic politics of modernity.

Thus, while it is correct to state that neoconservatism was conceived in opposition, it is more accurate to maintain that it was conceived in opposition to liberalism. Didn't neoconservatives consider themselves liberals in the early years? Yes, they did, but there were liberals and there were liberals. Through the 1960s, the neoconservatives saw themselves as liberal critics of liberalism or, more specifically, liberal critics of the liberal interpretation of liberalism. Their objections to liberalism were the product of two powerful forces—convictions derived from principle and experiences garnered in youth. Several of the neoconservatives had been socialists as young men, and they were all very familiar with people on the left. While conservatism was an abstraction—with a few notable exceptions, the neoconservatives did not know any American conservatives until the 1960s—liberalism was not. The neoconservatives knew the mind-set, the means, the lure, the aspirations, the background, and the people of the left, and were disgusted with its persistent faith in illusions they (the neoconservatives) had shed long ago, or avoided altogether.

The youthful experience of several of the neoconservatives with the left taught them much more than how Marxists think. First, it is important to realize that the socialism of these neoconservatives (Kristol, Lipset, Glazer, and Melvin Lasky) consisted largely in participation with a Trotskyist group at the City College of New York in the late 1930s. Their comrade Daniel Bell was a "social democrat." The domain of this group was Alcove One of the City College cafeteria, as opposed to Alcove Two, which housed the other political group on campus, the Stalinists, who outnumbered the Trotskyists by thirty to one. Thus, even as socialists or Trotskyists, Kristol and company developed intellectually by combating enemies on the left. While many neoconservatives (notably James Q. Wilson who said, "I didn't know what a Trotskyite was until Dan Bell explained it to me. I'm still not sure I can repeat the definition."[27]) were never socialists, they were all significantly influenced by Irving Kristol. At least in that way, the mode in which the young thinkers in Alcove One learned to analyze social issues has influenced almost all of the neoconservatives.

Recalling his days in Alcove One, Kristol has written, "Joining a radical movement when one is young is very much like falling in love when one is young. The girl may turn out to be rotten, but the experience of love is so valuable it can never be entirely undone by the ultimate disenchantment."[28] Bell offers the same analogy in his autobiographical essay, "First Love and Early Sorrows,"[29] and it is a telling one. For just as the lessons of love acquired in youth usually survive one's first romance, the ways to think and read that one learns as a student last well after the original subject matter has been exhausted. This is especially true for people like Kristol and Bell, who learned to think by studying Marxism. In order to understand Marxism well—and both Kristol and Bell do—one has to see politics as a comprehensive system, not as the sum of individual issues. Connections between seemingly diverse disciplines are necessary because everything is interrelated.

The neoconservatives abandoned socialism when they were young, generally because of some contact with the larger world. Kristol, for instance, who had never been west of the Hudson River before entering the army in the early 1940s, states,

> My de-radicalization proceeded very quickly. I got into the army with a Midwest regiment. It turned out that most of the guys there came from a town called Cicero, a town I had never heard of. I said to myself, I can't

> build socialism with these people. They'll probably take it over and make a racket out of it.[30]

While discarding their radicalism as young men, the neoconservatives maintained something which would prove much more important in the decades to come—a sociologically sophisticated way of looking at the way the world works. Trained to approach ideas as coherent systems rather than as conglomerations of isolated issues, the neoconservatives have always plunged beneath the surface of social questions to ascertain the internal logic (or lack of logic) of whatever situations or ideas they are addressing. Amid these intellectual depths, the neoconservatives have consistently discovered that at the roots of even the most basic issues are interlocking social structures and historically informed moral ideas. Engaging issues and social questions at this level, the neoconservatives have been compelled to address the seemingly disparate branches from what they recognize to be common roots. And at the roots of the most damning social questions, the neoconservatives consistently found a timid, naive, and desiccated liberalism.

In the 1970s and 1980s, Norman Podhoretz did not merely advocate higher defense spending; he targeted the rhetorical bastardizations of totalitarianism, the problems democracies have in combating an absolutist enemy, and what he called "the culture of appeasement," triggering "the failure of nerve" that has crippled anti-Communist efforts, including American defense spending. Irving Kristol has never been satisfied defending capitalism by saying that it works better than socialism; he has stressed that the free market must draw upon accumulated moral capital supplied by the bourgeois ethic—which, in turn, is defined by religion. The ultimate success and longevity of capitalism, Kristol has argued, will have more to do with whether it is consistent with Judeo-Christian notions of morality and justice than with how many goods are produced. Considering the cultural contradictions that a booming economy can yield, this is not a foregone conclusion—regardless of the fall of Communism or even the death of socialism. For the neoconservatives, no idea is an island unto itself; ideas are as naturally social as, following Aristotle, the men who conceive them.

From the early 1950s to the present day, neoconservatives have castigated liberalism for the same failures—ignoring the complexity of human action and the wisdom of human systems, a lack of resolve in confronting evil, a laissez-faire attitude toward human virtue, and an unwillingness to defend the critical ideas of American civilization from its discontents. Practically every neoconservative argument and position can be seen as a reaction to one of these left-wing ideas. Anti-Communism? That is obvious—much of the nascent neoconservative animosity toward Communism took the form of bitter attacks against American intellectuals who were not sufficiently anti-Communist. Opposition to the 1960s radicals? This, too, is self-explanatory; the neoconservative defense of American society was launched in response to the student radicalism and the tepid reaction of the liberal faculty. Capitalism? The neoconservatives noted that a non-Marxist anticapitalism resembling that of the Old Right had become the fundamental fact of left-wing politics in the mid-1970s. They surmised that nothing the left hated as much as capitalism could be that bad, so they investigated it. Shortly after, they produced a unique, comprehensive, and sociologically significant moral defense of the free market.[31] Religion? In the past several years, the neoconservatives have perceived a moral decline fueled by a militant secularism pervading the culture. Wanting to recall the notion of public virtue they deemed necessary for civilization, the neoconservatives have turned to the source of those values, religion. Consequently, they developed a defense of religion in the public square that applies to people of all religious faiths.

Does this consistent opposition to the left mean that the neoconservatives always had the same ideas, or that all neoconservatives think alike? Of course not. The neoconservatives have varied widely in their political positions, their political dispositions, and even their philosophical orientations. But the fact that several of them are married to each other (Gertrude Himmelfarb and Irving Kristol, Midge Decter and Norman Podhoretz, Brigette and Peter Berger), and all are close personal friends, helps to bring their thought into something of a critical mass. Moreover, they write for each other's magazines, constantly cite each other's work, and promote one another—just look at the acknowledgments, footnotes, or back cover blurbs of a neoconservative book.

The richness of neoconservatism is at least partially due to the fact that the neoconservatives bring individual expertise in a variety of fields to bear. Many of them are greatly distinguished among their chosen professions. Gertrude Himmelfarb is one of the world's great social historians; James Q. Wilson, America's premier criminologist, is a past president of the American Political Science Association; Michael Novak is an internationally recognized Christian theologian; Norman Podhoretz is an expert on Israel and Communism; Leon Kass is a medical doctor and biblical scholar; Joseph Epstein is a renowned literary critic; Hilton Kramer is the most respected American art critic; Peter Berger is a distinguished sociologist; Richard John Neuhaus is a Catholic priest with extensive experience ministering to an inner-city community; Robert Bork is one of America's most respected legal theorists; Daniel Patrick Moynihan is perhaps the most gifted thinker to serve in public office in this century; Irving Kristol drives it all. With such distinguished intellectuals from a variety of disciplines learning from one another as friends and contributors to the same journals, neoconservatism is blessed with a unique depth.

As with anyone or any group passionately engaged in the world of ideas over a half-century, their thought has changed over time—even though not nearly as much as is often charged. Neoconservative principles and ideas are evident in the work of Irving Kristol and Gertrude Himmelfarb throughout the past fifty years, and they were joined by others along the way. Some, like Richard John Neuhaus, came on board late because they had been associated with other schools of thought; others, like George Weigel, came on board as young men. Still others, such as Norman Podhoretz, started on the neoconservative train, got off for a few years, but caught up with it at a later point. Individual neoconservatives may have changed—as most people do—but the fundamental principles of neoconservatism have remained consistent since the 1950s when the issue of anti-Communism provided the opportunity for a liberal critique of liberalism to blossom.

This is not to deny that some of the political positions of neoconservatism have changed, or at least changed emphasis. Indeed, they have. In a 1993 essay reflecting on his days as a young liberal anti-Communist in the 1950s, Kristol recalls, "I was far from being a conservative, had no interest in 'market economics,' and the notion of voting Republican was as foreign to me as attending a Catholic mass."[32] Now, of course, Kristol is a conservative, one of the world's foremost philosophers of market economics, and has probably even attended Catholic mass. What happened?

Nothing drastic. The necessity and inevitability of change is an integral part of the logic of neoconservatism. Because neoconservatism is premised upon fundamental principles rather than specific policies, it has maintained a remarkable resiliency through several decades. Using their principles as intellectual instruments, the neoconservatives have always analyzed whatever liberalism has generated, registered an objection, and put forth a different idea. Exactly what position neoconservatives have produced in opposition at any given time is of relatively little consequence. If a particular idea does not seem to work, neoconservatives can return to their principles and find something better; political positions take care of themselves so long as principles are sound. This is not weakness, nor is it inconsistency. For a philosophical movement bent on remaining intellectually serious, consistency to principles often demands that manifestations of those principles must be altered.

A more prominent source of perceived change in neoconservatism concerns the nature of issues they discussed. As times have proceeded from the 1950s to the 1990s, political questions have become more fundamental. Unquestioned assumptions began to be questioned, and answered questions were opened once again. No one was prepared for this; modernity was supposed to progress into more technical issues, not revert to what everyone thought was settled decades earlier. This strange twist in the nature of ideological debate triggered several changes in emphases in neoconservative thought, but did nothing to its basic principles. Perhaps the most prominent example is that of the 1960s and the counterculture, when neoconservatives were said to have abandoned liberalism for what became known as neoconservatism.

Neoconservatism is often said to have begun in the late 1960s, in reaction to the counterculture. There is something to be said about beginning a study of neoconservatism in the late 1960s, but I think Mannheim's style of thought method demands that it begin earlier. While the neoconservatives were liberal critics of liberalism in the 1950s, a certain way of approaching social and political questions naturally developed into neoconservatism when the counterculture presented the opportunity in the 1960s. The attack the neoconservatives launched on the counterculture in the 1960s was the natural flowering of ideological seeds that had been planted long ago. Neoconservative attacks on the counterculture in the 1960s were passionate and distinctive, but the ideas behind them were not new and certainly did not signify an ideological transformation.

To say that the formative years of neoconservatism were spent in the late 1960s would imply that the neoconservatives would not have so strenuously objected to the counterculture in, say, 1954. But they would have. Neoconservatives always despised what Lionel Trilling called "the adversary culture"; there was just not much to say about it when it was largely confined to a few Beat poets in Greenwich Village and experimental colleges in the Pacific Northwest. However, the liberal anti-Communist criticism of anti-anti-Communism in the 1950s was every bit as trenchant as the neoconservative castigation of the counterculture some fifteen years later. Many of the arguments they used to discuss the left in the 1950s were sometimes repeated and almost always adapted—not changed—in the 1960s or after. In the 1960s, the neoconservatives defended the besieged institutions and ideas they thought had been safely in place long ago. Did this defense necessitate making alliances with conservatives and considering ideas that conservatives had put forth for many years? Yes, it did. Did it signify a sea change in the thought of the neoconservatives? Absolutely not. Everyone adapts to social upheaval, and every adaptation brings change. The way an intellectual group arrives at an idea, and develops, transforms, and alters that idea, is almost always more interesting and more important than the idea itself.

Neoconservatism is now coming to an end, as it becomes clear that only one generation of thinkers identifies itself as such. This is perhaps the truest testament to the success of neoconservatism in the following sense: what was once considered exclusively neoconservatism is now conservatism. Parts of what was once conservatism remain as such, but much of it is no longer with us. What we now know as conservatism—identified in the ideas of our intellectuals or the words of our politicians—is largely the legacy of the neoconservatives. To understand conservatism in American politics and thought today, there is no better way than to go to the roots—and study the history and development of neoconservatism.

Notes

1. William F. Buckley, contribution to *Commentary* symposium, "What Is a Liberal—Who Is Conservative?" *Commentary* (September 1976) p. 47.

2. James Burnham, *Suicide of the West: An Essay on the Meaning and Destiny of Liberalism* (New York: John Day, 1964) p. 280.

3. Peter Berger, "Ideologies, Myths and Moralities," in Irving Kristol and Paul Weaver, eds., *The Americans: 1976—Critical Choices for Americans, Volume II* (Lexington, Ky.: Lexington Books, 1976) p. 347.

4. William F. Buckley, "Did You Ever See a Dream Walking?" in William F. Buckley and Charles R. Kesler, eds., *Keeping the Tablets: Modern American Conservative Thought* (New York: Harper and Row, 1988) p. 21.

5. Peter Steinfels, *The Neoconservatives: The Men Who Are Changing America's Politics* (New York: Simon and Schuster, 1979) p. 4.

6. Interview with Richard John Neuhaus, January 10, 1994.

7. Seymour Martin Lipset, "Neoconservatism: Myth and Reality," *Society* (July/August 1988) p. 29.

8. Interview with Irving Kristol, January 26, 1994.

9. Irving Kristol, "Confessions of a True, Self-Confessed—Perhaps the Only—'Neoconservative'," *Public Opinion* (October/November 1979) p. 50.

10. Nathan Glazer, contribution to "Neoconservatism: Pro and Con," *Partisan Review* (Vol. 4, 1980) p. 498.

11. Jeff Weintraub, *Freedom and Community: The Republican Virtue Tradition and the Sociology of Liberty* (Berkeley: University of California Press, 1996).

12. Along these lines, James Q. Wilson has said, "To me, and I suppose to most neoconservatives, Alexis de Tocqueville is one of the most important authors. So is Aristotle. But I think what I find in de Tocqueville, in the Federalist Papers, and in Aristotle, is a combination of theory and practice, a desire to test ideas by the sober second thought of a decent citizen—to ask whether institutions can be made to display the best qualities of people without imposing upon

people the worst qualities of institutions" ("Neoconservatism: Pro and Con," p. 509). Tocqueville has also been a major inspiration to Irving Kristol. Kristol called Tocqueville "infinitely wise" in "Class and Sociology: 'The Shadow of Marxism'," *Commentary* (October 1958) p. 358. He repeated the compliment thirty years later in "The Spirit of '87," *The Public Interest* (Spring 1987) p. 8.

13. Jeff Weintraub, "Varieties and Vicissitudes of Public Space," in Philip Kasinetz, ed., *Metropolis: Center and Symbol of Our Times* (New York: New York University Press, 1995) p. 293. This concept is elaborated upon in Chapters 1 and 2 of *Freedom and Community.* It may be worth adding that while Weintraub agrees that important elements of the neoconservative perspective can be traced to the republican virtue tradition, he would emphasize that these represent only one possible understanding or manifestation of the principles of that tradition.

14. *Freedom and Community*, p. 15. Some might suggest that the concept of the "willed community" ignores important communities that are not willed, such as religion and family. However, the willed community applies mainly to political society, granting autonomy to institutions of civil society—like religions and families—that are not voluntary. Also, while one is born into one's religion, religion in certain senses can be considered a willed community. People choose to either keep their religion or adopt a new one, and the idea of proselytization revolves around members of a community convincing others to join that community. This notion is reinforced by the prohibition against an established church, which would, through government coercion, violate the conception of religion as a kind of willed community. Furthermore, families and religions help to nurture and develop the virtues necessary for people to emerge from civil society and participate as positive additions to willed communities.

16. Michael Walzer, "Nervous Liberals." Review of *The Neoconservatives: The Men Who Are Changing America's Politics* by Peter Steinfels. *New York Review of Books* (October 11, 1979) p. 5.

17. Karl Mannheim, "Conservative Thought," in Paul Kecskemeti, ed., *Essays on Sociology and Social Psychology* (London: Routledge, 1953) pp. 74–164.

18. "Conservative Thought," p. 74.

19. See, for instance, Norman Podhoretz's essay "Following Irving," in *The Neoconservative Imagination: Essays in Honor of Irving Kristol* (Washington: American Enterprise Institute, 1995).

20. Interview with George Weigel, January 25, 1994.

21. Irving Kristol, "The Most Successful Revolution: The Leaders All Died in Bed," *The American Heritage* (April 1974) p. 38.

22. James Q. Wilson, contribution to "Neoconservatism: Pro and Con," p. 509.

23. "Conservative Thought," pp. 95–96.

24. Quoted in Gertrude Himmelfarb, *Darwin and the Darwinian Revolution* (New York: Doubleday Anchor Books, 1959) p. 361.

25. Reinhold Niebuhr, *The Children of Light and the Children of Darkness* (New York: Scribner's, 1944) p. xi.

26. "Conservative Thought," p. 99.
27. James Q. Wilson, contribution to "Neoconservatism: Pro and Con," p. 508.
28. Irving Kristol, "Memoirs of a Trotskyist," *The New York Times Magazine* (January 24, 1977). Reprinted in *Reflections of a Neoconservative* (New York: Basic Books, 1983) p. 4.
29. Daniel Bell, "First Love and Early Sorrows," *Partisan Review* (No. 4, 1981) pp. 532–51.
30. Irving Kristol, "Second Thoughts: A Generational Perspective," in David Horowitz and Peter Collier, eds., *Second Thoughts: Former Radicals Look Back at the Sixties* (Lanham, Md.: Madison Books, 1989) p. 184.
31. Of course, others have been there before them, beginning with Adam Smith. The neoconservatives, however, are the only group to have amassed a defense of industrial capitalism (which developed after Smith's time). While the free exchange of goods and services between consenting adults has been defended by thinkers from Smith to the present, only the neoconservatives defend capitalism with reference to its cultural contradictions and blessings. One of the distinctive strengths of the neoconservatives' argument is to have developed a defense of capitalism which seriously confronts its cultural contradictions and blessings.
32. Irving Kristol, "My Cold War," *The National Interest* (Spring 1993) p. 142.

2

The Formative Years: Communism, Anti-Communism, and the Intellectual Life

When we act, if we call it action, it's only in a peripheral way. We do have sympathies with the (Communist) Party, and even, in a way, with its revolutionary aims. But maybe, sympathetic as we are, we prefer not to think about what the realities of such a party are.—John Laskell in Lionel Trilling's novel, *The Middle of the Journey*, 1947

It should be apparent that liberals in the twentieth century are confronted by a situation quite unfamiliar to their forebears. For they must contend not with fearless heretics, indigenous elements of the community who, like the abolitionists and revolutionists of old, scorn concealment, and who make no bones about their hostility to the principles of liberalism. They find themselves in the unique historical predicament of having to deal with native elements who, by secrecy and stratagem, serve the interests of a foreign power which believes itself entitled to speak for all mankind, and whose victory spells the end of all liberal civilization and with it the right to heresy. It is now plain that the Communist regimes of the world have turned out to be the greatest and cruelest heresy hunters in history, not merely in politics but in every branch of theory and practice.—Sidney Hook, 1953

Liberal Anti-Communism in Perspective

It is not always that a direct ancestor of an intellectual movement can be identified, but such is the case with neoconservatism. The ancestor is liberal anti-Communism, a broad but distinct intellectual grouping that encompassed a number of prominent and soon to be prominent thinkers, most of them Jews from New York. Who were these liberal anti-Communists? Sidney Hook, Diana Trilling, Lionel Trilling, Nathan Glazer, Gertrude Himmelfarb, Irving Kristol, George Orwell, Norman Podhoretz, Irving Howe, William Phillips, Saul Bellow, Mary McCarthy, Philip Rahv, David Riesman, Melvin Lasky, James Burnham, Maurice Goldbloom, Richard Rovere, Daniel Bell, Hannah Arendt, Dwight MacDonald, Reinhold Niebuhr, Seymour Martin Lipset, Moshe Decter, James Rorty, Leslie Fiedler, William Barrett, Elliot Cohen, Harold Rosenberg, Clement Greenberg, Meyer Shapiro, Lionel Abel, Alfred Kazin, Delmore Schwartz, Norman Thomas, Arnold Beichman, Robert Warshow, Jacques Barzun, Arthur M. Schlesinger, Arthur Koestler, David Bazelon, and Richard Hofstadter are just some of these intellectuals. Criteria for membership in this group were not ideologically restrictive; significant differences existed. But there were important points of agreement. They were liberals in the sense that they favored equality of opportunity for all people regardless of race and religion, a mixed economy with an active public sector, and tolerance for differing views and backgrounds backed by freedom of thought and expression. They believed Communism to be the enemy of liberalism, and the Soviet Union to be the greatest force of evil on earth.

In the Beginning: Socialism in Intellectual Arcadia

Pre-World War II America was a difficult place for Jewish intellectuals. They were generally proud to be Americans, but had a persistent sense that they were outsiders in a hostile Gentile culture. This identity crisis was often resolved through socialism. Jewish intellectuals never thought very much about dialectical materialism or the economics of socialism; these intellectuals were attracted to the socialist promise of a world without prejudice, involuntary association, or war. But there was, most importantly, the communal element, well described by Irving Howe in his 1982 memoirs, *A Margin of Hope*.

> Comparisons between radical politics and religious practice are likely to be glib, especially when used to dismiss the substance of the radical case; yet in thinking back to these years I'm forced to recognize, not very comfortably, that there were some parallels between the two. Everything seemed

to fall into place: ordered meaning, a world grasped through theory, a life shaped by purpose.[1]

The socialist faith brought together the New York intellectuals and Communist Party operatives in the 1930s. *Partisan Review*, the first journal of the New York intellectuals, was founded in 1934 as an organ of the John Reed Club, a Communist cell in Greenwich Village. Though not heavily involved with Communist activities, the editors of *Partisan Review* were nonetheless forthright and unrepentant about their political aspirations and purposes, declaring in their first editorial, "The defense of the Soviet Union is one of our principal tasks."[2]

The John Reed Club and *Partisan Review* became the chic organizations in Greenwich Village; intellectuals flocked to them and a vibrant community developed. Fund-raising, surprisingly, turned out to be easy for *Partisan Review* and the club. Rich Communists gave readily. *Partisan Review* intellectuals and their sponsors ran into trouble only once, when a fund-raising party was busted by the police for violating the Volstead Act, which enforced the Prohibition amendment. Bail was no problem; one club member simply posted a Soviet government bond.

As the *Partisan Review* intellectuals and the Communists began to work more closely, they realized that their interests and goals were quite divergent. Speaking in very broad terms of general goals, they agreed on most things. But an unpassable gulf of purpose and temperament parted the two. The *Partisan Review* intellectuals were literary people first and Communists a distant second. They were attracted to the self-proclaimed ideals of Communism, and saw no contradiction between Communist politics and standards in literature. The Communists, on the other hand, thought of Marxism as more than an intellectual theory, and did not have much use for free inquiry that veered from the Communist political path. Writers and artists were crucially important weapons in the class struggle, and literature was to be measured by how well it advanced political purposes. In his memoirs, *Partisan Review* editor in chief William Phillips records one representative incident.

> It was the time of the famous Scottsboro case, which involved the arrest of several young black men accused of raping two white girls. At a meeting of the club a letter from one of the blacks was read, which sounded like this: "I din't jazz no girls. I din't jazz nobody. Nobody jazz no girls," etc., for two or three pages. When the reading was over, one John Reed Club member jumped up and announced, "This is literature."[3]

Phillips did not think so, and neither did any of his intellectual comrades. The *Partisan Review* intellectuals realized that the Communists did not respect their ideas, but wanted to use their literary abilities for purely political purposes. They abandoned the Communists in 1936, and dedicated themselves to authenticity in literature and a vague socialism in politics and economics.

America the Beautiful?

In September 1947, Mary McCarthy published an essay in *Commentary*, provocatively titled, "America the Beautiful," boldly declaring that "We are a nation of 20 million bathtubs, with a humanitarian in every bathtub."[4] While this upbeat sentiment was not universal among the New York intellectuals, it certainly indicates an important change of attitude from the fellow-traveling days of the 1930s and 1940s. By the time World War II was over, the New York intellectuals had shed their Communism, but were still wrestling with their tenuous identities as Americans. Bitter fights about whether America should enter World War II had engaged two camps, one led by Dwight MacDonald and the other by Sidney Hook. MacDonald reasoned that while Hitler was horrible, the United States was in no position to judge because of her own great moral failings. This doctrine of moral equivalency employed by MacDonald would recur throughout the following decades in various forms, mostly relating to Communism and the Soviet Union. The liberal anti-Communists (and later, the neoconservatives) regarded the doctrine of moral equivalency as the quintessential example of the failure of liberals to make distinctions between imperfection and evil.

Hook was the first to articulate the dimensions of the left-wing doctrine of moral equivalency, and he did so in a scathing attack on MacDonald in *Partisan Review* in 1949. Granting that the United States has many serious fundamental problems, Hook nevertheless refuses to concede that America is in any way morally equivalent to Nazi Germany, declaring that the major issue of the day was not capitalism versus socialism, but freedom versus despotism.[5]

Partisan Review came around to Hook's position and advocated it with great eloquence after World War II. Several issues of *Partisan Review* featured riveting editorials defending the West against the Soviet Union. These editorials often took issue with intellectuals who morally equated the Soviet Union and the United States. Case in point is a 1948 *Partisan Review* editorial, "The Politics of Desperation."

> Frankly, we have little patience with those bohemian radicals who are more concerned with making a show of their purity and intransigence than with formulating a serious opposition to Stalinism. . . . In general, the political situation on the anti-Stalinist side of the fence is fluid and unpredictable. Stalinism, on the other hand, means absolute terror and dictatorship, and confronts us with the question of the sheer survival of our most elementary freedoms and human values. If anyone seriously believes that Stalinism and the status quo of democratic capitalism are equally bad, then he must conclude the situation is equally hopeless and begin to investigate the various means of committing suicide.[6]

The New York intellectuals were able to become more comfortable with America because America was becoming more comfortable with them. The expansion of higher education that accompanied the postwar boom provided them with university jobs. This newfound feeling did not come easily; it sometimes surprised the very intellectuals who had it. An anecdote involving the literary critic Alfred Kazin illustrates this point. In the late 1940s, Kazin wrote a review of Francis Parkman's book on the Oregon Trail in *Partisan Review.* In the review, Kazin mentioned the phrase "Our forests," only to invoke the retort from an editor, "Our forests, Alfred?"[7]

"Our forests, indeed!" was the answer of Kazin and many of the other New York intellectuals in a 1952 three-part *Partisan Review* symposium, "Our Country and Our Culture."[8] Lionel

Trilling, for instance, declared, "The American situation has changed in a way that is not merely relative. There is an unmistakable improvement in the present American cultural situation over that of, say, thirty years ago."[9] Some were more specific. For instance, the distinguished sociologist David Riesman praised Hollywood movies and chastised intellectuals for considering themselves above popular culture.[10] For Jewish intellectuals who just a few years before had great trouble reconciling their identities as Jews and as Americans, this represented quite a sea change.

As thinkers accepted by and generally accepting of their nation, the New York intellectuals naturally found themselves at the crux of the most important twin issues of the 1950s, Communism and anti-Communism. They were especially well-qualified anti-Communists; as Diana Trilling noted in 1950, "Most [liberal] anti-Communists have been through the Communist mill or frighteningly close to it, which has given them first-hand knowledge of the Communist technique."[11] The liberal anti-Communists believed that their experiences with Communism made them especially fit to confront the Stalinist danger. They not only could understand the socialists' arguments as well as anyone else, but, unlike most, they understood the unspoken, almost inchoate emotions that would drive someone to Communism. The Italian intellectual Ignazio Silone, writing in what has become the liberal anti-Communist manifesto, *The God That Failed*, proclaimed, "The final battle will be between the Communist and the ex-Communist."[12]

The hard anti-Communism that liberals articulated in *Commentary, The New Leader*, and *Partisan Review* generally centered around two larger ideological foci. First and foremost was that Communism is a system of absolute evil. Second was the demonstration that liberalism is not only distinct from Communism, but diametrically opposed to it in both theory and practice. The liberal anti-Communist view of the iniquity of Communism was informed primarily by three related factors: the passions of the ex-Marxists like Hook, Arthur Koestler, and James Burnham who had seen the monster face to face; the special awareness of totalitarianism generated in the aftermath of Hitler; and the belief that Stalinism was morally indistinguishable from Nazism. The last factor was the most important, because it was the driving force behind the others.

Melvin Lasky put it most succinctly. "The historical uniqueness of Nazism should not blind us to the fact that morally and politically it is identical with Stalinism."[13] Just as Hitler had terrorized the world with concentration camps, genocide, suppression of freedoms, and the smashing of religions and other mediating structures, Stalin had done the same, on a larger scale and in more countries. The liberal anti-Communists were dismayed that numerous intellectuals who had vigorously protested Hitler were either silent or apologetic when it came to Stalin. Writing about his employer, New York University, Professor Sidney Hook wrote,

> If we match Hitler's first six years with the six years that have elapsed since the cessation of hostilities, we find that Stalin has absorbed more countries, killed more people, extirpated more democratic institutions more thoroughly, than even the psychotic barbarian, Hitler. Where is the excitement, the moral indignation, the impassioned protest?[14]

In 1953, Diana Trilling concluded that the prime liberal fallacy of the day was to "see no resemblance at all between Communism and Fascism."[15]

The liberal anti-Communists believed that liberalism and anti-Communism depend on each other. The moral (and actual) equivalent of Nazism, Communism was the ultimate enemy of liberalism. Calling Communism "the most powerful existing institution which opposes such changes and reforms as liberalism proposes," Irving Kristol asked, "Why, then, should not liberals, and liberals especially, fear and hate it?"[16] To these intellectuals, a liberalism that did not incorporate a vociferous anti-Communism was not liberalism.

Liberal anti-Communists admonished that if liberals did not act upon this truth, their enemies on the right would destroy them. The liberal anti-Communists lived in dread that their brand of liberalism would be equated with Communism in the public mind, thus discrediting liberalism along with Communism. A 1946 *Partisan Review* editorial presents this point passionately.

> Yet what do "liberals" really stand to gain from their present frenetic support of Russia except their own political death? . . . . In a situation of impending or existing hostility between America and Russia, the Communists will be dealt with for what they are, outright foreign agents; but reactionaries, never remarkable for niceties of discrimination, have always been a little color-blind to the difference between pink and red friends of Russia, and the reaction, when it comes, would thus clamp a tight lid on all political liberties and perhaps even bring a ruthless suppression of civil liberties. If certain "liberals" insist on digging their own graves, that might seem to be their private affair; but we hope . . . [they know that they are] dragging down to their ruin . . . everyone else who genuinely desires the values that have been an essential part of traditional liberalism.[17]

A Conspiracy, Not a Heresy

The liberal anti-Communists considered both Nazism and Communism to be special kinds of evil well outside the bounds of acceptable thought or consideration. A free society, the liberal anti-Communists claimed, depends on a number of prerequisites, not the least of which is self-perpetuation. Because Communism aims to destroy the society in which freedoms flourish, the liberal anti-Communists reasoned that Communist ideas may legitimately be purged from a free society. As Hook reasoned,

> membership in the Communist Party unfits a person to serve his government for the same reason that membership in Murder, Inc. unfits a gangster—even if he has not yet been convicted of any crime—to serve on the police force.[18]

Or, as Hook asked of a liberal political adversary, "Would [Henry Steele] Commager argue that to deny a fervent apostle of euthanasia a post as director of a home for the aged and infirm is necessarily to deny him his rights?"[19]

James Burnham, an ex-Communist associated with the liberal anti-Communists before he became a conservative, eloquently articulated this idea in his 1947 book, *The Struggle for the World.*

> Suppose that a football team claimed to be the best in the country, and announced that it was ready to prove it by playing against "any other team." Let us further suppose that another group, calling itself a football

> team, challenged; but that this second group did not in fact accept the rules which define the game of football to be what it is. The second group, let us say, scored differently, refused to accept penalties, shot runners with pistols instead of tackling them, and so on. If our first claimant to the championship refused to take up the challenge, would we then denounce it for not making good on its offer to play "any other team"? We would, of course, not. We would say, rather, that the second group was not really a football team at all. We would say that you can play football only with those who accept the fundamental rules which define football, without which there would be no such thing as football.[20]

The difficult question for the liberal anti-Communists was to determine when the opponent was playing football. While the liberal anti-Communists did not believe that Communists had the right to serve in sensitive positions in the federal government, they were vigilant about protecting civil liberties. Liberal anti-Communists did not want to see a perfectly logical policy regarding Communists extrapolated to non-Communists or even fellow travelers. The distinction they agreed upon was Sidney Hook's: heresies were essential for the survival of liberal societies, while conspiracies were anathema to it. The difference between the two? Hook explained,

> A heresy is a set of unpopular ideas or opinions on matters of grave concern to the community. . . . A conspiracy, as distinct from a heresy, is a secret or underground movement which seeks to attain its ends not by normal political or education processes but playing outside the rules of the game. . . . A heresy does not shirk from publicity. It welcomes it. Not so a conspiracy. The signs of a conspiracy are secrecy, anonymity, the use of false names and labels, and the calculated lie.[21]

Any doubts should be decided in favor of the heresy. Communism was certainly a conspiracy, but that did not mean that all inklings of it could be treated as such. Liberal anti-Communists warned of irresponsible anti-Communists who served the Communist cause by using the label "Communist" promiscuously and stressed the point that the free play of legitimate ideas, broadly defined, was an essential component of liberty—even if that meant that some Communists would go undetected. As Sidney Hook insisted, Communist *ideas* are heresies while the Communist *movement* is a conspiracy.[22] For that reason, Hook argued that using the Communist newspaper *The Daily Worker* as a tool to expose the Communists was superior to suppressing it or even banning it from the classroom.[23]

The liberal anti-Communists realized that the issue of Communists in government was complicated by the very nature of Communism. Communists in important positions did not make their party memberships public. Rather, important Communists were told by their superiors in the United States or the Soviet Union to stay underground. This, according to Hook and others, made the suppression of Communism practically though not morally difficult. Suppressing Communism in theory was fine but, to be effective, the government would have to suppress all of its front and quasi-front groups, and that would have required a massive violation of civil liberties.[24]

Flank Right: Challenge from the Conservatives

The liberal anti-Communist fear that the right was attempting to conflate liberalism with Communism was accurate. The intellectual conservatives paid little or no attention to the distinctions that the liberal anti-Communists made between Communism and liberalism. While the liberal anti-Communists and the conservative anti-Communists shared many ideas regarding Communism, neither group recognized these similarities and a potential alliance instead became a feud. While the conservatives equated liberalism with Communism, the liberals did not take the conservatives very seriously, thus making the possibility of a fruitful exchange even more remote. Lionel Trilling's most famous line comes in his 1950 book, *The Liberal Imagination*: "Conservatives do not express themselves in ideas but only in action or in irritable mental gestures which seek to resemble ideas."[25] Trilling should have known better. As Gertrude Himmelfarb pointed out in *Commentary* in that same year, conservatism was filled with learned and respectable thinkers such as Russell Kirk, Richard Weaver, and Alfred Jay Nock.[26] However, the liberal anti-Communists were able to ignore the conservative intellectuals because they had little influence on American intellectual life prior to the mid-1950s.

George Nash, the foremost historian of postwar American conservatism, has pointed out that there were eight important liberal weekly journals of opinion in the 1950s whereas the conservatives had none.[27] The conservatives at the time were a smattering of intellectuals, who, while often brilliant, sometimes found themselves intellectually wandering among castles and serfs in the fifteenth century or in some laissez-faire utopia. There were three dominant schools of conservative thought, with a good number of unaffiliated extremists to go around.

The first brand of conservatives were the traditionalists, notably Erik Voegelin, Russell Kirk and Richard Weaver. With a hatred of modern civilization, with its perceived technological displacements of the spiritual, these intellectuals generally had some obscure figure in antiquity whom they thought initiated the decline of the West. For Voegelin it was Joachim of Flora, for Weaver it was William of Occam. They were very far removed from current political questions; from the perspective of William of Occam, what is the difference between socialism and capitalism, let alone Adlai and Ike?

Another group of conservatives were the libertarian champions of the free market. These intellectuals, led by Ludwig von Mises, Friederich von Hayek, Frank Chodorov, Milton Friedman, and Henry Hazlitt, rejected Keynesian economics and massive government spending for a pure free market. Even when flirting with the eccentricies that sometimes plague libertarians, such as private lighthouses, many of these intellectuals were very learned and wrote superb books and essays.

The third group of conservatives were the anti-Communists. All conservatives were anti-Communist, but this group made the issue its raison d'être. While many of them were ex-Communists, they skipped the stage of liberalism and proceeded directly to conservatism. Led by Whittaker Chambers and flanked by Frank Meyer, Max Eastman, Ralph de Toledano, Freda Utley, and others, these intellectuals disagreed on issues relating to religion and morality, but agreed that the New Deal was the first step to Communism.

The queen of the extremists was Ayn Rand, who made a theology out of selfishness. Her sweeping novels such as *Atlas Shrugged* and *The Fountainhead* drew a considerable following that bordered (and still borders) on the cultist. There was also the John Birch Society, whose fanatical anti-Communism was regarded by both liberal and conservative anti-Communists as destructive to the cause. The John Birch Society was obsessed with conspiracies; in one typical statement, its president, Robert Welch, called President Eisenhower a Communist—to which Russell Kirk replied, "Eisenhower is no Communist. He is a golfer."[28] Aside from these two organized groups were a variety of crudely prejudiced demagogues and their followers. *National Review* senior editor Richard Brookhiser accurately characterized the right prior to the mid-1950s as

> an intellectual rag-tag about as coherent as the Iranian parliament; robber barons and free enterprisers; Communists turned Americans; America Firsters turned McCarthyites; Midwestern Republicans and Confederates; with Peter Viereck on the sidelines whispering all the while that the True Prince was Franklin D. Roosevelt.[29]

All this changed with the arrival of William F. Buckley Jr, who gained national recognition as an undergraduate at Yale when he turned the editorial page of the *Yale Daily News* into a haven for conservative journalism. Two books that he published shortly after college, *God and Man at Yale* and *McCarthy and His Enemies*, were iconoclastic works that were widely read and widely despised by liberals.

Buckley's conservatism was a mixture of orthodox Catholicism, free market economics, and hard anti-Communism. Irving Kristol and others pointed out that these tenets were inherently contradictory; how can an adherent of orthodox Catholicism sanction the rapid social changes generated by the free market? Or for that matter, how could a laissez-faire economic philosophy be reconciled with hard anti-Communism, which required extraordinary government spending?[30] It was not so much that Kristol objected to any of Buckley's tenets of conservatism individually; Kristol regarded orthodox Catholicism, free-market economics, and hard anti-Communism as legitimate beliefs. But the idea of incorporating these views in a consistent political framework did not work for Kristol or his colleagues in the liberal anti-Communist camp. Trained to view politics as a system where ideas, institutions, and social forces complement and augment one another, the liberal anti-Communists demanded that a political philosophy have an overarching coherence.

Buckley's major goal at the time was to fight the encroachment of liberalism, and he concluded that the differences that all branches of conservatism had with liberalism overshadowed whatever differences existed within the conservative camp. He had a vision of joining the three disparate conservative factions into an intellectual front that could fight liberalism as a united force on several fronts. Buckley's weapon of choice was the weekly magazine; his colleague and friend Willie Schlamm wrote that Buckley had "the worst case of magazinitis"[31] he had ever seen, but it could be cured.

By the time *National Review* came to life in November 1955, Buckley was in the process of another feat that would prove as important to conservatism as that of bringing together libertarians, anti-Communists, and traditionalists. He was well on his way to purging the right of the poisonous elements that Brookhiser so richly described. *National Review*'s original editorial board had five Jews and a number of Catholics, thus engendering anger on the fringes of the right. Aloise Buckley Heath, Buckley's sister and one of his many relatives closely associated with the magazine, recollected, "Our most deeply buried fear [of *National Review* in the 1950s] was that Gerald L. K. Smith was the only other conservative in America."[32] Just as the liberal anti-Communists did not want fellow travelers to corrupt liberalism, *National Review* conservatives insisted that people like Smith not be permitted to pollute conservatism. Throughout Buckley's career, purging poisonous elements from the American conservative movement has been something of a calling.

In the 1950s, Buckley purged three groups from the conservative coalition—one libertarian, one anti-Communist, and one vaguely traditionalist. The first to go were Ayn Rand and her coterie of radical libertarians. Buckley considered Rand's disdain for Judeo-Christian morality anathema to conservatism and exorcised her by publishing a review of her book *Atlas Shrugged* by Whittaker Chambers. His review remains controversial to this day.

> Out of a lifetime of reading, I can recall no other book in which a tone of overriding arrogance was so implacably sustained. Its shrillness is without reprieve. Its dogmatism is without appeal . . . resistance to the Message cannot be tolerated because disagreement can never be merely honest, prudent, or just humanly fallible. Dissent from revelation so final can only be willfully wicked. There are ways of dealing with such wickedness, and, in fact, right reason itself enjoins them. From almost any page of *Atlas Shrugged*, a voice can be heard, from painful necessity, commanding: "To a gas chamber—go!"[33]

The second group to go were those associated with *The American Mercury*, a magazine that Buckley considered anti-Semitic. Buckley handled that by forbidding anyone on the *National Review* masthead to write for *The American Mercury*. The third group purged was the John Birch Society. At the risk of losing numerous subscribers and important financial contributors to *National Review*, Buckley launched several attacks on the John Birch Society in his magazine. *National Review* had quickly become the conservative standard-bearer, and neither Ayn Rand, nor the *American Mercury*, nor the John Birch Society could win a fight with it.

National Review in the 1950s unabashedly advanced the argument that the liberal anti-Communists hated: no liberalism could ever be a potential ally against Communism. Every kind of liberalism was considered a variant of or first step to Communism. This argument was ubiquitous and was generally packaged in one of three ways. One way is articulated by William Buckley in his book *Up from Liberalism*: the procedural guarantees of democratic liberalism are no match for the eschatological promises of the fanatical faith of Communism. A bourgeois society, with its stress on individual freedoms and small communities, was no match for a totalitarian monstrosity that controlled the lives of all of its citizens.[34]

But this argument did not encapsulate the conservative view on this matter. Buckley and *National Review* also maintained that liberalism and Communism are by definition indistinguishable—liberals are Communists without guts, or Communists are liberals in a hurry. Making an exception only for AFL-CIO President George Meany and sometimes Sidney Hook, *National Review* writers rarely distinguished between fellow-traveling leftists and liberal anti-Communists. *National Review* publisher William Rusher introduced himself to readers through a 1957 article calling liberals the "country cousins" of Communists.[35]

Even fusionist Frank Meyer, a fairly moderate *National Review* editor, promulgated this notion. In what may be *National Review*'s most succinct presentation of this argument, Meyer explained,

> 1) . . . contemporary Liberalism is in agreement with Communism on the most essential point—the necessity and desirability of socialism; 2) that it [Liberalism] regards all inherited value—theological, philosophical, political—as without intrinsic virtue or authority; 3) that, therefore, no irreconcilable differences exist between it and Communism—only differences as to method and means; and 4) that, in view of these characteristics of their ideology, the Liberals are unfit for the leadership of a free society, and intrinsically incapable of offering serious opposition to the Communist offensive.[36]

Liberal anti-Communists not only disagreed with this interpretation, but were angered by it. They had consistently distanced themselves from anti-anti-Communists and fellow travelers and did not appreciate the conservative claim that there was no real difference between the two. As a result, the liberal anti-Communists disparaged the conservatives mercilessly in their publications. In the April 1955 issue of *Commentary*, Dwight MacDonald launched an attack on *National Review* in 1955, "Scrambled Eggheads on the Right," which castigated the tone of *National Review* as "that of a religious revival" and referred to Buckley's mind as shallow.[37] In *The Reporter*, Irving Kristol conceded that Buckley was a charming and likable fellow, but charged that he and his magazine had a bit of the "crackpotty."[38]

In their attacks on the right, the liberal anti-Communists made it clear that it was not conservatism per se to which they were objecting, but the conservatism advanced by *National Review* and Buckley. The liberal anti-Communists had respect for what they considered true conservatism, a philosophy that sought to preserve existing institutions and maintain valuable traditions against the onslaught of what Michael Oakeshott, the distinguished conservative English philosopher, termed "rationalism in politics." When Buckley and his colleagues proved to be more interested in smashing liberalism than in advancing a prudent conservatism, the liberal anti-Communists replied that America had no real conservatives. Buckley and *National Review* writers readily admitted that if the liberal anti-Communists defined conservatism in strict libertarian or Burkean terms, they were not conservatives. They embodied a distinctly American breed of conservatism, one that the liberal anti-Communists were not able to consider respectfully, given that it equated liberalism with Communism.

Flank Left: Challenge from the Progressives

More potent adversaries of the liberal anti-Communists were the fellow travelers or anti-anti-Communists. In his now classic book *The Vital Center,* Arthur Schlesinger called these liberals "doughface progressives." Sidney Hook referred to them instead as "ritualistic liberals," and Irving Kristol preferred just "liberals." I will use the term "progressives," which was used by people across the political spectrum to describe them. The primary journals of the progressives were *The New Republic* and *The Nation,* and prominent progressive intellectuals included Fred Schuman, Lillian Hellman, Carey McWilliams, Leonard Bernstein, Henry Wallace, Harlow Shipley, Alan Barth, Zechariah Chafee, Freda Kirchwey, Henry Steele Commager, John Stewart Service, Owen Lattimore, and numerous professors at elite universities.

According to the liberal anti-Communists, the progressives did not understand the power of ideas or the role of ideology in shaping human events. The metaphysical benchmark of the progressives was faith in the goodness of human nature. The progressives were the naive "children of the light," whom Reinhold Niebuhr admonished for believing that because all people are good and share the same general goals, everyone can cooperate. Consistent with their unadulterated belief in human goodness, the progressives often wrote—as Dwight MacDonald did of the Nazis during World War II—that American criticism of Soviet totalitarianism was unacceptable until all forms of American injustice were eliminated. Their strategy of anti-Communism was, as a speaker at the Columbia University Bicentennial put it, to make America a nation "so just and equitable that no one will wish to betray it."[39]

An emblematic progressive view came from Fred Schuman, who wrote in "Horrors of Bolshevism, Inc.," a 1946 *The New Republic* article, that "[criticism of the USSR is] utterly misleading in the absence of a balanced perspective on the aspects of community experience and aspiration."[40] Another *New Republic* writer, Daniel Membane, pinpointed the evil of Communism: "The worst thing about Communism is that it produces ex-Communists."[41] Such astounding naïveté was, according to the liberal anti-Communists, a logical outgrowth of progressive thought. As Arthur Schlesinger bemoaned in 1947, "The USSR keeps coming through as a kind of enlarged Brook Farm community, complete with folk dancing in native costumes, joyous work in the fields and progressive kindergartens. Nothing in his system has prepared him for Stalin."[42] The progressives had no appreciation of evil.

Liberal anti-Communists attacked the progressives for having an insufficient appreciation of tragedy, caused by a naive faith in the inherent goodness of man. With individuals born good and corrupted by society, there are no limits to the improvements that well-intentioned people can enact when they put their minds together. Schlesinger again:

> Its persistent and sentimental optimism has endowed Doughface Progressivism with what in the middle of the twentieth century are fatal weaknesses: a weakness for impotence, because progressivism believes that history will make up for human error; a weakness for rhetoric, because it believes that man can be reformed by argument; a weakness for economic fetishism, because it believes that the good in man will be liberated by a change in economic institutions; a weakness for political myth, because Doughface optimism requires somewhere an act of faith in order to survive the contradictions of history. . . .[43]

According to the liberal anti-Communists, a major weakness of the progressives was in making distinctions—distinctions between liberalism and Communism, between the United States and the Soviet Union, and between theoretical musing and political reality. Distinctions require judgment, and judgment requires distinguishing between right and wrong. While the progressives shied away from this task, the liberal anti-Communists maintained that it was as necessary as it was difficult. Liberal anti-Communists charged that the progressive refusal to condemn Communism as an unadulterated evil sent a powerful message that Communism was a legitimate philosophy, indeed an extension of liberalism. For instance, Irving Kristol charged Henry Steele Commager with viewing Communism "out of the *left* corner of his eyes . . . [he seems] seduced by the insidious myth according to which Communism is a political trend continuous with liberalism and democratic socialism."[44] There was no question to the liberal anti-Communists that the worst manifestation of the progressives' simplistic view of human nature was an acceptance—though not espousal—of Communism.

The progressives granted credence to the Soviet experiment by engaging in high-level cultural exchanges with intellectuals in the Soviet bloc, which often disintegrated into anti-Western romps. The support for Communism at these conferences went beyond the theoretical musings of utopians and sometimes into downright approval of Stalin and his ways of dealing with writers and other intellectuals. But these conferences were not billed that way. They were cloaked in euphemism; terms such as peace, security, and freedom were ubiquitous and caused numerous intellectuals who should have known better to sign on as cosponsors.

The liberal anti-Communists reacted with disgust to these meetings and tried to disrupt them with a dissenting viewpoint whenever possible. Most memorable was the German Writers' Congress held in East Berlin in 1947. In the midst of this Stalinist conference, the twenty-seven-year-old American liberal anti-Communist Melvin Lasky rose and delivered a stunning oration at the risk of his physical safety. In a ringing tribute to the censored and imprisoned Soviet intellectuals, Lasky said, "We feel spiritual solidarity with writers and artists in Soviet Russia. . . . We know how soul-crushing it is to work and write when a political censor stands behind us and behind him stands the police." Lasky was promptly denounced by Soviet and fellow-traveling intellectuals as "a repulsive, war-mongering fascist," and "a cheap Hollywood imitation of Trotsky,"[45] but at least he left East Germany safely—a conclusion that was far from foregone.

These conferences reached a crescendo in 1949 at the Cultural and Scientific Conference for World Peace, held at the Waldorf-Astoria Hotel in New York. Intellectual historian Alexander Bloom calls this conference "the last gasp of the Popular Front."[46] Attended by a host of Communist and Socialist intellectuals in favor of those ideologies, this conference was cosponsored and attended by prominent American progressives. The liberal anti-Communists were furious, and several liberal anti-Communists infiltrated the conference (though not including Sidney Hook, whose request to speak was rebuffed). Dwight MacDonald (now a liberal anti-Communist) asked the Soviet writer Fadeyev why he allowed the Politburo to edit his novel *Young Guard*. "The Politburo's criticism helped my work greatly," was the reply. Nicholas Nabokov asked the Soviet composer Dmitri Shostakovich if he agreed with *Pravda* that the composers Stravinsky, Hindemith, and Schoenberg were "lackeys of imperialism" who should be banned from the Soviet Union. Shostakovich said yes.[47]

Fighting Conference with Conference

The liberal anti-Communists were not satisfied merely to infiltrate from within. A large-scale attack from without was needed, and the liberal anti-Communists delivered. Sidney Hook and the socialist Norman Thomas, the perennial presidential candidate and strong anti-Communist, organized an ad hoc group, Americans for Intellectual Freedom. This group was funded by David Dubinsky's International Ladies Garment Workers Union, which, like almost all other American unions, was a consistent bulwark against Communism in all forms and guises. Americans for International Freedom rented offices in the Waldorf-Astoria Hotel and attacked the conference until it ended, calling it "a perfect case study of how Communist propaganda is carried to writers, artists, scientists, and other intellectuals."[48] The first objective of the

Americans for Intellectual Freedom was to persuade the sponsors of the Waldorf conference to withdraw their support—Hook reasoned that one-quarter of the 650 sponsors would withdraw when the Communist influence on the conference was disclosed. Though some withdrew, there were not as many as Hook hoped for. The Americans for Intellectual Freedom also conducted a counter conference at Freedom House, which packed the 450-person room and was transmitted to either hundreds or thousands (depending on whose numbers are believed) of supporters in nearby Bryant Park.

The most important legacy of Americans for Intellectual Freedom was the impetus it provided the Congress for Cultural Freedom, which held conferences and sponsored journals to promote liberal anti-Communism around the world. Among the journals the congress funded were *Jiyu* in Japan, *Hiwar* in Lebanon, *Transition* in Uganda, *Mundo Nuevo* in Uraguay, *China Quarterly* in Taiwan, and *Quadrant* in Australia. However, the most successful journal, the one which Congress for Cultural Freedom President Michael Josselson called "our greatest asset,"[49] was the British magazine *Encounter*, edited by Irving Kristol and Stephen Spender.

Uncommon Allies: The Congress and Its Financiers

Even after the demise of the Congress for Cultural Freedom in the late 1950s, it was plagued by the issue of funding. In 1967, Tom Braden, a CIA operative in the 1950s, wrote an article in *The Saturday Evening Post* claiming that he directed CIA money to the Congress for Cultural Freedom to fund *Encounter* and other journals.[50] As the foremost historian of the congress, Peter Coleman, has shown, the reaction to Braden's revelation was different in each country. In Uganda, Rajat Neogy, the editor of *Transition*, was imprisoned in his country because he was said to be a "CIA agent." In Japan, editor Hoki Isihari's house was bombed, and he needed police protection. The French and Germans did not really care about the CIA involvement, but the Americans did.[51]

The reaction of the American progressives was predictable; they shuddered in horror that the liberal anti-Communists could have accepted CIA funding, which was said to manifest a lack of integrity and independence. Norman Podhoretz's dictum about the CIA penned in 1981 applies here. "Though some of us may have difficulty in understanding why there is anything wrong with working for the CIA, if we remind ourselves that what Communism was to Joe McCarthy, the CIA is to the *Nation* [we will understand why liberals have such animosity toward the CIA]."[52] When Braden revealed the involvement of the CIA with the Congress for Cultural Freedom, it was as though every suspicion that the progressives ever had about the liberal anti-Communists had come to fruition. The liberal anti-Communists were sellouts, intellectual tools of the political establishment. Jason Epstein's response in *The New York Review of Books*, "The CIA and the Intellectuals," was emblematic of the American liberal reaction; he asked of the liberal anti-Communists, "Weren't there at least some for whom the official limousines, the lectureships, the grants, and other allowances gave proof in the Calvinist sense of the predestined rightness of their choice?"[53]

None of the liberal anti-Communist intellectuals admitted knowledge of the CIA connection, but several had suspicions. Many of them knew that the international group was funded by the J. M. Kaplan Fund and Fairfield Foundation, a known conduit of CIA funds. The American Committee was the only national committee not to receive Fairfield money. This was significant because the CIA was prohibited from subsidizing groups within the United States. Diana Trilling had strong impressions that the congress was funded by the CIA for some time. Sometime in the 1950s, the chairman of the American Congress for Cultural Freedom, Norman Thomas, was desperate to raise money. He said that they did not have the money for the rent, but this did not mean bankruptcy. Mrs. Trilling explained,

> [Norman Thomas] would phone "Allen"; he returned from the telephone to tell us that a check for a thousand dollars would be in the mail the next morning. None of us could fail to know that the "Allen" who tided us over was Allen Dulles, head of the CIA, and that in the strictest sense it was even a breach of legality for him to give us help. But none of us, myself included, protested.[54]

Sidney Hook remembered the same story, but interpreted it differently. Hook wrote that Thomas indeed phoned Allen Dulles, but that Dulles's contribution was a personal one. Thomas and Dulles were friends from their undergraduate days at Princeton, and Dulles was just helping his friend with a donation of his own money.[55]

If the liberal anti-Communists were none too concerned when the funding sources of the congress were revealed, it was largely because they did not care. Daniel Bell, for instance, maintained that CIA funding would only be important if the financial sources affected the ideas produced, which it clearly did not.[56] Irving Kristol explained his beliefs on the matter in an article in *The New York Times Magazine* in 1968.

> I [did not] disapprove of the CIA or even of the secret subsidies (at certain times, in certain places, under certain conditions, for specific and limited purposes). Aside from the fact that the CIA, as a secret agency, seems to be staffed to an extraordinary extent by incorrigible blabbermouths, I have no more reason to despise it than, say, the Post Office. (Both are indispensable, both are exasperatingly inept.) No, I would have refused to go for two reasons: First, because I was (and am) exceedingly jealous of my reputation as an independent writer and thinker. Second, because, while in the Army in World War II, I had taken a solemn oath to myself that I would never, never again work as a functionary in a large organization, and especially not for the U.S. government.[57]

Kristol added that any allegations that the CIA or anyone else influenced the work of the congress or any of its publications was self-evidently fallacious. The notion that anyone—let alone the CIA—could influence the work of men of brazen independence like Ignazio Silone and Nicola Chiaramonte was mind-boggling to Kristol. "I would be scared silly of entrusting them with *anything*." As for Dwight MacDonald, an *Encounter* editor and regular contributor, Kristol asked, "Could the CIA have 'endorsed' him? Dwight has spent a fruitful life and distinguished career purposefully being a security risk to just about everyone and everything within the reach of his typewriter."[58]

Other liberal anti-Communists associated with the congress, such as Arthur Schlesinger and Sidney Hook, went further than

Kristol and Bell in their anti-anti-CIA sentiments. Schlesinger and Hook pointed out that progressives and conservatives each received plenty of money from foundations. The liberal anti-Communists were caught in something of a vacuum; they were unacceptable to both right-wing and left-wing foundations, and had few places to turn aside from the CIA. If foundations on the right and the left could fund intellectuals to advance their agenda, why not the CIA?[59]

Whose Backs Are Turned? The Hiss–Chambers Case

The great eruption between the liberal anti-Communists and the progressives occurred with the pivotal event of modern American intellectual history, the Hiss–Chambers affair. On its face, the case consisted of Whittaker Chambers, an admitted ex-Communist, claiming that Alger Hiss, a high-level official in the Roosevelt and Truman administrations, was a member of a Communist cell who provided important state secrets to the Soviet Union. Like the Dreyfus case in France a half-century before, the significance of the case went well beyond the issue of who was telling the truth. It became a battle over the moral legitimacy of American liberalism.

As the literature of thinkers from all across the ideological spectrum indicates, what was on trial, for better or for worse, was the New Deal and liberalism. The feeling on the left was "There but for the grace of God go I." Hiss was, in every respect, from his breeding to his education to his contacts to his resume, the quintessential New Deal liberal. He could be seen as a symbol of a generation. If many of the liberal intellectuals did not know Hiss, they probably had mutual friends, and if they did not, they easily could have. And the thought that Hiss could be a Communist—and thus verify the charges of their worst enemies—was too devastating to be treated with any degree of seriousness. If there was ever a case of cognitive dissonance in American politics, this was it. The almost religious faith in Hiss's innocence was, in fact, characteristic of many of the progressives' defenses of Hiss. Sidney Hook relates one anecdote about a conversation he had with a

Columbia University professor and diehard Hiss supporter. "One day I turned to him and asked, 'What kind of evidence would convince you that Chambers was telling the truth?' To which he replied: 'Even if Hiss himself were to confess his guilt, I wouldn't believe it.'"[60]

Indeed, the liberal anti-Communists and the conservatives did see Hiss as far more than an ordinary, and ultimately ineffectual, Communist spy. Looking at the unprecedented and incredible fervor generated by the case, Chambers claimed that he had indicted something much greater and much more important than Hiss. Indeed, Chambers saw Hiss as emblematic of liberalism and believed that he had not merely helped to bring one individual to justice but had tapped a domino in a massive sequence.

> The simple fact is that when I took my little sling and aimed at Communism, I also hit something else. What I hit was the forces of that great socialist revolution, which, in the name of liberalism, spasmodically, incompletely, somewhat formlessly, but always in the same direction, has been inching its ice cap over the nation for two decades.[61]

Chambers believed that the battle between freedom and Communism was not just a clash of political ideologies, but a cataclysmic conflict between two irreconcilably conflicting faiths. As he explained in the foreword of *Witness*, "[the case] was more than human tragedy. Much more than Alger Hiss or Whittaker Chambers was on trial in the trials of Alger Hiss. Two faiths were on trial."[62] One of these faiths was religious—a belief that man has inherent limits on his ability to remake the world because he is under God. The other faith was that man can ultimately reconstruct his environment and possibly even human nature to craft a radically better, ultimately utopian society.

The liberal anti-Communists had a grudging respect for Chambers. Some, notably Lionel Trilling, had known Chambers for many years. They all shared his fierce anti-Communism and admired his genius, but objected strongly when he said that liberalism was an extension of Communism. Moreover, the liberal anti-Communists did not share Chambers's contention that the battle over Communism was religious at the core. As Sidney Hook said in exasperation to *National Review* editor Ralph Toledano,

> Ralph, you know that I know Chambers is telling the truth. I know Hiss is lying. I know everything Chambers has told committees in testimony is absolutely true. But why does he have to bring God into it?[63]

The liberal anti-Communists found themselves in a fairly common position with regard to the Hiss case: neither right, left, nor in the middle. On one side were the progressives who maintained a religious faith in the innocence of Hiss and the villainy of Chambers despite the most extensive countervailing evidence. On the other side was the right, as represented by Chambers and his many lessors in the conservative intellectual community, who often did not distinguish between liberal anti-Communists and progressives, let alone fellow travelers and Communists. The liberal anti-Communists agreed with the position of the right (that Hiss was guilty) but could not accept the broad conclusions the conservatives drew from the case. Not willing to adulterate their principles and their logic to make allies, the liberal anti-Communists were shunned by all sides of the political spectrum.

McCarthy and His Enemies and His Enemies' Enemies

As with most of the other conflicts among the anti-Communists in the 1950s, the intellectual debate over Senator Joseph McCarthy had three distinct viewpoints: the conservatives on one side, the progressives on the other, and the liberal anti-Communists precariously planted somewhere in between. And as usual, the liberal anti-Communists attempted to maintain a line of sanity and hardheaded liberalism in the face of the hysteria generated by the progressives and the facile condemnations of liberalism by the right.

The conservative reaction to Senator McCarthy was heterogeneous. In the middle of the conservative spectrum were Buckley and his brother-in-law Brent Bozell, who, while agreeing with McCarthy that there were a number of security risks in the government who needed to be fired, found many of his methods repulsive. Thus, while Buckley and Bozell admittedly shared some of the same aims as McCarthy, they believed that his methods were a disgrace to his aims. This message became clouded as liberal intellectuals seemed to miss the numerous explicit condemnations of McCarthy in *McCarthy and His Enemies* in the numerous blistering reviews of the book.

There was, nonetheless, solid conservative support for McCarthy in the intellectual community. There were a few stalwarts who supported McCarthy strongly if for no other reason than the fact that their enemies were strongly opposed to him. *National Review* was receptive to these positions, as is evidenced by Willie Schlamm's eulogy of the senator in the magazine.

> I shall be perfectly satisfied to be called for the rest of my life a McCarthyite. . . . A McCarthyite is a person who is instructed, either by organic innocence or by true sophistication, to fight for his life and his verities . . . . In this grave we have put, for whatever future God has in His mind, a young man [McCarthy] who, in five gruesome years, was stoned by the genteel into ultimate fatigue. We do not crave his fate. We dread it. But we are ready to face it. We, too, have seen the gargoyles stare and sneer at us. We, too, are reaching out to crush them. We mean it. We are McCarthyites.[64]

The third position among the conservatives was represented by Whittaker Chambers who was, from the outset, unequivocally anti-McCarthy. Refusing to write the introduction to William Buckley's *McCarthy and His Enemies*, Chambers explained,

> One way whereby I can most easily help Communism is to associate myself publicly with Senator McCarthy; to give the enemy even a minor pretext for confusing the Hiss case with his activities, and rolling it all into a snarl with which to baffle, bedevil and divide public opinion.[65]

Not only would Chambers have nothing to do with McCarthy—in a rare entrance into political debate, Chambers told all his associates to do the same. As he warned Buckley, "For the Right to tie itself in any way to Senator McCarthy is suicide. Even if he were not what, poor man, he has become, he can't lead anybody because he can't think."[66] While some conservatives subscribed to a conservative version of the French expression *Il n'y a pas d'ennemi à gauche* (there is no enemy to the left), Chambers realized from the start what a lasting travesty McCarthy would be to anti-Communism.

Unlike the right, the progressives were not split over McCarthy. The progressive reaction was often characterized by hysterical anti-anti-Communism. The progressives seldom matched their denunciation of McCarthy with a condemnation of Communism. It was often as though McCarthy was the central evil and Communism his unfortunate target. As the progressive thinker Zechariah Chafee wrote, "The biggest danger to the United States is from stuffed shirts—stuffed shirts in positions of authority who seek to fill every government office and every teaching position with stuffed shirts."[67]

The disagreements the progressives had with McCarthy were not only over methods, style, and even concern for civil liberties—but for anti-Communism itself. For instance, the prominent progressive Telford Taylor maintained, "In an absolute sense, everyone is in a 'sensitive' position with respect to national security."[68] Therefore, Taylor and others reasoned, loyalty tests and oaths were inherently invidious because there could be no principled way of determining why a CIA operative should receive one and an art history professor should not. The progressives believed that the requirement that government officials take loyalty oaths to the United States was the first step toward a general repression of dissent. Bertrand Russell maintained that McCarthy had made the United States as repressive as the Soviet Union and President Robert Hutchins of the University of Chicago wrote, "Everywhere in the U.S. university professors . . . are silenced by the general atmosphere of repression that now prevails."[69]

Such invidious comparisons of American loyalty tests to totalitarian practices were not rare in the writings of the progressives. Just as some conservatives did not distinguish liberals from Communists, many progressives equated supporters of loyalty oaths with purveyors of the worst manifestations of evil. For instance, the respected British member of Parliament and intellectual R. H. S. Crosman considered loyalty tests as "morally corrupting as the Nuremberg laws."[70] In his book *Senator Joe McCarthy*, Richard Rovere writes of *The New York Times* theater critic Brooks Atkinson blaming a poor theater season on the curtailment of free speech sparked by McCarthy and of a rabbi in New York attributing a rise in panty raids by a fraternity to the fact that the carousing students have nothing else to do now that Senator McCarthy has chilled their political speech.[71]

In addition to warning of impending, if not present, mass denials of freedom in the United States propagated by McCarthy, progressives spoke often of nationwide pressure to "conform." They generally did not delve deeply into the issue of conformity; they almost always used it as a pejorative. For instance, Henry Steele Commager wrote, "What is the new loyalty? It is, above all, conformity. It is the uncritical and unquestioning acceptance of America as it is—the political institutions, the social relationships, the economic practices."[72] Hook, Kristol, and other liberal anti-Communists asserted that this view was simplistic liberal empty talk; conformity was sometimes desirable and sometimes detestable. While it is not good to hold a position on tax rates because one's neighbor does, who would decry conformity to the idea that rape is immoral? Kristol wrote in 1954, "Conformity, if we mean by that a profound consensus on moral and political first principle, is the condition for a decent society; without it, blunt terror must rule."[73]

One of the major issues of contention between the progressives on one side and the liberal anti-Communists and the conservatives on the other concerned the taking of the Fifth Amendment before congressional committees. While most of the progressives were not called before congressional committees, many Communist sympathizers were. Often, these sympathizers would take the Fifth Amendment when they appeared before the committee and would sometimes decline to answer any question—even "What is your name?"—on these grounds. The progressives defended these witnesses, stating their refusal to testify was an act of courage.

For the liberal anti-Communists and their conservative counterparts, the promiscuous use of the Fifth Amendment was a morally untenable act of cowardice. In a variety of essays and books, most notably Sidney Hook's *Common Sense and the Fifth Amendment*, the liberal anti-Communists railed against those who refused to stand by their principles when called upon to do so.

Hook questioned the propriety of the Fifth Amendment itself: "Is it self-evidently wrong to require a defendant or witness to give truthful testimony?"[74] The liberal anti-Communists believed that witnesses called before the various congressional investigative committees should tell the truth, defend their views against the philistines on the other side of the room, and damn the consequences—for what is higher than truth?

The liberal anti-Communists viewed the use of the Fifth Amendment as especially hypocritical in light of all the progressive talk about the need for "nonconformists" to speak their minds against the McCarthyite orthodoxy. The progressives were being given just that opportunity—in front of the whole country!—and were turning it down, out of fear. Hook compared the progressives' response, "On the advice of counsel, I plead the Fifth Amendment on the grounds that an answer might incriminate me," with the words of the Bible, "The wicked flee when no man pursueth: but the righteous are as bold as a lion," and with the courage of the socialist leader Eugene Debs who declared to those who sought to imprison him for political reasons, "I am in earnest—I will not equivocate—I will not excuse—I will not retreat a single inch—and I will be heard!"[75]

The liberal anti-Communists had an especially difficult balancing act when it came to McCarthy and the issues he addressed. On one hand, the liberal anti-Communists hated McCarthy. They believed his methods were both illiberal and anticonservative; his method of investigation by lie, innuendo, and unsubstantiated accusation was anathema to the foundations of democratic society that the liberal anti-Communists cherished. In the definitive liberal anti-Communist work on McCarthy, *McCarthy and the Communists*, written by Moshe Decter and James Rorty for the Congress for Cultural Freedom, three qualifications are listed which compose a good anti-Communist policy: "identify the enemy clearly, pinpoint the enemy unmistakably and expose the enemy persistently and relentlessly."[76] Decter and Rorty concluded that McCarthy blatantly violated these criteria, thus rendering his anti-Communism destructive and grossly counterproductive. They accused McCarthy of violating proper procedure in ten ways:

> Multiple untruth, abuse of documents, insinuation and innuendo, the slander amalgam, intimidation, attributing significance to the irrelevant, the fluff and diversionary gambit, the personal spy network, contempt for the law and unfounded charge of treason.[77]

These methods, combined with other appalling breaches of law and procedure, were more than sufficient to incite liberal anti-Communist animosity toward him. This hatred was compounded by what the liberal anti-Communists realized would be the unintended consequences of McCarthy's reign. Liberal anti-Communists were convinced that McCarthy was damaging the anti-Communist cause; the Communists and the anti-anti-Communists wanted nothing more than to be able to characterize anti-Communism as a philosophy indistinguishable from McCarthyism.

This theme of irresponsible people destroying otherwise good and necessary alliances was a recurring one for the liberal anti-Communists in the 1950s. First were the progressives, whose cavalier attitude toward Communism forced the liberal anti-Communists to spend much effort convincing the world that liberalism and Communism were inherently incompatible. Now, just as the progressives had split liberalism, McCarthy was splitting anti-Communism. Because McCarthy had made headway in associating reactionary politics with anti-Communism, the liberal anti-Communists had to convince the world that hard anti-Communism was incompatible with McCarthyism. Intellectually, this was an easy case to make. The liberal anti-Communists charged that McCarthy erred in focusing on Communists in government, a minor problem, while losing sight of Communists in the Soviet Union, a major problem. However, the combination of McCarthy's idiocy with the progressive and anti-anti-Communist exploitation of it proved to be very powerful. Neither the liberal nor the conservative anti-Communists were ever able to overcome it completely. From McCarthy's rise to the end of the Cold War, arguments equating anti-Communism with McCarthyism always had much resonance among intellectuals.

The liberal anti-Communists were determined not to let the ultimate conflict—the battle against Communism—be detoured by the junior senator from Wisconsin. The fact that McCarthy was a cancer on the American political system does not mean that everything he believed was false. As Martin Peretz recollects,

> Some things are true, even if Joe McCarthy believed them. There were Communists, disciplined, driven, dedicated, in those movements whose filial devotion was to foreign powers. Their filial devotion even extended to what Norman Mailer once called subpoena envy. Hoping for persecution. I can't tell you how many times during those days I would get a phone call in the middle of the night about someone's phone being tapped or someone's taxes being scrutinized.[78]

As Peretz suggests, the liberal anti-Communists saw the hysterical reaction of the progressives extend into the general culture and were alarmed that the fight against Communism was being abandoned for an attack on McCarthy. They endeavored to show that while McCarthy was a fool, he was not a threat to American freedom. Nathan Glazer encapsulated this position in a 1953 *Commentary* article, "[it is] a shame and an outrage that Senator McCarthy should remain in the Senate. Yet, I cannot see that [his position in the Senate] is an imminent danger to personal liberty in the United States."[79] The liberal anti-Communists believed that people should not lose sight of the fact that Communism—not McCarthy—was the real issue. *Commentary* Editor-in-Chief Elliot Cohen opined, "McCarthy remains in the [public] mind an unreliable, second-string blowhard; his only support as a great national figure is from the fascinated fears of the intelligentsia."[80] Hook elaborated on this view in *Partisan Review.*

> Our own vigilantes and reactionaries are much more like witches and straw scarecrows than are the paid and unpaid agents of the Kremlin who constitute the membership of the Communist Parties in all countries. They can be cleared out of the way by a little courage and a sense of humor. They have nuisance value especially because of their effects abroad.[81]

One area of nearly unanimous agreement among the liberal anti-Communists, even loosely defined, was that McCarthy did not represent a real threat to freedom. This was not an easy argument to make; there was a powerful contingent of intellectuals who maintained that McCarthy had sparked a general atmosphere of repression. The liberal anti-Communists pointed out that repression is blunt, and they saw few signs of it. Condemnation of McCarthy was, after all, standard fare in intellectual circles. As the Irving Howe explained, "At political gatherings, cocktail parties, academic sessions—McCarthyism, McCarthyism, until one grew sick of it."[82] The liberal anti-Communists found something slightly strange in everyone talking publicly about how they were being repressed and censored. They knew from personal experience that the fears of repression were unfounded; they were as anti-McCarthy as anyone else, and yet they never felt even a hint of danger in their work. As Richard Rovere wrote,

> I never felt under any compulsion to say anything but what I believed to be the truth about McCarthy and McCarthyism. I got a good deal of disagreeable mail, but I owned a capacious wastebasket, and that took care of the correspondence.[83]

Actually, in intellectual circles it was not a matter of fear to voice anti-McCarthy sentiments. To the contrary, the liberal anti-Communists considered it a professional hazard to be pro-McCarthy, or even anti-anti-McCarthy. Leslie Fiedler wrote in *Encounter,*

> It can be asserted with almost equal justice that there is nothing easier in America at the present moment than speaking ill of McCarthy. In academic circles, for instance, particularly in the East, it is generally the pro-McCarthy position which occasions resentment and even ostracism. . . . For intellectual respectability (and one can understand "intellectual" in its broadest possible scope), it is *de rigeur* that one consider McCarthyism a major threat to liberty.[84]

The liberal anti-Communist position against both McCarthy and the progressives was a precarious one indeed. In a politically polarized climate, the liberal anti-Communists had to demonstrate deftly that attacking McCarthy did not mean they sided with the progressives. While the New York intellectuals had once resolved the conflict between unpalatable alternatives on the right and the left with the philosophy, in the words of William Barrett, "to risk being wrong with Stalin for fear of being right with

Hearst,"[85] this was not to be the case for liberal anti-Communism in the 1950s.

The liberal anti-Communists, while finding numerous problems in the discretion given to security enforcement officials in many of the security programs, nevertheless supported them on the whole. For instance, Hook maintained that the Smith Act, which criminalized organizing for the purpose of overthrowing the government, was a positive piece of legislation, although he would modify it to stress action over advocacy.[86] Supporting security policies in theory and sometimes in reality, Hook always stressed prudence and the importance of respecting civil liberties.[87]

It is quite rare in intellectual history when all the arguments for a particular point of view are accurately encapsulated in one article. But for an understanding of liberal anti-Communism, Irving Kristol's *Commentary* essay in March 1952, "'Civil Liberties,' 1952—A Study in Confusion," is important and powerful. This essay was widely read, praised, and criticized, and still—today, many years after its publication—can generate heated discussion in certain circles. Kristol attacks anti-anti-Communists such as Chafee, Commager, Alan Barth, and William O. Douglas for defending the civil liberties of Communists when the goal of Communism is to overthrow the American democratic system that allows for free speech. Communism, Kristol maintains, "is an Idea, and it is of the essence of this Idea that it is also a conspiracy to subvert every social and political order it does not dominate." Kristol compares the Communists to the Nazis, stating that it would be just as absurd to allow a Nazi to teach in Flatbush as it would a Communist in Oshkosh. To permit Communists the same civil liberties as of the Americans is analogous to a "businessman . . . [paying] a handsome salary to someone pledged to his liquidation."

Kristol is especially suspicious of those who claim to be "victims" of the red scare. Contrary to progressives' rhetoric, few people actually lost a job on account of their political beliefs, and no one suffered worse than that. Kristol and his liberal anti-Communist colleagues considered those who bemoaned the red scare "Fifth Amendment Communists" because they were consistently shielding their ideas about overthrowing the system with a generous asset of the system itself—the Fifth Amendment.

> These martyrs whose testament is—"I refuse to answer on the grounds that it might incriminate me!" These "intellectuals" of Hollywood and radio who are outraged at a Congressman's insistence that they say what they actually believe. . . . Is this the vibrant voice of "nonconformity" and "dissent"? Are these the American rebels of today?

Kristol is very clear that liberals must dissociate themselves with unwavering decisiveness from Communism and fellow-traveling if they are to stand a chance when debating conservatives in the court of public opinion. He writes, "If American liberalism is not willing to discriminate between its achievements and its sins, it only disarms itself before Senator McCarthy, who is eager to have it appear that its achievements are its sins." After calling McCarthy a "vulgar demagogue" and divorcing himself from McCarthy's temperament and tactics, Kristol nonetheless establishes that the opposite of a wrong is not a right. In what has become the famous passage from that essay, Kristol writes,

> For there is one thing that the American people know about Senator McCarthy: he, like them, is unequivocally anti-Communist. About the spokesmen for American liberalism, they feel they know no such thing. And with some justification.[88]

Elliot Cohen predicted a major reaction to this essay in an editorial note about the article, and a large letters section was devoted to the piece in May 1952. While some letters criticized the essay, most were positive. The support catalogued in *Commentary* ranged from Ernest Angell of the ACLU to Norman Thomas. Particular support came in from the unions, as a laudatory letter from Arnold Beichman attests. Dissent came from the liberals attacked as well as from anti-Communist liberals who wished to adopt a different tone from that of Kristol. Important among these was Irving Howe, who used Kristol's article as a major impetus to start the journal *Dissent*, which would also be in the liberal anti-Communist camp, though it would accentuate liberalism and deemphasize anti-Communism. The impact of Kristol's article on

Howe was so great that he attacked Kristol for it seventeen years later in an exchange in *Commentary*. Kristol says that Michael Harrington needled him about the article until Harrington's death in the late 1980s.[89]

Liberal Anti-Communism in Retrospect

The fires of anti-Communism among the liberal anti-Communists abated—at least for the time being—when Senator Joseph McCarthy was censured by the Senate in 1954. While books and essays continued to be published on the issues raised by liberal anti-Communists throughout the 1950s, most of the arguments had been made by 1954. This is not to say that their battles were any less important; some of them continue to this day. Kristol's article on civil liberties and the Communists is still a point of controversy, and the Hiss-Chambers case still generates fierce disagreement. In the 1970s, the progressives used Watergate as proof that Richard Nixon was a dishonest man—and thus that Hiss was innocent. *Commentary* responded with a new study by Irving Younger concluding that Hiss was guilty.[90] *Commentary* was called to the issue again in 1993 when a Russian security officer, General Dmitri Volkogonov, claimed that he had thoroughly investigated old security files from the Soviet Union and did not find Hiss's name. *Commentary* debunked that myth—the historian could not possibly have gone through even a fraction of the files—and again published an article proving Hiss's guilt in an essay by Sam Tannenhaus.[91] It is hard to imagine the faith in the innocence of Hiss waning among his supporters, but it is harder still to imagine *Commentary* letting them have the last word.

If the Hiss case and McCarthy were the two great crises of liberal anti-Communism in the 1950s, the Vietnam War presented a third in the 1960s. While the liberal anti-Communists were close to becoming labeled neoconservatives by 1967 when *Commentary* held its symposium, "Liberal Anti-Communism Revisited," in which dozens of prominent intellectuals were asked to reflect on the meaning of liberal anti-Communism in light of the Vietnam War. The arguments presented in that symposium will be explored in the next chapter. Suffice it to say that the term liberal anti-Communist became less and less relevant as the days drew closer to neoconservatism.

But most of the ideas and trials of liberal anti-Communism have been adapted to inform neoconservatism. Many of the arguments of neoconservatism build directly upon the battles fought and ideas formulated in the days of liberal anti-Communism. While considering themselves to be liberals, the liberal anti-Communists directed most of their most powerful arguments against other liberals (the progressives). As Kristol reflected in 1993 on his days as a liberal anti-Communist, "It was the fundamental assumptions of contemporary liberalism that were my enemy."[92]

The liberal anti-Communists regarded liberalism as fragile and believed that its internal weaknesses (excessive tolerance toward enemies on the left, unwillingness to make distinctions, belief that everyone shares the same goals, etc.) could destroy it. In order to protect itself from opposition right and left, liberalism needed a strong core of beliefs that could see through cant, repair abused rhetoric, and separate itself from impostors bearing poison. Liberalism needed to know who its friends were but, more importantly, it needed to identify its enemies.

This duty was far from fulfilled by solely identifying enemies on the right. According to the liberal anti-Communists, the right was no great threat to liberalism. For progressives to assume that their primary adversaries were Buckley and McCarthy was, according to the liberal anti-Communists, an intellectually disingenuous betrayal of liberalism. The real enemy to liberalism was on the left; those, who, clothed in the comfortable rhetorical attire of the American democratic tradition, would abscond with its good name and replace it with something grossly illiberal. These enemies were much more difficult to counter than the right because this fight required the drawing of lines and the making of distinctions. With the right, drawing lines was no problem; the right was not trying to usurp liberalism; to the contrary, it denied, rejected, and impugned liberalism in any form. The right was perfectly honest that it wanted to destroy liberalism in all forms and guises.

Fighting the enemies on the left required that liberalism be properly defined with an acceptable range of beliefs and, correspondingly, an unacceptable range of beliefs. This, in turn, required stating that ideas directly and powerfully inform the conduct of human affairs and ultimately for the nature of human reality. Because not all human realities are alike, the ideas that define them cannot be alike; some must be better than others. The intellectual calling requires saying "We are right, and they are wrong!" in no uncertain terms.

Were liberal intellectuals—the progressives—willing to do this? The liberal anti-Communists believed that this question would not apply to one issue (anti-Communism in the case of the progressives in the 1950s), but would assume other forms as changing times offered different opportunities to either defend or abandon liberalism. If the progressives could blithely allow the Communists to usurp the language of liberalism and bastardize it for their own pernicious political purposes, this signaled something very inauspicious about the future.

In 1954, Irving Kristol warned, "For Communist propaganda despite all its striking failures, has gained one enormous—though subtle—success it has induced in the West, and particularly among Western intellectuals, a bad conscience about opposing Communism."[93] If the Communists won this battle, the United States would have a very difficult time mustering the intellectual confidence it needed to fight the menace in the East. The progressive doctrine of moral equivalence simultaneously distorts the East and bastardizes the virtues of the West, thus grossly harming its fight against Communism. The West could not win without a clear idea of why the East was the enemy and without an equally clear idea of why it was morally superior to its adversary. And what good is a liberalism that cannot defend America against the Soviet Union?

Hence it was not just that the liberal anti-Communists opposed the progressives in an effort to save liberalism. This was one factor; the liberal anti-Communists did, of course, want to save liberalism by sharply distinguishing it from anything even vaguely related to Communism. But the progressives were making that task more and more difficult. And the liberal anti-Communists opposed the progressives not because the progressives were liberals, but because they were intellectual gluttons who did not care what they put in their ideological bodies. In other words, they hated the progressives because they were progressives.

Notes

1. Irving Howe, *A Margin of Hope: An Intellectual Autobiography* (San Diego: Harcourt Brace Jovanovich, 1982) p. 14.
2. Editorial Statement, *Partisan Review* (February/March 1934) p. 2.
3. William Phillips, *A Partisan View: Five Decades of the Literary Life* (New York: Stein and Day, 1983) p. 34. Phillips, perhaps setting a record for job security, has served at the helm of *Partisan Review* for over sixty years.
4. Mary McCarthy, "America the Beautiful," *Commentary* (September 1947) p. 204.
5. Sidney Hook, "The Philosophical Battlefield," *Partisan Review* (March/April 1949) p. 252.
6. Editorial, "The Politics of Desperation," *Partisan Review* (April 1948) p. 450.
7. Norman Podhoretz, *Making It* (New York: Random House, 1967) p. 123.
8. "Our Country and Our Culture" was an ongoing symposium which began in the July/August issue of *Partisan Review* in 1952 and lasted through two more issues. Nearly all the prominent New York intellectuals at the time contributed.
9. Lionel Trilling, contribution to "Our Country and Our Culture," *Partisan Review* (July/August 1952) p. 318.
10. David Riesman, contribution to "Our Country and Our Culture," p. 311.
11. Diana Trilling, "A Memorandum on the Hiss Case," *Partisan Review* (1950) p. 229.
12. R. H. S. Crosman, ed., *The God That Failed*, (New York: Harper and Row, 1949) p. 113.
13. Melvin Lasky, "Why the Kremlin Extorts Confessions," *Commentary* (January 1952) p. 5.
14. Sidney Hook, *Heresy—Yes, Conspiracy—No!* (New York: John Day, 1953) p. 82.
15. Diana Trilling, "From an Autumn Journal," *Partisan Review* (January/February 1953) p. 26.
16. Irving Kristol, "On Negative Liberalism," *Encounter* (January 1954) p. 2.
17. Editorial, "The Liberal Fifth Column," *Partisan Review* (Summer 1946) p. 292.
18. Sidney Hook, *Common Sense and the Fifth Amendment*, (New York: Criterion Books, 1957) p. 78.

19. Sidney Hook, "Unpragmatic Liberalism," *The New Republic* (May 14, 1954) p. 20.
20. James Burnham, *The Struggle for the World*, (New York: John Day, 1947) p. 205.
21. *Heresy—Yes, Conspiracy—No!* pp. 21–22.
22. *Heresy—Yes, Conspiracy—No!* p. 22.
23. *Heresy—Yes, Conspiracy—No!* p. 131.
24. Maurice Goldbloom, "The Communist Conspiracy," review of *The Struggle for the World* by James Burnham. *Commentary* (July 1947) p. 97. See also Daniel Bell, " 'Hard' and 'Soft' Anti-Communism," *The New Leader* (May 17, 1954) pp. 23–25.
25. Lionel Trilling, *The Liberal Imagination.* (New York: Viking Press, 1950) p. ix.
26. Gertrude Himmelfarb, "Prophets of the New Conservatism," *Commentary* (January 1950) pp. 78–85.
27. George Nash, *The Conservative Intellectual Movement in the United States Since 1945* (New York: Basic Books, 1976) p. 27.
28. Quoted in John Diggins, *Up from Communism: Conservative Odysseys in Intellectual Life* (New York: Harper and Row, 1975) p. 407.
29. Quoted in Anne Carson Daly, "*The Conservative Mind* at Forty," *Intercollegiate Review* (Fall 1993) pp. 46–47.
30. Irving Kristol, "On the Burning Deck," review of *Up from Liberalism* by William F. Buckley. *Reporter* (November 26, 1959) p. 46.
31. John Judis, *William Buckley: Patron Saint of the Conservatives* (New York: Simon and Schuster, 1988) p. 115.
32. *William Buckley: Patron Saint of the Conservatives*, p. 470.
33. Whittaker Chambers, "Big Sister Is Watching You," review of *Atlas Shrugged* by Ayn Rand. *National Review* (December 28, 1957) p. 596.
34. William Buckley, *Up From Liberalism* (New York: McDowell, Obolensky, 1959) p. 115.
35. William Rusher, "Report from the Publisher," *National Review* (July 27, 1957) p. 101.
36. Frank Meyer, "Principles and Heresies," *National Review* (June 14, 1958) p. 566.
37. Dwight MacDonald, "Scrambled Eggheads on the Right," *Commentary* (April 1955) p. 372. This article was commissioned by Assistant Editor Norman Podhoretz.
38. "On the Burning Deck," p. 48.
39. As quoted in Sidney Hook, "Uncommon Sense About Security and Freedom," *The New Leader* (June 21, 1954) p. 8.
40. Fred Schuman, "Horrors of Bolshevism, Inc.," *The New Republic,* (May 6, 1946) p. 668.
41. As quoted in *Up From Communism*, p. 207.
42. Arthur Schlesinger, *The Vital Center* (Boston: Houghton Mifflin, 1949) p. 37.

43. *The Vital Center*, p. 40.

44. Quoted in Alexander Bloom, *Prodigal Sons: The New York Intellectuals and Their World* (New York: Oxford University Press, 1986) p. 237.

45. As quoted in Peter Coleman, *The Liberal Conspiracy: the Congress for Cultural Freedom and the Struggle for the Mind of Postwar Europe* (New York: Free Press, 1989) pp. 4, 5.

46. *Prodigal Sons: The New York Intellectuals and Their World*, p. 260.

47. *The Liberal Conspiracy*, p. 103.

48. *Prodigal Sons: The New York Intellectuals and Their World*, p. 260. For an excellent discussion of the Americans for Intellectual Freedom and its relationship to the Waldorf conference, see Neil Jumonville's *Critical Crossings: The New York Intellectuals in Postwar America* (Berkeley: University of California Press, 1991) pp. 28–35.

49. *The Liberal Conspiracy*, p. 59.

50. Tom Braden, "Why I'm Glad the CIA Is Immoral," *Saturday Evening Post* (May 20, 1967) pp. 10–14. The revelations about the relationship between the CIA and the Congress are on page 12.

51. *The Liberal Conspiracy*, p. 229.

52. Norman Podhoretz, "The Future Danger," *Commentary* (April 1981) p. 46.

53. Jason Epstein, "The CIA and the Intellectuals," *New York Review of Books* (April 20, 1967) p. 19.

54. Diana Trilling, "I was a member . . . ," *We Must March My Darlings* (New York: Harcourt Brace Jovanovich Harvest, 1978) pp. 60–61.

55. Sidney Hook, *Out of Step* (New York: Harper and Row, 1987) p. 425.

56. Daniel Bell, contribution to "Liberal Anti-Communism Revisited," *Commentary* (September 1987) p. 37.

57. Irving Kristol, "Memoirs of a 'Cold Warrior,' " *New York Times Magazine* (February 11, 1968) p. 15.

58. "Memoirs of a 'Cold Warrior,' " p. 17.

59. *Out of Step*, pp. 452, 455.

60. Sidney Hook, "An Autobiographical Fragment: The Strange Case of Whittaker Chambers." *Encounter* (January 1976) p. 78.

61. Whittaker Chambers, *Witness* (New York: Random House, 1953) p. 741.

62. *Witness*, p. 3.

63. Oliver Bath, "Warm Friday," *National Review* (May 4, 1984) p. 42.

64. Willie Schlamm, "Across McCarthy's Grave," *National Review* (May 18, 1957) p. 471.

65. As quoted in George van Dusen, "The Continuing Hiss: Whittaker Chambers, Alger Hiss and *National Review* Conservatism," *Citartha* (November 1971) p. 75.

66. As quoted in William Buckley, *Rumbles Left and Right: A Book About Troublesome People and Ideas* (New York: Putnam, 1963) p. 189.

67. Zechariah Chafee, introduction to Alan Barth's *The Loyalty of Free Men* (New York: Viking Press, 1951) p. xix.

68. *Common Sense and the Fifth Amendment*, p. 82.
69. Robert Hutchins, "The Freedom of the University," *Ethics* (January 1951) p. 97.
70. R. H. S. Crosman, "The Plight of U.S. Liberalism," *New Statesman and Nation* (October 16, 1954) p. 460.
71. Richard Rovere, *Senator Joe McCarthy* (New York: Harcourt Brace, 1959) p. 8.
72. Henry Steele Commager, *Freedom, Loyalty, Dissent* (New York: Oxford University Press, 1954) p. 141.
73. Irving Kristol, "Liberty and the Communists," *Partisan Review* (July/August 1954) p. 493.
74. *Common Sense and the Fifth Amendment*, p. 23.
75. *Common Sense and the Fifth Amendment*, p. 105.
76. Moshe Decter and James Rorty, *McCarthy and the Communists* (Boston: Beacon Press, 1954) p. 18.
77. *McCarthy and the Communists*, p. 84.
78. Quoted in Peter Collier and David Horowitz, *Second Thoughts: Former Radicals Look Back at the Sixties* (Lanham: Madison Books, 1989) p. 172.
79. Nathan Glazer, "The Method of Senator Joe McCarthy," *Commentary* (March 1953) p. 266.
80. Elliot Cohen, "The Free American Citizen, 1952," *Commentary* (September 1952) p. 229.
81. Sidney Hook, contribution to "Our Country and Our Culture," p. 574.
82. *A Margin of Hope*, p. 223.
83. *Senator Joe McCarthy*, p. 269.
84. Leslie Fiedler, "McCarthy," *Encounter* (August 1954) p. 13.
85. William Barrett, "Cultural Conference at the Waldorf," *Commentary* (May 1949) p. 487.
86. Sidney Hook, "Does the Smith Act Threaten Our Liberties?" *Commentary* (January 1953) pp. 63–73.
87. See Sidney Hook, "Uncommon Sense About Security and Freedom," *The New Leader* (June 21, 1954).
88. Irving Kristol, " 'Civil Liberties,' 1952—A Study in Confusion," *Commentary* (March 1952) pp. 235, 236, 234, 239, 229, 234.
89. Interview with Irving Kristol, January 26, 1994.
90. Irving Younger, "Was Alger Hiss Guilty?" *Commentary* (August 1975) pp. 23–37.
91. Sam Tannenhaus, "Hiss: Guilty as Charged," *Commentary* (April 1993) pp. 32–37.
92. Irving Kristol, "My Cold War," *The National Interest* (Spring 1993) p. 143.
93. "On Negative Liberalism," p. 3.

3

Mugged by Reality: The Counterculture and Ideology in the Sixties

When I think of the student rebellion today, and of the disasters threatening and in some measure already actual on the campuses today—the massed battles between students and police, the destruction of card catalogues and lecture halls (and the threat to major research libraries), the destruction of computer tapes and research notes, the arming of many black students and the terrorization in many cases of other black and white students—I do not think initially in terms of the major reforms that are required on the university campus, but I think of the politics, and even the tactics, that would defend the university. For I have made some commitments: that an orderly democracy is better than government by the expressive and violent outbursts of the most committed; that the university embodies values that transcend the given characteristics of a society or the specific disasters of an administration; that the faults of our society, grave as they are, do not require—indeed, would in no way be advanced by—the destruction of those fragile institutions which have been developed over centuries to transmit and expand knowledge. These are strongly held commitments, so strongly that my first reaction to student disruption—and it is not only an emotional one—is to consider how the disrupters can be isolated and weakened, how their influence, which is now enormous among students, can be reduced, how dissension among them can be encouraged, and how they can finally be removed from a community they wish to destroy.—Nathan Glazer, 1969

Prelude to the 1960s

The postwar boom, combined with the G.I. Bill, triggered an expansion of higher education on an unprecedented scale. For the first time, Jewish intellectuals were offered job security and social recognition as they filled the numerous teaching posts in universities that had been created. The larger intellectual culture began to appreciate Jews as well; Jews were welcome to write for high-circulation magazines such as *The New Yorker* and *Harper's*. Deciding to do so, however, was not always an easy one: the threat of being considered a "sellout" (as branching out beyond *Commentary* and *Partisan Review* was called) by fellow New York intellectuals was still an important, if slowly disappearing, concern.

While there were several liberal anti-Communist journals that featured the same authors writing on the same topics in the early 1950s, this uniformity began to crack by the middle of the decade. One group of intellectuals, led by Irving Howe, broke off from the liberal anti-Communism of *Commentary, Partisan Review*, and *The New Leader* to form a new journal, *Dissent*. While maintaining loose ties to the liberal anti-Communist camp, *Dissent* wanted to place a far greater stress on the first part of that label. In an important 1954 *Partisan Review* essay, "This Age of Conformity," which served as the launching point for *Dissent*, Irving Howe accuses the liberal anti-Communist writers of abandoning the intellectual's duty to criticize and becoming too comfortable with American society.[1] Howe claimed that the *Commentary* intellectuals focused on attacking Communists—an utterly safe activity—at the expense of dealing with the injustices of American society. Wanting to promulgate radical cultural criticism and political analysis while remaining within the larger rubric of liberal anti-Communism, Howe founded *Dissent* in 1955.

The Background of Norman Podhoretz

Something of a child prodigy growing up in Brooklyn, Norman Podhoretz accepted a scholarship to Columbia University upon graduation from college. While only a few miles apart geographically, Podhoretz nonetheless reflected in his 1967 memoirs, "One of the longest journeys in the world is the journey from Brooklyn to Manhattan."[2] Columbia turned out to be the perfect school for Podhoretz, as it would have been for any bright student burning with intellectual curiosity. Philosophers, critics, and authors such as Lionel Trilling, Moses Hadas, Mark van Doren, F. W. Dupee, Andrew Chiapee, and Richard Chase worked in close contact with the students from freshman year through graduation. The students, in proper awe of their accomplished professors, had their minds sparked as they became absorbed in the Western tradition of literature and thought.

In this atmosphere, Podhoretz flourished and established himself as the best of the brightest, earning a rare A+ from Trilling and another from Dupee and becoming Trilling's protégé. Podhoretz's success at Columbia won him a scholarship to Cambridge University, which, he discovered, was even farther from Brooklyn than Manhattan. To say the least, he was not accustomed to the Cambridge environment where he was provided with a commodious bedroom, living room, and servant.

Of more lasting importance than the shock generated by the irony of a poor Jewish boy from Brooklyn having a servant in England is the first exposure Podhoretz had to the world of political debate. This introduction arrived by accident. While studying literature with students from all over the world, Podhoretz found himself in the midst of rampant anti-Americanism. He spent many hours convincing foreigners that American women were not frigid and that American civil liberties were not about to be repealed by Senator McCarthy.

Podhoretz's literary training provided him with the intellectual foundation he needed to understand and attack the left. The themes of meliorism, simplicity, and radicalism that he saw in the politics of the left were easy for him to refute; he had confronted these questions before in his study of literature and he had only to remember the answers. Podhoretz's tangible resource in these debates was *Commentary*, and particularly Irving Kristol's article on Communists and civil liberties, which he considered at the time to be bold and correct.[3] All the while, he continued to establish himself as a literary phenomenon, winning the accolades of the internationally renowned British critic R. F. Leavis.

Podhoretz was tempted to remain at Cambridge, but instead returned to the United States to work as an assistant editor at *Commentary*. A two-year army stint did not significantly interrupt Podhoretz's literary ascendancy; he wrote consistently for *Commentary* and practically every other liberal anti-Communist journal of note throughout the 1950s. While the topics of his essays ranged from William Faulkner to nuclear war, they are thematically consistent. They reveal the skepticism of a literary critic inclined to doubt any simple answers or easy slogans to social, political, and literary questions—which are inherently complicated. Discussions of neoconservatism often operate from the assumption that Podhoretz and his colleagues were liberals in the 1950s, but there is little of what modern readers would consider liberalism in Podhoretz's early writings. Although accepting the basic liberal tenets of political liberalism such as support for labor, social security, and civil rights, Podhoretz had no use for the philosophy of liberalism—nor the conception of human nature that it embodied. Rejecting the meliorist, rationalist, and utopian themes of liberalism, Podhoretz had a great appreciation for the commonplace, noting that it did not come about easily or without reason. In a 1957 essay, Podhoretz accused liberalism of being unable to "take a sufficiently complicated view of reality," characterizing it as

> a conglomeration of attitudes suitable only to the naive, the callow, the rash: in short, the immature. Its view of the world was seen to be an undignified, indeed dangerous philosophy for the leading nation in the West to entertain.[4]

While Podhoretz eschewed conservatism as he did liberalism, his early writings reveal a respect for the commonplace and the everyday at the expense of utopianism. Thus, beginning in the 1950s, Podhoretz was democratic in his regard for the average American and his distaste for those who disdained bourgeois society and morality. This sense becomes quite clear in his seminal 1958 *Partisan Review* essay, "The Know-Nothing Bohemians."

In this essay, Podhoretz excoriates the Beats, several of whom he knew at Columbia. He maintains that their disdain for bourgeois morality translates into a dangerous nihilism, charging that the Beats manifest "the revolution of the spiritually underprivileged and the crippled of soul—young men who can't think straight and so hate anyone who can. . . ." The message of their animosity toward private property and the middle class was, according to Podhoretz, clear. "Kill the intellectuals who can talk coherently, kill the people who can sit still for five minutes at a time, kill those incomprehensible characters who are capable of getting seriously involved with a woman, a job, a cause."[5]

Podhoretz's essay on the Beats generated quite a bit of controversy in the intellectual community and spoke to a rift that would widen later. A short time after the essay was published, Podhoretz received a telephone call late at night from Jack Kerouac and Allen Ginsberg, who were at a party at Kerouac's apartment in Greenwich Village. "Come on down!" they urged. Although he was a grown man with a family, Podhoretz accepted the invitation to party with the Beats in the wee hours of the morning—lest he look like the bourgeois square they thought he was. He put on a suit and tie and went down to the Village where he argued the themes of his *Partisan Review* essay with its subjects. As he was about to leave, Ginsberg pulled him aside and said, "We're going to get your children."[6] The fight was joined. Podhoretz was provided a major weapon in this fight; in 1959 he was named editor in chief of *Commentary*.

Commentary and the Zeitgeist

But Podhoretz would not take up arms right away—at least not in the way his encounter with Kerouac foreshadowed. As J. David Hoeveler writes in his excellent book, *Watch on the Right: Conservative Intellectuals in the Reagan Era*, "Podhoretz, a man who seemed to be always just a little bit ahead of the times, believed he had anticipated and shaped the course of the leftward turn of the 1960s."[7] When magazines change, their changes are usually not sudden. Magazines are not like sports teams whose fortunes can be dramatically altered with a new coach or a top draft pick; rather, changes in magazines generally occur gradually as the worldview of their editors are affected by events in the polity or the culture. Important ideas and events ranging from the Hitler-Stalin Pact in 1939 to student radicalism in the 1960s to multiculturalism in the 1990s have challenged preconceptions and triggered realignment as old alliances are broken, new ones are made, and the very terms of the debate are transformed. It is rare that a magazine, especially an established one, changes overnight, but this is exactly what happened when Podhoretz took over *Commentary.*

Podhoretz had not been a radical in his youth, but felt the Zeitgeist of the 1960s when he assumed the job at *Commentary* and was determined to infuse the journal with a dose of radicalism.[8] The key factor behind Podhoretz's experimentation with radicalism was the death of Joseph Stalin and his replacement by Nikita Khrushchev. While maintaining his strong anti-Communism, Podhoretz did not think that the Soviet threat was as urgent now that Stalin was dead. The debate over whether the evil of the Soviet system was attributable to Stalin or to the intrinsic nature of Communism was prevalent at the time. It had surfaced in *Commentary* as far back in 1953, when Paul Willen argued in an essay, "Can Stalin Have a Successor? Why the Dictator's Shoes Can't Be Filled,"[9] that a hard anti-Communism was necessary only to counter the totalitarian system erected by and embodied in Stalin.

With Stalin dead, Podhoretz believed that American intellectuals could afford to experiment with ideas like pacifism and opposition to nuclear weapons.

> It was not that I thought the hard anti-Communist position had been proven wrong; on the contrary, never for a single moment did I doubt the soundness of [hard anti-Communist] ideas about the character of Stalin's regime inside the Soviet Union or about his aggressive designs on the rest of the world, or about the need for a determined American resistance to those designs. What I did begin to question was whether these ideas were still applicable to the Soviet Union under Khrushchev.[10]

Many of these articles contained praise for the peace movement. As William Phillips argues in a 1962 *Commentary* essay, left-wing intellectuals became attracted to the peace movement in the early 1960s when Communism and fellow-traveling became unacceptable forms of radicalism.[11] In the December 1962 issue, Nathan Glazer opined, "[America] needs a peace movement . . . more than ever to counter the much larger party of wild men who have an insufferable response to nuclear weapons and an insufficient love of life . . . ."[12] A 1960 piece by the renowned sociologist David Riesman and his colleague Malcolm Maccoby refers to "the ulcer of the cold war which exposes the failure of a style of life."[13]

Podhoretz was determined not to allow his flirtation with radicalism blind *Commentary* to the harsh realities of human nature and geopolitical structures. He realized that while he was searching for an acceptable form of radicalism, he had not found it. He was looking for a conservative radicalism—a radicalism that married anti-Communism to social experimentation in the domestic sphere. In order to achieve the hardheaded pacifism he sought, Podhoretz included essays that incorporated radically different ideas in the same issue of *Commentary*. For instance, in the same issue that Riesman and Maccoby penned their essay impugning the role of the United States in the Cold War, Richard Lowenthal maintained that Khrushchev was the logical heir to Stalin.[14] Theodore Draper, a formidable scholar and a regular contributor to *Commentary* for many years, expanded on Lowenthal's position in several articles during that period.[15] In July 1961, Irving Kristol published an essay attacking the idea of unilateral disarmament as advanced by H. Stuart Hughes in *Commentary*.[16]

More important than these largely theoretical pieces regarding defense policy was the coverage *Commentary* gave in the early 1960s to the Vietnam War. While very few publications in these years gave much thought to the Vietnam War or its potential ramifications, Podhoretz sensed early on that the conflict in Vietnam was worth the consideration of his journal. *Commentary* ran anti-Communist essays by Hans Morganthau, Oscar Gass, Maurice Goldbloom, and Joseph Zasloff expressing a desire to help the Vietnamese to be freed from the oppression of the Vietcong.[17] Nonetheless, these writers perceived that military action would be too complicated to be successful, and advised the United States to avoid a military engagement in Vietnam. Morganthau's essay in May 1962, "Vietnam: Another Korea?"[18] best articulates this sentiment. He writes that while the Communist threat is present and dangerous, a substantial American military engagement in Vietnam would be no more successful than the effort in Korea, and would in fact yield more casualties. He maintains that instead of military force, the United States should impose political sanctions on North Vietnam.

As these essays attest, the experimentation with utopian foreign policy ideas in *Commentary* was limited. Theoretical pacifism may have found a home in the pages of several issues, but realism was the governing philosophy of most actual discussions of serious policy. The real radicalism in the early years of *Commentary* was not found in the realm of foreign affairs, but of cultural criticism. In his opening statement as the editor of *Commentary*, Podhoretz explains,

> We are the heirs of a tradition going back to the philosophers of the Enlightenment which commits us, whether we like it or not, to acting out the great adventure of modernity to the limit. But the pressures of the cold war have gradually transformed us into a society devoting all its energies to holding a defensive line not only against the very real threat of Soviet power but against the promise of our own future potentialities.[19]

There were several important voices of radicalism presented in *Commentary*. Norman Mailer, Norman O. Brown, and Herbert Marcuse all published essays in the 1960s. However, the primary voice of cultural radicalism voiced in *Commentary* was that of Paul Goodman, a radical writer in whom Podhoretz took a special interest. In the 1950s, Goodman wrote a book, *Growing Up Absurd*, which was rejected by nineteen publishers. After these rejections, Goodman showed the manuscript to Podhoretz, who thought it was terrific. Podhoretz arranged to have *Growing Up Absurd* published through Jason Epstein, then the head of Random House. When the book was released, it became an instant best-seller. Podhoretz published three chapters of the book in *Commentary* in February and March of 1960 and in March of 1961.

Goodman's essays in *Commentary* were radical cultural criticism. He writes that the values of middle America are sorely in need of change because the average American cares for nothing more than his job and his standard of living and has no vision or real goals. These problems are endemic of larger cultural concerns, and relate to an unnecessarily strict definition of sexual morality and delinquency. Legalizing pornography, Goodman claimed, would have "beautiful cultural advantages."[20]

Commentary remained fairly conservative on issues concerning politics and social institutions, and did not question the fundamental tenets of American politics and did not advocate any type of socialist economics. Capitalism was criticized, but only when it fit directly into the rubric of cultural criticism. And no alternative was offered in its stead.

Podhoretz's decision to place limits on the types of radicalism that *Commentary* showcased remained firm even when he was presented with good opportunities to stretch those boundaries. He rejected an early version of the founding document of the New Left, the Port Huron agreement, as vulgar, infantile, and altogether intellectually unworthy for publication in *Commentary*. Podhoretz and the radicals whose essays he published in *Commentary* did not believe in large government or, for that matter, large anything. Social problems were not to be addressed to large structures which minimized the individual and possibly alienated him; they were to be solved locally by people working in tight-knit communities. As Nathan Glazer recollected in 1970,

> This was a radicalism that had a good deal in common with conservatism—the bias against government intervention in various areas, the willingness to let people decide for themselves how to spend their money, the belief that the theoretical and political structures reared by liberals to control policy in the foreign and domestic realms would no longer work, the allergy to Communist repression, the attraction toward the small.[21]

But Podhoretz's effort to balance radical cultural criticism with traditional analysis did not satisfy the old-time *Commentary* regulars, many of whom were furious with him. These intellectuals believed the liberal anti-Communist consensus to be fragile, and thought that Podhoretz's experimentation was potentially harmful. Irving Kristol, always harboring a deep disdain for radicalism, was not pleased with Podhoretz. Lionel Trilling was even more upset, considering his protégé's flirtation with radicalism to be a direct repudiation of his tutelage.[22]

The Birth of *The New York Review of Books*

The primacy of *Commentary* on the New York intellectual scene was challenged in 1963 with the founding of *The New York*

Review of Books. Through the late 1950s and early 1960s, the New York intellectuals saw a niche in the literary market for a good publication of book reviews. By the early 1960s, there were only three major publications which focused specifically on book reviews, *The Saturday Review* and the Sunday book review sections of *The New York Times* and the *Herald Tribune*. None of these met the demanding standards of the New York intellectuals.

There was nothing but talk about forming a new journal that would cover book reviews until Jason Epstein decided to put his mind to it. This idea had been something of a project for him for years; he had said in the late 1950s, "There's only one person in the country who could do it [start the review] and I'm busy."[23] Epstein managed to free himself from his duties as the young star of the publishing industry in 1962 with the newspaper strike in New York. He arranged for a $4,000 bank loan and appointed his wife, Barbara, and a *Harper's* editor, Robert Silvers, as the new editors of this journal-to-be. The model of the publication was the *London Times Literary Supplement*, and the new magazine was to be a distinctly family publication, with writers derived almost solely from the established New York intellectual scene.[24] A list of the first writers reads like a who's who of the New York intellectuals; the premier year of *The New York Review of Books* featured articles by Hannah Arendt, W. H. Auden, F. W. Dupee, Ralph Ellison, Nathan Glazer, Paul Goodman, Clement Greenberg, Lillian Hellman, Irving Howe, Alfred Kazin, Irving Kristol, Robert Lowell, Dwight MacDonald, Norman Mailer, Stephen Marcus, Mary McCarthy, William Phillips, Philip Rahv, Susan Sontag, Stephen Spender, William Styron, Gore Vidal, Robert Penn Warren, and Edmund Wilson. During the next two years, the *Review* published contributions from Daniel Bell, Midge Decter, Gertrude Himmelfarb, Norman Podhoretz, and Harold Rosenberg.

The New York Review of Books opened to great acclaim, having filled a gap in the American intellectual landscape. And it did so by staying within the New York literary family. If intellectual incest were a crime, the editors of *The New York Review of Books* would have been executed. Conflict of interest is generally overlooked in book reviewing, but *The New York Review of Books* abused the privilege. Historian Richard Hofstadter's characterization of the journal's early years is right on target—*The New York Review of Each Other's Books*.[25]

In the first two years of *The New York Review of Books*, the New York intellectuals maintained an uncharacteristic lack of acrimony. The only conflicts arising from *The New York Review of Books* at its inception were between Mary McCarthy and Norman Mailer over a parody Mailer wrote of an Elizabeth Hardwick piece, and between Mailer and Rahv because Mailer was upset that Rahv was commissioned to review a book instead of him.[26] Aside from that, the New York intellectuals reveled together in the glory of their new and successful publication. As Podhoretz wrote in 1963, "If *The New York Review* were to succeed in establishing itself on a permanent footing . . . everyone I know would certainly be happy. . . ."[27]

The Beginning of the Rift

As Podhoretz suggests, there was no competition between *The New York Review of Books* and *Commentary* at the inception of the newer publication. The two journals had an amicable relationship and shared writers—for one year. In 1964, Podhoretz asked Nathan Glazer, who was teaching at the University of California at Berkeley, to write an article for *Commentary* on the free speech movement at Berkeley. During the free speech movement in 1964, students at Berkeley had conducted protests and sit-ins, occupied buildings, and "liberated" People's Park in an event that consecrated Berkeley as the nation's focal point of radicalism. Glazer said that he would like to do a piece on the student upheaval for *Commentary*, but was already commissioned to write one for *The New York Review of Books*. Podhoretz found this a bit odd because he was under the impression that *The New York Review of Books* was just that—a journal that reviewed books—and was worried that his territory was being encroached upon.

A few weeks later, Glazer called Podhoretz and asked him if he still wanted the essay on the free speech movement. Podhoretz said he did want it, but wondered why it was not going into *The*

New York Review of Books. Glazer said that Robert Silvers had rejected it because it was too long. This was strange because *The New York Review of Books* was notorious for publishing exceptionally long articles.

The confusion was elucidated when *The New York Review of Books* published an essay on the free speech movement by John Schaar and Sheldon Wolin, which unequivocally sided with the students. Glazer's essay, which appeared in *Commentary,* is moderate in its treatment of both the administration and the students. Glazer's only criticism of the students concerns their demand for complete immunity for anything they might do. However, this apparently went too far for *The New York Review of Books*. Podhoretz, who was never that kind of radical, knew that he had a fight brewing.

In the two years following the Glazer/Schaar-Wolin controversy, *The New York Review of Books* continued to follow a radical line which went well beyond what Podhoretz would have considered for *Commentary* even in 1960 or 1961. Starting in 1965, *The New York Review of Books* ran articles on the Vietnam War questioning not only the wisdom of U.S. military engagement, but the morality of anti-Communism. While *The New York Review of Books* occasionally published essays by mainstream intellectuals like Hans Morganthau on Vietnam, it also veered far in the other direction, publishing poems by the left-wing Buddhist monk Thich Nhat Hanh. The radicalism of *The New York Review of Books* reached a pinnacle in a letter published in December 1965 by the former *Commentary* contributor Staughton Lynd. Lynd writes, "May I inquire why it is immoral to desire a Vietcong victory?" He proceeds to compare the Vietcong with the American Founding Fathers and said that the Communist demands boil down to "Give me liberty or give me death."[28]

The radicalism advanced in the pages of *The New York Review of Books* in 1964 and 1965 caused Podhoretz to seriously reevaluate his own experimentation with radicalism. As he had stressed since he assumed the top job at *Commentary* in 1960, his radicalism might challenge basic ideas about how to manifest certain fundamental principles, but those principles would not change. No matter what *Commentary* said about the Cold War or the arms race, Podhoretz believed that America was the greatest country on earth, Communism was evil, and standards of excellence in literature and the arts were inviolable. Perhaps a bit more emphasis should be put on America's failings than her successes, but in no way should that change the basic assumptions the New York intellectuals had grown to accept and to cherish.

The Questions of Race and Social Change

In 1965 and 1966, *The New York Review of Books* and *Commentary* began to split over political issues. As the Glazer-Schaar/Wolin incident foreshadows, *The New York Review of Books* was going in a radical direction while *Commentary* was retreating from its radicalism. In the mid-1960s, *Commentary* embodied a chastened liberalism; its writers advocated liberal policies in areas such as civil rights, welfare programs, and the Vietnam War while shunning utopian notions about the potential of politics. As a result of this political perspective, *Commentary* intellectuals were recognized as a distinct group, soon to be called neoconservative. While the term "neoconservative" was used actively until the early 1970s, it is an accurate description of the *Commentary* intellectuals from the mid-1960s on. The same people who were called neoconservatives in the 1970s—Podhoretz, Glazer, Kristol, Himmelfarb, Decter, Bell, Daniel Patrick Moynihan, James Q. Wilson—developed the positions in the 1960s that would earn them the appellation "neoconservative" in the next decade.

On the most important political issues of the day, the neoconservatives were firmly entrenched in the liberal camp. They were strong supporters of civil rights. Since the 1950s, all the New York intellectual magazines ran articles supporting civil rights legislation. There was no hedging on this issue. As Irving Kristol wrote in 1965, "I believe the Negro's struggle for civic equality to be absolutely just, and the use of militant methods in this struggle to be perfectly legitimate."[29] While the neoconservatives supported civil rights with as much fervor as anyone else, they were less sanguine about the possibility that civil rights legislation would ultimately accomplish what liberals hoped it would. The neoconservatives saw racial issues as infinitely complicated and beyond the ability of well-intentioned people to solve. While always supporting civil rights and government spending on antipoverty measures, *Commentary* essays in the 1960s maintained that storybook integration and eradication of black poverty would not follow the passage of any legislation or spending bills.

Those who had high hopes for integration figured that blacks, when duly enfranchised, would join the American melting pot and follow the same pattern as other ethnic groups. The concept of the melting pot was essential to the idea of integration; the melting pot, after all, is integration by definition. But the neoconservatives were skeptical about the existence of a melting pot in the first place, and this informed their skepticism about the possibilities for integration. In their seminal work on ethnicity, *Beyond the Melting Pot*, Nathan Glazer and Daniel Patrick Moynihan maintained that there could never be a world without involuntary association and ethnic or tribal ties—precisely the mechanisms that stood in the way of the liberal conception of integration. Ethnicity and race are, for better or for worse, categories people use to group themselves, and nothing can be done about that.

According to Glazer and Moynihan, the presence of these solid ethnic ties not only would complicate integration, but would make the enforcement of antidiscrimination legislation very difficult. They pointed to the persistence of guilds and unions—avenues to good jobs that mark the beginning of upward mobility. These organizations often recruited from a particular ethnic group and, whenever possible, on the basis of familiar connection. For no reason of prejudice, non-Italians or non-Irishmen or non-whatevers would not be able to enter certain occupations easily. Glazer and Moynihan asked, would the process of teaching one's son or nephew one's trade now be considered discrimination?

The same situation was true of social clubs. Like guilds, the social life in most American cities was determined largely by ethnicity. Italians, the Irish, blacks, and Jews live, socialize and marry within their own groups. These groups have not necessarily discriminated out of prejudice; rather, they simply associate with the people with whom they share a common heritage. If the liberal idea of integration depends on people of various races and ethnic groups mixing heavily and if ethnic groups tend to stick to their own, where would the opportunities for integration be? The neoconservatives did not see where and were skeptical of the idea that integration as understood by liberals would occur. Glazer and Moynihan wrote, "we may discover that discrimination is only the first crude barrier to integration, and that people are more complicated than either racists or those who deny the reality of race believe."[30]

In short, they believed that the liberal project regarding integration was doomed to fail because it was predicated on what Glazer called "a world, a society, that does not exist, except in ideology."[31] According to the neoconservatives, if the liberal paradigm failed on one hand because it was predicated on an imaginary world without ethnic or religious loyalties, it also failed in not exacting a specific definition for discrimination. The latter reason expanded beyond the problems that would be generated by indelible ethnic ties. The neoconservatives pointed out that every human activity involves discrimination of some sort—after all, what is choice if not discrimination for the desired and against the undesired? Because there are a myriad of different factors, some conscious and some unconscious, which account for a choice, it is extraordinarily difficult to isolate a particular factor, such as race. And to demand that a particular factor be isolated to such a strict standard that it could be enforced by law seemed nearly impossible. Without the ability to carefully delineate between racist and nonracist practices, determining discrimination would be extraordinarily difficult. The perception that the government could isolate illegitimate discrimination and punish it with exacting specificity struck the neoconservatives as another example of liberal utopian naïveté.

Even more discouraging to the neoconservatives was the realization that prejudice would be nearly impossible to eliminate, let alone by criminalizing discrimination. *Commentary* addressed this problem well before the burgeoning of civil rights legislation in a tortured essay by Dan Jacobson, a South African writer, published in May 1953. Jacobson, a self-professed liberal, wrote, "I am racially prejudiced, and I don't believe in my prejudices."[32] Despite the fact that his reason can dictate that his prejudice is wrong, his prejudice is too entrenched to be changed by his conscious volition, let alone by a government program. If this was the case with such a forthright liberal intellectual, why would an entire society be any different?

This idea of the intractability of prejudice formed the basis for one of the most controversial and well-known essays ever run in *Commentary*, Norman Podhoretz's "My Negro Problem—and Ours," published in February 1963. This piece was inspired by Podhoretz's good friend and long time *Commentary* contributor James Baldwin. In 1962, Podhoretz commissioned Baldwin to write an essay on the burgeoning movement of Black Muslims. Baldwin agreed and the two men had numerous discussions relating to the article. However, when the due date for the essay passed, Baldwin was nowhere to be found. Podhoretz finally located him and asked for the essay. This was impossible, Baldwin admitted, because he had submitted it to *The New Yorker*, which paid him twenty times as much as *Commentary* offered.

This violated the ultimate taboo of the literary world. Writers simply do not promise an article to one magazine and give it to another because the latter can pay more, and Podhoretz was furious. Baldwin's essay, "The Fire Next Time," was an immediate sensation. In venting his rage to others in literary circles, Podhoretz was told by many people to forgive Baldwin because he was black. This infuriated Podhoretz even more.

At lunch one afternoon, Podhoretz told Baldwin in no uncertain terms what he thought of blacks who claimed that they were oppressed and needed special privilege based on past discrimination when the Jews had the same problems and were not complaining. Podhoretz told Baldwin of his youth in an integrated neighborhood, where the black students did not study or work and spent their days terrorizing the white kids. Liberals were forever talking about integration, but what did they know of it? Podhoretz had grown up living next to blacks, and his experience was nothing like liberals said it should have been. Podhoretz describes their conversation, "as I talked, Baldwin's eyes blazed even more fiercely than usual. 'You ought,' he whispered when I had finished, 'to write all that down.' "[33]

And so "My Negro Problem—And Ours" was published. In

this essay, Podhoretz writes of his experience with blacks as a child. "I was . . . afraid of Negroes. And I still hated them with all my heart." He writes of being attacked by his black schoolmates when he did well in school or in athletic events. The black students hated him for his skin color and for his work habits. Their lifestyles were different from his, and Podhoretz claims that the seeds for the differences in achievement in adulthood were evident in their youth.

> *We* all went home every day for a lunch of spinach and potatoes; *they* roamed around during lunch hour, munching on candy bars. In winter *we* had to wear itchy woolen hats and mittens and cumbersome galoshes; *they* were bareheaded and loose as they pleased. *We* rarely played hooky, or got into serious trouble in school, for all our street-corner bravado; *they* were defiant, forever staying out (to do what delicious things?), forever making disturbances in class and in the halls, forever being sent to the principal and returning uncowed. But most important of all, *they* were tough; beautifully, enviably tough, not giving a damn for anyone or anything. To hell with the teacher, the truant officer, the cop; to hell with the whole of the adult world that held *us* in its grip. . . .

Podhoretz explains that to his liberal shame, his feelings toward Negroes have not changed. He writes, "Now that Brooklyn is behind me, do I fear and envy them and hate them still? The answer is yes." He admits that these feelings are "twisted and sick," but asserts that they are shared by a large number of whites. Similarly, Podhoretz claims (citing Baldwin) that all Negroes hate whites. In such a state of race relations, there can be only one solution—which is emphatically not integration, conventionally understood. It is miscegenation, which will make the differences between the two races go away by literally eliminating them.

> If I were asked today whether I would like a daughter of mine to marry one [negro], I would have to answer: "No, I wouldn't like it at all." I would rail and rave and rant and tear my hair. And then I hope I would have the courage to curse myself for raving and ranting, and to give her my blessing. How dare I withhold it at the behest of the child I once was and against the man I now have a duty to be?[34]

This essay, which was discussed by practically every political intellectual in America at the time, has since been reprinted in dozens of anthologies. The reaction to the article was—and is—heated, but mixed. Some admired its brutal honesty, and others liked it because it suited their political purposes. The psychologist Kenneth Clark was in the latter group. He used it to show that northern liberal whites were really as racist as the crude southern reactionaries. Others had different interpretations; in 1963, Stokely Carmichael, then a respected black activist associated with the Student Non-Violent Coordinating Committee (SNCC) called Podhoretz a "racist" at a speech in Philadelphia. Podhoretz seriously considered suing Carmichael for libel because the term racist "possessed an enormous force, second only to the word 'Nazi'," and would be damaging to his career. Remembering the editor's interest in liberal libel laws, Podhoretz decided against it.[35]

Neoconservative writings on the complicated nature of the American racial situation extended beyond discussions of the inviolability of ethnicity and the intractability of prejudice. The civil rights struggle had been a great moral crusade, but it was over. The poetry of Martin Luther King, Jr. would have to yield to the unglamorous prose of reality. In a 1967 *Commentary* essay, Daniel Patrick Moynihan offered,

> The President of a new Asian nation once remarked to an American Assistant Secretary of State that his predecessor, the first President, had a glorious job. "He had only to go about the country shouting, 'Freedom!' For me it's different. For me it's all arithmetic." Just such a day was approaching for the Negro leaders.[36]

Moynihan might have included liberal intellectuals as well. Everyone even loosely affiliated with liberalism agreed with the goals of the civil rights legislation—the guarantee of freedom and equality before the law for all citizens. However, with no consensus on the ends of economic and social change, agreement on the means would be almost impossible. No liberal believed that nothing should be done. Action was imperative despite the fact that no one was sure what success would look like or how to go about achieving it.

While the neoconservatives were not sure what they wanted to do, they were sure what they did not want to do. First, they did not want to point to the civil rights legislation, call a victory, and forget about the problems in black America. They wanted to provide blacks with the apparatus with which to take advantage of their freedom, and they believed that the government had a large responsibility toward that end. But the neoconservatives were not sure that the liberal paradigm of spending more money on urban problems was going to be effective.

The neoconservatives foresaw that numerous complications and perverse incentives would be generated by government social programs. While they generally did not phrase it as such nor begin to seriously confront it until the late 1960s, the neoconservatives always accorded primacy to culture when considering urban problems. Large programs that did not solve the problems they were intended to solve would not merely waste money—they could provide incentives that could exacerbate terrible problems. It was not just a matter of wasting money, a natural part of any experimentation, but of making terrible conditions even worse. The truly devastating unintended consequences of government social programs would not squandered resources, but the subsidizing and reinforcing of destructive behavior. The neoconservatives wrote of this as early as 1958, when Nathan Glazer published a report on Puerto Ricans in *Commentary*. Glazer writes that discrimination is far from the only reason that accounts for the poverty of Puerto Ricans. Rather, he maintains that the poverty of Puerto Ricans is due in large part to welfare dependency, which leads to the breakup of families. He concludes that their comfort with government services leads to "the active adapting of a people to all of the services of a modern welfare state [which] makes their condition possible."[37] Although Glazer sees some government programs as counterproductive producers of perverse incentives, he does not advocate terminating them or radically changing them.

Despite having no use for liberals in the 1960s, the neoconservatives nonetheless generally supported liberal welfare programs. The neoconservatives supported the programs while disagreeing with almost all of the reasons why they were enacted in the first place. This view is most evident in a 1966 *New York Times Maga-*

zine essay by Irving Kristol, "The Negro Today Is Like the Immigrant Yesterday." In this essay, Kristol maintains that welfare is predicated upon the principle that those on the dole want to find work and support themselves. Kristol agrees with this view, maintaining that welfare recipients are sincerely interested in self-help and that accusations of "self-perpetuating and self-generating dependency are spectral rather than sociological."[38] He further states that welfare benefits are too stingy and should be increased.

Nonetheless, Kristol contends that conservatives are correct in labeling the welfare system a "vicious cycle" which encourages people to have more children while remaining on the dole. Correspondingly, liberals should not be surprised when a more generous welfare system leads to more welfare recipients. While supporting generous welfare payments, he was aware that the unintended consequences of increased funding would be detrimental to the recipients. This paradox could not remain unresolved forever. Kristol and the neoconservatives eventually had to choose one or the other.

Or did they? While the discussion of welfare programs in the mid-1960s generally revolved around the state, the willingness of Kristol and others to point out the weakness of the state-run system led to a mode of thinking that they would expand upon in later years. In a 1963 *Harper's* article, "Is The Welfare State Obsolete?", Kristol ponders alternative ways of providing needed public services. He suggests, "After years of experience with New York's subway system, I am not at all averse to seeing it owned and operated by General Motors. Perhaps what is good for General Motors will be good for me. It couldn't be worse."

Aside from privatization of public functions, Kristol writes that the role of nongovernmental public institutions—such as church, neighborhood, and community groups—should assume much of the responsibility for social service. The important consideration to keep in mind is not the means—there is nothing inherently good about government welfare programs—but the end of helping people. And if people can be better helped through private institutions, so be it. Kristol again:

> A more relevant response would be to concede the desirability of the ends pursued while focusing attention on new methods of achieving them. We

> might then find that the idea of a welfare state does not necessarily imply that the state should itself always dispense all the welfare. Perhaps it would suffice for the state to establish a legal framework for a society in which individual welfare is recognized as a *social* responsibility without at the same time necessarily being a direct responsibility of the *state*.[39]

While Kristol's political writings in the mid-1960s were practically rather than ideologically driven, they were always informed by a revulsion to cant and intellectual sloppiness. Most of the cant in the 1960s was liberal, and Kristol devastated it, often employing an incisive dry wit—and sounding conservative in the process. Case in point is his 1967 article published in *The New York Times Magazine*.

> Bronx Borough President Herman Badillo grandly promises 100,000 new jobs in the glamorous, exciting, but unfortunately non-existent "automatic learning" industry; a little old shoe factory is apparently beneath his dignity.[40]

Kristol's discussion of a potential businessman in New York City provides another example of the commonsense, nonideological back-door conservatism that characterized his political thought in the 1960s. Having no principled commitment to the free market yet, Kristol nonetheless sympathized with businessmen under attack from the left in that same 1967 essay.

> [A] small businessman with a factory to establish would have to be out of his mind to locate it in New York City. The unions would cause him infinite trouble, the politicians would denounce him for polluting the atmosphere, the civil rights groups would picket him for trading with South Africa; SANE would excoriate him for producing war material—in short, he would be treated as a public nuisance rather than a public benefactor. Inevitably he asks himself: Who needs it?[41]

The Birth of *The Public Interest*

To study the new exploding public sector, Irving Kristol and Daniel Bell founded a journal, *The Public Interest*, in 1965. *The Public Interest*, though well within the rubric of liberalism in its early years, sought to explore many of the technical questions posed by the new and expansive programs. As Bloom suggests, Daniel Bell accurately articulated the goal of *The Public Interest* in a 1961 *Dissent* article. "A utopia has to specify where one wants to go, how to get there, the costs of the enterprise, and some realization of, and justification for, who is to pay."[42]

The design of *The Public Interest* was to be nonideological, which meant that the writers presupposed nothing; they simply wanted to acquire knowledge and make judgments based on the information they received. The name of the journal comes from Walter Lippman's statement: "The public interest may be presumed to be what men would choose if they saw clearly, thought rationally, acted disinterestedly and benevolently."[43] The goal of *The Public Interest* was to provide the information necessary for public policy decisions to be made rationally. The enemy was ideology, where dogmatic principles determined ends. As Bell wrote in that 1961 *Dissent* article,

> ideologists are "terrible simplifiers." Ideology makes it unnecessary for people to confront individual issues on their individual merits. One simply turns to the ideological vending machine, and out comes the prepared formulae. When these beliefs are suffused by apocalyptic fervor, ideas become weapons, and with dreadful results.[44]

Instead of ideology, the ordering of the modern world was to be determined by technical skill and the knowledge of experts. With agreement on the constitution of the good life, the only interesting question was how to attain those ends. As Nathan Glazer reflected on the early *Public Interest* in its twentieth anniversary issue, "All could agree on a course of action that satisfied more or less the interests of workers, employers, property owners and tenants, farmers and consumers, renters and investors."[45]

In their introduction to the first issue of the journal, Kristol and Bell wrote that the nature of ideology is to preconceive reality while the social scientist uses his tools to determine reality on the basis of the available evidence and knowledge. They believed that this was the wave of the future and that it was for the good. Glazer maintained this idea through the 1960s. For instance, he wrote in 1968,

> there are fewer and fewer major areas of American domestic policy in which the old-fashioned conflict between interests representing clearly reactionary forces, and the interests of the society in general, still remain central. . . . I would argue, complex technical issues have superseded the crude power struggle between the forces of reaction [and] the forces of progress.[46]

The Public Interest was consciously aimed at elites—university professors, upper-level government bureaucrats, policy makers and thinkers, journalists, and activists. The editors of *The Public Interest* thought that government policy would be more or less determined by these people, who were best qualified to draft and execute the social programs. Daniel Patrick Moynihan explained this point in the inaugural issue of *The Public Interest.*

> The creation of a society that can put an end to the "animal miseries" and stupid controversies that afflict most peoples would be an extraordinary achievement of the human spirit. . . . The prospect that the more primitive social issues of American politics are at last to be resolved need only mean that we may now turn to issues more demanding of human ingenuity than that of how to put an end to poverty in the richest nation in the world.[47]

The Public Interest began with the belief that the welfare state could be successful if constructed in the right way and infused by the correct incentives. As James Q. Wilson has noted, the first year of *The Public Interest* contained major articles by several prominent scholars advancing arguments from the thesis that important policy issues could be solved if confronted rationally.[48] While the early ideas of the contributors and editors of *The Public Interest* were rationalistic, they were not idealistic in the way that many of the intellectuals and planners in and close to government were. There is nothing in *The Public Interest* supporting "community action" or any other popular ideas of the day that signified a radical break with traditional city politics and government programs.

Kristol attributes the different expectations that government officials and *Public Interest* editors had for government programs to differences in their backgrounds. The bureaucrats and planners were largely born into privilege and had little contact with actual poor people. As a result, they were able to believe that the only difference between the poor and themselves was money. In addition, by virtue of their birthright and lives, they assumed that what Kristol called the "long, slow traditional climb up the ladder of economic mobility" could be circumvented by intelligent government programs. *Public Interest* contributors, on the other hand, knew poverty firsthand from their youths and had no illusions about the poor or the ability of policy makers to significantly alter the situation for the better.[49]

Thus, when the evidence began to accumulate that the Great Society was not reaping the expected gains, *Public Interest* editors and contributors were neither surprised nor unprepared. And *The Public Interest* wasted no time in revealing the failures of the welfare state. An early issue published parts of the Coleman Report, a report on education by James Coleman, one of America's preeminent social scientists.[50] Coleman conducted an exhaustive study of all the inputs regarding education, from class size to athletic facilities to school funding, and determined that the overriding determinant of success in educational performance was the family life of the children.

Articles that suggested the limits of public policy became prevalent in *The Public Interest*, especially regarding school busing and public housing. If there is one theme which can be culled from early issues of *The Public Interest*, it is the "law of unintended consequences." Government planners generally advanced their ideas based on the intended consequences of their programs—this input into education would lead to the diminution in class size, which would lead to better student performance; that jobs program would provide work for inner-city teenagers, which would move them from crime into productive activity, and so on.

But the neoconservatives concentrated on the unintended results of social action: the family breakdown encouraged by welfare, the homelessness encouraged by rent control, the shiftlessness allowed for in government jobs programs. Such unintended consequences accompanied every reform; as Aaron Wildavsky wrote, "Unanticipated consequences are the rule, not the exception, of social action."[51] The neoconservatives demonstrated how endemic unintended consequences were in government action; even the most seemingly innocuous measures invited them. In a

1960 *Encounter* article, Kristol considered the Garden State Parkway in New Jersey by writing,

> the toll collectors were instructed to say "thank you" to each passing motorist, which innovation [*sic*] so affected the motorists that they became positively maudlin, thanking the collectors profusely in return, sometimes backing up to do so; the upshot of this high-minded reform is that traffic on the Parkway is now in one perpetual snarl, with the Parkway authorities threatening to discipline motorists who don't keep moving.[52]

It was not for opposition to friendliness on the nation's thoroughfares that *The Public Interest* became known as conservative, but by writing of what Glazer calls "the limits of social policy,"[53] and by pointing out the problems that were produced by liberal solutions. As Kristol suggested in 1985,

> Rigorous statistical analysis always does tend to throw cold (or at least cooling) water on reformist enthusiasm—hence the reputation earned by *The Public Interest*, from its earliest days, of being in some sense "conservative." In fact, only a minority of *Public Interest* contributors have ever been conservatives, or even "neoconservatives." But there is no doubt that if you go around constantly chastening utopian enthusiasm, or offering reasons for curbing reformist enthusiasm, you are bound to find yourself regarded as a conservative element.[54]

The stress on the law of unintended consequences changed neoconservatism. For one thing, it ended the trial separation between neoconservatism and ideology. The technical analyses of the writers and editors of *The Public Interest* that consistently demonstrated the devastating unintended consequences of governmental programs made them rethink the emphasis they placed on the efficacy of expert knowledge and technical solutions. Somehow, failure after failure could not be the result of coincidence, recurring bad luck, or the product of poor organization. As the decade progressed, the neoconservatives began to realize that the rational solutions they proposed to solve complex social problems were overly simplistic and optimistic. Looking back on his confidence not long before, Glazer wrote in 1969,

> the problem of poverty and inequality, it seemed, could be handled by a tax cut, an Area Redevelopment Administration program for the by-passed

areas, a manpower training program for workers displaced by automation. The poverty program was still, in those days, a juvenile-delinquency-fighting program. Life was simpler then![55]

Life became more complicated when the neoconservatives abandoned the meliorism of the past and began to concentrate on the cultural causes and consequences of poverty and government solutions to poverty. The intellectuals around *The Public Interest* realized that their models and those of government planners presupposed a rational individual who wants to partake in the bourgeois culture of hard work, individual achievement, close families, and educational advancement. Often, programs designed for people with one set of values were meant to serve the underclass, which often lived by a very different code. Rational policy analysis was predicated on a population with similar values and goals. With that foundation exploded, the editors of *The Public Interest* surmised that such analysis was radically devalued. As James Q. Wilson concluded in 1969, "Modern economies, however affluent, have great difficulty in doing much for anybody who finds life on the street more attractive than life in the factory."[56] And for those who found life on the street more attractive than life in the factory, the meliorism of social scientists would have to yield to ideology and its teacher, political philosophy. As Kristol noted in 1971,

> Controversies over matters of political philosophy, since they are controversies over fundamental beliefs, are exceedingly dangerous for any nation. They certainly ought not to happen too often, for they then make civilized political life very difficult to sustain. But they ought to—they inevitably will—arise occasionally. We seem to be living through such a moment right now; and the first thing to do is consciously to face up to this critical fact and make it manifest in all its implications. We must go behind the small questions in order to contemplate the larger answers they tacitly demand.[57]

The Moynihan Report, Campus Corollaries, and the Fallout

What became known as the Moynihan Report was actually a paper produced by the Office of Policy Planning and Research in the Department of Labor in March 1965, entitled "The Case for National Action: The Negro Family."[58] The intended audience of this report, written mainly by Daniel Patrick Moynihan, was approximately one hundred upper-level officials in the Johnson administration.[59] Its intent was to provide ideas for President Johnson's major civil rights address at Howard University in June 1965.

The report was a short and rudimentary discussion of the condition of blacks in America. Moynihan began the report stating, first, that

> the racist virus in the American blood stream still afflicts us: Negroes will encounter serious personal prejudice for at least another generation. Second, three centuries of sometimes unimaginable mistreatment have taken their toll on the Negro people.

Moynihan attributes the genesis of the racist virus to slavery, which he holds was the worst form of slavery the world has ever known because of its uniquely debilitating effects on the black family. The damage inflicted on the black family by slavery remains the major barrier to black advancement.

The Moynihan Report is replete with statistics regarding the startlingly high rates of black illegitimacy, welfare participation, and single-parent families. Moynihan calls the breakdown of the family a "tangle of pathology," and maintains that the government's major role in the post-civil rights era is to strengthen the black family. The report proposed no new policy solutions; Moynihan wanted to articulate the grave problem and discuss the solutions later.

The report remained private until the summer. President Johnson delivered his much acclaimed speech in June, which was widely and correctly perceived to be just the beginning of a major government effort to augment the economic and social conditions of blacks. However, in July, the report was leaked to Mary McGrory of the *Washington Star* and later to other reporters. Copies of this "confidential" report soon began to make their way around the Beltway, making it a well-known secret. *Newsweek* ran a two-page article on the report, fully aware of the dangers of releasing it. The unsigned article declares, "The Negro family problem was scarcely news to social scientists. But its very intimacy has excluded it from the public dialogue of civil rights; it reaches too deep into white prejudices and Negro sensitivities."[60] Needless to say, civil rights leaders wanted to know what was in this report and demanded that it be made public.

The report grew in importance in mid-August 1965. The occasion was the riots in Watts, which the administration had a difficult time explaining considering the enormous gains in civil rights in 1964 and 1965. The press used the Moynihan Report, which was becoming more and more widely (though unofficially) available, as the administration's explanation for the rioting. In the mainstream press to a small extent and in the major sectors of the civil rights community to a much greater extent, the Moynihan Report was interpreted to have "blamed the victim." For instance, James Farmer, president of the Congress of Racial Equality, writes,

> By laying the primary blame for present-day inequalities on the pathological condition of the Negro family and community, Moynihan has provided a massive academic cop-out for the white conscience and clearly implied that Negroes in this nation will never secure a substantial measure of freedom until we learn to behave ourselves and stop buying Cadillacs instead of bread.[61]

The discussion by William Ryan in *The Nation* and reprinted in the magazine of the National Association for the Advancement of Colored People, *Crisis*, was even more virulent. Ryan accuses Moynihan of purveying a

> new form of subtle racism . . . and seduc[ing] the reader into believing that it is not racism and discrimination but the weaknesses and defects of the Negro himself that account for the present status of inequality between Negro and white.[62]

Moynihan was personally devastated by the reaction to his work and the subsequent mauling of his reputation. He explained,

> I had spent much of my adult life working for racial equality, had helped to put together the antipoverty program, had set the theme and written the

first draft of President Johnson's address at Howard University, which he was to describe as the finest civil rights speech he ever gave, only to find myself suddenly a symbol of reaction.[63]

Moynihan looked to the liberal and university communities for support and found little. There were a couple of isolated liberals; the prominent sociologist Kenneth Clark was one. Clark said, "It's a kind of wolf pack operating in a very undignified way. If Pat is a racist, I am. He highlights the total pattern of segregation and discrimination. Is a doctor responsible for a disease simply because he diagnoses it?"[64] But as Clark's own statement suggests, he was one of the very few members of the liberal intellectual community who defended Moynihan. If most liberal intellectuals did not themselves condemn Moynihan of racism, they did not defend him from the radicals who did.

The neoconservatives were furious at the liberal collapse around Moynihan. They perceived this reaction as intellectually and personally disingenuous as well as downright immoral—Moynihan was well known in the academic community and no one could seriously claim that he was a racist. Still, his colleagues would not defend him. The neoconservatives contrasted the liberal reaction to the Moynihan Report with that of *National Review*, which praised the report and defended its author. Moynihan commented,

> My God, I was not a racist, I was not a bigot, but all the good guys were calling me a racist, [while] here was this fellow Buckley saying these thoughtful things. Glazer and I began to notice that we were getting treated in *National Review* with a much higher level of intellectual honesty [than in liberal publications.][65]

This abandonment of Moynihan was not an isolated incident—similar events were common in the 1960s and early 1970s. Edward Banfield, a renowned social scientist at Harvard, wrote a book, *The Unheavenly City*, which detailed the failure of many antipoverty programs. As with the Moynihan Report, the reaction to this book was ferocious. Banfield was made the bane of liberal intellectuals and was forced out of Harvard by his colleagues, many of whom refused to speak to him after publication of the book.

Another Harvard professor, Richard J. Herrnstein, was also the victim of left-wing inquisitors on college campuses. In 1971, he wrote an article in *Atlantic Monthly* asserting that an individual's genetic makeup affects his intelligence and that his intelligence affects success in life; therefore, one's genetic makeup affects success in life.[66] Herrnstein's article generated a fury among campus radicals. Wherever he went to speak shortly after the article was published, he was viciously hounded and given death threats. He had to flee from one speech in an unmarked police car. The response of liberal intellectuals to the Herrnstein case was, as with Moynihan and Banfield, equivocal. While Herrnstein's liberal colleagues did not like the tactics of the opposition, they refused to support him against charges of racism leveled by the radicals.

In these and in several less prominent cases, the neoconservatives saw the pursuit of truth being sacrificed on the altar of left-wing orthodoxy, and were determined to lead the countercharge. With respected thinkers and rigorous scholars such as Moynihan, Banfield, and Herrnstein being run off elite campuses for not conforming with a particular ideology, freedom of thought was clearly in jeopardy. Podhoretz summarizes the neoconservative concern with the state of the universities by the early 1970s.

> The upshot [of the Banfield, Moynihan, and Herrnstein incidents] is an atmosphere which is no longer conducive to fearless inquiry or even to playful speculation and which, far from encouraging, positively obstructs the development of independence of mind and of the critical spirit. Thus do our colleges and universities continue their degenerative mutation from sanctuaries for free discussion into inquisitorial agents of a dogmatic secular faith.[67]

James Q. Wilson, a professor at Harvard at the time of the Banfield, Herrnstein, and Moynihan incidents, wrote an essay in *Commentary*, "Liberalism and Liberal Education," which maintains that the same forces that silenced those three scholars chilled debate over the campus. "Political correctness" became an important issue in the early 1990s, but Wilson predicted it two decades earlier. He wrote that the radicals created an intellectual climate where dissent from any number of liberal orthodoxies—especially those concerning race and Vietnam—was violently condemned as fascist or worse. Wilson states that he has been a member of five institutions in his life—the Catholic Church, the University of the Redlands, the U.S. Navy, the University of Chicago, and Harvard University. "If I were required to rank them by the extent to which free and uninhibited discussion were possible within them, I am very much afraid that the Harvard of 1972 would not rank near the top." Extrapolating from his experience at Harvard, he wrote,

> [it is] within higher education that one finds today many . . . of the most serious threats to certain liberal values—the harassment of unpopular views, the use of force to prevent certain persons from speaking, the adoption of quota systems either to reduce the admissions of certain kinds of students or enhance the admissions of other kinds, and the politicization of the university to make it an arena for the exchange of manifestoes rather than a forum for the discussion of ideas.[68]

The neoconservatives believed that liberal intellectuals had become, in large part, entranced by the causes of radical students and minorities to the point where they could no longer sense who the enemies of true liberalism were. Wilson says that while George Wallace was afraid of being "out-segged" by anyone to his right, liberal intellectuals did not want to be "out-civil righted" by anyone to their left.[69] Liberal professors were afraid that the defense of existing institutions or traditions against the onslaught of black radicals would be considered "right-wing" and against civil rights. They did not connect the student radicalism with their own values or their own jobs. In short, they did not understand the power of ideas.[70] The radicals were subverting nearly everything for which the liberal ideals of scholarship stood, and liberal intellectuals just watched. Daniel Bell and Irving Kristol commented, "The past five years have been, for American universities, the most dramatic in their history. The drama, indeed, is so flamboyant that sober contemplation is exceedingly difficult."[71] And despite the most rabid protests and violent denunciations of the way of life that liberal intellectuals had cultivated, they did not defend themselves, let alone confront the radicals.

Liberalism, Neal Kozodoy has argued, was destroyed by its greatest strength. "[Tolerance] has regressed from being the chief glory and strength of liberalism to being one of its chief weaknesses—its Achilles heel—rendering it all but impotent in the face of determined assaults upon it by radical movements of all kinds, especially but not exclusively those emanating from the Left."[72] The intellectual child of the desiccated liberalism of the progressives, it was almost the actual child as well. Liberalism could not ignore these radical movements, and if it could not fight them, that left only one alternative. Nathan Glazer explains that liberal intellectuals

> accept the idea that people need not be taught to work hard, or to study in order to qualify, or to be judged in accordance with impersonal and universal criteria. They have accepted the idea that they ought to support revolutionaries because revolutionaries have access to the grass roots, and they have accepted the idea that they should not support moderates because moderates are Uncle Toms whose belief in the bourgeois virtues cuts them off from their own people.[73]

Gertrude Himmelfarb, who was a professor and recognized as an eminent historian by the 1960s, maintains that many of the professors she knew were very committed to their students and took great pride in the educational enterprise. They suffered a "failure of imagination." Not recognizing the cultural revolution that was occurring before them, many intellectuals believed that the radicalism was just a passing phase that should not be taken too seriously. Himmelfarb remembers Lionel Trilling telling her, "We mustn't put ourselves in a position of antagonizing the students. They are, after all, our children." Spoiling their children instead of disciplining them, the liberal intellectuals stepped aside as the onslaught of radicalism ran unhindered.[74]

The liberalism of the 1960s was the ideological offspring of the liberalism of the progressives in the 1950s, and many of the radicals in the 1960s were the biological offspring of the progressives of the 1950s. The neoconservatives, especially Midge Decter and Nathan Glazer, have pointed out that the notion that the student radicals were rebels against authority was fallacious. Instead, many of them were "red diaper babies," perhaps "going too far," but showing the same spirit that their parents had a generation ago.[75]

The students were lauded by their parents and professors as "brilliant," even "the best generation ever" because of the passion they devoted to political issues. Liberals who voiced these beliefs generally viewed political passion in amoral terms; activism and participation were good no matter what cause they served. And when the students dropped out and acted in ways that even the most liberal adults disdained, many of these adults did not see their complicity and, indeed, encouragement. The neoconservatives, however, saw the radical actions as logical consequences of an adult culture that did not object in any significant way to early student criticisms of America and bourgeois society as iniquitous. As Irving Kristol wrote in 1965 when student unrest was starting,

> Many of the same middle-aged critics who so fervently and eloquently condemned the silent generation are now considerably upset and puzzled at the way students are "misbehaving" these days. One wanted the young to be idealistic, perhaps even somewhat radical, possibly even a bit militant—but not like this! It used to be said that the revolution devours its children. It now appears that these children have devoured this revolution.[76]

Kristol maintained that the inability of liberals to defend liberalism not only contributed to the personal tragedy of many radical students, but dealt a serious blow to the university. Students came to college looking for intellectual and moral guidance, and found their professors caving in to radicals impugning the standards of such guidance. Youth need role models, guidance, authority, and direction. To be told that such things are illegitimate is not only disillusioning, but ultimately destructive. The students and, ultimately, society are the victims of this relativism. Kristol maintained in a 1974 *Psychology Today* interview,

> We tell young people in our universities that we don't know what the good life is. And we don't ask them to find out what it is, but just to question everything that pretends to be good. That is exactly what they do and they then show, which is true, that things that pretend to be good are not as good as they seem. But that kind of questioning makes for an empty

> and exacerbating existence. Society has put them in an unfair position by giving them enough education to think about these matters but without giving them any guidance as to how to think. I think people who have no inherited values by which to live and who have not come up with a new set of values to live by—well, I think such people will find the universe to be a hostile place and the reaction to hostility is aggression.[77]

Joshua Muravchik, a neoconservative who graduated from the City College of New York in 1969, witnessed student radicalism firsthand. After radical black students took over the school, claiming to be victims of "genocide," Muravchik, a campus socialist organizer, attempted to marshal a voice of sanity in support of the institution that was, after all, providing free education to its student rebels. Given that the radicals were launching a full-fledged assault on the university and on liberal ideals, Muravchik figured that he could forge a coalition between nonradical students and professors. He was mistaken.

> I went to the best, most senior, most well-respected, naturally liberal professors and said, "What this is building up to is getting more and more out of hand—it's crazy—and before it gets more out of hand, people ought to get together and offer a voice of reason." We had a bunch of students, but we need some faculty as well. And the professors said, "Gee, you're right, but it's not mine to handle."

Looking back on his experience and similar occurrences elsewhere, Muravchik notes, "The astonishing thing was how successful that assault [on the university] was. Liberals just collapsed. This I don't understand. I didn't understand it then, I don't understand it now."[78]

Nor, for that matter, did many of the other neoconservatives. While the liberals did not recognize their true enemies, the New Left could not have told them more explicitly. The wrath of the New Left was explicitly directed against liberalism. The New Left thought that liberalism was a weak philosophy crippled by a fear to seriously transform society. Consequently, the New Left sought to destroy liberal institutions such as the university and dominate the Democratic Party. Robert Nisbet, for instance, a forthrightly conservative professor throughout his career, remembers his amazement at not being assailed by the radicals while his liberal colleagues were vilified.[79]

In a 1967 essay, Daniel Patrick Moynihan explained that true liberals should realize that they should ally themselves with conservatives against radicals. This would result in a potential political realignment for the neoconservatives.

> Liberals must see more clearly that their essential interest is in the stability of the social order; and given the present threats to that stability, they must seek out and make much more effective alliances with political conservatives who share their interest and recognize that unyielding rigidity is just as great a threat to continuity of the social order as an anarchic desire for change. . . . For too long we have been prisoners of the rhetoric that Republicans do not know or care about the social problems of the nation.[80]

While agreeing with his neoconservative colleagues that liberal intellectuals demonstrated a lack of resolve in confronting the radicals, Podhoretz added another consideration. Perhaps, he suggests, campus liberals did not object to the radical onslaught because they subconsciously cheered the chilling of conservative ideas or criticism. The liberals did not like Herrnstein any more than did the radicals, and might have silently enjoyed seeing him suppressed. Sure, the radicals launched broad attacks on "liberalism," but these attacks never threatened individual liberals or the freedom to articulate liberal ideas. But the attacks did usurp the academic freedom of conservatives like Herrnstein, whose ideas on intelligence challenged the central liberal conception that society can be endlessly manipulated. For this, at least some liberals may have been willing to tolerate some of the more boorish behavior of the radicals.[81]

In several essays, Irving Kristol used the inability of liberal professors to defend liberalism as a starting point for a broader attack on intellectuals. He regarded liberal intellectuals as morally confused, unable to instruct their students—their charges—on the basic rules of political propriety, but utterly unhesitant to lecture the nation on all manner of public policy.[82] This notion probably informed Kristol's definition of intellectuals penned in 1968, "An intellectual may be defined as a man who speaks with general authority about a subject on which he has no particular competence."[83] Two years later, Kristol encapsulated his criticism of intellectuals in *The New York Times Magazine.*

> There is no reason to think there is not the slightest shred of evidence—that the organized, collective intelligence of professors has anything whatsoever to contribute to our social, economic, political, or moral problems . . . Never has one had better cause to appreciate the cogency of William F. Buckley's observation that he would rather be governed by the first 2,000 names in the Boston telephone directory than by the Harvard faculty.[84]

Kristol developed this anti-intellectual theme in the following decades as he saw academics become more and more willing to embrace radical ideologies that threatened the very core of liberal education and scholarship. Peter Steinfels calls the neoconservatives "counter-intellectuals,"[85] an incisive and accurate appellation.

The New Left and Its Complications

Just as the neoconservatives perceived that the true threat to liberalism in the 1950s came from those on the left—the Communists, fellow travelers, and progressives—in the 1960s they saw the primary threat to liberalism coming from those on the left as well. The New Left was formed on college campuses in the early 1960s with the objective of radically transforming society. Even the salient issues of the New Left—civil rights and opposition to the Vietnam War—were secondary to what they considered the spiritual crisis afflicting affluent Western bourgeois capitalist society. Unlike previous left factions, this faction was in large part the product of suburban wealth.

The neoconservatives, who worked to lift themselves from poverty to their dream of a bourgeois lifestyle, believed that the students were monumentally spoiled. Their ancestors left the old country for one reason: the hope that their descendants could enjoy the promise of America. Countless others died for America in foreign wars. For what? So disgruntled, affluent kids could complain, protest, and denigrate the values that provided the luxury to be able to do so? Elsie O'Shaughnessy wrote in a revealing 1994 *Vanity Fair* profile of Daniel Patrick Moynihan,

> Moynihan's animosity toward the children of privilege—[whom he called] the "rich college fucks"—would resurface in the late 1960s, when he saw the anti-war movement on college campuses as part of "a mindless assault on the civic and social order," as he has written, when "nihilistic terrorism made its appearance as children of the upper middle class began to blow up themselves, and on occasion, others, as they expressed their disapproval with this or that government policy."[86]

The neoconservatives regarded them as immature, utterly devoid of intellectual seriousness and ultimately dangerous to society. The New Left was vaguely Marxist, not so vaguely authoritarian, and fervently anti-anti-Communist, as is demonstrated by the characterization of anti-Communism as "the equivalence of rape"[87] by two of the leading luminaries on the New Left, Tom Hayden and Staughton Lynd. Kristol writes that political discussion with the New Left was impossible because they did not have any political ideas and frankly did not care about politics. Trying to discuss progressive measures like Social Security and Medicare with the New Left, Kristol found, was an exercise in futility. "Whenever I have mentioned this legislation in conversation, I have received an icy stare of incomprehension and disdain, as if I were some kind of political idiot who actually believed what I read in the *New York Times*."[88]

A cultural movement masquerading as a political movement can have no political responsibility. The New Left allowed itself to transform into a progressive free-for-all where political positions were chosen according to what the establishment did not believe. Daniel Bell and Irving Kristol wrote in 1969,

> For the radical student body, circa 1969, there is no authentic interest in such rational politics, for there is really no conception of clear goals which can be fought for, negotiated, or compromised. For the "politics of confrontation" the goal is not really the satisfying of grievances but the destruction of authority itself.[89]

Leslie Fiedler, a New York intellectual who was not a neoconservative, compared the New Left to the radicals of the 1930s.

"We went in for Talmudic exegesis—you go in for holy rolling."[90] The "we-you" distinction that Fiedler draws was important to the neoconservatives. While the neoconservatives never had much use for any left, they refused to apply a doctrine of moral equivalence to the Old Left, as embodied by the socialists and even Communists in the 1930s, and the radicals of the New Left. For all its faults, the Old Left maintained a commitment to economic growth and to the essential values of bourgeois society. Kristol writes of the difference between the Old Left and the New Left in a 1968 *Fortune* article.

> If we must have a Left (and such appears to be our destiny), no reasonable man can doubt that the Old Left was enormously preferable to the New. The Old Left, or at least the part of it traditionally classed as "democratic socialist," can now be seen to have been an authentic part of the Western political tradition. After all, democratic socialism did try to evolve a social program that made some intellectual sense, if only on the surface. It took the economics seriously, even if this economics was faulty and amateurish. It did genuinely believe in liberal-democratic values, even if somewhat equivocally. And it did propose some distinct standards against which it might be judged, even if the result was to refute itself.[91]

The neoconservatives argued that the true ancestor of the New Left was not the Old Left, but the Old Right. Both the New Left and the New Right had contempt for liberal democracy and capitalist progress, indeed for what they regarded as the spiritual crisis of modernity. Their ways of reorganizing society were often radically different, but their diagnosis was, in many ways, strikingly similar. Such an alliance between Russell Kirk and Tom Hayden may seem bizarre, but as Irving Kristol noted in a 1970 article on this phenomenon, "revolts against modern civilization contain their own logic."[92]

Unlike the Old Right, the New Left hated traditional conceptions of religion. Nonetheless, the neoconservatives suggested, both had a theocentric view of the world and wanted to reorganize society along those lines. The faiths might be different, but that did not detract from their fundamentally similar critique of modernity. Daniel Patrick Moynihan suggested in 1967, "Who are these outrageous young people? I suggest to you they are

Christians on the scene of second-century Rome."[93] In another essay, Moynihan elaborated on the religious metaphor of the New Left. Pointing out that the New Left had so few of the attributes of a traditional political movement, he advances the idea that the New Left and the concerns they raise are religious in nature.

> I would offer, from the world of politics, the thought that the principal issues of the moment are not political. They are seen as such: that is the essential clue to their nature. But the crisis of the time is not political, it is in essence religious. It is a religious crisis of large numbers of intensely moral, even godly, people who no longer hope for God. Hence, the quest for divinity assumes a secular form, but with an intensity of conviction that is genuinely new to our politics.[94]

The neoconservatives suggested that the New Left could only be understood as a quasi-religious movement fundamentally at war with American society. The distinctions between the Democratic and Republican parties were no more significant to the New Left than was the choice between Stevenson and Eisenhower for the traditional conservatives of the 1950s. As Irving Kristol suggested in 1970,

> Our young radicals are far less dismayed at America's failure to become what it ought to be than they are contemptuous of what it thinks it ought to be. For them, as for Oscar Wilde, it is not the average American who is disgusting; it is the ideal American.[95]

The neoconservatives despised the New Left and its conception of America. The contempt they had for the New Left cannot be overestimated. Norman Podhoretz and the *Commentary* writers considered the New Left to be a negation of liberalism and an embrace of nihilism which was doing considerable damage to a generation of American youth and to the very fabric of American society. Such people were beyond annoying; they were wreaking potentially permanent damage on crucial American institutions. Lionel Trilling had warned of an adversary culture centering around the intellectual life in the 1950s. There was nothing much to this when the adversary culture was composed primarily of Beat poets. But when the adversary culture began to spread throughout the intellectual and student populations of America the neoconservatives perceived a full-fledged assault. The New Left, in short, stood for the elimination of practically everything the neoconservatives valued. As Jeanne Kirkpatrick described,

> The New Politics is the expression of the political counter-culture; it is united by its opposition to the traditional political culture, and it challenges that culture's central beliefs: the belief that politics is based on self-interest; that conflict is a permanent feature of politics; that the pursuit of individual purpose is socially beneficial; that freedom is rooted in law; that equality of opportunity and individual achievement constitute a just basis of reward; that power is an instrument necessary to social and international peace . . . that those who cannot work should be supported by public funds and those who will not should be treated less generously; that authority rests on force as well as consent . . . that work (read discipline) has intrinsic value for persons and societies; that citizenship requires obedience to laws with which one disagrees; that violation of the law should be punished; that order is a prerequisite to both liberty and justice; that patriotism is a social virtue; that the U.S. is basically a decent and successful—though imperfect—society.[96]

Neoconservatives and the Vietnam War

While the neoconservatives despised the New Left, their basic political positions were not affected by the fact that the New Left shared some of them. The neoconservatives' commitment to civil rights was unfazed, as was their support for a generous welfare state. The political distinction between the New Left and the neoconservatives became most pronounced with the Vietnam War. The Vietnam War put the neoconservatives in the familiar position of defending a liberal position while vociferously opposing the attitude and reasons of those who shared their position.

As the discussion of the Vietnam War in *Commentary* in the early 1960s indicates, most of the neoconservatives opposed the Vietnam War from the start. From the early 1960s through the end of the war, most of the neoconservatives supported unilateral immediate withdrawal. Not so, however, for Irving Kristol. He believed that the United States should not pull out of Vietnam because doing so would be a sign of American weakness. Maintaining, "I happen to think that the Administration's 'domino theory' is . . . perfectly correct,''[97] Kristol wrote in 1968 that an American failure of nerve might lead nations like India to think the United States will not do anything to prevent them from acquiring a nuclear bomb. Thus, if the domino effect does not apply to Southeast Asia, it will take effect in other, and potentially more dangerous, parts of the world.

While supporting the war—or, more accurately, opposing an American pullout—Kristol saw no prospect for victory, primarily because the South Vietnamese were incapable of governing themselves. He had none of the confidence of the men in the upper echelons of the Kennedy and Johnson administrations that American aid could bring democracy and liberal government to the Vietnamese. In a 1966 *Encounter* piece, Kristol maintained that the liberal arrogance that asserts that all people can be liberal democrats if only educated properly is akin to the conservative arrogance that American military power can accomplish any goal.[98] Admitting that the South Vietnamese leader Diem was corrupt and could not be trusted, Kristol confessed,

> I cannot place my hope in political-religious leaders whose mode of protest is to make funeral pyres of themselves. Such men doubtless have great virtues, but it is unlikely that a capacity for effective government can be reckoned among them.[99]

According to Kristol, the lack of leadership among the South Vietnamese is only one of the many impediments that make the goals of the United States impossible. A functioning democracy requires a rare and exquisite cultural apparatus, which the South Vietnamese did not have.

> The plain truth is that South Vietnam, like South Korea, is barely capable of decent self-government under the very best of conditions. It lacks the political traditions, the educated classes, the civic spirit that makes self-government workable. . . . No amount of American aid, no amount of exhortation, no amount of good advice can change this basic condition. . . . The most we can hope for in South Vietnam is what we have achieved in South Korea; that is, to remove this little, backward nation from the front line of the cold war so that it can stew quietly in its own political juice.[100]

Kristol's support for the Vietnam War was influenced by his contempt for many of those who opposed it. Even aside from his loathing for those on the New Left who imported anti-Americanism into their efforts to end the fighting in Vietnam, he had little use for many liberals on this issue (as on many others). In his 1968 endorsement of Hubert Humphrey for president in *The New Republic*, he castigated those who assumed that Vice President Humphrey only supported the Vietnam War out of institutional loyalty.

> [Let] us begin by dismissing the accusation against the Vice President that he has, during these past four years, "prostituted himself" by supporting the Administration's policy in Vietnam. This accusation is both stupid and contemptible. It is stupid because, in the nature of things, none of us has any way of knowing what private doubts and reservations Mr. Humphrey might have had about various aspects of this policy. He would have been less than human had he not had any such doubts; he would have been less than worthy of his high office had he insinuated them into the public ear.[101]

Unlike left-wing opponents of the Vietnam War, the neoconservatives did not view American involvement in Vietnam as an indication of American iniquity or proof that America should not become engaged in military conflict. It was not, as Daniel Patrick Moynihan wrote, a symptom of any systemic failure.[102] The neoconservatives believed that American involvement in the war was a single error based on the specific circumstances of the situation. It was no precedent. As Nathan Glazer wrote,

> I cannot accept the idea that the fundamental character of American society, its political or economic life, is the prime cause of the horrors of Vietnam. In the end, I cannot help believing, the Vietnam War must be understood as the result of a series of monumental errors. The key point to me is this: America would not have had to be very different from what it is for some President to have gotten us out of Vietnam rather than deeper and deeper into it.[103]

In another essay, Glazer maintained that a major problem the liberal professoriat had with confronting the New Left concerned a misunderstanding of how to approach the Vietnam War. Liberal intellectuals simply did not understand that they could strongly object to both the war and the anti-war movement, as represented by the New Left. When it came to the New Left, the typical reaction of liberals was, "we agree with your ends, but not necessarily with your means." The neoconservatives believed this to be as destructive to society as the ideas of the New Left. The liberals did not understand that the purpose of the New Left was not to stop racism or end the war in Vietnam, but to fundamentally reorder American society. And it was evident that the New Left was not interested in democratic ideals. Take freedom, the neoconservatives offered, for example. If the New Left supported freedom, how would they justify robbing their classmates of their freedom to join ROTC by attempting to ban the military from campus? Glazer suggested the proper liberal response to the New Left.

> We disagree totally with your means, which we find abhorrent, we disagree totally with your ends, which are the destruction of any free and civil society; some of the slogans you have raised to advance your ends nevertheless point to real faults which should be corrected by this institution, which has shown by its past actions on various issues that it is capable of rational change without the assistance of violence from those who wish to destroy it, and we will consider them.[104]

While the New Left movement among the students infuriated neoconservatives, it was not as astounding to them as the infiltration of the ideas of radicalism into many middle-aged intellectuals. This went beyond youthful stupidity or the inability of liberals to defend liberalism on college campuses; this involved the older people who actively supported the students—and not just refused to condemn them. Kristol relates an anecdote about Alfred Kazin, a New York intellectual and one of the most respected American literary critics since the 1940s.

> Bea [Gertrude Himmelfarb] wrote an essay on a Victorian subject and Alfred denounced her for not discussing the Vietnam War. She said, "What do you mean discuss the Vietnam War? It's about Victorian England!" Kazin replied, "Never mind, you could have got it in."[105]

The neoconservatives could understand the appeal of utopianism to impressionable students but it was a different matter when veterans of the old intellectual battles over Stalin—like Kazin—took up the same banner. And this is exactly what happened in 1967 when *The New York Review of Books* not only caught the Zeitgeist but helped to spread it. The relative congeniality of the New York intellectual community, which was embodied in both *Commentary* and *The New York Review of Books* so gracefully in the early 1960s, saw the initial disagreement over the Glazer/Schaar-Wolin controversy in 1964 expand and eventually explode.

The Radicalism of *The New York Review of Books*

Hints of the burgeoning radicalism had been present in *The New York Review of Books* in 1965 and 1966, but these were just hints. The late 1960s politicized much of what had not previously been political, and writers not known for their interest in public policy such as Noam Chomsky, Philip Rahv, and Christopher Lasch began to write about politics for *The New York Review of Books*. The result of the combination of politicization and radicalism was the most controversial year ever in a New York intellectual journal—a controversy which would leave scars and memories long after *The New York Review of Books* abandoned politics for history and culture. This year started with the Christmas issue of 1966, featuring a blistering David Levine cartoon of President Johnson as a pig eating a globe.

In the February 23, 1967 issue of *The New York Review of Books*, Noam Chomsky published "The Responsibility of the Intellectuals." He compares Bell, Kristol, Walt Whitman Rostow, Arthur Schlesinger, and Henry Kissinger to death-camp paymasters.[106] The war in Vietnam was, according to Chomsky, in large part the fault of liberal anti-Communist intellectuals.

This theme of liberal anti-Communist iniquity surfaced again in the April 20, 1967 issue of *The New York Review of Books* with an essay by Jason Epstein—"The CIA and the Intellectuals." In this essay, he excoriates the liberal anti-Communists for accepting CIA funding while working with the Congress for Cultural Freedom, implying that their work was influenced by their financial backers.

> There was . . . a genuine community of interest and conviction between the entrepreneurs of American cold war diplomacy and those intellectuals who, to put it bluntly, were hired to perform tasks which often turned out to be a form of public relations in support of American cold war policies.[107]

All of the contentious articles published in the first half of 1967—and there were more than the few discussed above—were just a harbinger of the August 24, 1967 issue of *The New York Review of Books*. Philip Nobile is correct in comparing this issue to Ralph Branca's pitch—the journal will forever be remembered for this one issue.[108] It is unnecessary to read very far in order to see why—the most jolting aspect of the issue was its cover. The bottom half is occupied by a diagram and instruction guide for a Molotov cocktail, the weapon of choice for rioters in American cities. If the neoconservatives could have been asked for an example of what would signify the worst aspects of their opposition, they could not have conceived of something better. In the uproar that followed, the editors maintained that it was a joke, that everyone who wanted to make a Molotov cocktail could do so, that readers of the *Review* were not the violent types, and that reports from Newark indicated that the formula did not work, anyway. This rationale was not appreciated, and what became known as the "Molotov Cocktail issue" earned infamy almost overnight.

More than the cover was radical in this issue. There was Andrew Kopkind's "Soul Power," a book review of Martin Luther King's *Where Do We Go from Here: Chaos or Community?* In this short article, Kopkind expresses the beliefs of much of the New Left concerning accepted standards, the relevance of intellectual predecessors, and the tactics of the fight to come.

> The old words are meaningless, the old explanations irrelevant, the old remedies useless. It is the worst of times. This is the best of times . . . the continuity of an age has been cut out, that we have arrived at an infrequent fulcrum of history, and that what comes now will be vastly different from what went before. . . . Important literature is in the underground press, the speeches of Malcolm, the works of Faron, the songs of the Rolling Stones and Arethra Franklin. The rest all sounds like the Moynihan Report . . . explaining everything, understanding nothing, changing no one.[109]

The liberal anti-Communists could withstand this disrespect for elders and aversion to literature because they had been experiencing such events since the mid-1930s. However, what they had neither intellectual preparation nor tolerance for was one Kopkind line in particular—a line that is now enshrined in New York intellectual history as one of the most shocking statements in a mainstream journal. "Morality, like politics, starts at the barrel of a gun." A blistering letter from Louis Coser, an opponent of neoconservatism, two months later, summarizes the response of the New York intellectuals not associated with *The New York Review of Books*. "Has it occurred to Mr. Kopkind or the editors that this is but a restatement of the *Der Stermer* doctrine, 'When I hear the word culture I draw my revolver'?"[110]

The New York Review of Books maintained its radicalism despite the criticism generated by that issue. For instance, a December 7 article, "On Resistance" by Noam Chomsky, calls the Pentagon "the most hideous institution on earth," and Senator Mike Mansfield "an American intellectual in the best sense; a scholarly, reasonable man—the kind of man who is the terror of our age."[111] These articles, interspersed with advertisements such as "For $7.50 a year you can be feared and envied. . . . Imagine the reaction of your Jewish friends . . . as you quote I. F. Stone's critique of Zionism," or "if you want to bring a Molotov cocktail to your next cocktail party, arm yourself with Tom Hayden's 'The Occupation of Newark,'" characterized the attitude of the attitude of the New Left and consecrated the permanent split between the two camps of the current and former liberal anti-Communists.

The Response to Radical Chic

In 1967, writers for *The New York Review of Books* challenged even the broadest limits of intellectual discourse. According to most of the New York intellectuals (not just the neoconservatives), *NYRB* had provided an intellectual voice and moral leadership to the abhorred New Left. *Commentary* was the journal that intellectuals of all stripes joined in order to launch a full-blown offensive against the New Left in general and *The New York Review of Books* in particular. While these attacks came from all different ideological quarters and over a myriad of issues, three *Commentary* essays stand out as emblematic in their passionate condemnation of the New Left and *NYRB*. These essays, penned by Irving Howe, Diana Trilling, and Dennis Wrong, stand as monuments to the intellectual and personal animosity which was erected between *NYRB* and the rest of the New York intellectual scene.

The first of these, "The New York Intellectuals: A Chronicle and a Critique" by Irving Howe, was published in *Commentary* in October 1968. Howe provides a thorough history of the New York intellectual scene before launching into a blistering attack against the accomplices of the New Left. He and Philip Rahv had, shortly before, ruined their friendship in a debate over the meaning of socialism published in *The New York Review of Books*. Fresh from this blistering fight, Howe's gloves were off and he was swinging.

Howe writes as a socialist disgusted with what he perceives as the illiberal attitudes of the counterculture and the New Left. He is horrified at the sight of his old friends backing the illiberal reaction in the name of staying in tune with the Zeitgeist. He calls the New Left "ambitious, self-assured, at ease with prosperity while conspicuously alienated, unmarred by the traumas of the totalitarian age, bored with memories of defeat, and attracted to the idea of power."

After castigating the New Left and their motives, Howe attacks their common sense and intelligence. He accuses the radicals of proposing "a revolution, I would call it a counterrevolution, in sensibility . . . it is a spreading blot of anti-intellectualism . . . it declares itself through a refusal of both coherence and definition." He further accuses them of believing that "everything touched by older men reeks of betrayal," and subsequently castigates them for adopting the worst qualities of anarchists and authoritarianism. After accusing the New Left of consorting with illiberal and anti-Semitic forces, Howe wrote,

> The new sensibility is impatient with ideas. It is impatient with literary structures of complexity and coherence, only yesterday the catchwords of

> our criticism. It wants instead works of literature—though literature may be the wrong word—that will be as absolute as the sun, as unarguable as orgasm, and as delicious as a lollipop. It schemes to throw off the weight of nuance and ambiguity, legacies of high consciousness and tired blood. It is weary of the habit of reflection, the making of distinctions, the squareness of dialectic, the tarnished gold of inherited wisdom. It cares nothing for the haunted memories of old Jews. It has no taste for the ethical nail-biting of those writers of the Left who suffered defeat and could never again accept the narcotic of certainty. It is sick of those magnifications of irony that Mann gave us, sick of those visions of entrapment to which Kafka led us, sick of those shufflings of daily horror and grace that Joyce left us. It breathes contempt for rationality, impatience with mind, and a hostility to the artifices and decorum of high culture. It despises liberal values, liberal caution, liberal virtues. It is bored with the past: for the past is a fink.

While this passage encapsulates the position of the liberal anti-Communists in the *Commentary* crowd and says it all, Howe continues. He devotes over a page to accusing *The New York Review of Books* of being a living manifestation of radical chic where "liberal values and norms are treated with something very close to contempt."

In the last paragraph of this essay, he declares the New York intellectual experience over and the liberal anti-Communist consensus dead. While declaring that "such breakups are inevitable," he accords no hope for the future. With *The New York Review of Books* crowd surrendering the notion of intellectual seriousness, he despairs for the future of intellectual thought with all of the work of the liberal anti-Communists buried by the new sensibility.[112]

After Howe sent *The New York Review of Books* reeling with this unmitigated polemic, *Commentary* attacked again the next month. In November 1968, Diana Trilling published "On the Steps of Low Library," a long and impassioned account of the student revolt at Columbia University.[113] Trilling's sharp pen was aimed at the students and at several of her colleagues in the New York intellectual community.

The revolt at Columbia was supported by some members of the New York intellectual community who had caught the Zeitgeist and did not want to miss an actual revolution. The renowned literary critic F. W. Dupee called Dwight MacDonald during the Columbia uprising and shouted, "You must come up right away, Dwight. It's a revolution! You may never get another chance to see one." MacDonald came right away, and shared the enthusiasm of his friend. After students urinated out of the windows of the office of President Kirk of Columbia University, MacDonald commented, "If anybody's windows can be peed out of, it's his windows. He was such a big stuffed shirt and of course they got rid of him, thank God."[114] The neoconservatives knew that MacDonald was—to put it mildly—eccentric, but this was too much. Soon after the rebellion at Columbia, he attended a party and saw Midge Decter. Trying to make small talk, she commented that it was terrible that the students were destroying the life work of professors. MacDonald replied, "Obviously, you care more about material values than human values." A heated argument ensued.[115]

Partially because the Columbia revolt was a product of seasoned adults as well as naive students, Trilling's essay is fraught with a sense of ruin and incorporates a pessimistic look toward the future. She had a special bond to Columbia because of the life she spent there and through her husband's association with the university either as a student or a professor since 1918. It was at Columbia where she developed her beliefs in the promise of liberalism and the sanctity of literature and culture. Seeing Columbia University under siege, Diana Trilling felt as though she had suffered a grievous personal loss.

She perceived the revolt at Columbia as a revolt against liberalism more than anything else, explaining:

> The sit-in was anti-liberal in its lawlessness and in its refusal of reasonable process. It was anti-liberal in its scorn for the entire liberal good-will with which the largest part of the faculty tried to meet it. In fact, the demonstration was a demonstration against liberalism—more (if the two can be separated for purposes of comparison) than Mark Rudd's "bullshit" expressed a lack of personal respect for his teachers, it communicated the contempt of the revolution for any embodiment of liberal purpose, liberal hope and confidence such as the faculty predominantly represents. . . .

She writes that the anti-liberalism of the Columbia revolt is evident not only in its ideas but in its tone. She believes that liberalism, properly understood, is concerned with rational mental facilities, thoughtful consideration, and introspective deliberation. In the call for direct action generated by emotional stimuli, the radicals were acting in a way which contradicted the central premises of liberalism. Just as *Partisan Review* editorialized throughout the 1940s that the failure of liberalism to challenge Communism would help the right wing, Diana Trilling writes that the forces of reaction would be aided by the antics of the New Left.

Commentary's third major attack on the New Left took the form of a direct assault against *The New York Review of Books* through a Dennis Wrong essay, "The Case of *The New York Review*."[116] Wrong begins his essay by celebrating the rich early history of *NYRB* and states that it is only natural that the journal moved from literature to politics as "the Vietnam War provided the focus." He further concedes that *The New York Review of Books* moved away from radical politics after 1967, and that Stokely Carmichael, Tom Hayden, and Andrew Kopkind were no longer to be found in its pages. Wrong also states that *The New York Review of Books* is "more disciplined and less self-indulgent" than either *The Village Voice* or *Ramparts*. But none of this, Wrong concludes, makes up for 1967.

Calling *The New York Review of Books* "anti-American," Wrong asserts that its writers are guilty of intellectual treason. At the very least, their efforts will succeed in helping the "Reagans, Mitchells, and Agnews" of America. He criticizes the New Left for succumbing to "irrationality and moral authoritarianism," free from the demands of "civility, tolerance, and intellectual rigor." He concludes his essay by stating that *NYRB* writers do not respect the hard-fought lessons of the anti-Stalinist intellectuals of the 1940s.

How Bad Is It for the Jews? The Neoconservatives and the New Left

The neoconservatives consistently criticized the New Left for castigating America's civil religion—democracy and the belief in progress through established institutions and pathways. While this was bad enough, attacking the real, as opposed to the civil, religion of most neoconservatives was simply unacceptable. According to the neoconservatives, the New Left worked actively against Jewish interests by either directly or indirectly condemning Israel and traditional Jewish ways of social mobility in America.

The neoconservatives believed that the New Left was bad for the Jews even when Jews were not explicitly targeted by the radicals. The neoconservatives noted that the major targets of New Left animus—teachers and small businessmen in cities, university professors, landlords, attorneys, accountants, doctors, and other professionals—include an overwhelming number of Jews. Nathan Glazer explained,

> All the roles that Jews play are roles that the New Left disapproves of, and wishes to reduce. . . . It attacks the principles of merit and non-discrimination on which they are based. It attacks scholastic bases for entry into college. It attacks the role and authority of professors as well as teachers. It is critical of course of all private business, and of its whole associated institutional complex—lawyers, stockbrokers, accountants, etc.—in which Jews are prominent. The kinds of society it admires have no place for occupations in which Jews have tended to cluster in recent history.[117]

The anti-Jewish bias of the New Left remained more or less under the surface until Israel's stunning victory in the Six Day War. In 1967, Israel was attacked by six Arab countries poised at her border, all of which greatly outnumbered Israel in both manpower and weaponry. Nevertheless, Israel won the war in a victory that generated great enthusiasm for Israel in the West and reinvigorated the religious identity of many American Jews who were becoming secular and assimilated. The massive attack launched against Israel reminded Jews and Gentiles alike of the resiliency, dedication, and strength of Jews.

While this victory provided Jews with a renewed sense of pride and strength, it also reminded Jews of their continued vulnerability. Once again, Jews were forced to confront a stark reality: no matter what they did to mask or avoid it, they would forever be Jews, with all the attendant historical responsibility. American Jews responded to the Six Day War with massive financial and moral support. After the 1967 war, polls showed that 99 percent of American Jews were very supportive of Israel and her actions during the conflict.[118] While Israel had always been viewed positively by most American Jews, the overwhelming support had never approached 1967 levels. In less than a week's time, Israel had become the civil religion of American Jewry.

While this victory propelled Israel to unprecedented popularity, she was diminished in the eyes of the New Left. The New Left did not focus on the fact that Israel was attacked without provocation by a half-dozen Arab countries intent on annihilating the Jewish state. Instead, the New Left concentrated on the fact that Israel won the war, which meant that the Jews were no longer a member of an oppressed minority, but the operators of an imperialistic government.

The New Left often expressed its animus toward Jews by using the term "Zionist" instead of "Jew" when Israel or American Jews were criticized. This rhetorical sleight-of-hand was ubiquitous, and responsible leaders sought to expose such fraudulence. For instance, to a questioner talking about "Zionist businessmen," Martin Luther King angrily replied: "Don't talk like that. When people criticize Zionists, they mean Jews. You're talking anti-Semitism!"[119] According to the neoconservatives, the New Left's equations of Zionism with imperialism was a major boon for anti-Semites across the political spectrum. As Edward Alexander wrote in a 1988 *Society* article, "Anti-Semites have been able to express Jew-hatred with impunity since 1967."[120]

But sometimes the anti-Jewish sentiment of the New Left was not clothed in the language of Zionism. Martin Peretz, a wealthy radical in the 1960s, recalls funding a New Left conference in Chicago. The conference quickly disintegrated into an anti-Semitic romp, with speakers proclaiming they were sick of hearing about the Holocaust although, as Peretz points out, no one had mentioned it.[121] Disgusted, Peretz left his own conference and wrote a powerful *Commentary* essay, "The American Left and Israel."[122]

But other radical Jews did not respond as Peretz did to such anti-Semitic outbreaks. Jewish money funded much of the counterculture and Jews consistently supported this radicalism no matter how directly it ran contrary to fundamental Jewish interests. In a 1971 *Commentary* article, Nathan Glazer wrote that Jews were also disproportionately represented in movements advocating drug legalization, pornography, liberalization of abortion laws, peace at all costs in Vietnam, welfare rights, busing and other liberal and radical movements in the 1960s and 1970s.[123] As Glazer wrote in 1969, while left-wing Jews did not riot and pillage themselves, their ideas and their money contributed significantly to the ethos that spawned the violence.

> We must acknowledge that white intellectuals, and that—to repeat—means in large measure Jewish intellectuals, have taught violence, justified violence, rationalized violence. Anti-Semitism is only a parrot of this whole syndrome, for if the members of the middle class do not deserve to hold on to their property, their positions, or even their lives, then certainly the Jews, the most middle-class, are going to be placed at the head of the column marked for liquidation.[124]

This was a major concern to the neoconservatives and was the subject of one of *Commentary*'s most powerful issues, devoted to "Revolutionism and the Jews" and published in February 1971.[125] Essays by Glazer, Walter Lacquer, and Robert Alter denounced liberal Jews for their role in the New Left. These writers focused on two reasons why the visible Jewish presence in the counterculture was dangerous. First, Glazer and Lacquer predicted a massive backlash against the left-wing agenda once the issue of the Vietnam War was settled. When people looked to see who was behind the eradication of traditional morality, and who supported the movements that tore the American social fabric, they would not have to look very far to find Jews, and lots of them. The fact that Jews were really to blame for many of the sources of radical cultural turns, combined with the understanding that Jews have traditionally been used as scapegoats, pointed to a backlash of anti-Semitism that would follow the Vietnam War.

According to Nathan Glazer, a related question accompanied the self-destructive attitude of left-wing Jews to the bourgeois lifestyle. If America is as racist and as inherently prejudiced as the New Left claims, how did the Jews prosper as they have? Glazer reasoned that if prejudice was so powerful, prevalent, and endemic in America, it would surely have stopped Jews from succeeding. However, it obviously did not. This contradicts the liberal contention that prejudice prevents the progress of oppressed groups. Unless of course, the Jews were involved in rigging the system in some sort of conspiracy which sacrificed other minority groups. This was the logical conclusion that Glazer drew from the radical belief in American iniquity, but the neoconservatives perceived the New Left as being either hopelessly oblivious or unbelievably sanguine about it.[126]

Political Realignment in the Face of the New Left

Throughout the 1960s, neoconservatives believed that they remained true to the principles of liberalism that they saw imperiled but not destroyed in earlier days—the liberalism (or chastened liberalism) of Lionel Trilling, Reinhold Niebuhr, Franklin Roosevelt, Harry Truman, and John F. Kennedy. But when liberals and the left shunned these models for radical substitutes, the neoconservatives did not see a place for themselves in liberalism—not anywhere in any kind of liberalism. In the early 1970s, Irving Kristol famously defined a neoconservative as "a liberal who had been mugged by reality."[127]

The "Revolutionism and the Jews" issue sent a signal to the editors of *National Review* that the neoconservatives were a full-fledged ally. The March 9, 1971 issue of *National Review* offered an editorial invitation to *Commentary* entitled "C'mon In, the Water's Fine." Praising *Commentary* and its writers, *National Review* maintained that *Commentary* was a full-fledged conservative magazine and a valuable ally in the struggle against the left.

Despite the invitation of *National Review, Commentary* was not ready to accept the full embrace of the right. The editors and writers for *Commentary* hated what had become of American liberalism, but could not fully accept conservatism—especially with regard to the political issues of the day. While *Commentary* was thoroughly disgusted with liberal intellectuals and politicians in the early 1970s, many of the neoconservatives (though not Irving Kristol) still held numerous liberal views. These views were illustrated in a monthly column begun by Norman Podhoretz, "Issues," which usually summarized and defended an article in that issue of *Commentary.* When attacking the New Left, Podhoretz's "Issues" columns and the articles they supported were powerful condemnations of the radicalism he saw corrupting American institutions and society. These views, however, had no consistent policy implications. Like Kristol in the mid-1960s, Podhoretz was determined to stick to the principles of neoconservatism while not completely rejecting the liberal answer to policy questions. He often saw a discrepancy, but refused to sacrifice intellectual honesty to achieve a consistent political stance.

As with Norman Podhoretz, *Commentary*'s politics did not always neatly follow its ideology. In May 1971, Nathan Glazer wrote an essay advocating immediate withdrawal of all troops from Vietnam, a position which was supported by Podhoretz in his "Issues" column. The next month, Podhoretz reluctantly came out for legalization of marijuana. In a discussion of an Alexander Bickel essay in November 1972, Podhoretz reluctantly supported an absolutist interpretation of the First Amendment. His views of the free market were also in the mainstream of liberal thought in the 1970s; in February 1973, he argued, "The rich often pay less than their fair share of taxes."[128]

Reflecting this period of ideological transformation, *Commentary* did not come down strongly on the side of either presidential candidate in 1972. In September of 1972, *Commentary* ran opposing essays by Nathan Glazer, who endorsed George McGovern, and Milton Himmelfarb, who endorsed Nixon. Podhoretz took no public position, merely maintaining in the "Issues" column that Jews could vote for either candidate with a clear conscience. Irving Kristol and Gertrude Himmelfarb did not equivocate on this matter; they were leaders of "Professors for Nixon."

Liberals and the Final Abandonment of Liberalism

Having repudiated the New Left, the neoconservatives looked to the reaction of mainstream liberalism to the counterculture. Well aware of the abandonment of Moynihan, Banfield, and

Herrnstein by liberal intellectuals, neoconservatives were able to definitively answer the questions that had plagued them for some time. Would liberals be able to defend liberalism against the onslaught of the New Left? Would liberals be able to see the radical students for what they really were—at best, myopic nihilists; at worst aspiring terrorists in a totalitarian thrall? And how could they misjudge the radical students, considering that their offices were being (literally) raided and their integrity as scholars and as people viciously impugned? Surely, the neoconservatives hoped, even if liberals could not defend liberalism from Communists in the 1950s, they could do so to the New Left, a direct threat to the university life. It all made such logical sense but, alas, was not to be. Just as liberals had failed to defend liberalism in the past, they failed yet again. And with this, the neoconservatives said good-bye to liberalism.

The liberal reaction to the New Left was one of puzzled approval. The methods of the New Left were often called into question—did Columbia University students really have to urinate on the carpet in President Kirk's office? But the spirit and the "idealism" of the students were admired. The neoconservatives, on the other hand, understood the radicals' intention to be wreaking havoc on American politics, society, and culture—and found them abominable. Irving Kristol elaborated,

> In our society and in our culture, with its pathetic belief in progress and its grotesque accent of youth, it is almost impossible to speak candidly about the students. Thus, though most thoughtful people will condemn the "excesses" committed by rebellious students, they will in the same breath pay tribute to their "idealism" and their sense of "commitment."[129]

Chris DeMuth, president of the American Enterprise Institute, recalled affectionately in a toast at Irving Kristol's seventy-fifth birthday party,

> My first encounter with Irving was at lunch with Edward C. Banfield on August 29, 1968. The previous evening the Democrats had nominated Hubert Humphrey for president, and there had been bloody riots in the streets of Chicago. Kristol and Banfield began immediately and in the strongest of terms to denounce the rioters and sympathize with Mayor

> Daley and the Chicago police. When I interjected a few muddled sentimentalities about the idealism of the demonstrators, they turned on me ruthlessly and relentlessly.[130]

The neoconservatives pointed out how the inclination to support the motives, intentions, and idealism of the students resulted in gross moral confusion. In a 1970 *Commentary* article, Robert Nisbet used the report of the Scranton Commission on violence as an example. While maintaining that student violence and harassment are wrong, the report nonetheless concedes that the just and passionate desires of youth to eliminate war, poverty, pollution, and a whole host of assorted evils were being ignored by the majority culture. Thus, the Scranton Commission was saying that while the radical critique of America was correct—America was as bad as the radicals said—the students should not act radically to change society.[131]

The neoconservatives saw this as yet another manifestation of the lack of seriousness with which liberals regarded ideas. Conservatives, neoconservatives, and radicals all realized that radical critiques of society invite radical action to remake it. Man is a moral animal, and will not be satisfied in an immoral society. Hence, if someone is morally offended, and his offense is legitimized by trusted authority, tumultuous change is inevitable. This radical desire was bound to be thwarted. Democracy is a deliberative form of government where decisions are made slowly and, one hopes, carefully. This basic notion directly conflicts with the human reaction to injustice, which is to correct it immediately. Daniel Bell remarked in *Encounter*,

> When a nation has publicly admitted moral guilt, it is difficult to say no to the ones it has offended. And when a nation admits moral guilt, but goes slow in restitution, then the explosive mixture becomes even more inflammable.[132]

The same misunderstanding of ideology which plagued the Scranton Commission was found to be prevalent among university faculty. University faculty often joined students in their opposition to the "establishment" and "authority," apparently not realizing that they were the ones being assailed. Sidney Hook told the story of a faculty meeting at New York University, where he taught philosophy. At the meeting he describes, students came to justify their violent actions against the university.

> The black student, who was wearing a hat, was the first to speak when they reached the platform. Turning to the teachers, he said, pointing to his hat, "My mudder told me that wearing a hat indoors is a mark of disrespect for the people present." And then an unbelievable thing happened. Two thirds of the faculty present rose to their feet in a standing ovation and vigorously applauded the students. One member of the audience shouted in indignation, "Throw the bums out!" which led to renewed applause. The two white students delivered tirades against the government, the university, the faculty, the war, and capitalism.[133]

The accusations that the liberal anti-Communists leveled at the progressives regarding the latter's paranoia about McCarthy were resurrected in the 1960s. Rather, many liberals generally spoke of "repression" (directed against them) and oppression whenever possible. As Walter Goodman reported in *Commentary*, "Cocktail-party conversation in liberal circles starts from the understanding that those who are out to get us are well along in the process, and proceeds to further calamities."[134] Rumors like the one that President Nixon was going to cancel the 1972 election were rampant and believed by some liberal intellectuals. The respected political scientist and *New York Review of Books* contributor Benjamin DeMott even remarked that he was voting for Nixon over McGovern because McGovern's victory would just delay the inevitable arrival of fascism in America.[135]

The neoconservatives contrasted the ominous paranoia possessed by many liberals born out of "threats" from the right with the real danger from the left. While liberals had always dealt with right-wing groups with swift and sure condemnation, they could not distinguish between the true liberalism and the illiberalism of the New Left. Or, as Sidney Hook noted in a different context, between a heresy and a conspiracy. As Arnold Beichman wrote in 1969,

> Were the attack on academic freedom from the John Birch Society or from followers of George Wallace or from some reactionary and philistine State Legislature, the Columbia faculty, like any faculty in America would know

> exactly what to do. The response would be swift, heroic, and efficacious. Yet these same intellectuals, many of whom were able to mount a powerful propaganda assault against President Johnson and Vietnam, are still unable to contain the "Left" assault from within, even though the SDS and its allies represent little more than five percent of Columbia's 17,500 students.[136]

As is fitting for a group of intellectuals that placed a primacy on the importance on ideas, the neoconservatives saw the combination of liberal acquiescence to the New Left and paranoia to imagined threats from elsewhere taking a toll on American politics and culture. In the 1960s, the cultural dislocations that were born of the liberal intelligentsia spread to the general public though a variety of mechanisms, notably entertainment. Bourgeois society was far from immune to the hits it was taking from the left and from liberals who refused to defend liberalism from the left. The neoconservatives consistently stressed that overly ambitious demands on government or culture would not cause the would-be-reformers to examine their hubris, but would generate a crisis in the legitimacy of fundamental institutions and ideas as hopes were thwarted and aspirations are frustrated. Institutions and ideas can take only so much of a beating before the society upon which they rest is shaken. This, the neoconservatives reasoned, could have profound implications for the future. Not only were liberal intellectuals afraid to defend bourgeois society, but bourgeois society was forgetting how to defend itself. Irving Kristol explained in 1970,

> One wonders: how can a bourgeois society survive in a cultural ambiance that derides every traditional bourgeois virtue and celebrates promiscuity, homosexuality, drugs, political terrorism—anything, in short, that is in bourgeois eyes perverse . . . there is something positively absurd in the spectacle of prosperous suburban fathers flocking to see—and evidently enjoying *The Graduate*—or of prosperous, chic, suburban mothers unconcernedly humming "Mrs. Robinson" to themselves as they cheerfully drive off to do their duties as den mothers. This peculiar schizophrenia, suffusing itself through the bourgeois masses of our urban society, may be fun while it lasts; but one may reasonably suppose that, sooner or later, people will decide they would rather not die laughing at themselves, and that some violent convulsions will ensue.[137]

The Sixties in Perspective

The 1960s are commonly understood to be the Kronstadt—the event that forever changes the *Weltanschauung*—of the neoconservatives. But it was not so much their Kronstadt as social manifestation of the liberal ideas they assailed in the 1950s. Though the liberal anti-Communists thought the progressives were woefully blind to the realities of Communism, everyone was at least nominally anti-Communist. And while the liberal anti-Communists worried that the lack of a progressive backbone might help to erode the will of America to fight Communism abroad, they had no fear of Communism being established in America. While the left's lack of moral seriousness, personified by its inability to recognize the existence of evil or even tragedy and its reluctance to make meaningful distinctions all came to the fore in the 1950s, these weaknesses were not immediately ready to corrode the body politic. The liberal anti-Communists tried to destroy these pernicious notions before they could do any damage. The future—whose precise manifestations always escape human prediction—was at issue.

The aspect of the 1960s that infuriated neoconservatives most was the inability of liberals to defend liberalism against the radical onslaught. Precursors of this failure of nerve are evident in the writings of progressives from the 1950s. If progressives could not take a hard stand against Communists, who could they take a stand against? If they could not exorcise fellow travelers, whose company would they reject? If they could not compete in intellectual slow-pitch softball, what were they to do when the balls came whizzing at them at ninety miles an hour?

They would strike out. The issues of the 1960s were complicated and commanded a level of sophistication that the progressives failed to demonstrate in the decade before, when politics was much easier. How so? For example, consider the relationship between anti-Communism and American power in the two decades. Believing that Stalinism is evil and must be combated by the only force in the world capable of doing so is easy. Holding that U.S. involvement in Vietnam is grievously wrong but that the

United States is still a great moral force for good in the world is more complicated and needs a more sophisticated defense. This belief requires strong confidence in the fundamental goodness of American institutions that plain anti-Stalinism does not. Because the progressives were hard-pressed to condemn their left and support America in the age of Stalin, the neoconservatives did not expect that the progressives would be able to dissociate themselves from the radicals in the 1960s.

This same love of America (as it is, not as it might be if . . .) resided at the core of neoconservative beliefs on issues and ideas. While many on the left saw the civil rights movement as a move to correct a representative sample of a pervasive American iniquity, the neoconservatives saw it as a logical step in the unfolding of America's promise. Neoconservatives stressed that peaceful change and lasting prosperity depend on a confidence in the ability of people and institutions to carry out that change and achieve justice. In short, bourgeois society and American life needed a strong defense if the goals advocated by liberals were to be achieved.

The devastating critiques that Norman Podhoretz and Irving Kristol leveled at liberalism in the 1950s assumed new meaning in the new decade. When Podhoretz considered the Beats in the 1950s, he refused to dismiss them as an irrelevant band of silly rhymers. But he sensed that the nihilistic attitude of the Beats might not be limited to a contained group in Greenwich Village. The same can be said about Kristol's attacks on the progressives. In the 1950s, Kristol stressed that a refusal to defend bourgeois society and American life was at the core of the progressives' inability to take a strong stance against Communism. While the latter was crucially important, the former was more significant because it could weaken the resolve against Communism and generate nefarious consequences later.

According to Kristol and the other neoconservatives, no societal arrangement—no matter how secure it appears or how much economic prosperity it generates—is indestructible because it rests on a foundation of ideas. It takes a long time for ideas to develop to the point where they acquire the strength and support to buttress a society. But it takes a much shorter time for those ideas to be questioned, attacked, and imperiled by other ideas. The war of ideas does not submit to the rules of egalitarianism. Ideas in the mind of a few intellectuals can, in short time, have a tremendous influence on society. This is not nice, good, or fair; it is simply true. Kristol wrote,

> The modern world, and the crisis of modernity we are now experiencing, was created by ideas and by the passions which these ideas unleashed. . . . I know that it will be hard for some to believe that ideas can be so important. This underestimation of ideas is a peculiarly bourgeois fallacy, especially powerful in the most bourgeois of nations, our own United States. For two centuries, the very important people who managed the affairs of this society could not believe in the importance of ideas—until one day they were shocked to discover that their children, having been captured and shaped by certain ideas, were either rebelling against their authority or seceding from their society. The truth is that ideas are all-important. The massive and seemingly-solid institutions of any society—the economic institutions, the political institutions, the religious institutions—are always at the mercy of the ideas in the heads of the people who populate these institutions. The leverage of ideas is so immense that a slight change in the intellectual climate can and will—perhaps slowly, but nevertheless inexorably—twist a familiar institution into an unrecognizable shape.[138]

The neoconservatives have always been alert to the way in which a change in the intellectual climate could reverberate in politics and in the culture. Warriors on the front of ideas, they retire to the more prosaic and less important arena of public policy when the day is done. Throughout the 1960s and early 1970s, neoconservative ideology and political positions often conflicted. When Irving Kristol supported more welfare payments despite admitting that such a plan would generate a cycle of dependence or when Norman Podhoretz passionately denounced the left while supporting the legalization of marijuana, each was open to the possibility that his position would change. Neoconservatives want their philosophical principles to have political implications, but realized that would not always be a neat or easy task. Philosophical principles have to be consistently reinterpreted when confronted by different issues, and that reinterpretation will not always yield linear results. Even in the end, different people may interpret the same principles quite differently.

While this poses no problem (actually it is a strength) for neoconservatism as a philosophical movement, it complicated the relationship of neoconservatism to the political culture. Irving Kristol and Gertrude Himmelfarb solved this problem in the early 1970s by becoming Republicans and endorsing Richard Nixon for president in 1972. Most other neoconservatives did not do this, but the conversion of Himmelfarb and Kristol meant that many knew a Republican well for the first time in their lives. When *National Review* extended a hand with the assurance that the water is fine and, more importantly, when Irving Kristol introduced a collection of essays, several of which were first published in *Commentary*, with the statement, "My instincts are—I have indeed come to believe that an adult's normal political instincts should be—conservative,"[139] it was not difficult to see which direction neoconservatism was taking on political issues. Liberalism was becoming consistently worse, and conservatism (by contrast if for no other reason) consistently appeared more appealing. As the issues of the next decade accentuated the lines between the left and everyone else even more clearly, the inevitable neoconservative move to the right proceeded swiftly, smoothly, and without apology.

Notes

1. Irving Howe, "This Age of Conformity," *Partisan Review* (January/February 1954) pp. 18, 11.
2. Norman Podhoretz, *Making It* (New York: Random House, 1967) p. 3.
3. Interview with Norman Podhoretz, January 11, 1994.
4. Norman Podhoretz, *Doings and Undoings: The Fifties and After in American Writing* (New York: Farrar, Straus, 1964) pp. 106, 107.
5. Norman Podhoretz, "The Know-Nothing Bohemians," *Partisan Review* (Spring 1958), pp. 316, 318.
6. Interview with Midge Decter, November 27, 1993.
7. J. David Hoeveler, *Watch on the Right: Conservative Intellectuals in the Reagan Era* (Madison: University of Wisconsin Press, 1991) p. 11.
8. Jeffrey Hart's changing views of Norman Podhoretz illustrate Podhoretz's intellectual journey. In Hart's 1964 book, *The American Dissent: A Decade of Modern Conservatism*, he called Podhoretz "a faithful servant of the zeitgeist" (p. 246). Hart, who became an occasional contributor to *Commentary*, wrote of

Norman Podhoretz in 1986, "the neoconservatives in my opinion should be embraced, congratulated, celebrated. I have known Norman Podhoretz for years and have read everything he has written. . . . Podhoretz continues to wage a splendid campaign for sanity and decency on the cultural and political front, and in point of courage and intelligence he need give place to no one" ("Gang Warfare in Chicago," *National Review*, June 6, 1986, p. 33).

9. Paul Willen, "Can Stalin Have a Successor? Why the Dictator's Shoes Can't be Filled." *Commentary* (July 1953) pp. 36–44.

10. Norman Podhoretz, *Breaking Ranks: A Political Memoir* (New York: Harper and Row, 1979) p. 204.

11. William Phillips, "What Happened in the 30's," *Commentary* (September 1962) pp. 204–12.

12. Nathan Glazer, "Cuba and the Peace Movement," *Commentary* (December 1962) p. 519.

13. David Riesman and Malcolm Maccoby, "The American Crisis," *Commentary* (June 1960) p. 472.

14. Richard Lowenthal, "Totalitarianism Reconsidered," *Commentary* (June 1960) pp. 504–12.

15. Two of Draper's articles from the early 1960s in *Commentary* are "Beyond Berlin: Is There a New Balance of Forces," in November 1961 (pp. 302–10) and "Five Years of Castro's Cuba," in January 1964 (pp. 25–37).

16. Irving Kristol, "Deterrence," *Commentary* (July 1961) pp. 64–67. Hughes's article is "The Strategy of Deterrence," *Commentary* (March 1961) pp. 185–92.

17. Oscar Gass and Hans Morganthau wrote often for *Commentary* in the early 1960s, writing around six times a year each. Joseph Zasloff's prescient article is "The Problem of South Vietnam" (February 1962) pp. 126–35.

18. Hans Morgenthau, "Vietnam: Another Korea?" *Commentary* (May 1962), pp. 369–74.

19. Norman Podhoretz, "The Issue," *Commentary* (February 1960) p. 184.

20. Paul Goodman, "Pornography, Art and Censorship," *Commentary* (March 1961) p. 212.

21. Nathan Glazer, "On Being Deradicalized," *Commentary* (October 1970) p. 75.

22. *Breaking Ranks*, p. 174.

23. Philip Nobile, *Intellectual Skywriting: Literary Politics and The New York Review of Books* (New York: Charterhouse, 1974) pp. 18–19.

24. Norman Podhoretz uses the term "family" in *Making It* to describe the New York intellectuals. He breaks the intellectuals down into how close they are to the center of the family, all the way out to "kissing cousins."

25. *Intellectual Skywriting*, p. 29.

26. Alexander Bloom, *Prodigal Sons: The New York Intellectuals and Their World* (New York: Oxford University Press, 1986) p. 326.

27. *Doings and Undoings*, p. 264.

28. Staughton Lynd, "An Exchange," (With Irving Howe) *The New York Review of Books* (December 23, 1965) p. 28.
29. Irving Kristol, "A Few Kind Words for Uncle Tom," *Harper's* (February 1965) p. 96.
30. Nathan Glazer and Daniel Patrick Moynihan, *Beyond the Melting Pot: The Negroes, Puerto Ricans, Jews, and Irish of New York* (Cambridge: M. I. T. Press, 1963) pp. 290, 66.
31. Nathan Glazer, *Ethnic Dilemmas* (Cambridge: Harvard University Press, 1983) p. 42.
32. Dan Jacobson, "A White Liberal Trapped by His Prejudices," *Commentary* (May 1953) p. 454.
33. *Making It*, p. 342.
34. Norman Podhoretz, "My Negro Problem—And Ours," *Commentary* (February 1963) pp. 93, 98, 99, 101.
35. *Breaking Ranks*, pp. 141–42.
36. Daniel Patrick Moynihan, "The President and the Negro," *Commentary* (February 1967) p. 38.
37. Nathan Glazer, "New York's Puerto Ricans," *Commentary* (November 1958) p. 471.
38. Irving Kristol, "The Negro Today Is Like the Immigrant Yesterday," *New York Times Magazine* (September 11, 1966) p. 132.
39. Irving Kristol, "Is the Welfare State Obsolete?" *Harper's* (May 1963) p. 42.
40. Irving Kristol, "It's Not a Bad Crisis to Live In," *New York Times Magazine* (January 22, 1967) p. 26.
41. "It's Not a Bad Crisis to Live In," p. 72.
42. Daniel Bell, "Ideology and the Beau Geste," *Dissent* (Winter 1961) p. 75. Alexander Bloom's insightful discussion of this quote is on page 328 of *Prodigal Sons: The New York Intellectuals and Their World.*
43. Irving Kristol and Daniel Bell, "What Is the Public Interest?" *The Public Interest* (Fall 1965) p. 4.
44. "Ideology and the Beau Geste," p. 75.
45. Nathan Glazer, "Interests and Passions," *The Public Interest* (Fall 1985) p. 19.
46. Nathan Glazer, "The New Left and Its Limits," *Commentary* (July 1968) p. 35.
47. Daniel Patrick Moynihan, "The Professionalization of Reform," *The Public Interest* (Fall 1965) pp. 1–22.
48. James Q. Wilson, "On the Rediscovery of Character," *The Public Interest* (Fall 1985) p. 4.
49. Interview with Irving Kristol, January 26, 1994, and "Skepticism, Meliorism and *The Public Interest.*" *The Public Interest* (Fall 1985) p. 33.
50. James Coleman, "Equal Schools or Equal Students?" *The Public Interest* (Summer 1966) pp. 70–75.

51. Aaron Wildavsky, "Using Public Funds to Serve Private Interests," *Society* (January/February 1979) p. 41.

52. Irving Kristol, "An Odd Lot," *Encounter* (December 1960) p. 62.

53. Nathan Glazer, "The Limits of Social Policy," *Commentary* (September 1971).

54. "Skepticism, Meliorism and *The Public Interest*," p. 32.

55. Nathan Glazer, "A New Look at the Melting Pot," *The Public Interest* (Summer 1969) p. 183.

56. James Q. Wilson, "Black and White Tragedy," *Encounter* (October 1969) p. 66.

57. Irving Kristol, "From Priorities to Goals," *The Public Interest* (Summer 1971) p. 4.

58. Daniel Patrick Moynihan, "The Case for National Action: The Negro Family," Office of Policy Planning and Research, U.S. Department of Labor, March 1965.

59. Harry McPherson, a top aide to Lyndon Johnson, suggests that the intended audience may have been more than the hundred officials that are commonly cited. He writes, "[100 copies] was too many if you were trying to keep it close, and it was too few if you were trying to make it just one more government document. A hundred seemed about right for giving it a rarity and importance, and to know that it was supposed to be treated confidentially made it all the more grist for the Washington mill and more exciting to people." Quoted in Elsie O'Shaughnessy, "The Moynihan Mystique," *Vanity Fair* (May 1994) p. 62.

60. "New Crisis: The Negro Family," *Newsweek* (August 9, 1965) p. 32.

61. James Farmer, "The Core of It," (December 18, 1965) syndicated column.

62. William Ryan, "Savage Discovery: The Moynihan Report," *The Nation* (November 22, 1965).

63. Daniel Patrick Moynihan, *Coping: On the Practice of Government* (New York: Random House, 1973) p. 21.

64. Quoted in Michael Novak "Race and Truth," *Commentary* (December 1976) p. 56.

65. John Judis, *William Buckley: Patron Saint of the Conservatives* (New York: Simon and Schuster, 1988) p. 327.

66. Richard Herrnstein, "I.Q.," *Atlantic Monthly* (September 1971) pp. 47–64.

67. Norman Podhoretz, "The New Inquisitors," *Commentary* (April 1973) p. 8.

68. James Q. Wilson, "Liberalism versus Liberal Education," *Commentary* (June 1972) pp. 50–51.

69. Interview with James Q. Wilson, March 13, 1994.

70. See Daniel Bell, "Columbia and the New Left," in *Confrontation: The Student Rebellion and the Universities*, ed. Daniel Bell and Irving Kristol (New York: Basic Books, 1968) p. 101.

71. "Introduction," in *Confrontation: The Student Rebellion and the Universities*, p. vii.

72. Neal Kozodoy, "Religion and Tolerance," *Freedom Review* (January/February 1993) p. 72.

73. Nathan Glazer, "Blacks, Jews and Intellectuals," *Commentary* (April 1969) p. 37.

74. Interview with Gertrude Himmelfarb, March 24, 1994.

75. See Nathan Glazer, "The Jewish Role in Student Activism," *Fortune* (January 1969) p. 126, and Midge Decter, "A Letter to the Young (and their parents)," *Atlantic Monthly* (February 1975) p. 36.

76. Irving Kristol, "What's Bugging the Students." *Atlantic Monthly* (February 1965) p. 108.

77. Robert Glasgow, "An Interview with Irving Kristol," *Psychology Today* (February 1974) p. 78.

78. Interview with Joshua Muravchik. March 20, 1994

79. Robert Nisbet, "Still Questing," *The Intercollegiate Review* (Fall 1993) p. 42.

80. Daniel Patrick Moynihan, "The Politics of Stability," *The New Leader* (October 9, 1967) p. 7.

81. "The New Inquisitors," p. 8

82. Irving Kristol, "Teaching in, Speaking Out: The Controversy over Viet Nam,'" *Encounter* (August 1965) p. 65, 68.

83. Irving Kristol, "American Intellectuals and Foreign Policy," *Foreign Affairs* (July 1967) p. 594.

84. Irving Kristol, "What Business Is a University In?" *New York Times Magazine* (November 23, 1969) p. 106.

85. Peter Steinfels, *The Neoconservatives: The Men Who Are Changing America's Politics* (New York: Simon and Schuster, 1979) p. 189.

86. "The Moynihan Mystique," p. 58. The "rich college fucks" comment comes from a conversation between Moynihan and the reporter Timothy Crouse in 1976 discussed in the article. "'What sort of background do you come from?'" The candidate (Moynihan) asked the journalist (Crouse). Crouse confessed it was "upper middle class." "Aaaaaah," said Moynihan. "A rich Harvard kid. Or, as we used to say where I come from, a rich college fuck." p. 52.

87. Quoted in Richard Rodosh, "On Irving Howe," *Partisan Review* (Fall 1993) p. 345.

88. "What's Bugging the Students," p. 109.

89. "Introduction" in *Confrontation: The Student Rebellion and the Universities*, p. xi.

90. Quoted in John Diggins, *The Rise and Fall of the American Left* (New York: Norton, 1992), p. 233.

91. Irving Kristol, "Why It's Hard to Be Nice to the Old Left." *Fortune* (August 1968) p. 175.

92. Irving Kristol, "Barbarians from Within," *Fortune* (March 1970) p. 191.

93. Daniel Patrick Moynihan, "Nirvana Now," *The American Scholar* (Autumn 1967) p. 541. Similarly, Irving Kristol writes of the New Left, "It resembles nothing so much as the fantasies of various heretical sects of the early Christian era who anticipated a Second Coming in their lifetime and prepared themselves by seceding from civil society on earth." "The Improbable Guru of Surrealistic Politics," *Fortune* (July 1969) p. 174.

94. Daniel Patrick Moynihan, "Politics as the Art of the Impossible," *The American Scholar* (Autumn 1968) p. 578.

95. Irving Kristol, "'When Virtue Loses All Her Loveliness'—Some Reflections on Capitalism and 'The Free Society,'" *The Public Interest* (Fall 1970) p. 4.

96. Jeanne Kirkpatrick, "The Revolt of the Masses," *Commentary* (February 1973) p. 60

97. Irving Kristol, "We Can't Resign as 'Policeman of the World,'" *The New York Times Magazine* (May 12, 1968) p. 13.

98. Irving Kristol, "A New Isolationism? Letter from New York," *Encounter* (June 1966) p. 52.

99. Irving Kristol, "Facing the Facts in Vietnam," *The New Leader* (September 30, 1963) p. 8.

100. "Facing the Facts in Vietnam," p. 8.

101. Irving Kristol, "Why I Am for Humphrey," *The New Republic* (June 8, 1968) p. 22.

102. *Coping*, p. 18.

103. "The New Left and Its Limits," p. 39

104. Nathan Glazer, "The Campus Crucible," *Atlantic* (July 1969) p. 52.

105. Interview with Irving Kristol, January 26, 1994.

106. Noam Chomsky, "The Responsibility of the Intellectuals," *New York Review of Books* (February 23, 1967) pp. 16–26.

107. Jason Epstein, "The CIA and the Intellectuals," *The New York Review of Books* (April 20, 1967) p. 20.

108. *Intellectual Skywriting*, p. 50.

109. Andrew Kopkind, "Soul Power." Review of *Where Do We Go From Here: Chaos or Community?* by Martin Luther King. *The New York Review of Books* (August 24, 1967) p. 3

110. Louis Coser, letter to The *New York Review of Books* (October 26, 1967) p. 44. Coser's impassioned response illustrates the breadth of the opposition to *The New York Review of Books* at the time. For Coser was anything but a neoconservative—he was actually an opponent. For a blistering attack on neoconservatives, see "Midge Decter and the Boys on the Beach," *Dissent* (Spring 1981) p. 217.

111. Noam Chomsky, "On Resistance," *The New York Review of Books* (December 7, 1967) pp. 4, 6.

112. Irving Howe, "The New York Intellectuals: A Chronicle and a Critique," *Commentary* (October 1968).

113. Diana Trilling, "On the Steps of Low Library," *Commentary* (November 1969) pp. 29–56.
114. Gertrude Himmelfarb, "The Politics of Dissent," *Commentary* (July 1994) p. 35.
115. Interview with Midge Decter, November 24, 1993.
116. Dennis Wrong, "The Case of *The New York Review*," *Commentary* (November 1970) pp. 49–63.
117. Nathan Glazer, "Jewish Interests and the New Left," *Midstream* (January 1971) p. 35.
118. Arthur Hertzberg, "Israel and American Jewry," *Commentary* (August 1967) p. 70.
119. Quoted in Seymour Martin Lipset, "The Socialism of Fools: The Left, the Jews and Israel," *Encounter* (December 1969) p. 24.
120. Edward Alexander, "Gore Vidal's Anti-Jewish Nationalism," *Society* (March/April 1988) p. 79.
121. Interview with Martin Peretz, April 25, 1994.
122. Martin Peretz, "The American Left and Israel," *Commentary* (November 1967).
123. See Nathan Glazer, "The Role of the Intellectuals," *Commentary* (February 1971) pp. 55–61.
124. "Blacks, Jews, and the Intellectuals." *Commentary* (April 1969) p. 36.
125. These articles are Robert Alter's "Appropriating the Religious Tradition," pp. 47–54, Nathan Glazer's "The Role of the Intellectuals," pp. 55–61 and Walter Lacquer's "New York and Jerusalem," pp. 38–46.
126. Nathan Glazer, "The Exposed American Jew," *Commentary* (June 1975) pp. 25–30.
127. This is one of the oft-quoted remarks of neoconservatism. One citation is, "Neo-conservative Guru to America's New Order: Q and A: Irving Kristol," (*MacLeans*, January 19, 1981, p. 9). In this interview, Kristol says that he made the comment a few years earlier.
128. Norman Podhoretz, "The Intellectual and the Pursuit of Happiness," *Commentary* (February 1973) p. 7.
129. Irving Kristol, *On the Democratic Idea in America* (New York: Harper and Row, 1972) p. 114.
130. Chris DeMuth, "Toasts and Remarks Delivered at a Dinner in Honor of Irving Kristol on His Seventy-fifth Birthday" (Washington: American Enterprise Institute, January 21, 1995).
131. Robert Nisbet, "An Epistle to the Americans," *Commentary* (December 1970) p. 41.
132. Daniel Bell, "Unstable America," *Encounter* (June 1970) p. 13.
133. Sidney Hook, *Out of Step: An Unquiet Life in the 20th Century* (New York: Harper and Row, 1987) p. 555
134. Walter Goodman, "The Question of Repression," *Commentary* (August 1970) p. 23.

135. *Coping*, p. 19.
136. Arnold Beichman, "Letter from Columbia," *Encounter* (May 1969) p. 19.
137. Irving Kristol, "Urban Civilization and its Discontents," *Commentary* (July 1970) pp. 34–35.
138. "Utopianism, Ancient and Modern," *Imprimus* (April 1973) reprinted in *Two Cheers for Capitalism* (New York: Basic Books, 1978) p. 169.
139. *On the Democratic Idea in America*, p. vii.

4

Old Battles and New Enemies: Ethnic Dilemmas and Political Realignment

The 1960s ended, however, not with a revolution but with the election of Richard Nixon: Richard Nixon, who better than any single figure in American public life seemed to epitomize everything in opposition to which the adversary culture had always defined itself. But the response to this defeat was not a new withdrawal. It was, on the contrary, a new determination to mount an effective political challenge, this time "working within the system" to get rid of the usurper who had seized the throne and to place political power at long last into the proper hands. This effort, which called itself the New Politics, sought to forge a coalition of two disparate elements: Those who were, or felt themselves to be, deprived of the full benefits of middle-class comfort and security (the blacks and the poor) and those who were, or felt themselves to be, deprived of the full benefits of political power (the New Class). Operating through the candidacy of George McGovern for president, the New Politics came infinitely closer to actual power than any political movement associated with the adversary culture had ever done before. . . . Full political power, then, had not been achieved, but obviously great progress had been made.—Norman Podhoretz, 1979

With respect to political things, most people were equal, and therefore most things distributed politically should be distributed equally. This implied that you favor civil rights laws, you favor ending inhibitions on people expressing political rights, you oppose manifestly unjust distributions of public good and services. Now suddenly comes the arrival of quotas and goals, affirmative action, and a form of advanced ethnic political patronage in which what is being sought for is more, not the good but the more. And at this point most people in society feel that an elemental standard of justice has been either violated or made obscure. Now that is an area in which one can show the linkage between a philosophical conception that is not trivial, a set of empirical observations, and a comment on public policy.—James Q. Wilson, 1980

The Return to Ideology

The neoconservative literary scholar Joseph Epstein best encapsulated the neoconservative take on the 1960s in a 1988 essay.

> The sixties, I have come to believe, are something of a political Rorschach test. Tell me what you think of that period and I shall tell you what your politics are. Tell me that you think the period both good and bad, with much to be said for and against it, and you are, whether you know it or not, a liberal. Tell me that you think the sixties a banner time in American life, a period of unparalleled idealism, a splendid opportunity sadly missed, and you are doubtless a radical, sentimental or otherwise. Tell me that you think the sixties a time of horrendous dislocation, a disaster nearly averted, a damn near thing, but a thing nonetheless for which we are still paying and shall continue to pay. . . . Well, I am not sure what you are precisely, but your views, friend, are close to mine and I am pleased to meet you.[1]

It was John Updike who said the 1970s were the decade when the sixties had finally percolated down to everybody, but it might have well been Irving Kristol, Midge Decter, or Daniel Patrick Moynihan.[2] In many ways, the politics of the 1970s took what was worst in the 1960s and exacerbated it. Neoconservatives spent the 1970s fighting against what liberalism had become. As the neoconservatives saw it, 1970s liberalism could not discriminate between civil rights and quotas, had little to say about anti-Semitism at home or abroad, and read into America's failure in Vietnam a broad argument against the moral legitimacy of American military engagement.

The issues of the 1970s were interconnected in a variety of ways. The Soviet agenda was executed in large part by the Third World, which in turn was often anti-Zionist and anti-Semitic. Nevertheless, the Third World was romanticized and celebrated by the left on several continents. The neoconservatives noted that some of the greatest champions of the Third World were prominent radical American blacks, many of whom had worked closely with Jews in the civil rights movement. Confrontations between blacks and Jews over the Third World and Israel were magnified by conflicts over affirmative action and the proper role of Jewish public employees—especially teachers—in black neighborhoods in American cities such as Newark and New York. Of course, the connections are much deeper and at times more subtle than this cursory analysis suggests—and they will be developed—but this should not detract from the fact that the issues and disputes of the 1970s elude facile compartmentalization.

These connections signify something greater than a mere coincidence or even a confluence of thought. They speak to the prevailing intellectual culture, which was characterized by a return to fundamental principles and a reexamination of basic philosophical assumptions—in short, ideology. Nonideological thinking is geared to solving one problem before moving to the next. It assumes rational actors who largely share basic assumptions and ultimate aims. On the other hand, as Daniel Bell noted in 1961, ideological thinking creates a situation where "ideas become weapons."[3]

If it is just a matter of which inputs from a known quantity will produce the agreed outcome, compromises can be made and differences can be split without much difficulty. However, if what is being debated are fundamental conceptions of human nature, human potential, and the limits of human action, deep-seated emotions are bound to flare up as fundamental philosophies confront one another in ideological combat. The issues of the 1970s, especially race and religion, lent themselves especially well to these passions. In such an ideological climate, it was inevitable that old alliances would fall apart and new ones would be formed.

While the intellectual debates of the 1970s were characterized by interrelated topics united by ideology, there was one pivotal issue that fueled the others—race. Perhaps never in American intellectual history have the parameters of a debate been so dramatically and so quickly changed as with the issue of race during the 1960s and 1970s. In the early 1960s, liberals fought hard for equal rights for blacks and achieved all their legislative aims. The Civil Rights Acts of 1964 and 1965 and the Voting Rights Act of 1965 mandated equality before the law throughout the United States. Seldom are victories in democracies so astounding and so absolute—generally, the by-products of the compromise inherent in the system are aims still unattained and goals yet to be fulfilled.

Affirmative Action . . . or Discrimination?

The usurpation of language and history concerning affirmative action was a focal point for neoconservative thought. In a *Commentary* article, "Why Racial Preference Is Illegal and Immoral," the philosopher Carl Cohen writes of how affirmative action led to the substitution of the word "disadvantaged" for "blacks" or other minorities when "not all minorities are disadvantaged, and not all those disadvantaged are minorities."[4] Thus, large groups of people are classified as "disadvantaged" and other groups of people are considered "advantaged" regardless of their individual backgrounds or particular situations—a twist that Cohen and the neoconservatives regarded as intellectually unjust to the blacks who are not "disadvantaged."

Several neoconservatives, most notably Nathan Glazer, have discussed extensively how bastardization of language resulted in a sea change in the conception of affirmative action in numerous ways. Contributors to *The Public Interest* and *Commentary* showed that affirmative action originated under President Kennedy as a way for companies to seek people of different racial and ethnic backgrounds by advertising job positions clearly and widely. In the Civil Rights Act of 1964, the definition of "affirmative action" was expanded somewhat to include penalizing employers who were found guilty of discrimination on the basis of race and sex. The fundamental idea of the civil rights movement—that race should never be a factor in anything—was codified.

Shortly after, affirmative action programs were transformed to the point where all members of an ever broadening number of "minority" groups received preferential treatment regardless of their particular circumstances. No longer was color-blindness the benchmark for liberal discussions of race relations. As Glazer and Moynihan commented in a 1974 *Commentary* essay, "Nothing was more dramatic than the rise of this practice [of quotas] on the part of the American government in the 1960s, at the very moment it was being declared abhorrent and illegal."[5] The enforcement mechanisms of antidiscrimination laws were also rearranged; no longer was an accused party innocent of discrimination until proven guilty. Supreme Court decisions put the burden on proving *nondiscrimination* on the accused. By the 1970s, all nonreligious institutions, whether corporate, governmental, educational, or nonprofit, were required to be able to justify and defend the ethnic composition of their employees. If the ethnic composition of their employees did not correspond to the ethnic makeup of the surrounding area, institutions could be considered guilty of discrimination unless they proved otherwise—a nearly impossible task.

Consequently and, the neoconservatives claimed, quite logically, these institutions turned to quotas to protect themselves. Quotas, of course, violated the central principle of the Civil Rights Acts and of the traditional liberal conception of race relations. Neoconservatives had fought so hard for civil rights and had won a resounding victory only to have their efforts completely transformed by their former allies. Irving Kristol asked in 1974,

> Who would ever have thought, twenty or even ten years ago, that we in the United States would live to see the day when a government agency would ask institutions of higher learning to take a racial census of their faculties, specifying the proportion of "Indo-Europeans" (traditionally, just another term for "Aryans")? And who could have anticipated that this would happen with little public controversy, and with considerable support from the liberal community? How on earth did this fantastic situation come about?[6]

The neoconservatives have consistently opposed affirmative action on principle and in practice. Quite simply, the neoconservatives maintained that race should never be a factor in hiring, admissions, or anything else. They have consistently maintained that the idea of racial collectivism embodied in affirmative action contravenes a fundamental premise of Western society, that justice adheres in the individual. Affirmative action imbues an entire class of people with guilt they may not deserve and another class with victim status they are not necessarily due. And for the neoconservatives—who hated discrimination and fought for civil rights—affirmative action constitutes a trivialization of the heinous moral crimes of racism and discrimination.

Richard John Neuhaus and Peter Berger addressed the issue of affirmative action in their 1975 American Enterprise Institute monograph, *To Empower People: The Role of Mediating Structures in Public Policy*, by making a distinction between a society of proscription and a society of prescription. In a formulation that encapsulates the neoconservative position on affirmative action, Neuhaus and Berger assert that racial discrimination should be proscribed tirelessly. However, this in no way should imply a policy of prescription, where the "correct" racial or ethnic composition of an institution is determined a priori, without regard to specific individuals.[7]

Affirmative action was even more pernicious to the neoconservatives because of the undemocratic way in which it was established. Though a policy that pervades broad sectors of the nation, it has never had popular support. Affirmative action was almost always the result of dictates of the federal bureaucracy and the liberal courts, unelected and accountable to no one. Through decisions and mandates that placed the burden of proof in discrimination cases on employers, bureaucrats and judges discarded the intention of the framers of the civil rights laws and instead mandated their political preference for quotas. The neoconservatives consistently pointed out that those who drafted the Civil Rights Act of 1964 and the Voting Rights Act of 1965 explicitly denied that their legislation should be interpreted as the courts and bureaucrats were interpreting it in the 1970s. This line of argument enabled the neoconservatives to demonstrate that their disagreement with liberals concerning affirmative action was not limited to the interpretation of laws or the value of a policy, but spoke to larger issues of intellectual honesty and democratic fidelity.

One crucial reason behind the neoconservative animus toward quotas related to the question, "Is it good for the Jews?" On most issues, the neoconservatives have asserted that few political issues are clearly good or bad for the Jews and that Jews should, for the most part, develop political positions without referencing them to Judaism. However, with affirmative action—and with several other ideological issues in the 1970s—the question "Is it good for the Jews?" became unavoidable.

For decades, Jews had fought against quotas which were used to keep them out of universities, law firms, medical schools, country clubs, and investment banks. Jews had progressed despite the quotas, largely by establishing their own institutions such as the Albert Einstein Medical Center in response to discrimination at Cornell Medical School or investment banks such as Lehman Brothers in response to discrimination by the white-shoe banking houses. Nevertheless, Jews felt the pain and suffered the consequences of quotas and consistently fought for the abolition of race, religion, and ethnicity as factors in admission and hiring practices.[8] To see these same measures of discrimination resurrected—by liberals!—was, to put it mildly, ironic. Few Jewish groups and no neoconservative accepted the liberal explanation that quotas are exclusive, while the "goals and timetables" of affirmative action are inclusive. To the neoconservatives and most Jewish groups, a quota is a quota.[9]

The neoconservative claim that affirmative action is bad for the Jews went beyond a theoretical opposition to quotas, though that important claim should not be minimized. In addition to their principled objection to race-based classifications, the neoconservatives believed that the tangible and practical manifestations of affirmative action were harmful to Jews. The very institutions that were at the forefront of the quota revolution—the government, universities, professions, even corporations—had large concentrations of Jews. After being shut out of these institutions by pro active discrimination, Jews were about to be the victims of reverse discrimination. As Daniel Patrick Moynihan declared in a 1968 *Atlantic Monthly* essay, "Let me be blunt. If ethnic quotas are to be imposed on American universities and similarly quasi-public institutions, it is Jews who will be almost driven out."[10]

While affirmative action and quotas may have begun with blacks, such programs were significantly expanded to other ethnic groups. Hispanics followed first and they were subsequently joined by a coterie of other groups from Eskimos to Aleuts. According to the neoconservatives, the expansion of affirmative action to these groups exacerbated the grave problems generated by affirmative action applied to blacks. Neoconservatives argued that extending affirmative action to a host of minority groups conveys the message that the United States is a hopelessly prejudiced nation needing stern guidance to ensure that it does not discriminate. The implication behind the strict rules and tightly enforced regulations that compose affirmative action is that prejudice and bigotry will run rampant unless employers and institutions are tightly controlled by government regulations. If Americans were so hopelessly racist that quotas were necessary, affirmative action would be a mere palliative that would not come close to dealing with America's fundamental immorality and intractable problems.

Affirmative Action and Black Progress

According to the neoconservatives, the most damning aspect of affirmative action was the detrimental and destructive effect it has on its intended beneficiaries. Nathan Glazer makes this argument the centerpiece of *Affirmative Discrimination*.

> If the conditions of the black population can be improved by these programs, then undoubtedly that would be the best reason for them. For me, no consideration of principle—such as that merit should be rewarded, or that governmental programs should not discriminate on grounds of race or ethnic group—would stand in the way of a program of preferential hiring if it made some substantial progress in reducing the severe problems of the low-income black population and of the inner cities.[11]

Neoconservatives contended that affirmative action is strictly a middle-class phenomenon; it does nothing for the blacks who need help—those suffering in the inner city. A child who cannot walk home from school without the fear of being shot will not be helped by a program of preferential treatment for blacks at prestigious colleges and in large corporations.[12] The neoconservatives consider affirmative action a way for liberals to avoid the real problems of black America, many of which are cultural, unpleasant to discuss, and even harder to solve.

The neoconservatives have maintained that affirmative action harms blacks by generating a backlash and increasing the racism for which affirmative action is supposed to compensate. People can generally accept being rejected from a job or a university if they know that the decision was made fairly—if it is based on what people deserve—on their merits. However, just as blacks have resented being treated unequally because of their race, nonminorities (whoever that will include depends on who is considered a minority) will resent being rejected on the basis of characteristics over which they have no control.

A major concern of the neoconservatives with affirmative action has been the culture of dependency that it generates. When minority groups demand or receive preferential treatment, they rely on the allegedly dominant culture to provide them with jobs and places in universities. This dependency relationship is not only humiliating to the recipient, but it maintains an "us versus them paradigm" that is contrary to racial equality. Orlando Patterson ponders this in *The Public Interest.*

> There is something inherently demeaning about begging help from your offender. It gives the offender the moral status of a god. The victim who cries, "Help me! You have crippled me, now make me whole again," is simply contemptible. There is nothing ethnocentric about the contempt we feel for such a plea. The literature, legends, and myths of almost every known culture makes this point in the inevitable motif of the defeated hero who spurns the victor's help, licks his wounds, restores himself through sheer force of will (and, occasionally a little help from the gods—his own gods). . . . There can be no moral equality where there is a dependency relationship among men; there will always be a dependency relationship where the victim strives for equality by vainly seeking the assistance of his victimizer.[13]

Likewise, the dependent—and hence unequal—relationship between groups receiving preferential treatment and those not receiving it is perpetuated by asserting that blacks need or even want affirmative action. The best way for blacks to overcome prejudice, Nathan Glazer argued, is by demonstrating that they can excel without special treatment.[14] Affirmative action may cause white communities to wonder whether there are intrinsically negative qualities about minorities that necessitate special treatment. Thomas Sowell voiced this concern in a 1970 *New York Times Magazine* essay.

> When the failures of many programs become too great to disguise, or to hide under euphemisms and apologetics, the conclusion that will be drawn in many quarters will not be that these were half-baked schemes, but that black people just don't have it.[15]

The justifications for affirmation action about which Sowell writes may not be voiced in polite company, but the neoconservatives contend that they are the ugly and unavoidable questions of affirmative action. As Irving Kristol has noted, "I cannot accept the notion that black Americans are a crippled people who cannot cope with the world except under 'our' benevolent guidance. I doubt very much that they accept it, either."[16]

As Kristol's comment suggests, neoconservatives considered affirmative action to be the benchmark of a larger liberal philosophy of condescension to blacks. Race should not be a factor in hiring or admissions; likewise, it should not be a factor in applying moral judgment. To explain away criminal behavior by blacks is, according to the neoconservatives, a form of racism—liberal racism. Daniel Patrick Moynihan explains, "Liberals must somehow overcome the curious condescension that takes the form of defending and explaining away anything, however outrageous, which Negroes, individually or collectively, might do."[17]

The neoconservatives wrote that liberals often refused to criticize blacks or even to hold them to the same standards of behavior and achievement as whites for fear of being considered racist. And when radicals blamed most problems of black America on racism or refused to hold blacks and whites to the same standards of conduct and merit, liberals were loathe to contradict them for fear of being labeled racist or reactionary. The radicals preyed on liberal weakness, knowing that the charge "racist" would—no matter how unfounded—not be easily dismissed. Neoconservatives regard the charge of "racism" as often an intellectual arrest; it is an indelible stigma regardless of guilt or innocence. As Michael Novak, a neoconservative by the mid-1970s, wrote in *Commentary*,

> The word racist now functions as did the word pink in the 50s: the whip across the face used by demagogues; the slap meant to cripple careers and to dry up sources of scholarly funding; the occasion for disruptions of free speech; and the broad brush of derogation and character assassination.[18]

Neoconservatives noted the irony of liberals, who had championed equality of men regardless of race only a few years ago, defending different standards for blacks and whites. The neoconservatives considered this intellectually illegitimate and, more importantly, destructive and patronizing to those who were held to the lower standard. Novak addressed this point in another *Commentary* article from the same period.

> If you grant no responsibility or hope for their own advancement to blacks, but treat their needs as in every respect due to a form of victimization, then no one calls you a racist; you are regarded, instead, as a friend to blacks. "Don't blame the victim" is the slogan of such friendship. But if, on the other hand, you assert that blacks are equal to whites in potency, moral spirit, dignity, responsibility, and power over their own future, and deny that they are mere pawns and victims, then you set off a chorus of alarums and find yourself on treacherous emotional territory.[19]

In this article, Novak maintains that one of the most significant causalities of the liberal dogmatism on racial issues is that of open discourse. With the charge of racism so promiscuous—and damning—discussion of racial issues is chilled.

> Certain opinions pass without inspection; others—on plainly ideological grounds—are rejected without inspection. It is as though no one dares to think, no one dares to question. The overriding current requirement is that one march in rank. Intellectual muggers stand ready to discipline those who stray. New extortion rackets function: conform, or take your punishment.[20]

As Novak's statement implies, the neoconservatives have been greatly disturbed by the liberal reaction to the intellectual naggings performed by radicals. The radical assault on traditional standards of acceptability—which the liberals either tolerated or co-opted—worked in two ways. The first is an insidious relativism, which, in the name of tolerance, prohibits strong criticism of immoral behavior and action for fear of passing judgment. Just as the liberal anti-Communists criticized Progressivism in the 1950s for failing to make crucial moral distinctions, the neoconservatives criticized liberals in the 1970s for failing to uphold and enforce similar standards.[21]

Second is the result of this relativism. According to the neoconservatives, the inability of the left to exorcise unacceptable forms of discourse led to a tolerance of authoritarian suppression of opinions on certain controversial issues. Having no use for traditional liberal beliefs concerning free expression, the radicals—as with the Herrnstein, Moynihan, and Banfield cases to name a few—often worked actively to chill the articulation of ideas they hated. And the liberals, afraid even to say that the authoritarianism of the left was unacceptable, surrendered as their professed values were assaulted. The neoconservatives have used the issue of race to illustrate this phenomenon, for it is in this controversial area that the liberal surrender to radical modes of discussion is most evident.

Ethnic Dilemmas

Michael Novak, a lay Catholic theologian and philosopher, was recognized in intellectual circles in the late 1960s as a radical leftist. His best-known work at the time, *A Theology for Radical Politics*, followed the usual radical line of castigating liberals. In that book, he charged, "it is the liberal way of life and mind that represents the evil of America." He continues,

> The enemy in America, then, is the tyrannical and indifferent majority: the good people, the churchgoers, the typical Americans, the ones who have been taught that to be an American is by that fact to be moral, just, free, generous and trustworthy. So long as such a majority controls the destiny of America, it appears, the nation will remain militarist, racist, and counterrevolutionary; the wealth of the United States will increase, conscience will be suffocated; the wretched of the earth will suffer yet more. . . .[22]

Novak's politics began to change in 1970 when he traveled the country writing speeches for Sargent Shriver, who was campaigning for Democratic congressional candidates. Descending from the towers of academe and working with ordinary Americans, Novak saw that the people he met along the campaign trail in no way resembled the descriptions of Americans in *A Theology for Radical Politics*. He recalls, "Comparing the actual American people to the vision of America cherished in the literary snobbery that I took part in, I was subverted. I came to think there was more health in the people than in their literary elites, including me."[23]

This conversion was aided by a reevaluation about the connection between Novak's radical politics and the situation of his family, who had escaped oppression in Slovakia to come to America.

> One of the features of being on the left that most disquieted me was the "bad faith" in which it placed me. In arguing for left-wing positions, I found myself putting down other Americans, trying to shock "the complacent" (as I thought them) and writing of U.S. "militarism" and "imperialism." But who was I to be anything but grateful to this country that had taken in an impoverished and much oppressed family of former serfs from Slovakia, and that had given to me and countless others opportunities unprecedented in history?[24]

Novak's 1971 book, *The Rise of the Unmeltable Ethics: Politics and Culture in the 1970s*, represents something like a halfway point in his development from the embrace of radicalism in 1969 through a complete rejection of radicalism in 1975. The book cannot be classified as liberal or conservative. Novak sought to celebrate a group of minorities who had been the object of neglect or the subject of scorn among liberals—the group he endearingly called PIGS: Polish, Irish, Greeks, Slavs.

Novak's project is not political. In the climate of awareness to ethnicity, he wants white ethnics to be freed from liberal stereotypes and to gain a modicum of respect from the larger culture. Novak charges that liberals castigate the largely ethnic working class as unenlightened, racist rednecks whose claims for group pride are simply covers for racism, and calls for a black-ethnic front against their common enemy—the WASP.

In analyzing this book, the left generally overlooked Novak's condemnation of American capitalism and focused on his favorable treatment of the PIGS. For instance, Earl Shorris wrote of Novak's book in *The Nation*, "'Ethnic interests' is the new euphemism for racism."[25] Garry Wills's criticism in *The New York Times Book Review* was more significant because Wills, a former protégé of William Buckley, was a respected scholar in all quarters. Wills called *The Rise of the Unmeltable Ethnics* an "immoral book" whose purpose is to "extend the already vast repertoire of American resentments."[26] The neoconservatives, while they may not have agreed with everything in the book, nonetheless respected Novak's argument and his courage to make it. Robert Alter praised the book in *Commentary*, maintaining that Novak deftly combined an economics of the left with a decidedly conservative take on ethnicity in a forthright and original work.[27]

While the neoconservatives did not celebrate ethnicity per se to the extent that Novak did, they, too, voiced concerns over the ways the left regarded white ethnics. In 1970, Nathan Glazer noted that there is no language with which to speak about ethnicity free of the charges of racism or at least ethnocentrism. While people speak of assimilation through the language of the melting pot, there is no corresponding language of ethnicity untainted by the specter of racism.[28]

In their discussions of affirmative action and ethnicity, the neoconservatives crafted their own language—distinct from that of the melting pot or of supporters of quotas—which they considered consistent with the principles of true liberalism. Daniel Patrick Moynihan and Nathan Glazer wrote in *Beyond the Melting Pot* that people tend to maintain an attachment to their ethnic group long after the actual blood tie has been diluted to the point of dissipation. The neoconservatives had no objection to this when the goal was community solidarity or historical understanding. They found nothing wrong with an individual whose claim to Irish or black heritage consists of one great-grandmother, so long as that individual is simply seeking community with neighbors or continuity with the past. However, the neoconservatives dropped their support when the purpose of recovering long-lost ancestry was to obtain preferential treatment or victim status. When society rewards people for a certain ethnicity and encourages them to seek an identity to earn special treatment, the natural consequences are resentment and balkanization. Nathan Glazer explained in *Affirmative Discrimination*,

> Individuals find subtle pressures to make use of their group affiliation not necessarily because of any desire to be associated with a group but because

> groups become the basis for rights, and those who want to claim certain rights must do so as a member of an affected or protected class. New lines of conflict are created by government action. New resentments, new turfs are to be protected.[29]

Glazer and the other neoconservatives have maintained that a group that is placed outside the mainstream and targeted for preferential treatment is denied the opportunity to share in the heritage of the ideals of unity and harmony upon which racial justice is based. When people search their background for something that makes them different and proceed to accentuate this difference to advance in a society that rewards ethnic identity, the notions of shared destiny and common values are lost.

And yet that is what the neoconservatives perceived as happening in the 1970s. The traditional liberal paradigm for race relations in the 1960s incorporated all citizens, regardless of their skin color, into the general rubric of American society. This, after all, was the theme behind integration; as the argument runs, when blacks and whites are finally permitted live together, they will see how much they have in common and the result will be harmony. The neoconservatives argued that whether this ever could have worked in practice is a question that liberals never permitted to be answered. Harmony between ethnic and racial groups is engendered by stressing commonalities in culture, hopes, and aspiration. Affirmative action accentuates difference.

Black Anti-Semitism

One major by-product of the neoconservative, and hence Jewish, opposition to affirmative action and the issues it generated was the complete break of the civil rights coalition of blacks and Jews. In a 1979 *Commentary* article, Murray Friedman cited the results of a survey commissioned by the National Conference of Christians and Jews: 17 to 32 percent of whites agreed with a series of negative stereotypes of Jews, while blacks agreed in a range of 37 to 56 percent. Although black anti-Semitism had always been a problem, it was exacerbated by black resentment to the Jewish opposition to affirmative action.

As Kenneth Clark and James Baldwin discussed in *Commentary* in the 1940s, anti-Semitism had always been prominent in the black community.[30] Black anti-Semitism remained a lifelong concern of Baldwin. In a 1967 *New York Times Magazine* article, he wrote that black anti-Semitism is not against the Jews per se, but against whites in general.[31] Most of the whites with whom inner-city blacks came into contact were Jews—social workers, teachers, doctors, lawyers, etc.—and the connection between Jews and whites was made. This, however, was no excuse for Baldwin or the neoconservatives.

The rise in black anti-Semitism in the 1970s accompanied the rise of anti-Semitism among radicals of all races. The gradual unfolding of black anti-Semitism began after the death of Martin Luther King, who called anti-Semitism "anti-man and anti-God," and said that blacks have a special responsibility to combat it.[32] Following the assassination of King, however, there was no leader with the desire and influence to end anti-Semitic rhetoric in the black community.

A major eruption of left-wing politics and black anti-Semitism occurred in the New York City teachers strike in Ocean Hill/Brownsville. In 1968, the Ford Foundation provided New York City with a grant with which to embark on a program of decentralized, community schooling. This experiment was to take place in Ocean Hill, a poor district that was 75 percent black and 20 percent Puerto Rican. The district still received money from the state—in addition to its grant from the Ford Foundation—and had almost complete autonomy with regard to how to spend it.

The plan degenerated into a radical romp of the worst kind. The newly empowered "community leaders," many of them "parents" (having children in the schools was not a requirement for this designation), often sent virulent politicized messages to their young charges. Middle School Principal Leslie Campbell exhorted the young teenagers, "Don't steal toothpaste and combs, steal things we can use. You know what I mean, brothers. . . . When the enemy taps you on the shoulder, send him to the cemetery. You know who your enemy is."[33] Following this speech, several teachers were physically attacked by their students and required hospitalization.

In addition to these generic threats to the teachers in Ocean Hill, lurking not so far below the surface, and often rising above the surface, was anti-Semitism. It was no secret that the teachers were primarily Jewish and the community leaders were primarily black. Anti-Semitic literature and pamphlets were distributed by the "community leaders"; a typical example was a poem to union leader Albert Shanker read over a radio station by a black teacher, "Hey, Jew boy, with that yarmulke on your head / You pale-faced Jew boy—I wish you were dead."[34] A widely circulated pamphlet referred to the Jewish faculty as "the Middle East murderers of colored people . . . blood-sucking exploiters and murderers. . . ." Consequently, the teachers went on strike three times to protest the physical violence against them and the unjust treatment of their colleagues—some of whom had been fired without explanation.

These events did much to damage relationships between blacks and Jews, which had been in a steady process of erosion since the end of the civil rights movement. Never before were the two groups pitted so directly against each other; no euphemisms could disguise the fact that black "community leaders" were aligned against Jewish teachers. The dichotomy was painful and obvious, and members of these groups as well as the general public were forced to choose sides and make enemies.

The teachers strike also highlighted rifts in the intellectual community. In the November 1968 issue of *Ramparts*, Sol Stern wrote that the teachers would probably vote for George Wallace. Liberals such as Murray Kempton, Jason Epstein, James Wechsler, Jimmy Breslin, and Nat Hentoff agreed with Stern's sentiment if not his electoral analysis and blamed the strikes on white racism. *Dissent* ran the best essay on the subject, "Tragedy at Ocean Hill, by Thomas Brooks, defending the teachers while providing a thorough history of the event.[35] Martin Meyer wrote a book, *The Teachers Strike*, defending the teachers.

While the more Nazi-like anti-Semitism voiced at Ocean Hill stayed outside the mainstream, the neoconservatives were concerned about black anti-Semitism that went far beyond the traditional resentment to whites. Instead of following the lead of James Baldwin and Martin Luther King in excoriating all types of anti-

Semitism, many black leaders such as Jesse Jackson and Andrew Young tolerated and even encouraged it. Consequently, black anti-Semitism became a major object of discussion in *Commentary* as represented in important articles by Earl Raab, Maurice Goldbloom, Murray Friedman, and Carl Gershman.

Jesse Jackson earned the animosity of the neoconservatives in the 1970s. In a typical statement, Jackson called the refusal of the State Department to meet with the Palestinian Liberation Organization (PLO) in the 1970s "an international absurdity and a crime against the civilized world."[36] These anti-Zionist views assumed institutional significance in 1979 when Andrew Young, a prominent black leader serving as the United States Ambassador to the United Nations, met with a representative of the PLO in direct violation of explicit instructions from President Carter. Young was forced to resign, but he never apologized for meeting with the PLO. Instead, he called Carter's policy "ridiculous" and stated that blacks "now believe that the Palestinians are oppressed and will act accordingly" and should no longer be "convinced that the Jews were the oppressed people."[37]

Always perceptive to the cultural underpinnings of political positions, the neoconservatives looked toward the source of many of the ideas which generated black anti-Semitism. In 1965, Jews and blacks marched arm in arm in civil rights marches; ten years later, the relationship between the two groups was characterized by the worst kind of bitterness. Who was responsible? The neoconservatives looked to those who formulated the ideas, to those who provided the initial intellectual firepower for affirmative action and anti-Zionism. The ideas that had triggered the black-Jewish rift were not only prevalent among black leaders, but were at the forefront of liberalism. And, the neoconservatives noted, many of the intellectuals and financiers who made black radicalism and affirmative possible were Jews. According to Nathan Glazer,

> The expansion and inflammation of anti-Semitism among blacks, while fed by material already present at the grass roots, has largely been the work of the black intelligentsia—to use an unfortunately indispensable word—abetted and assisted by a white, predominantly Jewish, intelligentsia. When

> we attack black anti-Semitism, let us be perfectly clear that we are attacking the fruits of five years of growing rage and irrationality, centered among radial college students, but encouraged by a wide range of white intellectuals, many of them Jewish.[38]

This may seem paradoxical. After all, if much of what was objectively "bad for the Jews" was related to black anti-Semitism, how could black anti-Semitism be aided and abetted by Jews? Wouldn't they have the most direct self-interest in preventing what the neoconservatives claimed was occurring? On the surface, perhaps, but the neoconservatives pointed out that some liberal Jews were quick to become self-hating and that anti-Semitism was, as it always had been, the province of Jews as well as Gentiles. As Martin Peretz recollects about the 1960s, "Self-interest was itself suspect. If you could see someone else's interest that was against that of your own group, that made you seem to yourself and to others more universal in your orientation, more just in a certain way."[39]

Israel, Jews, and the Left

The main problem, the neoconservatives asserted, was not self-consciously anti-Semitic Jews; there were precious few of them. The real concern was liberal Jews who, as Martin Peretz suggests, found self-interest invidious and sacrificed Jewish concerns when they conflicted with the left-wing agenda. The radicals' abandonment of Israel after the 1967 war permeated deeply into both liberal and moderate thought in the 1970s. The neoconservatives regarded Jews outside Israel as almost constitutionally unable to support Israel in the war of ideas. Ruth Wisse demonstrates how Jewish liberalism precludes a full-fledged rhetorical battle with the sworn enemies of the faith.

> Hoping that the Arabs will turn friendly "if not tomorrow then the day after," in the words of a popular Hebrew song, Israel and its supporters are genuinely disinclined to answer the propaganda against them, much less strike back in kind, lest by exacerbating tensions they only make things worse.[40]

The neoconservatives were determined to compensate for the failure of will they saw pervading liberal Jewry. The neoconservative effort to launch an intellectual defense of Israel was led by Norman Podhoretz through both his writing and his editing. Throughout the 1970s and beyond, Podhoretz marshaled and developed the best pro-Israel thinkers from around the globe as *Commentary* became the foremost Zionist publication in the world.

Podhoretz's mission to provide a pro-Israel voice in the intellectual community was difficult, considering the lack of support for Israel in the intellectual community. On one side were the traditional anti-Zionists, sometimes called Arabists, who would not defend Israel for fear of offending the Arabs. However, the far greater threat to Podhoretz's ideas came from liberals who attacked Israel for her domestic policies. These attacks came in a variety of ways. The least virulent, but most prevalent, attacks are encapsulated in the argument of Rabbi Joacham Prinz: "What we think is right and just in our own country must be right and just in Israel. What we find in America—the imperfections of democracy that we recognize and seek to correct—must also be considered faulty in Israel."[41]

The neoconservatives viewed this crude universalism just as they viewed the pieties of the progressives in the 1950s—as simplistic and idealistic examples of utopian naïveté freed from any real understanding of human nature. The neoconservatives stressed that the United States and Israel live in very different neighborhoods and have very different security situations. By comparing Israel with the United States, these liberal intellectuals were not comparing the Jewish state to the Arab neighbors with whom she had to deal on a daily basis. It was rarely pointed out that none of the twenty-one Arab states surrounding Israel is a democracy and that none has shown any hesitancy to wage war on Israel directly or through terrorism. If Israel, a tiny nation surrounded by belligerent and powerful neighbors, approached military engagements in the deliberate way as did the United States, she would have been destroyed in infancy or at any number of subsequent instances. The Arabs have attacked Israel several times in her short history and Israel has had to maintain eternal vigilance. Even when the Arabs were not attacking, Arab terrorists were poised throughout Israel and, as the tragedy at the Munich Olympics in 1972 showed, all over the world, waiting for the opportunity to destroy the Jewish state. The neoconservatives believed that liberals should focus instead on the fact that Israel is by far the best friend of human rights in the Middle East and should leave the security arrangements to those who live and die by them.

Just as neoconservatives objected when Israel was compared to the United States, they objected even more to *how* the Western press compared Israel to the Arab nations. Neoconservatives have maintained that the media apply a double standard that results in a situation where Arab acts of terror are minimized while Israeli acts of defense are magnified to look like unprovoked acts of belligerence. Thus, Israel is not only being held to an unjust standard when compared to the United States, but is not provided a fair hearing when compared to Arab nations.[42]

Who is at fault for this? As always, the neoconservatives looked to those who created the ideological climate—the intellectuals. The facile liberal analysis of Israel will, given time, have tremendous consequences. Norman Podhoretz declared in a 1976 *Commentary* article, "The Abandonment of Israel,"

> If a nuclear war should ever erupt in the Middle East, then, be it on the heads of all those in the United States and elsewhere—inside government and out, in the foundations and universities, in the councils and in the press—who under cover of self-deceptions and euphemisms and outright lies are "negotiating over the survival of Israel" instead of making the survival of that brave and besieged and beleaguered country, the only democracy in the Middle East and one of the few left anywhere on the face of the earth, the primary aim for their policies and the primary wish of their hearts.[43]

The neoconservative fury over Israel, which had been brewing over a number of policy and theoretical issues in the 1970s and early 1980s, reached a crescendo in 1982 with the Israeli incursion into Lebanon. Terrorists in Lebanon had been shelling Israelis with Katyusha rockets from across the border for years. Civil society had long ago broken down in Lebanon, due in large part to the efforts of the Syrian dictator Hafez al-Assad, who at one point had leveled the entire Syrian city of Hamas in order to eliminate an opposing political sect. Under the rule of Palestinians, Lebanon was dominated by roaming gangs of terrorists who often attacked Israel.

The liberal Western press regarded this action as an inexcusable act of imperialism. It was presented as though Israel were "taking over" Lebanon. The neoconservatives regarded this as silly at best—why would Israel want Lebanon? Several prominent liberal columnists said that Jews were treating the Palestinians as the Nazis had treated the Jews.

Norman Podhoretz explored the liberal reaction to the Israel-Lebanon situation in an article which became discussed all over the world, "J'Accuse," published in *Commentary* in September 1982. Throughout the 1970s and beyond, neoconservatives were accused of altering the terms of the debate about Israel by accusing its opponents of anti-Semitism. But all the neoconservatives use the term anti-Semitism sparingly, if at all. Sparingly, though, does not mean never. In "J'Accuse," Podhoretz states which of the critics of Israel were operating from anti-Semitism and the reasons why he believed so. He defines legitimate criticism of Israel as that which does not apply a double standard to Israel and the rest of the world. If someone criticizes Arabs and Israelis for not abiding by U.S. human rights standards, he may be naive and wrong, but is not necessarily anti-Semitic. However, when Israel is judged according to a far higher standard than other nations and when the rhetoric used to characterize the Jewish state incorporates a comparison to Nazi Germany, the motive of anti-Semitism cannot be overlooked. And that is just what Podhoretz saw happening in the late 1970s and early 1980s. He wrote in "J'Accuse,"

> In thinking about how Israel can be called Nazi-like, while reading dozens of vitriolic attacks on Israel, I have resisted the answer that nevertheless leaps irresistibly into the mind. The answer, of course, is that we are dealing with an eruption of anti-Semitism. . . . I accuse all those who have joined in these attacks not merely of anti-Semitism but of the broader sin of faithlessness to the interests of the United States and indeed to the values of Western civilization as a whole.[44]

The problems that neoconservatives had with the left and Israel were not limited to the radicals whose anti-Israel bias was clear or to naive opponents of Israeli human rights policy who disregarded its geopolitical situation. Perhaps the most difficult opponents the neoconservatives had to confront were ostensibly pro-Israel liberal Jews. While often supporting Israel over the demands of the Third World and even avoiding the naïveté of Rabbi Prinz, these Jews nevertheless supported the liberal line on the Cold War and the defense budget. The neoconservatives maintained that support for Israel without a hard-line stance toward the Soviet Union was useless. Israel needed American money, but she needed American weaponry even more. The Arabs had Soviet equipment, and Israel needed something commensurate. American weaponry was indispensable for Israel in several wars, and the development of top-notch American weaponry demanded a substantial defense budget. Pro-Israel liberals often did not seem to realize that weapons had to exist for Israel to use them. As Martin Peretz writes of pro-Israel Democrats who oppose high defense spending, "It means the eagerness of Democrats to provide weapons to Israel which these Democrats don't think the United States should build at all."[45]

According to the neoconservatives, this situation provided an easy answer to the following question when applied to American politics: Is it good for the Jews? Midge Decter explains,

> In a world full of ambiguities and puzzlements, one thing is absolutely easy both to define and locate: that is the Jewish interest. The continued security —and in those happy places where the term applies, well-being—of the Jews, worldwide, rests with a strong, vital, prosperous, self-confident United States.[46]

The Third World and the United Nations

Consistent with the restless nature of ideology, the ideas that the neoconservatives considered bad for the Jews did not remain dormant in the pages of American magazines and syndicated columns. Rather, they spread and influenced leaders in the Third World, who articulated their views in the United Nations. To many Jews, it was ironic that the United Nations had become a forum for anti-Semitism of any kind, considering that Jews had always been among its greatest supporters. Liberal Jews believed that the universalistic ethos embraced by the United Nations was superior to nationalistic ideas, which were said to nurture anti-Semitism.

But even in the 1950s, when *Commentary* voiced pro-United Nations and anti-Zionist sentiments, those who would become neoconservatives never accepted liberal universalism. Irving Kristol, for instance, wrote in 1956 that the Third World and the West would never come together in common cause because their values, goals and visions are diametrically different.[47] Though disappointed, the neoconservatives were not surprised when the United States exploded into a frenzy of anti-Semitism in the 1970s. And they were certainly not hesitant to resolutely break with the United Nations.

In 1983, serving as the U.S. ambassador to the United Nations, Charles Lichtenstein said in response to a proposal that the United Nations move from New York City, "We will put no impediment in your way, and we will be down at the dock bidding you a fond farewell as you sail off into the sunset."[48] Irving Kristol sent Lichtenstein a congratulatory telegram. Kristol would probably have liked to see Lichtenstein's dream come true; in a 1985 *National Interest* article, he called the United Nations "a playground for irresponsible or hostile governments to create mischief for the United States."[49] Or, as Kristol proposed at a 1987 American Enterprise Institute conference, "I just want to go on record as saying that I thoroughly deplore in this serious conversation on foreign policy, any mention of the UN Charter."[50]

Jeanne Kirkpatrick, who served as the ambassador to the United Nations in the 1980s, maintained that the United Nations was founded on a fallacy. While the U.N. Charter assumed that its member nations would embody democratic principles, the Soviet Union and its client states never had such intentions. By acting as though the United Nations was a liberal democratic body for the purpose of serving common ends, the United States was living a lie.[51]

The neoconservatives have always claimed that ideas work, in the not too long term, to transform human reality. The developments in the United Nations manifested this. Just as American radicals accused the United States of colonialism and imperialism during the Vietnam War, the Third World did so in the 1970s. The domestic disputes in which the neoconservatives engaged now applied to the international arena; the ideas simply traveled from one forum to the other, wrecking havoc everywhere they settled. This did not perplex the neoconservatives; Kristol, for instance, explained, "In an era of ideological politics, which is ours, foreign policy tends to be a continuation of domestic policy by other means."[52]

The same abandonment of individual accountability among American liberals that neoconservatives criticized in the 1960s was seen in the United Nations through resolutions such as the Declaration on the Establishment of a New Economic Order (1974), the Programme of Action on the Establishment of a New International Economic Order (1974), the Charter of Economic Rights and Duties of States (1975), the Constitution of the United Nations Industrial Development Organization (1979), and others. The theme behind these resolutions, often phrased in euphemisms, was that multinational corporations and American cold war maneuvering were responsible for the inability of the political instability and gross poverty of the Third World. Anti-Americanism had become a theme of the left throughout the world. Daniel Patrick Moynihan cites Russian writer and long-time Soviet political prisoner Alexander Solzhenitsyn on the irony of the anti-Americanism of much of the Third World in the United Nations.

> The United States of America has long shown itself to be the most magnanimous, the most generous country in the world. Wherever there is a flood, an earthquake, a fire, a natural disaster, disease, who is the first to help? The United States. Who helps the most and unselfishly? The United States. And what do we hear in reply? Reproaches, curses, "Yankee Go Home." American cultural centers are burned, and the representatives of the Third World jump on tables to vote against the United States.[53]

While American liberals did not always embrace the more radical resolutions to reach the U.N. floor, they refused to condemn them resolutely. As in the 1960s, the neoconservatives saw two types of people on the left. First were those who, while generally agreeing with and benefiting from Western capitalism, did not have the intellectual confidence to rebut radical challenges to it, especially from people of color. These progressives were petrified of being called racist or appearing unsympathetic to the professed needs of the "oppressed" Third World. At the same time, the progressives did not see that the ideas of the Third World could be a threat to the West or to Third World nations themselves. While Western liberals may have objected to the way something was phrased or to the rhetoric used to defend a point, they had no substantive opposition to the ideas that often directly implicated them. Second were those genuinely radical leftists who manipulated the liberals. As with Communists in the 1950s and the student radicals in the 1960s, leftists in the 1970s set the agenda that the progressives followed or apologized for. The neoconservatives noted that Third World issues were especially fruitful for many of these radicals who promoted anti capitalism, anti Americanism, and anti-Semitism wherever they could.

The neoconservatives noted that the same liberals who had substituted collective guilt for individual accountability with the criminal justice system and affirmative action in the United States were now blaming the problems of the Third World on the West. According to the neoconservatives, the contention that Third World countries were mere puppets of the West, subservient to its every capricious whim, denied whole nations of their moral agency. Just as the neoconservatives maintained that individuals in the United States should be held accountable for their actions, they believed that Third World nations should be considered responsible for their successes or failures. Anything less would be patronizing to the Third World. George Weigel refers to the "racism" that is behind the belief that "the Arabs [are] fractious children who really don't know any better, and thus have to be appeased."[54]

This is not to say the neoconservatives denied that Western actions affected Third World conditions and are, in some ways, responsible for the poverty of those nations. In an important 1976 *Commentary* article, "Western Guilt and Third World Poverty," the British development economist P. T. Bauer specifically cites two ways in which the West has contributed to Third World poverty. First, the West exported tremendous advances in health care to the Third World. This naturally lowered the rates of infant mortality and thus led to a population boom in the Third World. With more people and the same amount of money, the obvious result is a decline in living standards. Thus, Bauer and others claimed that a major Western contribution to Third World poverty has really been a blessing in other ways.[55]

The second reason Bauer advances, however, has no corresponding benefits. He states that Third World leaders have for generations been trained at elite schools in Europe, most notably the London School of Economics. At these schools, the promising young men of the Third World were taught that capitalism is oppressive, the West is responsible for problems of developing countries, and economic and cultural life should be politicized. The devastating consequences of the left-wing domination of American universities were even worse in the Third World because there were few sources of opposing views in Third World nations. If a bright student in the United States wanted another viewpoint from the one taught at his liberal college, he could transfer, seek out dissident professors, or subscribe to *Commentary*. This was not true in the Third World, which had few literate people and thus very little opportunity to develop ideas to challenge those that were being taught to the elite African and Asian students at the London School of Economics. And with the elite being taught dependency theory, socialism, and anti-Americanism, there was little that could be done to prevent these ideas from being implemented in the Third World.

Just as the Third World was saturating the United Nations with anti-Western propaganda fired with intellectual ammunition furnished by Western intellectuals, the Third World did not blame solely the West for its problems. The Third World found an additional target—Jews. The anti-Semitism of these nations sometimes took the form of vicious attacks on Israel, Zionism, or Zionists. Israel was the consistent focus of opprobrium in the General Assembly of the United Nations until it almost became a joke to blame Israel for any problem. These efforts culminated in a U.N. resolution, "Zionism Is a Form of Racism and Racial Discrimination." The fight for the passage of this resolution was led by Idi Amin, the dictator of Uganda who ate his first wife after she crossed him.[56] In 1974, Amin rose to the floor of the United Nations and delivered a speech that summarized the arguments for the resolution.

> The United States of America has been colonized by the Zionists who hold all the tools of development and power. They own virtually all the banking institutions, the major manufacturing and processing industries and the major means of communication; and have so much infiltrated the CIA that they are posing a great threat to nations and peoples which may be opposed to the atrocious Zionist movement. They have turned the CIA into a murder squad to eliminate any form of just resistance anywhere in the world. . . . How can we expect freedom, peace and justice in the world when such a powerful nation as the United States of America is in the hands of the Zionists? I call upon the people of the United States of America whose forefathers founded this State "conceived in liberty and dedicated to the proposition that all men were born equal" to rid their society of the Zionists in order that the true citizens of this nation may control their own destiny and exploit the natural resources of their country to their own benefit. I call for the expulsion of Israel from the United Nations and the extinction of Israel as a State, so that the territorial integrity of Palestine may be ensured and upheld.[57]

After the speech, Amin received a standing ovation, which continued even after he left the room. The next night, the secretary-general of the United Nations hosted a party in his honor. With this type of reaction, no one was surprised when Amin's resolution passed easily: seventy nations voted yes, twenty-nine voted no, and sixteen abstained. Those in favor were almost all either Arab nations or Soviet-bloc countries, and those opposed were primarily the Atlantic Alliance and a few Latin American states. The U.S. delegation did not confront the passage of the resolution with its usual sense of sheepish resignation. Rather, the resolution was contested with a passionate denunciation delivered by the U.S. ambassador to the United Nations, Daniel Patrick Moynihan—a speech that launched Moynihan's subsequent career in the Senate.

Moynihan, of course, had always been one of the leading neoconservative intellectuals. Several years after the Moynihan Report was released, its author went to work for Richard Nixon as his domestic policy adviser. A few years after leaving that post, Moynihan became the U.S. ambassador to India. Toward the end of his stay in India, Moynihan penned what would be one of *Commentary*'s most important articles—"The United States in Opposition."

In that essay, Moynihan writes that the United States has been blind to the blatant anti-Americanism that the Soviet bloc and the Arab nations voiced enthusiastically in the United Nations. It is a classic case of what the neoconservatives have been hearkening back to since the 1960s—the inability of liberals to defend liberalism. Moynihan asked,

> Why has the United States dealt so unsuccessfully with these nations and their distinct ideology? . . . It was done, moreover, with the blind acquiescence and even agreement of the United States which kept endorsing principles for whose logical outcome it was wholly unprepared and with which it could never actually go along.[58]

Moynihan maintains the United States must take the U.N.'s leftism seriously and defend herself against it. The world, Moynihan explains, is divided between two blocs, the liberty party and the equality party. The nations of liberty—the free West—have not attempted to enforce equality of result because to do so (even if desirable) would constitute a massive infringement of freedom. The parties of equality—the Communist governments—have instituted totalitarian structures aimed at coercing equality of condition. The parties of liberty have produced more equality than have the parties of equality. Moynihan states that it is about time the West faces reality and defends the liberty party against the despots and tyrants masquerading as the party of equality.

Moynihan's article generated a fervor throughout the world. Podhoretz anticipated this and released the essay in a press conference, which was the only press conference he ever called to announce the publication of a *Commentary* article. Numerous newspapers, television stations, and radio stations picked it up, and Secretary of State Henry Kissinger telephoned Moynihan to tell him his article was "staggeringly good." The Central Committee of the Soviet Union had it translated into Russian. And, on the basis of "The United States in Opposition," President Gerald Ford appointed Moynihan ambassador to the United Nations.[59]

When the "Zionism Is a Form of Racism and Racial Discrimination" resolution was passed, Moynihan was ready to put the concepts he articulated in "The United States in Opposition" into action on the floor of the United Nations. Podhoretz took an active role in drafting Moynihan's speech to the United Nations, which was delivered on November 10, 1975. Moynihan's powerful speech manifested the most important principles of neoconservatism. The importance of ideas, the crucial meaning of language, the hatred of racism, and the fear that the term (and, hence, the reality) of racism was bastardized by the left, the manipulation of liberalism by illiberal despotic impostors—it is all here.

> The United States rises to declare before the General Assembly of the United Nations, and before the world, that it does not acknowledge, it will not abide by, it will never acquiesce in this infamous act. . . . It is precisely a concern of civilization, for civilized values that are or should be precious to all mankind, that arouses us at this moment to such special passion. . . .
>
> The terrible lie that has been told here will have terrible consequences. Not only will people begin to say, indeed they have already begun to say, that the United Nations is a place where lies are told. Far more serious, grave and perhaps irreparable harm will be done to the cause of human rights. The harm will arise first because it will strip from racism the precise and abhorrent meaning that it still precariously holds today. How will peoples of the world feel about racism, and about the need to struggle against it, when they are told that it is an idea so broad as to include the Jewish national liberation movement? . . .
>
> This is the danger, and then a final danger that is the most serious of all. Which is that the damage we now do to the idea of human rights and the language of human rights could well be irreversible. . . . Most of the world believes in newer methods of political thought, in philosophies that do not accept the individual as distinct from and prior to the State, in philosophies that therefore do not provide any justification for the idea of human rights and philosophies that have no words by which to explain their value. If we destroy the words that were given to us by past centuries, we will not have words to replace them, for philosophy today has no such words.
>
> But there are those of us who have not forsaken these older words, still

so new to much of the world. Not forsaken them now, not here, not anywhere, not ever.

The United States of America declares that it does not acknowledge, it will not abide by, it will never acquiesce in this infamous act.[60]

Moynihan's speech was not well received by most of the Western world. *The New York Times* condemned his speech for being divisive and too critical of the Third World, as did the British ambassador to the United Nations, Ivor Richard, who compared Moynihan to King Lear raging in the storm. The Arabs and the Soviets responded with a conference in Tripoli on the subject of "Zionism and Racism," co-sponsored by the International Organization for the Elimination of All Forms of Racial Discrimination and the Libyan Bar Association. The titles of the speeches at the conference indicate its theme: "Intellectual Origins of Imperialism and Zionism" (Edward Said), "Zionism and Racism: Contrasting Perspectives and Perceptions" (L. Humphrey Walz), "Racism: A Basic Principle of Zionism" (Stefan Goranov), "Zionist Manipulations to Induce Immigration to Israel" (Alfred M. Lilienthal), "The Jewish National Fund: An Instrument of Discrimination" (Walter Lehn), and "Zionism and Imperialism" (Guy Bajoit).

Communism and Its Apologists . . . Again

The anti-Semitic rhetoric and the positions advanced by Arab and Third World nations in the United Nations were not inspired solely by the Western left. Rather, the Soviet Union, providing intellectual inspiration and financial and military support, served as another major impetus to the politics of the Third World. Throughout the 1970s, the Soviet Union shepherded the anti-Western and anti-Semitic polemics through the United Nations in the name of equality, freedom, democracy, and justice. The quintessential example of this is an amendment the Soviet Union proposed to the Convention on the Elimination of Racial Discrimination in 1965.

State Parties condemn anti-Semitism, Zionism, Nazism, neo-Nazism and all other forms of the policy and ideology of colonialism, national and race

> hatred and exclusiveness and shall take action as appropriate for the speedy eradication of those inhuman ideas and practices in the territories subject to their jurisdiction.

The equation of Zionism with Nazism and racism—an argument the neoconservatives fought when used by the radical American left—was now being used by the Soviet Union in the United Nations. In a supreme act of chutzpah, the Soviet Union sponsored a resolution condemning anti-Semitism and Zionism in one sentence. In this effort and other similar ones, the Soviet Union gathered the votes of the world's Communist and Arab nations.

The neoconservatives regarded the Soviet Union and much of the Third World as equally venal enemies of the United States and of freedom. And the real shame was that American liberals—who controlled much of the opinion-making elite and diplomatic corps—did not realize this and did nothing to counter it. Liberals kept trying to reason, kept trying to understand the other side, kept trying to find common ground with those who wanted not to coexist, but to bury them.

As had happened often in the history of neoconservatism, much of the discussion in *Commentary* of the Third World and Israel revolved around the misappropriation of words and the bastardization of language. The neoconservatives were very sensitive to this abuse of language; in different essays, Fred Ilke and Daniel Patrick Moynihan have called it "semantic infiltration."[61] This "semantic infiltration" was taken seriously by the neoconservatives. Ideas have consequences, ideas are expressed in words, and disputes over meanings of words are as crucial as the ideas themselves. As Moynihan explained in a 1978 *Policy Review* essay,

> the West's political culture is endangered by the fact that the vocabulary and the symbols of political progress are being expropriated by the opponents of our values. Democracy, as we understand it, is under assault from totalitarians masquerading as democrats. . . . Nonetheless, we persist in dignifying these enemies of freedom with the terminology of freedom—so that we persistently misdescribe the political forces arrayed against us.[62]

Since the 1950s, the liberal anti-Communists and neoconservatives accused the left of adulterating language to misrepresent ideas, but the left had gone to new extremes in this regard in the 1970s. In that decade, neoconservatives perceived the forces of totalitarianism advancing themselves both intellectually and militarily by perverting the sacred terms of the Western civil religion.

The philosophical difference between the neoconservatives and the left can be distilled to disagreement over one word: evil. For the left, human failings are the product of unfortunate environments. The neoconservatives stress individual moral accountability, allowing for the possibility that some people are simply corrupt or evil. Correspondingly, these people can make corrupt or evil nation-states. An underlying theme behind the neoconservative critique of the Third World and the United Nations in the 1970s is that the forces of evil, the Soviet Union and many Third World leaders, confronted the West on the West's liberal democratic terms. Not realizing that the only factor that moved their enemies was force and the only language they spoke was power, Western liberals all too often acquiesced to the demands and charges of the Third World and the Soviet Union. And when the Third World and the Soviet Union went back on agreements, clearly manipulated international bodies, and altogether did not deal in good faith, much of the West was surprised. The neoconservatives, however, were not. They believed they were living in an era of high-tech intellectual warfare, where, as Midge Decter wrote, "Either Communism in some variant or Western-style democracy in some variant must prevail. It is a case of 'them or us.' "[63]

Neoconservatives and Double Standards

In addition to exposing the rhetorical hypocrisy of the Communists, the neoconservatives were determined to expose the realities of Communist ideology and political posturing as well. In the 1970s, *Commentary* ran several articles on Communism that called for a realization that the United States was confronting a mortal enemy, not a negotiating or trading partner. The neoconservative effort to counter Communism both on the level of theory and in the arena of practice was led by Podhoretz through both his writing and his editing.

Podhoretz's first major article on Communism, "Making the World Safe for Communism," was published in *Commentary* in April 1976. He writes that the Communists should be considered as nothing less than "the most determined, ferocious and barbarous enemies ever to have appeared on the earth."[64] Podhoretz built upon this idea in an essay he published in 1981, "The Future Danger." Podhoretz argues that Communism is even more dangerous than Nazism because the Nazis—unlike the Communists—never captured the imagination of Western intellectuals. Harking back to an argument that was prevalent in the 1950s, Podhoretz writes that Communism and Nazism are alike in other important ways. He writes that the Soviet Union is a manifestation of the historian Earl Ravenel's statement, "Imagine Hitler with nuclear weapons," and there is to be no doubt as to who has the responsibility to stop these present-day Nazis. "[The] conflict between the United States and the Soviet Union is a clash between two civilizations. More accurately, it is a clash between civilization and barbarianism."[65]

All the neoconservative ideas about the United Nations, evil, and the Communist threat culminated in Jeanne Kirkpatrick's "Dictatorships and Double Standards," published in the November 1979 issue of *Commentary*. This essay was widely read and cited; one reader, Ronald Reagan, liked it so much that he appointed Kirkpatrick ambassador to the United Nations when he became president. All of Reagan's high-level foreign policy appointees were required to read it after he took office.[66]

The subject of "Dictatorships and Double Standards" is the Western error in automatically shunning non-Communist authoritarian governments. It was not that authoritarian governments were in any way admirable; Kirkpatrick said in 1985, "morally responsible people recognize that there are degrees of evil."[67] Throughout the 1970s, a common argument against the neoconservative conception of an activist anti-Communist foreign policy was that it would necessitate an unpalatable alliance with right-wing authoritarian regimes. Irving Kristol predicted this position in a 1965 article published in *The New York Times Magazine*.

> There are still some people around who think it wrong for the United States, under any conditions, to ally itself with nondemocratic regimes. But they are the kind of people who also think there is something immoral about comic books, and their voices do not resound in the land.[68]

By the 1970s, these voices did resound in the land. What, these critics asked, was the point of an anti-Communist policy if it necessitated aligning America with repressive, authoritarian nations? While by no means countenancing the authoritarian governments, the neoconservatives maintained that the United States would sometimes have to choose between the lesser of two evils. And to the neoconservatives, there was no doubt which evil was lesser. As Norman Podhoretz explained,

> Certain authoritarian regimes and right-wing dictatorships were included in the [anti-Communist] alliance. But in view of the fact that such associations were important in holding back the single greatest and most powerful threat to freedom on the face of the earth, they could be justified as an unfortunate political and military necessity.[69]

In "Dictatorships and Double Standards," Kirkpatrick writes of the paradox of the Carter administration's policy of punishing El Salvador, Nicaragua, and Iran for human rights abuses while trading and negotiating with the Soviet Union and other Communist totalitarian governments. She considers this process counterproductive at best; rejecting authoritarian governments in Nicaragua and Iran led to far worse situations under Manuel Ortega and the Ayatollah Khomeini. Given the record of right-wing authoritarian governments in contrast to Communist nations, she finds the choice of the Carter administration to shun the former and solicit the latter even more disturbing. She writes,

> Traditional autocrats leave in place existing allocations of wealth, power, status, and other resources which in most traditional societies favor an affluent few and maintain masses in poverty. But they worship traditional gods and observe traditional taboos. They do not disturb the habitual rhythms of work and leisure, habitual places of residence, habitual patterns

> of family and personal relations. Because the miseries of traditional life are familiar, they are bearable to ordinary people who, growing up in the society, learn to cope, as children born to untouchables in India acquire the skills and attitudes necessary for survival in the miserable roles they are destined to fill. Such societies create no refugees.
>
> Precisely the opposite is true of revolutionary Communist regimes. They create refugees by the million because they claim jurisdiction over the whole life of the society and make demands for change that so violate internalized values and habits that inhabitants flee by the tens of thousands in the remarkable expectation that their attitudes, values, and goals will "fit" better in a foreign country than in their native land.

Analyzing this situation, Kirkpatrick asks why Communist governments are treated so much better than are authoritarian ones. Certainly not because of Western stupidity or even lack of knowledge of the Communist-inspired terror. Rather, she concludes that Westerners have been beguiled by Marxist rhetoric into an chastened attitude to the horrific Communist reality.

> [Communists have] an ideology rooted in a version of the same values that sparked the Enlightenment and the democratic revolutions of the 18th century. . . . Marxist revolutionaries speak the language of a hopeful future while traditional autocrats speak the language of an unattractive past. Because left-wing revolutionaries invoke the symbols and values of democracy—emphasizing egalitarianism rather than hierarchy and privilege, liberty rather than order, activity rather than passivity—they are again and again accepted as partisans in the cause of freedom and democracy.[70]

The Neoconservatives and Liberalism's Failure of Nerve

The stark nature of the conflict between civilization and barbarianism demanded action commensurate with its importance. First, this meant an end to détente, the policy of reconciliation and peaceful coexistence with the Soviet Union that had begun under President Richard Nixon. Theodore Draper, Robert Tucker, Edward Luttwak, Walter Lacquer, and others took to the pages of *Commentary* to explain how President Nixon's efforts towards détente and compromise with the Soviet Union constituted a threat to human freedom and, ultimately, world peace. Instead of reconciliation with the Communists, *Commentary* writers called for a massive buildup of both conventional and nuclear weapons and a willingness to engage American troops and weapons militarily if necessary.

While the neoconservatives never actually advocated using military force against a Communist or Arab regime in the mid-1970s, a series of articles in *Commentary* in that decade suggested that they would have had no moral objections to doing so. The author of these articles, which generated worldwide attention, was Robert Tucker, whose "Oil: The Issue of American Intervention" was published in January 1975 and expanded on in later issues. Tucker's thesis was that the United States should threaten to use its military to guarantee the flow of oil that was being threatened by the Arab cartel. A storm of protest erupted in response to the articles, but the neoconservatives maintained that it is legitimate for a nation to use its military to ensure the protection of its economic lifeblood.

More important than the specific actions of the U.S. military was the philosophy on which the hawkishness of *Commentary* in the 1970s was based. Underlying hard anti-Communism was opposition to the "Vietnam Syndrome"—the idea that the use of American force is morally illegitimate and bound to fail. In 1977, Norman Podhoretz asked a question that was central to neoconservatism at that time: "Has the United States recovered from Vietnam?" The answer provided by Podhoretz and his neoconservative colleagues was no. "I think that far from having put Vietnam behind us, we are still living with it in a thousand different ways. It is there everywhere, a ubiquitous if often eerie invisible presence in our political culture."[71] As Midge Decter explained,

> defeat . . . is not good for people. And it is no better for nations than for individuals. It humiliates, raises doubts, heightens acrimony, increases recourse to tricksy [*sic*] euphemism, and stirs up all those lurking and treacherously seductive fantasies of escape. Most of all, it paralyzes, and once again does so no less to nations than to individuals.[72]

The neoconservatives regarded the potential importance of a weak American political culture in the world climate of the 1970s to be of devastating proportions. If the United States could not acquire the moral fortitude to defend the ideals that she represents, the world would belong to the Soviets. Decter admonished,

> If America, because of a terrible mistake made in the name of the Cold War, with all the bitterness and humiliation attendant thereto, ceases to continue that struggle . . . , a vast proportion of the earth's surface will to one extent or another eventually be Bolshevised. . . . There is no argument, there is only choice.[73]

The pernicious specter of Vietnam was most apparent in the American insecurity regarding use of her military. This natural by-product of the anti-Americanism of the left had already been manifested in the weakness of the United States with regard to the United Nations and the Third World. By the mid-1970s, the neoconservatives began to fear that a crippling hesitancy was overtaking important and ever expanding sectors of the United States at a crucial juncture in its history. Patrick Glynn articulated this point in a *Commentary* essay, "Why an American Arms Buildup Is Morally Necessary."

> To whole sectors of our culture, it should be recognized, moral thinking finds its starting point in the rejection of received moral and political values. This loss of faith has had a profound effect on the perspective that many people bring to national defense. In particular, it has undermined in many minds the idea that the United States, at least as a political entity, is something basically good and worth preserving. Thus while protest is inevitably directed against the weapons, for many people it is the United States government that is the real object of distrust. At its roots, the contention of these people is not that the administration has a bad defense policy, but that in the end the United States government is hardly worth defending.[74]

The neoconservatives, led by Norman Podhoretz, hoped that a clarification of the original American goals regarding Vietnam would relieve the stink of bad intentions that the left tried to associate with the defeat. Resurrecting arguments from the late 1960s, the neoconservatives once again set out to demonstrate that the loss in Vietnam was merely a failure of circumstance, not motive or morality. Podhoretz declared in 1980,

> The greater practical wisdom or tactical prudence would have counseled nonintervention into Vietnam—on the ground that the chances of success were so slight—says nothing about the principle, or about its applicability to situations where the local conditions might be more favorable to military action.[75]

Podhoretz wrote two books about America's involvement in Vietnam, *Why We Were in Vietnam* and *The Present Danger*; the latter became required reading in the first Reagan administration. Podhoretz and his *Commentary* writers maintained that the American effort in Vietnam had been conceived from a sincere desire to stop Communism from spreading its imperialistic and totalitarianism might. Americans had nothing to gain from entering Vietnam—not land, not money, not power. According to the neoconservatives, the American effort in Vietnam was a product of one of the noblest traits of the American character—altruism in service of principles.

The arguments from history that the neoconservatives used in the 1970s went back further than the previous decade; the arguments the liberal anti-Communists had with the progressives in the early 1950s were applicable once again. In a 1976 *Commentary* symposium, Sidney Hook maintained that the attitude of the left toward Communism in the 1970s was worse than the attitude of Western liberals who appeased Adolf Hitler in the 1930s at Munich. While no one could imagine the scope of totalitarianism and the extent of the danger of appeasement in the 1930s, this excuse no longer applied during Communist days. The surrender of a hard anti-Communist policy after Vietnam would be as potentially devastating as the agreement at Munich, but it would be a product of sheer weakness and utter moral cowardice rather than naïveté.[76]

As ideological determinists, the neoconservatives were confident that America's recovery from Vietnam would be determined by the ideas she used to view the experience and its possibilities for the future. The ultimate deciding factor in how America confronted her defeat would be determined by ideas. Would America pick herself up and look to the crucial battles in the future? Or, would she berate herself for past mistakes, questioning her legitimacy to be anything more than, say, Belgium? If the United States made the wrong choice, the neoconservatives knew exactly who would be responsible. Walter Lacquer warned,

> Since a realistic and effective policy cannot be insured today without an analysis of what went wrong in the past and why, it may be well that the battle against America's decline in the world will be won or lost not in foreign parts, but in the committee rooms, conference halls, and editorial offices in Washington and New York.[77]

The Neoconservatives and the Culture of Appeasement

In a major 1977 article published in *Harper's*, "The Culture of Appeasement," Norman Podhoretz termed the weakness and cowardice of the left in the aftermath of Vietnam "the culture of appeasement." The neoconservatives believed that an activist foreign policy needs a culture that is forthrightly patriotic, and not for sentimental reasons. The culture could not appease its adversaries; it had to be self-affirming if America was to muster the moral fortitude to reverse the failure of nerve that plagued it. This affirming patriotism would entail a belief in the moral destiny of America and a confidence in its ability to yield its power for good in the world. Only such a sentiment could generate the great sacrifice and will demanded by the anti-Communist effort. As Irving Kristol wrote, "for any kind of 'mature' foreign policy to exist, Americans must also continue to have faith in the ideals the nation is supposed to represent, and in the nation as an incarnation of these ideals. . . ."[78]

Part of this maturity entailed an extraordinarily large and powerful military, which Democrats continually rejected. The antimilitary sentiment of liberalism became a central concern for neoconservatives starting in the mid-1970s. As Podhoretz explained in "The Culture of Appeasement,"

> While the Soviet Union engages in the most massive military buildup in the history of the world, we haggle over every weapon. We treat our own military leaders as though they were wearing the uniform of a foreign power. Everything they tell us about our military needs is greeted with hostility. . . .[79]

With the Soviet Union spending and acting indiscriminately, the neoconservatives were greatly dismayed that Democrats pondered and argued about every weapon. In a 1981 *Commentary* essay, Podhoretz compared a Senate debate over weaponry in the 1970s to a scene from Shakespeare: "one Senator after another, sounding like Goneril and Regan asking King Lear why he need so many knights in his entourage ('What need you five-and-twenty, ten, or five? What need one?')."[80]

How could the intellectual left, which was primarily responsible for the culture of appeasement, have had such great influence? The neoconservatives argued that the ideas that started on the intellectual left were no longer confined to that small sector. While the neoconservatives had fought a menagerie of radical professors, racial agitators, student protesters, and assorted anti-Semites for years, they perceived a broader acceptance of these ideas into the common culture in the 1970s. As Midge Decter explained,

> I can't remember when I last heard a millionaire, or a successful journalist, or a well-heeled academic, or even a politician, of the so-called liberal persuasion, say a genuinely kind word about the system that made possible his own considerable elevation in it. But what I would say is that they are spoiled rotten and cosmicly greedy.[81]

As Decter suggests, neoconservatives saw many of the ideas they had vigorously countered in the universities being spread across the country via the media and through popular entertainment. American ideas, they claimed, are democratic to a fault. They are not the playthings of intellectuals. The ideas advanced by intellectuals in one generation will significantly contribute to a general outlook and way of life in the next generation—if not sooner.[82]

The neoconservatives maintained that many groups bore responsibility for the culture of appeasement. Decter penned a number of essays blasting feminism for questioning the foundations of bourgeois society.[83] Norman Podhoretz suggested that homosexual writers did the same.[84] But the culture of appeasement did not just come to people; they had to welcome it, or at least not contest it. The neoconservatives specifically charged two seemingly disparate groups with promulgating the culture of appeasement—the anti-American counterculture and profit-seeking businessmen. Peter Berger explains why these two groups became targets of neoconservatism.

> Most American intellectuals have since Vietnam come to believe that the exercise of American power is immoral. But what has been less noticed is that Vietnam has also changed the mind of a substantial segment of the economic elite as to the economic advantages of world power: it has given rise to the idea that the maintenance of American world power is unprofitable.[85]

The culture of appeasement promulgated by these groups had to be analyzed in the most serious of ways. Nothing less than Munich should serve as a comparison point. "Meanwhile," Podhoretz concluded, "the parallels with England in 1937 are here, and this revival of the culture of appeasement ought to be troubling our sleep."[86]

Business, Labor, and Communism

While the neoconservatives knew how to confront the left on issues relating to Communism, the challenge to their position by Republican businessmen presented a different problem. Thinkers from Lenin to Joseph Schumpeter to Daniel Bell have maintained that capitalism could not sustain itself because capitalists would pursue profit at the expense of combating their political enemies.[87] This was not really a new idea even when Lenin said it; it has long been a prominent idea in political philosophy that the forces of commerce work in opposition to those of battle. None less than Tocqueville wrote, "Violent political passions have little hold on men whose whole thoughts are bent on the pursuit of well being. Their excitement about small matters makes them calm about great ones."[88] Could a bourgeois society transcend its private concerns and muster the will for collective struggle when it was not directly attacked? This question would never be answered.

The neoconservatives saw Tocqueville's observation being manifested among businessmen in a time when excitement with large matters was essential. Neoconservatives saw the attitudes of the businessmen stemming from two sources. On a fundamental level, a military build up would be very expensive—which would mean higher taxes that most businessmen opposed. It also meant that trade with Communist countries would be restricted and that profitable opportunities would be forsaken.

The neoconservatives hoped the businessmen would realize that the anti-Communist cause was not only a great moral calling, but was in their long-term self-interest. But they were not confident this would be the result. *Commentary* ran several articles which explored this theme, neatly encapsulated in a title of an April 1979 essay by Carl Gershman, "Selling Them the Rope." Perhaps the most representative of this theme was "Banks, Tanks and Freedom," published by someone with the pseudonym of John Van Meer in the December 1982 issue. Van Meer excoriates various businessmen for their remarkable apathy toward Communism. He writes of a prominent New York banker who says that General Jaruzelski, the Polish Communist strongman, is a good leader because he ended the Solidarity strikes, which aided in the repayment of debts. Van Meer writes that perhaps the most representative of philistine businessmen was Thomas Theobald of Citibank who asked, "Who knows which political system works? The only test we care about is: can they pay their bills?"[89]

The neoconservatives contrasted this nihilism with the foreign policy beliefs of organized labor. Throughout most of the 1970s, the neoconservatives aligned themselves with labor unions on numerous issues. George Meany, president of the AFL-CIO, shared the neoconservative disgust with the counterculture and never wavered in his hard anti-Communism. As Sidney Hook stated, "[the AFL-CIO] more than any other [group] has . . . refused to accept the illusions of détente with the enemies of human freedom as a guide to our foreign policy . . . overall it still represents the best hope for the immediate future."[90]

Unlike businessmen and like the neoconservatives, the AFL-CIO did not let any concerns—economic or otherwise—interfere with the all-important task of confronting Communists.

In a 1981 *Commentary* essay, Podhoretz contrasted unions and corporations with regard to their responses to Communism.

> While . . . the chairman of Pepsi Cola and other luminaries of American business with more strategically important goods to sell were rushing to Moscow laden with the "rope" that Lenin famously predicted the capitalists would provide for their own execution at the hands of Soviet hangmen, the AFL-CIO under George Meany and Lane Kirkland was thinking and voicing other thoughts.[91]

Liberalism and the Jews

The January 1980 issue of *Commentary* features a symposium entitled "Liberalism and the Jews" which, through a coterie of passionate and sometimes pained contributions, encapsulates the neoconservative attitude toward liberalism and ambivalence toward the future following an intellectually tumultuous decade. Witnessing the transformation of liberalism from inclusive opportunity, anti-Communism, open inquiry, economic growth and civil rights into statism, anti-anti-Communism, quotas and acquiescence to bigoted radicals, the neoconservatives joined Elliott Abrams in asking, "Who deserted whom?"[92] The answer, provided by Abrams and the other neoconservatives, is that liberalism had betrayed the Jews. Once upon a time, liberalism and Jewry was a quasi-sacred match; liberalism was the only political philosophy for a people in need of religious pluralism, merit-based criteria, and a strong America. This was so ingrained in the Jewish psyche that Werner Dannhauser had to remind the readers of the *Commentary* symposium that, "No 11th—or 614th—commandment exists to the effect that a Jew shall be a liberal."[93]

It is a good thing that there was no such commandment, because the neoconservatives who responded to this symposium would have violated it. Paying due homage to the liberalism of old, the neoconservatives nonetheless agreed with the statement of Gertrude Himmelfarb.

> Reality has a way of catching up with us. If latter-day liberals have exposed their tenuous commitment to individualism and democracy, if affirmative

> action has shown itself to be yet another form of negative discrimination, if the historic sympathy with Jews as the underdogs of society has evidently given way to new causes and new victims, we may begin to question our own commitment to liberalism. We may begin to suspect that the liberalism that brought us into modernity, that gave us our freedom as individuals and tolerated us as Jews, has been replaced by a new liberalism that is inhospitable to us both as individuals and as Jews. We may conclude that a quite different philosophy is required if we are to survive in the modern world, survive as individuals and survive as Jews.[94]

Midge Decter wrote that the harm that liberalism has done to America cannot be separated from the its effect on Jews.

> The new liberalism is bad for the Jews not only because it endorses quotas, has come to extend its highly selective tolerance to anti-Semitism, and regards the PLO (as it once regarded the Vietcong) as a worthy instrument for national self-chastisement. It is above all bad for the Jews because it is bad for the whole country. It has disrupted our delicate civic arrangements, it has distorted our political process, it has undermined our sense of life and tried (unsuccessfully, I believe) to devalue our love of country, it has apologized for crimes against us and our friends, it has taken satisfaction in our humiliation, and it is in general sapping our vitality.[95]

Though dissatisfied with and betrayed by liberalism, the neoconservatives did not rush to the open arms of the Republican Party. Elliott Abrams offered an explanation. "For the sentimental link to the party of Truman and Johnson is strong . . . as is the sentiment that Republicans aren't 'our kind of people.' The GOP, with its flavor of small-town Midwestern business America, holds no comfort for Jews."[96] Frankly, Himmelfarb conceded, "We are, for the moment, homeless. . . ."[97]

Carter, Reagan, and the Neoconservatives

If the neoconservatives were not exactly politically homeless in 1976 (four years before Gertrude Himmelfarb confirmed that they were), they were defaulting on their mortgage payments to the Democratic Party. With no enthusiasm, the neoconservatives decided to join their allies in the labor movement and endorse Jimmy Carter, who had solicited their support and had promised they would have a role in his administration. Upon assuming the presidency, Carter wasted no time in disappointing the neoconservatives. He not only did not appoint them, but neglected their ideas. Abrams summarized the neoconservative influence in the Carter administration. "We got one unbelievably minor job. It was a special negotiator position. Not for Polynesia. Not Macronesia. But Micronesia. The Carter administration turned out to be ideological, a New Left administration."[98]

More importantly, the neoconservatives were disillusioned by Carter's attitude toward the Soviet Union. On May 22, 1977, Carter delivered a speech at Notre Dame, declaring his relief that America had overcome its "inordinate fear of Communism" and proposing that the United States join with the Soviets to work on joint development projects in the Third World. Carter followed this speech by the placing the name of the U.N. ambassador immediately beneath that of the secretary of state on the directory of the State Department. This ethos of cooperation and negotiation with Soviets remained a staple of the Carter administration, and the neoconservatives were infuriated. They moved further and further away from the Democratic Party. The relationship between the neoconservatives and the Democrats conflicted directly in January 1980, when President Carter and Vice President Walter Mondale called a group of the younger neoconservatives to the White House to discuss their ambivalence toward him regarding the 1980 election. The neoconservatives were willing to hear Carter's case, but he was abrupt, rude, and did not seem to care much about their support.[99] The neoconservatives were not in a forgiving mood with regard to their president after March 1, 1980, when the United States voted for Resolution 465 in the United Nations, which reads, "all measures taken by Israel to change the physical character, democratic composition, institutional structure or status of the Palestinian and other Arab territories occupied there since 1967, including Jerusalem, or any part thereof, have no legal validity." Senator Daniel Patrick Moynihan remarked in *Commentary*, "In a word, according to Resolution 465, Israel is an outlaw state, guilty of war crimes. (Not the Vietnamese invaders of Cambodia, or the Soviets in Afghanistan. Israel!)."[100]

The other neoconservatives were as furious as their colleague in the Senate. Carter's subsequent admission that the vote was a mistake did not placate the neoconservatives, especially considering the position of the Democratic Platform of 1980 on the Third World, which read, "[before President Carter] relations with the Third World were at their nadir. The United States appeared hostile and indifferent to the developing world's aspirations for greater justice, respect and dignity. All this has changed."

Though he testified to his disgust in *Commentary*, Moynihan had no choice but to support President Carter, whether or not he would have been otherwise inclined to do so.[101] Arnold Beichman, for one, did not; he declared in *Commentary*, "The only way I could support the 1980 Democratic presidential candidate . . . is if he should be Daniel P. Moynihan."[102] Moynihan was not running, and Beichman, joined by many other neoconservatives, pulled the Republican lever for the first time in his life when he voted for Ronald Reagan.

Neoconservatism and the 1970s in Retrospect

Ideas have consequences! Always a crucial aspect and inviolable principle of neoconservative thought, manifestations of this truism drove neoconservatism throughout the 1970s. In some cases, this idea came to life through the traditional warning against radical ideas that liberals refused to take seriously. This applied to black anti-Semitism, the United Nations, Third World radicalism, the Communist threat, and more. But the impact of these arguments had diminished by the 1970s; they were shopworn and generally unheeded. Though criticizing liberals for abandoning liberalism was as pressing as ever, this line of argument was, in many ways, rapidly becoming an intellectual antique, a relic from a bygone era.

Why, if relevant as ever, a relic? Because, in many respects, the warnings of liberals to defend liberalism voiced in the 1960s were no longer germane because there was nothing left to defend. Liberals had not defended liberalism and, just as the neoconservatives admonished, it collapsed under the assault of radicalism. And like any self-respecting invader who has overrun its prey, radicals took over liberalism, expropriating its language, altering its culture, and invading its institutions. By the 1970s, liberals of the Trilling-Niebuhr-Roosevelt-Truman-Kennedy-Humphrey-Scoop Jackson variety had two choices. They could, in one way or another, break with liberalism into some sort of conservatism or they could be co-opted by the radicals. This was not an easy decision nor was it an easy reality to confront. But it was true, and the few liberals who stubbornly attempted to defend the position they traditionally held were regarded as remainders of a quaint philosophy from the distant past hopelessly lost in the politics of nostalgia.

Traditional liberals had fought hard for civil rights in order to codify the principle that one's skin color should be irrelevant to institutions. Less than a decade following the passing of the landmark Civil Rights Act of 1964, that belief was considered anything from conservative to reactionary to downright racist. In its place were quotas—disguised in the agreeable language of affirmative action, goals, and timetables or whatnot—but quotas, which, of course, had been used against minorities for so many decades. How could the fruits of victory be the ideas of the losers championed by the winners? Only if the winners had changed. And that is what the neoconservatives said had happened. The winners—traditional liberals—were no more; radicals had taken their place. The radicals shared with the racists support for group justice based on race and, having taken over liberalism, by and large received what they desired.

The total corruption of liberalism was probably most apparent in, but by no means limited to, quotas. The failure of nerve was a potentially more important example of the co-option of liberalism by the radicals. The traditional liberal position with regard to Vietnam from the early 1960s on was simply that America should not enter the conflict in Southeast Asia for strategic reasons. Yes, Communism is evil. Yes, Communism must be stopped. Yes, America is the only nation in the world that can do so and should whenever possible. But it is not possible in Vietnam, and we should pull out immediately before we suffer even more in a fight we simply cannot win.

But the only people saying this in the 1970s were Norman

Podhoretz and his writers. The standard liberal response in this period was indistinguishable from the radical viewpoint held for decades: the possibilities of winning a foreign war against Communism are irrelevant because the United States is not in a moral position to do so. Dwight MacDonald voiced this opinion in his 1939 *Partisan Review* dispute with Sidney Hook over American involvement in World War II. By itself, it was nothing new. But its broad support was new, and it frightened, though did not surprise, the neoconservatives. As Martin Peretz said, the dicey career of freedom in the world depends on American power.[103] According to the neoconservatives, American power does not operate with guns and manpower alone; it must draw heavily on intellectual capital. Without ideas fueling confidence in America and in the good she can do around the world, the potential for American power would be rendered inoperative. The withdrawal of American military power from the realm of geopolitical possibilities would not be a world of isolated nations engaged in no more than a few regional skirmishes, but a world dominated by the Soviet Union and its Communist puppets and lackeys. In the zero-sum conflict known as the Cold War, one set of ideas would win. If the supposed chaperons of liberal democratic ideas did not have the intellectual fortitude to help their ideas win, Communist ideas would win. It was that simple.

Where did neoconservatism stand at the end of the decade? As an enemy of liberalism and alienated to liberals, for sure. But in conservatism? With the exception of Irving Kristol and Gertrude Himmelfarb, who never had a problem with conservatism per se, the "c" word was becoming considerably more palatable. Issue after issue drove the neoconservatives further and further away from liberalism and if the neoconservatives weren't going to accept *National Review*'s 1971 offer to "C'mon In, the Water's Fine" right away, they were rapidly being pushed into the pool. It took a decade to do it, but most neoconservatives went from George McGovern (reluctantly) in 1972 to Ronald Reagan (enthusiastically) in 1980.

Though they crafted an increasingly close alliance with *National Review* and even the Republican Party, the neoconservatives were not moving to the right while everyone else was staying the same.

Liberalism completely cracked up, but conservatism had changed profoundly. While neither *National Review* nor the Republican Party supported civil rights with any degree of enthusiasm in the 1960s, they were strong supporters of the original civil rights vision by the 1970s. And they had made their peace, however diffidently, with a limited welfare state.

Even though the differences between the neoconservatives and the *National Review* conservatives on political issues were outwardly minimal by 1980, the common claim that neoconservatism and prefixless conservatism had become the same is false, for two reasons. First, neoconservatism offered a different focus than regular conservatism. One rather evident manifestation is that the neoconservatives tirelessly stressed that liberalism, 1970s style, was distinctively bad for the Jews. The United Nations was anti-Semitic, the Third World was anti-Semitic, the Communists were anti-Semitic, affirmative action was anti-Jewish if not anti-Semitic, several prominent liberal black leaders were anti-Semitic, the New Left was anti-Jew and probably anti-Semitic, and vast sectors of the left might as well be anti-Semitic, having decided that Jews were no longer victims and sided with the terrorist enemies of Israel.

The Jewish factor was an important distinction between neoconservatism and the rest of conservatism, but it was far from the only difference. As a philosophical movement distinguished by a characteristic style of thought, neoconservatism is not defined by the political positions taken by its adherents. The way in which neoconservatives write about the social world is different from that of any other group of thinkers, and these differences cannot be reduced to a stance on any political issue. Neoconservative ideas are the product of an intellectual journey of decades, and—to put it mildly—cannot be reduced to anything simple or easily identified, such as a political party or a political issue. A group that arrives at what could be called conservative political positions through Reinhold Niebhur, Lionel Trilling, education in Marxism in college, liberal anti-Communism, support for civil rights, an experimentation with radicalism followed a total repudiation of radicalism, dedicated support for Israel underscored by a consistent sense of betrayal and abandonment by old allies will be remarkably different from a group that inherits those same political positions at birth or another group that comes to those positions via orthodoxy in religion, an early state of animosity with the left, ambivalence bordering on disapproval toward civil rights, hard, confrontational anti-Communism, laissez-faire economics, and a faith in Catholicism. As the 1970s yielded to the 1980s, many took the fact that both Norman Podhoretz and William Buckley supported the same candidates as evidence that differences between neoconservatism and other forms of conservatism were muted. To say that neoconservatives are the same as conservatives and that the "neo" prefix is obsolete—at least for the group of intellectuals who were always identified by it—discards all the crucial background material that is essential for comprehending the complex, nonlinear nature of philosophical systems. In a strictly political context, the prefix "neo" might have become irrelevant by the election of Ronald Reagan—but neoconservatism has always been far more than strictly political.

Notes

1. Joseph Epstein, "A Virtucrat Remembers," in John Bunzel, ed., *Political Passages: Journeys of Change Through Two Decades* (New York: Basic Books, 1988) p. 34.
2. Quoted in Thomas Mallon's review of Peggy Noonan, *Life, Liberty and the Pursuit of Happiness*, in *The American Spectator* (July 1994) p. 64.
3. Daniel Bell, "Ideology and the Beau Geste," *Dissent* (Winter 1961) p. 75.
4. Carl Cohen, "Why Racial Preference Is Illegal and Immoral," *Commentary* (June 1979) p. 45.
5. Daniel Patrick Moynihan and Nathan Glazer, "Why Ethnicity?" *Commentary* (October 1974) p. 34.
6. Irving Kristol, "How Hiring Quotas Came to the Campuses," *Fortune* (September 1974) p. 203.
7. Richard John Neuhaus and Peter Berger, *To Empower People: The Role of Mediating Structures in Public Policy* (Washington: American Enterprise Institute, 1975) p. 15.
8. For an interesting discussion of this, see the chapter "The Jews" in *Beyond the Melting Pot*, p. 143–85.
9. See Midge Decter, "The Professor and the 'L' Word," *Commentary* (February 1989) p. 44.

10. Daniel Patrick Moynihan, "The New Racialism," *Atlantic Monthly* (August 1968) p. 40.

11. Nathan Glazer, *Affirmative Discrimination: Ethnic Inequality and Public Policy* (New York: Basic Books, 1975) p. 73.

12. See Thomas Sowell, *The Economics and Politics of Race: An International Perspective* (New York: Morrow, 1983) p. 200–201.

13. Orlando Patterson, "The Moral Crisis of the Black American," *The Public Interest* (Summer 1973) p. 52.

14. Nathan Glazer, *Ethnic Dilemmas*, p. 101. See also Richard Scammon and Ben Wattenberg, "Black Progress and Liberal Rhetoric," *Commentary* (April 1973) p. 44.

15. Thomas Sowell, "Colleges Are Skipping Over Competent Blacks to Admit 'Authentic' Ghetto Types," *New York Times Magazine* (December 13, 1970) p. 49.

16. "Irving Kristol Writes," *Commentary* (February 1973) p. 24. Response to letters about "About Equality," *Commentary* (November 1972) pp. 41–59.

17. Daniel Patrick Moynihan, "The Politics of Stability," *The New Leader* (October 9, 1967) p. 9.

18. Michael Novak, Contribution to *Commentary* Symposium, "What is a Liberal—Who Is Conservative?" *Commentary* (September 1976) p. 84.

19. Michael Novak, "Race and Truth," *Commentary* (December 1976) p. 58.

20. "Race and Truth," p. 54.

21. Neal Kozodoy, "Religion and Tolerance," *Freedom Review* (January/February 1991) p. 72.

22. Michael Novak, *A Theology for Radical Politics* (New York: Herder and Herder, 1969) p. 25, 79.

23. Michael Novak, "Engagement but No Security," *Commonweal* (January 30, 1981) p. 45.

24. Michael Novak, "Errand into the Wilderness," in *Political Passages*, p. 262.

25. Earl Shorris, "The Jews of the New Right," *Nation* (May 8, 1982) p. 558.

26. Garry Wills, review of *The Rise of the Unmeltable Ethnics: Politics and Culture in the 1970s* by Michael Novak, *New York Times Book Review* (April 23, 1972) pp. 27–28.

27. Robert Alter, "A Fever of Ethnicity," Review of *The Rise of the Unmeltable Ethnics: Politics and Culture in the 1970s* by Michael Novak, *Commentary* (June 1972) p. 70.

28. Nathan Glazer, "Ethnicity and the Schools," *Commentary* (September 1970) p. 56.

29. *Affirmative Discrimination*, p. 75.

30. Kenneth Clark, "Candor About Negro-Jewish Relations," *Commentary* (February 1946) pp. 8–14; James Baldwin, "The Harlem Ghetto: Winter 1948,"

Commentary (February 1948) pp. 165–70. Baldwin's essay, which is one of the most riveting ever to run in *Commentary*, concludes with the haunting words, "Georgia has the Negro and Harlem has the Jew."

31. "The Harlem Ghetto: Winter of 1948," p. 170, and "Negroes Are Anti-Semitic Because They're Anti-White," (*The New York Times Magazine* April 9, 1967).

32. Quoted in Murray Friedman. "Black Anti-Semitism on the Rise," *Commentary* (October 1979) p. 35. At another point, King called anti-Semitism "wrong, unjust, and evil." Quoted in Jack Kemp, "Blacks, Jews, Liberals, and Crime," *National Review* (May 16, 1994) p. 40.

33. Thomas Brooks, "Tragedy at Ocean Hill," *Dissent* (January/February 1969) p. 33.

34. Martin Meyer, *The Teachers Strike* (New York: Harper and Row, 1969)

35. "Tragedy at Ocean Hill."

36. Quoted in Carl Gershman, "The Andrew Young Affair," *Commentary* (November 1979) p. 29. The State Department had a policy against meeting with terrorist groups.

37. Quoted in "The Andrew Young Affair," p. 26.

38. Quoted in Nathan Glazer, "Blacks, Jews and Intellectuals," *Commentary* (April 1969) p. 35.

39. Interview with Martin Peretz, April 25, 1994.

40. Ruth Wisse, *If I Am Not for Myself: The Liberal Betrayal of the Jews* (New York: Free Press, 1993) p. 5.

41. Joacham Prinz quoted in Gary Jacobsohn, *Apple of Gold: Constitutionalism in Israel and the United States* (Princeton: Princeton University Press, 1992) p. 58.

42. See, for instance, David Bar-Illan, "'60 Minutes' and the Temple Mount," *Commentary* (February 1991) pp. 17–24.

43. Norman Podhoretz, "The Abandonment of Israel," *Commentary* (July 1976) p. 31.

44. Norman Podhoretz, "J'Accuse," *Commentary* (September 1982) p. 31.

45. Peter Collier and David Horowitz, *Second Thoughts: Former Radicals Look Back at the Sixties* (Lanham, Md.: Madison Books, 1989) p. 170.

46. Midge Decter, contribution to *Commentary* Symposium, "Liberalism and the Jews," *Commentary* (January 1980) p. 31.

47. Irving Kristol, "Not One World." Review of *American Politics in a Revolutionary World* by Chester Bowles, *Commentary* (August 1956).

48. Charles Lichtenstein, reply to a proposal to move the United Nations from New York City, September 19, 1983.

49. Irving Kristol, "Foreign Policy in an Age of Ideology," *The National Interest* (Fall 1985) p. 11.

50. Irving Kristol, contribution to *The Reagan Doctrine and Beyond*, American Enterprise Institute Symposium (Washington: American Enterprise Institute for Public Policy Research, 1987).

51. Jeane Kirkpatrick, contribution to "Has the United States Met Its Major Challenges Since 1945?" *Commentary* (November 1945) pp. 50–52.
52. Irving Kristol, "A Transatlantic 'Misunderstanding': The Case of Central America," *Encounter* (March 1988) p. 9.
53. Quoted in Daniel Patrick Moynihan, *A Dangerous Place* (New York: Little, Brown, 1976) p. 76.
54. 54. George Weigel, "A War About America," *Commonweal* (February 22, 1991) p. 121.
55. P. T. Bauer, "Western Guilt and Third World Poverty," *Commentary* (January 1976) pp. 31–38.
56. Amin's culinary delights are discussed in Paul Johnson's *Modern Times* (New York: Harper and Row, 1983—Harper Colophon edition) p. 536.
57. *A Dangerous Place,* p. 158.
58. Daniel Patrick Moynihan, "The United States in Opposition," *Commentary* (March 1975) p. 35.
59. *A Dangerous Place*, pp. 49, 55.
60. Daniel Patrick Moynihan, address to the United Nations, November 10, 1975.
61. Ilke's use is quoted in Norman Podhoretz, "Vietnam and the Crisis of Containment," in William F. Buckley and Charles Kesler, eds., *Keeping the Tablets: Modern American Conservative Thought* (New York: Harper and Row, 1988) p. 379. Moynihan's citation is "Words and Foreign Policy," *Policy Review* (Fall 1978) p. 70.
62. "Words and Foreign Policy," p. 71.
63. Midge Decter, contribution to "Has the United States Met Its Major Challenges since 1945?" *Commentary* (November 1985) pp. 33–34, 36.
64. Norman Podhoretz, "Making the World Safe for Communism," *Commentary* (April 1976) p. 41.
65. Norman Podhoretz, "The Future Danger," *Commentary* (April 1981) p. 35.
66. Interview with Elliot Abrams, March 25, 1994.
67. Quoted in Adam Wolfson, "The World According to Kirkpatrick: Is Ronald Reagan Listening?" *Policy Review* (Winter 1985) p. 70.
68. Irving Kristol, "The 20th Century Began in 1945," *New York Times Magazine* (May 2, 1965) p. 84.
69. Norman Podhoretz, *The Present Danger: Do We Have the Will to Reverse the Decline of American Power?* (New York: Simon and Schuster, 1980) p. 100.
70. Jeanne Kirkpatrick, "Dictatorships and Double Standards," *Commentary* (November 1979) p. 42.
71. Norman Podhoretz, "The Culture of Appeasement," *Harper's* (October 1977) p. 25.
72. Midge Decter, contribution to "America Now: A Failure of Nerve?" *Commentary* (July 1976) p. 29.
73. Midge Decter, contribution to "America Now: A Failure of Nerve?" p. 30.

74. Patrick Glynn, "Why an American Arms Build-up Is Morally Necessary," *Commentary* (February 1984) pp. 17–18.

75. *The Present Danger: Do We Have the Will to Resist the Forward Surge of Soviet Imperialism?* p. 19.

76. Sidney Hook, contribution to "America Now: A Failure of Nerve?" p. 41.

77. Walter Lacquer, "Containment for the 80s," *Commentary* (October 1980) p. 42.

78. Irving Kristol, contribution to "America Now: A Failure of Nerve?" p. 54.

79. "The Culture of Appeasement," p. 26.

80. "The Future Danger," p. 32.

81. Midge Decter, contribution to "America Now: A Failure of Nerve?" p. 31.

82. Gertrude Himmelfarb, "Does the West Still Exist?" Committee for the Free World Symposium (New York: Orwell Press, 1990) p. 88.

83. See Midge Decter, *The New Chastity and Other Arguments against Women's Liberation* (New York: Coward, McCann and Geoghegan, 1971).

84. "The Culture of Appeasement," p. 31.

85. Peter Berger, "The Greening of U.S. Foreign Policy," *Commentary* (March 1976) p. 24.

86. "The Culture of Appeasement," pp. 31, 32.

87. For a more complete discussion of these ideas, see Chapter 5, "Capitalist Celebrations and Bourgeois Critiques."

88. Alexis de Tocqueville, *Democracy in America,* vol. 1 (New York: Vintage Classics, 1990), p. 120. For the neoconservative reaction to this idea, see Chapter 5, "Capitalist Celebrations and Bourgeois Critiques."

89. John Van Meer, "Banks, Tanks and Freedom," *Commentary* (December 1982) p. 17.

90. Sidney Hook, contribution to "America Now: A Failure of Nerve?" p. 43.

91. "The Future Danger," p. 32.

92. Elliot Abrams, contribution to "Liberalism and the Jews," *Commentary* (January 1980) p. 17.

93. Werner Dannhauser, contribution to "Liberalism and the Jews," p. 30.

94. Gertrude Himmelfarb, contribution to "Liberalism and the Jews," p. 44.

95. Midge Decter, contribution to "Liberalism and the Jews," p. 32.

96. Elliot Abrams, contribution to "Liberalism and the Jews," p. 17.

97. Gertrude Himmelfarb, contribution to "Liberalism and the Jews," p. 44.

98. Quoted in Sidney Blumenthal, *The Rise of the Counter-Establishment: From Conservative Ideology to Political Power* (New York: Times Books, 1986) p. 128.

99. Interview with Elliot Abrams, March 25, 1994.

100. Daniel Patrick Moynihan, "'Joining the Jackals': The U.S. at the UN 1977–1980," *Commentary* (February 1981) p. 29.

101. "Joining the Jackals," p. 23.

102. Arnold Beichman, contribution to "Liberalism and the Jews," p. 20.

103. Interview with Martin Peretz, April 25, 1994.

5

Capitalist Celebrations and Bourgeois Critiques

Democratic Capitalism is not just a system but a way of life. Its ethos includes a special evolution of pluralism; respect for contingency and unintended consequences; a sense of sin; and a new and distinctive conception of community, the individual, and the family.—Michael Novak, 1982

The Last Vestige of Our Liberalism

By the middle of the 1970s, the neoconservatives had established a distinctive viewpoint on a variety of issues. From Communism to quotas, from Israel to busing, from feminism to civil rights, from higher education to pornography, the neoconservative worldview was well articulated in journals, books, and op-ed pages. As Alan Wolfe, a critic of neoconservatism, wrote in 1985 (but could have written earlier),

> Not only have neoconservative ideas grown in acceptability, but neoconservative writers seem to be everywhere at once. Name any subject, and there is a neoconservative who has addressed it: poverty (Charles Murray), New York City (Roger Starr), the audience for classical music (Samuel Lipman), God (Michael Novak).[1]

In 1979, Wolfe's neoconservative authority on God quoted a former student of his as remarking, "I obtained one of the rarest commodities in the world, an unpublished thought of Michael Novak,"[2] and the same could be said of almost all the other neoconservatives. The neoconservatives are probably the most prolific group of intellectuals in American history—neoconservative thought on practically every issue in the past forty years is extensively developed. Yet, in this sea of ideas, economics escaped neoconservative consideration until the 1970s. But in the late 1970s and early 1980s, the neoconservatives developed an economic philosophy that proved to be their most important direct contribution to public policy. By the end of the 1980s, Jeane Kirkpatrick said—as have many other neoconservatives in one form or another—"The single most important change in my views in the last decade has been a much greater appreciation of market economics."[3] Simply, Midge Decter recollects, "[Economics was] the last vestige of our liberalism. Most of us had not been that interested in economics. It is fine, but [there was no] recognition that this was a key part of the whole package."[4]

As with most of neoconservatism, the interest in capitalism started with Irving Kristol. Since his days as a soldier in World War II, he regarded socialism as simplistic stupidity. And he had none of the animus toward businessmen that many intellectuals had. As he wrote in a 1960 *Encounter* piece,

> Like most intellectuals, I have had certain clear and preconceived notions about how capitalism works in America. The economy is dominated by an interlocking directorate of Big Business which, while breaching competition and "free enterprise," manages things to suit its own convenience and, sometimes, the common good. Unlike my friends on the Left, I have not been outraged by this state of affairs, since it always seemed reasonable to me that something as important as Big Business should be managed by hard-faced professionals than by, say, the editors of *The New Left Review*.[5]

Always opposed to egalitarianism and utopian political schemes of the right and left, Kristol had no use for liberal plans to equalize incomes or conservative support for laissez-faire economics. Before the 1970s, he favored honest, rigorous thinking on economic issues—apparently without regard to what ideological positions it supported. Lavishly extolling John Kenneth Galbraith's anticapitalist book *The Affluent Society* in a 1958 *Commentary* review, Kristol bestowed equal praise upon Friedrich von Hayek's *The Constitution of Liberty* two years later.[6] If he was leaning to either side, it was to Hayek; he commented in a 1960 *Yale Review* essay, "The only class that would suffer if these [income] taxes were reduced would be the tax lawyers."[7]

In a 1964 letter to *The New Republic*, Kristol addressed indirectly the theoretical roles of the state and of the individual in economic decision making. He was responding to an article that stated that a Ford Foundation grant to the ballet was subsidized by the government because the Ford Foundation has tax exempt status.

> The government grants me tax deductions for my two young children. Does that mean the rearing of my children is being subsidized by government money? I think not. It is being paid for by my money. A tax exemption is not some kind of benign and magnanimous dispensation. It is as much a part of the taxation laws as the law itself. Many people seem to be under the impression that the government has original ownership of all the money in the country, and then in its wisdom decides to let the citizenry keep some part of it. The opposite strikes me as more in accord with both the real and the ideal.[8]

The most forthright statement of Kristol's early economic views came through in a 1957 *Commentary* piece.

> It is really more than time that someone said a good word for the Horatio Alger novels. The moral of these stories is that, even if one is born very poor, one can still end up rich and successful if one is good-looking, intelligent, healthy, diligent, ambitious and extremely lucky. I can think of no truer sociological observation.[9]

This observation was to be deepened, by Kristol and the other neoconservatives. But what few suspected was that the revulsion to simplistic liberalism would be translated into the most comprehensive moral defense of the free market since Adam Smith's *The Wealth of Nations*. That is what the neoconservatives, in several seminal books and numerous essays and columns, have provided.

The Birth of an Idea: Supply-Side Economics

In the 1970s, Kristol became friendly with Robert Bartley, the editor of the *Wall Street Journal* editorial page. Bartley and Kristol were much taken by one another, and Kristol was placed on the *Wall Street Journal* Board of Contributors, a position which entailed a monthly column on the op-ed page. While serving on the board, Kristol studied economics, in part by befriending several of the brightest minds in economic thought whom he simultaneously learned from and mentored. The formation and eventual reality of supply-side economics is a case study in how, by thinking and acting in ways that transcend established modes, Irving Kristol and those he tapped and coordinated made an obscure idea the economic policy of the United States.

In 1971, the bane of much of respectable Washington was Arthur Laffer. Trained in economics at Yale in the early 1960s, Laffer received an M.B.A. from Stanford before joining the economics faculty at the University of Chicago. He became a protégé of the chairman of the Economics Department, George Schultz, who was appointed to head the Office of Management and Budget under President Richard Nixon. Schultz brought in Laffer as his chief economist. In 1970, Laffer earned some fame in generating a number that became famous—"1065," or 1.65 trillion, his prediction for the nation's GNP the next year. This was considered by many in Congress, the press and the economics profession to be a wildly optimistic figure put forth by the Nixon administration in an effort to win reelection in 1972. The Democrats went ballistic; Senator William Proxmire took to the Senate floor to decry "Art Laffer and his money machine!" Even established economists scoffed at Laffer's figure, and Laffer was left with few allies.[10]

At that time, Jude Wanniski was a young political writer for the *National Observer*, a Dow Jones publication. Wanniski introduced himself to Laffer, and the two became fast friends. Wanniski used Laffer as something of a tutor, given that Wanniski did not know much about economics. When Wanniski switched to another Dow Jones publication, the *Wall Street Journal*, in 1972, he called Laffer every morning for his mentor's take on the news of the day.

In 1974, Wanniski met Laffer's close associate, Robert Mundell. After spending a day with Mundell at a conference at the American Enterprise Institute, Wanniski came to believe that Mundell and Laffer had a revolutionary idea that he wanted to make the policy of the nation. Wanniski took to the op-ed page of the *Wall Street Journal* with an article whose pedestrian title should not detract from the revolutionary process it started, "It's Time to Cut Taxes." This article, which spelled out the foundations of the supply-side perspective, consists of an interview with Mundell. It had Wanniski's byline, but it was all Mundell. The article was read widely, and one of the readers was Irving Kristol, who had been following Wanniski's work at the *Wall Street Journal* and wanted Wanniski to contribute an essay to *The Public Interest.* He knew that Wanniski was concerned about the way the press handled Laffer, and asked Wanniski to lunch to discuss an article on the economic ignorance of the press corps. Wanniski recalls,

> Irving spent the lunch attacking the press for its economic ignorance. This had to do with the oil crisis. The press was blaming Exxon and Mobil. Everyone was blaming the oil industry, and business circles were alarmed about the press writing all this radical stuff. In the air was a massive takeover of the industry. Irving asked me to write a piece for *The Public Interest* on the economic ignorance of the press corps. Irving argued that we had to call the press to account. I said journalists reflect, they don't create. The problem we have is not the ignorance of journalists; we have the ignorance of economists. Irving said, "You want to write that instead?"[11]

Wanniski did, and published "The Mundell-Laffer Hypothesis, A New View of the World Economy" in the Spring 1975 issue of *The Public Interest.* The essay articulated the basic principles of supply-side economics. Wanniski presented it as an economic philosophy that stimulates growth by invigorating the relationship between consumer and producer. Unlike most economic theories, this hypothesis—which would become known as supply-side economics—was strikingly simple and appealed directly to human ingenuity. The key principle behind it is that people will work harder when they are allowed to keep their money. When people work harder, they make more money. When they earn more money, the government has more money to tax. If in the short run, government revenues decrease, that is fine because the government should not spend so much anyway.

The most enduring part of this essay was footnote 4, which articulated "the law of diminishing returns," the theory that once tax rates hit a certain level, people would stop working as hard and the government would not receive any increased revenue.

While it was not labeled as such in the article, this idea was translated into what became known as the "Laffer curve," which clearly illustrated the law of diminishing returns, thus making supply-side economics accessible to everyone.

The famous Laffer curve was conceived at the Two Continents Restaurant in Washington, D.C. Wanniski, wanting to sell the idea of supply-side economics to anyone who would listen, arranged to have dinner with Laffer and President Gerald Ford's assistant, Donald Rumsfeld. Rumsfeld did not have time to go and sent his aide, Richard Cheney, in his place. In the course of the dinner, Laffer whipped out a pen, took a cocktail napkin, and drew a graph to show to Cheney. On one axis was government revenue, on the other was tax rates. The curve showed how government revenue increases when taxes are raised at very low rates and diminishes when the taxes hit a certain point on the curve to the point where higher tax rates actually decrease government revenue. This became known as the Laffer curve.

Following the conference at the American Enterprise Institute, Wanniski set out with his articles and ideas to convince policy makers to implement supply-side economics. After being rebuffed by several prominent politicians, he found a willing protégé in a former quarterback and now two-term congressman from Buffalo, Jack Kemp. Wanniski and Kemp became quite close, and assembled a cadre of young congressmen, staffers, and professors who wanted to help spread the supply-side message. One of the key members of this group was David Stockman, a young congressman from rural Michigan and former John Anderson staffer.

1977 was an important year for Wanniski and supply-side economics, and not just because Kemp was starting the political process moving. Kristol, through contacts at the American Enterprise Institute, the Smith-Richardson Foundation and the *Wall Street Journal*, arranged for Wanniski to receive a fellowship at AEI to write a book presenting the supply-side case. On the fellowship, Wanniski wrote his book, *The Way the World Works*, which became the foundational work of supply-side economics, around which legions of young true believers rallied. *The Way the World Works* was published by Basic Books, and Wanniski's editor there was Midge Decter. David Stockman recalls,

> One day he [Kemp] handed me the manuscript of a book that would soon burst on the world in a blaze of illumination: Jude Wanniski's *The Way the World Works*. . . . His book hit me with the force of revelation. It reordered everything I had previously known or thought about economics.[12]

In addition to providing the means for Wanniski to write this book, Kristol bestowed on supply-side economics a crucial air of respectability. According to Jude Wanniski, critics could have dismissed him, Laffer, and Mundell as irresponsible firebrands whose ideas should not be taken seriously. However, this could not be done with Kristol, who was widely respected on all sides of the political spectrum. With Irving Kristol a supply-side partisan, Wanniski, Laffer, and even Kemp could not be dismissed as mavericks hawking a radical scheme—as their opposition sometimes tried to do.[13] Kristol advised the younger men on the philosophical underpinnings of supply-side economics, published the supply-side writers, arranged for their funding, and lent his valuable name to the project. About the only thing that Kristol did not do was title Wanniski's book; that honor belonged to Wanniski's young daughter, who, when asked by a neighbor what Daddy does, replied that he was writing a book on "the way the world works."[14]

While serving (with his reputation as much as with his ideas) as an invaluable ombudsman between the intellectual and business communities, Kristol was able to provide insights regarding supply-side economics that Wanniski and others needed. While Wanniski, Kemp, Laffer, and Mundell concentrated on the economics of the supply-side idea, Kristol considered the concept from a cultural angle. Economists, Kristol argued, were forever developing sophisticated models that missed the point. He stressed that professional economists could use a little common sense.

> Economic growth, after all, is not a mystery of nature like the black holes in distant galaxies. It is a consequence of purposive action by human beings very much like ourselves. . . . It is something that humanity has been intimately involved with for over two centuries now, and, if we are of a certain age, it is something we have personally witnessed and experienced in our lifetimes. . . .[15]

Supply-side economics spoke to this sense, manifesting a vision of instilling the power of creative economic possibility into the hands of the ordinary citizen with the vision and the determination to transform a vision into a reality. More than numbers, graphs, or equations, it was poetry. Ben Wattenberg summed up this sentiment: "Supply-side economics? The numbers may not work, but economics is symbolic. Forget the numbers. It's growth economics. . . ."[16] Irving Kristol stressed that the theme of entrepreneurship incorporated into supply-side economics is a terrific message for conservatives. More than tax rates or revenue generated, supply-side economics was about hungry capital searching for creative people bubbling with ingenuity and fresh ideas starving to be funded. How would the left answer *that*? In the anticapitalist climate of the late 1970s, supply-side economics was the way in which conservatives could demonstrate that the free market best spoke to the aspirations of the ordinary citizen and manifested the American dream. Conservatives always had a problem presenting a communitarian vision for the good life, but here was their chance.

The supply-side idea would be best articulated in a 1980 book by George Gilder, *Wealth and Poverty*. Working with Midge Decter, Gilder was inspired by the other major work on economics edited by Decter, *The Way the World Works*. "Wanniski's book . . . is one of the great inspirational works of economic literature . . . and in many ways my book follows the supply-side trail that Wanniski so boldly blazed."[17] The active and public support of Kemp, Stockman and President Reagan helped make the book a best-seller, and the most popular work on economics since Milton Friedman's *Capitalism and Freedom*.

Courting a Philosophical Prude: The Neoconservatives Approach Capitalism

While neoconservative ideas traditionally are articulated in journals and magazines, neoconservative thought on capitalism is found primarily in books. Irving Kristol's *Two Cheers for Capital-*

ism, Michael Novak's *The Spirit of Democratic Capitalism* and *The Catholic Ethic and The Spirit of Capitalism*, Daniel Bell's *The Cultural Contradictions of Capitalism*, Peter Berger's *The Capitalist Revolution: Fifty Propositions about Prosperity, Equality, and Liberty*, George Gilder's *Wealth and Poverty*, Jude Wanniski's *The Way the World Works*, Richard John Neuhaus's *Doing Well and Doing Good: The Challenge to the Christian Capitalist*, and books edited by Michael Novak of symposia at the American Enterprise Institute, compose the bulk of the neoconservative conversation on the free market. And a conversation it really is; these books address one another, expand on each other's ideas, and point out disagreements while building upon and refining arguments.

As with much of their thought, neoconservatives' treatment of capitalism began as a reaction to the left. The neoconservatives had a solid grip on left-wing views on economics because, with the exception of Kristol, they had shared some of those views only a short time ago. Neoconservatives believed that the thinking of the left on economics was shallow, uninformed, and often knee-jerk socialist. While the left could not be Communist because of all that was known about Soviet cultural and social life, left-leaning thinkers aligned themselves with the broad category of socialism which was rarely defined specifically. These "socialists" had no plans for how a socialist economy would function. They were not even sure how they wanted to redistribute the income that was created. The neoconservatives noted the lack of specificity on the left concerning economic issues and came to the conclusion that the left was more anticapitalist than prosocialist. In a 1983 *Commentary* essay, Joseph Epstein wrote,

> If one wonders what remains of leftism once the hunger for Communism is removed, the answer, I suppose, is a hunger for socialism. But since most American intellectuals who hold this view have never been able to give a shred of a hint of a clue as to what it is they have in mind by socialism, I think it might be less disingenuous, a good deal more straightforward, to say that at the center of left-wing anti-Communism is the hatred of capitalism.[18]

The lack of definitive goals permitted socialists to criticize capitalism without having to seriously confront the fact that people in free market societies live far better than those who do not. The left could always concede this, but maintain that such people would live so much better if only this or that form of socialism was enacted. As William Barrett wrote of his days in socialist intellectual circles, "You did not have to defend the imperfections of any existing regime. As one more intolerable socialism after another came into existence, you could simply shrug each off as not being 'real socialism.' "[19]

A benefit of advocating an entirely general socialism is the ability to claim that "Real socialism has never been tried." This has been a common refrain of the left, which can conceive of numerous reasons why the failure of collectivism had nothing to do with their particular variety of socialism. This claim—and its implicit assertion of immunity from moral accountability—has always disturbed neoconservatives. For the nature of politics is that no ideology or program is really tried as its most orthodox adherents would like; the inevitability of compromise eliminates the possibility for purity. In that sense, nothing is "ever really tried."

The neoconservatives regarded the anticapitalism of the left to be a variant of anti-Americanism. By criticizing the economic structure of a society, intellectuals would, by extension, criticize how people spend their days, who gets what, and how social roles are allocated. Leftism in the 1970s and 1980s being but an extension of the radicalism of the 1960s, the anticapitalism of the left was but an extrapolation of the cultural divide that was formed in the 1960s. With many of the former radicals now professors in universities or important figures in left-wing organizations, anticapitalism was a logical way for the left to demonstrate its animosity for American society.

While the anti-Americanism of the intellectuals was a phenomenon that had existed, disappeared, and come back in full blossom, a distaste for capitalism among intellectuals was nothing new. The neoconservatives regarded the unthinking opposition to capitalism on the left as a continuation of a long-standing literary and intellectual tradition. A consistent theme in neoconservative writing is the negative treatment of capitalism in literature and philosophy practically since the beginning of philosophy. According to Irving Kristol, "The cultural history of the capitalist epoch is not much more than a record of the varying way such dissatisfaction could be expressed—in poetry, in the novel, in painting, and today even in the movies."[20] Daniel Bell elaborates on Kristol's point.

> Romantic or traditionalist, Enlightenment or irrationalist, vitalist or naturalist, humanist or racialist, religious or atheist—in this entire range of passions and beliefs, scarcely one respectable intellectual figure defended the sober, unheroic, prudential, let alone acquisitive, entrepreneurial, or money-making pursuits of the bourgeois world.[21]

The neoconservatives have argued that social thought has generally bypassed the mechanics of production and consumption in order to confront the lofty and heroic themes that excite the literary imagination. Homer, Shakespeare, Milton, and Dante do not write of how wonderful it is to borrow at 3 percent and lend at 6 percent—they write of life and death, romantic love, human courage, and patriotic self-sacrifice. As Epstein maintained, "No writer I ever encountered as an undergraduate at the University of Chicago so much as suggested that business had anything to do with the good life."[22] The other neoconservatives have the same response as Epstein and credit the almost blind opposition of most social thinkers to free market in large part to the lack of a serious intellectual consideration of capitalism in literature and philosophy.

The neoconservatives believe that the negative treatment of capitalism in literature is crucially important and transcends the confined walls of academia where it ferments. A central tenet of neoconservatism concerns the way in which a social system morally legitimates itself. Neoconservatives believe that society consistently asks itself, "Is this right? Is it moral?"—even when something ostensibly "works." As Irving Kristol writes,

> My reading of history is that, in the same way as men cannot for long tolerate a sense of spiritual meaningless in their individual lives, so they cannot for long accept a society in which power, privilege, and property are not distributed according to some morally meaningful criteria.[23]

Thus, norms of justice apply to economics as they do to every other sector of society. To the neoconservatives, economics is much more than the allocation of resources. Kristol noted in 1964, "All economic systems have their peculiar imperfections, and no people ever accepts and endures an economic system for economic reasons alone. They must think that it is somehow 'right.' "[24] Productivity and efficiency are important, but are impotent unaccompanied by a forthright moral message. Kristol again: "Efficiency is not a moral virtue and by itself never legitimizes anything."[25] If defenders of capitalism rely on arguments of efficiency or productivity, they will lose to any opponent that presents an economic system that seems morally legitimate.

According to the neoconservatives, the lack of a serious moral defense has crippled efforts to strengthen capitalism. The people loudly answering the central question of society (Is it just?) are usually intellectuals, and their answers—subtly, of course—often form the basis of broad societal perceptions. Given the nearly universal condemnation of capitalism by intellectuals, the moral legitimacy of the free market system is put in jeopardy.

Why have intellectuals disliked capitalism so much? The neoconservatives offer no easy answer. There is always resentment: the free market economy does not make intellectuals rich. Furthermore, intellectuals are not attracted to a fundamentally prosaic system that is immediately concerned with producing the appropriate goods for the most people in the most efficient way possible. Economics is not inherently romantic; it is not usually a sphere where people challenge themselves to the limit and rise above adversity to win a coup for a glorious cause. Neoconservatives point out that this assessment is not always just—some of America's most successful entrepreneurs have fulfilled any definition of heroism. Nevertheless, capitalist values are not generally connected with physical courage, awesome sacrifice, or charity. Prometheus did not steal investment advice for mankind, he stole fire. Peter Berger points out,

> [capitalism] is particularly deprived of mythic potency. . . . The hypothesis would be falsified on the day when poets sing the praises of the Dow Jones and when large numbers of people are ready to risk their lives in defense of the Fortune 500. This does not seem like a probable eventuality.[26]

The ideas of economist Joseph Schumpeter concerning intellectuals and politics in his 1942 classic, *Capitalism, Socialism, and Democracy,* have significantly influenced the neoconservatives, and serve as a basis for much of their economic thought.[27] Most of their ideas on this subject are modern adaptations and applications of Schumpeter. He explains that capitalism rationalizes human behavior, thus purging from it the romantic ideals that inform other areas of life.

> Capitalist civilization is rationalistic "and anti-heroic." The two go together of course. Success in industry and commerce requires a lot of stamina, yet industrial and commercial activity is essentially unheroic in the knight's sense—no flourishing of swords about it, not much physical prowess, no chance to gallop the armored horse into the enemy, preferably a heretic or heathen—and the ideology that glorifies the idea of fighting for fighting's sake and of victory for victory's sake understandably withers in the office among all the columns of figures.[28]

While people may be satisfied with such a system that leads to the creation of such wealth, it is satisfying only on this one level. Capitalism does not seek grand conceptions of social justice and is unapologetic about unfortunate facts of life such as human inequality. It allows people to channel their energies and abilities into the arena that they enjoy best and find most useful, but makes no claim to address directly egalitarian concerns. Because capitalism is primarily functional and does not attempt to address deep issues, it generally does not captivate the heroic imagination. As Richard John Neuhaus writes, "Other spheres of human activity—politics, literature, the arts, family life—lend themselves to soaring visions of the true, the good, and the beautiful. It is not easy to wax inspiring about economics."[29]

The neoconservatives knew there was something to capitalism besides money, beyond acquisition—something moral that spoke to the ways society organize themselves. They wanted to see how this system worked, and how people—and values—fit into the equation. It is from this point that the neoconservatives began their consideration of capitalism.

Democratic Capitalism as True Liberalism

Since the days of liberal anti-Communism, the neoconservatives have consistently tried to show how liberals have subverted the fundamental principles of liberalism. In the 1950s, neoconservatives explained how treating Communism as a heresy rather than a conspiracy would ultimately undermine the ideas of free speech and open discourse that are the cornerstones of liberalism. In the 1960s, the neoconservatives criticized conflating liberty with license in the counterculture while castigating liberal intellectuals for countenancing the radicals who called Daniel Patrick Moynihan, Edward Banfield, and Richard J. Herrnstein racist. In the 1970s, neoconservatives wrote of how interpreting civil rights laws to mandate quotas was contrary to the quintessential liberal principle that no one should be judged by an involuntary characteristic such as the color of his skin. This pattern would be consistent with the neoconservative discussion of the free market. Through a variety of arguments, the neoconservatives wrote of how traditional liberal ideals are best served by capitalism.

The primary liberal idea that the neoconservatives believed was advanced by capitalism was that no one should be chained to what Lionel Trilling called "my station and its duties."[30] The core of traditional liberalism is that an individual should be able to rise as high as his abilities allow regardless of his familiar legacy. Just as this idea is a cornerstone of liberalism, it has always been a crucial component of neoconservative thought. As Decter wrote in 1976,

> I would bet that there are not six participants in this [*Commentary*] symposium [of intellectuals] who do not, as I do, owe the comfort of their lives, the cultivation of their minds, the softness of their hands—or to state the proposition with an extremism not entirely inappropriate to this century, who do not owe the fact that they are not buried in a pauper's grave or even are not literally gone up in smoke—to the idea that their grandfathers or their fathers or they themselves were not to be confined to their station at birth. Whatever other product of liberalism I may deplore, I must not forget that this idea is one to which I owe my very existence.[31]

Liberal critics of the free market miss the point when they stress that there is a wide gap between the rich and the poor in capitalist societies. First, Irving Kristol notes, the very fact that economists sweat over statistics purporting to demonstrate economic inequality in America proves that there is, relatively speaking, not much of it.[32] Even given that there is inequality, the crucial fact is that wealth in democratic capitalist societies is mobile. Inherited fortunes dissipate quickly, and new ones are built by hardworking and enterprising people. As Kristol wrote, "The rich will always be with us, but in the course of several generations, the old rich will gradually be superseded by the new rich, since the ability to respond to market opportunities is not—nor has anyone ever claimed it to be—an inherited human characteristic."[33] American history is replete with stories of people earning fortunes and then losing them.

Because of the mobility afforded by capitalism, the neoconservatives maintain that a free economy is the most effective antidiscrimination plan ever tried. Groups that have been the traditional victims of prejudice have often transcended their condition by providing a new product at a better price.

No discriminatory law or emotional prejudice can prevent a person with ingenuity, diligence, and creativity from prospering in a free market economy. Prejudice may prevent a member of a minority group from marrying someone's daughter, it may prevent him from moving next door, it may even prevent him from opening a business in a particular town, but there will always be a market in which he can enter and prosper. George Gilder uses Jews and Japanese Americans as manifestations of this theory. Both victims of systematic discrimination in America, these groups now rank one and two in per capita earnings among all ethnic groups.[34]

The neoconservatives contend that capitalism further satisfies liberal goals by providing for a broad range of individual choices. In a free market economy, the types of goods produced are not determined by an a priori notion of what should be consumed. Rather, they are determined by the desires and needs of ordinary people. The neoconservatives regard this as a true form of democracy; capitalism responds directly to the desires of the people by producing goods that suit them. If ordinary people do not want a good, it will not be sold, no matter what anyone with a fancy vocabulary, degree, title, or lineage says.

The freedom that capitalism generates through broad choices has philosophical importance beyond the array of goods and services offered. Capitalism liberates individuals to order their lives independently. Michael Novak explains,

> A democratic capitalist regime promises three liberations by institutional means—liberation from tyranny and torture; liberation from the oppression of conscience, information, and ideas; and liberation from poverty. The construction of a social order that achieves these is not designed to fill the soul, or to teach a philosophy, or to give instruction in how to live. It is designed to create space, within which the soul may make its own choices, and within which spiritual leaders and spiritual associations may do their own necessary and creative work.[35]

In *The Spirit of Democratic Capitalism*, Novak expands on the way in which capitalism services ordinary people. He believes that money is put to the best use when it is in the hands of those who earned it rather than in government coffers. While the left often castigates the luxuries that capitalism produces, Novak maintains that the true principles of liberalism allow for individuals to spend their money in ways that make them happy. Suggesting that people should be taxed so that money will not go to private good X but to public good Y entails transferring the agency and decision-making ability of ordinary people to a group of elites. Novak writes,

> It is wise to trust the ordinary wisdom of plain human beings on juries, in the voting booth, in the development of public dialogue, in the ordinary decencies of daily living. So also, it would seem, a wise society trusts individuals to spend their hard-earned dollars as they judge best. Choices made by some in the marketplace will often seem to others less than rational. This is true, as well, of the religious practices and moral principles to which individuals commit themselves.[36]

The neoconservatives had even more problems with opposition to capitalism because of the only plausible alternative to the free market—a large and powerful government in some kind of socialist system. As neoconservatives stressed in criticizing leftist economics, socialism could take any number of forms. It could be a system of government planning that tells industry what and how much to produce or it could be a confiscatory tax system that redirects capital from would-be investors to the state. The neoconservatives believe that hair-splitting arguments between types of socialism are irrelevant, for only the market can provide the opportunity, choices, and dispersion of power necessary for a free people. The traditional liberal benefits garnered from capitalism would be lost when large government invariably corrodes the freedom engendered by capitalism. Novak recollects discussions he had in the 1970s:

> the alternative [to capitalism] was big government for everybody. For example, the argument over the oil companies was that there were seven sisters who had practically a monopoly hold on the nation's oil supply and nation's oil decisions. What's the left-wing cure for that? Too much concentration of power—the left-wing cure is that the government takes charge. What kind of argument is that? Dividing something seven ways is too much concentration, but putting it under one roof, that's the cure. That's ridiculous.[37]

Compassion's Colleague: Capitalism or Big Government?

In a 1980 *Partisan Review* symposium, Nathan Glazer, who never wrote much about capitalism, analyzes economics from the perspective of his area of expertise, social policy.

> It's not that I think the profit motive is great and noble, but it does seem to impose a modest economy and efficiency. A private landlord, if you look at all of the figures, does a better job with old housing, better for the tenants in terms of the resources being put in, than the public landlords do. He might do even better if he had part of those subsidies that we give to public landlords.[38]

The neoconservatives maintain that the skills of businessmen are every bit as impressive, if not more so, than those of intellectuals. They reject a political culture where, as Kristol declared, "The Post Office gets away with murder while AT&T is crucified for every fault, simply because in the one case management's motives are assumed to be 'pure' while in the other they are by definition 'impure.' "[39] There is no competition between the world of the mind and the world of commerce—both perform differently valuable functions. If the intellectual life is sometimes considered "higher," that is because it is the intellectuals who do the considering. Novak writes,

> The chief executive officers of major corporations have as much claim to high talent as do the top five hundred intellectuals and professors, the top five hundred scientists, or the top five hundred musicians, painters and sculptors of the land. Their inventions and organizational innovations, their capacities for leadership and practical judgment, are assets which benefit their fellow citizens.[40]

Many of the neoconservative writings on capitalism are directed at capturing the moral sentiments traditionally dominated by the left. The neoconservatives are especially sensitive to the charge that capitalism fosters greed. Neoconservatives regard the profit motive as a perfectly legitimate and necessary—though not by itself morally praiseworthy—fact of life.[41] Putting aside the ingenuity sparked by the pursuit of economic profit, neoconservatives point out that nonmarket operations depend entirely on the prosperity of corporations and wealthy individuals. Novak charged in 1980,

> Public television advertises itself, for example, as "television for people, not profits." The truth is that public television is financed entirely by the excess of profit over cost; it does not earn its own way but is parasitic on profits made by others.[42]

Nor, Novak holds, are profits the consequence of an individualist quest for acquisition. While it is true that capitalism draws to a large extent upon self-interest, such a concept of self-interest must be appended with a Tocquevilleian "rightly understood." For even those who strive to accumulate as much money as possible cannot spend it themselves; most of the time, they give it to their families. Novak terms this phenomenon, perhaps the social centerpiece of capitalism, "familial socialism."[43]

Just as the motivation for profit is not the product of greedy self-interest, money is not made that way either. Novak has written that capitalist transactions are conducted primarily in committees with people working in concert toward a common goal. A corporation is a social institution, and buying and selling are social activities. An individual concerned solely with personal profit will not prosper in a corporate or entrepreneurial environment where teamwork and interpersonal relationships are crucial. It is no coincidence, therefore, that "for many, the workplace is a kind of second family. . . ."[44]

Capitalism, the neoconservatives claim, is far from the impersonal system that the left often claims it is. If an individual does not understand and appreciate the needs and concerns of his fellow man—it does not matter who he is or who he thinks he is—he will not know what to produce to make their lives more pleasant. Only the person who knows firsthand what would enrich the lives of his fellow citizens and is able to put himself in their stead will know what kind of product or service is demanded in a market economy. Moreover, if an individual cannot relate well to other people, he will be ostracized from the myriad of personal interactions—large and small—that constitute capitalism. As Novak holds, an individual who is not "other-regarding" will, in a capitalist market, encounter "hostile resistance, rejection, and social alienation."[45]

This need for an entrepreneur to be "other-regarding" indirectly performs an indispensable moral function by instilling virtue in the individual. Because the free market is so competitive, people have to consistently produce a quality product, or else they will be outdone by someone who will. If a businessman develops a reputation for dishonesty, shoddy work, irresponsibility, tardiness, obstinacy, or rudeness, customers will shun him. Likewise, even amoral men are morally disciplined by the market. As University of Iowa economist Donald McCloskey wrote in *The American Scholar*,

> A reputation for fair dealing is necessary for a roofer whose trade is limited to a town with a population of fifty thousand. One bad roof and he is finished in Iowa City, and so he practices virtue with care. By now he would not put on a bad roof even if he could get away with it, and he behaves like a growing child internalizing virtues once forced on him.[46]

According to Gertrude Himmelfarb, the primacy that capitalism places on the bourgeois virtues is perhaps the most striking symbol of the democratic values it inculcates. These virtues are within the grasp of ordinary people; no one is ostracized from the potential for success in a capitalist economy. Himmelfarb writes,

> Those modest, mundane, lowly virtues—hard work, sobriety, frugality, foresight—are within the capacity of everyone. They do not assume any special breeding, or social status, or talent, or valor, or grace—or even money. They are common virtues within the reach of common people. They are preeminently democratic virtues.[47]

Novak points out that the communal nature of capitalism is far from theoretical; the Americans whom he knows do not fit the stereotype of the hard-driving greedy profit-mongers that are often portrayed in leftist descriptions of capitalism. Instead of judging capitalism by its villains, Novak has suggested that it should be judged by its ordinary practitioners.

> When I think of the many families in America known to me, most of the descriptions of Americans common to sociological and literary conventions do not seem to fit. In particular, descriptions like "the consumer society," "greed," and "materialism" seem very wide off the mark. . . . Faced with a problem, Americans almost by instinct form a committee.[48]

Is this to suggest that the baneful qualities of greed and unenlightened self-interest are banished from capitalist societies? Of course not. Novak and the other neoconservatives have contended that greed is not a capitalist failing, but a human failing; indeed, it is one of the seven deadly sins.[49]

George Gilder goes even further than Novak in his condemnation of the notion of capitalism as a system that fosters greed. While anticapitalists decry "greed," they rarely define it. Gilder defines it for them. "Greed is an appetite for unneeded and unearned wealth and power. The truly greedy seek comfort and security first. They seek goods and clout they have not earned." He finds that capitalists reject the ethos of greed; they work hard for what they earn.

> This case for capitalism as a Faustian pact, by which we trade greed for wealth, is simple hogwash. America's entrepreneurs are not more greedy than Harry Homeless or Suzy Saintly. Even without making comparison to their opportunities for indolence, one can see that they work fanatically hard. In proportion to their holdings or their output, and their contributions to the human race, they consume less than any other group of people in the history of the world.[50]

To find greed, the place to look is not at those who work hard and earn a lot. Gilder suggests a few places.

> If you want to see a carnival of greed, watch Jesse Jackson regale an audience of welfare mothers on the "economic violence" of capitalism, or watch a conference of leftist college professors denouncing the economic system that provides their freedom, tenure, long vacations, and other expensive privileges while they pursue their Marxist ego-trip at the expense of capitalism.[51]

Gilder contrasts this greed with the behavior of capitalists. While most neoconservatives concentrated on the morality of capitalism, he has focused on capitalists.[52] This distinction speaks to the stress that Gilder puts on giving capitalism a human face, by making an understanding of the actual work of the free market accessible and palatable to ordinary people. He believes that most defenses of capitalism are flawed for a similar reason that most criticisms of capitalism are flawed: both assume that capitalists are greedy, self-interested individuals.

> "Businessmen are bastards": This crude view of men of commerce, once pronounced by President John F. Kennedy, sums up the sentiments of socialist thinkers in America and around the world, from Jane Fonda to the remaining followers of the late Chairman Mao. In fact, the idea that businessmen are bastards is such a cliché among the progressive and enlightened men of the Left that most of them would be hurt and startled if a businessman responded by calling them the bigots they obviously are. . . . In essence . . . [free market] economists answer President Kennedy by saying, "Yes, businessmen are bastards, but the best thing to do is let them loose, to fight it out among themselves, and may the best bastard win."[53]

Neoconservatives hold that when capitalists are portrayed as greedy, self-interested profit-seekers, the argument is over. Capitalists—and capitalism—lose. Gilder writes that any moral defense of capitalism must begin and end by accentuating the virtues of capitalists. And he finds capitalists quite virtuous.

> To defend capitalism, even to understand it, one has to comprehend that businessmen are not bastards, but the heroes of the modern age—crucial vessels of those generous and creative impulses that give hope to an ever more populous humanity in overcoming its continuing scarcities and conflicts. In a world always divided in part between the givers and the takers, businessmen are among the most persistent and ingenious of donors; and all of us who benefit should be thankful. . . .[54]

Gilder stretches this notion further, contending that capitalism is a form of altruism because it entails giving of oneself through investment with no predetermined return. This idea is a frequently discussed part of *Wealth and Poverty*, and it is one with which the neoconservatives largely disagree. The neoconservatives want to reserve altruism for truly selfless people who serve and sacrifice as a matter of course, and with no obvious benefit for themselves. As Gilder recounts in his preface to the 1993 edition of *Wealth and Poverty*,

> From William F. Buckley, Jr., who debated with me on "Firing Line," to the late Ayn Rand, who devoted part of her last speech to denouncing me, to Irving Kristol and Michael Novak, my most trusted mentors firmly spurned my idea of a profound affinity between the altruistic themes of the Judeo-Christian tradition and the practical imperatives of supply-side capitalism.[55]

While Kristol found *Wealth and Poverty* to be a magnificent book that provides capitalism with some necessary dazzle, he nonetheless has criticized Gilder for providing capitalism with too many cheers. Kristol maintains that Gilder does not appreciate the limits of the free market and the moral necessity of human qualities that have nothing to do with economics.

> There is one important point, however, on which I have to register a strong disagreement with Gilder. . . . [Bourgeois capitalist virtues] do not add up to a complete moral code that a society can base itself on. Not only are certain virtues neglected—where is charity? physical courage? patriotic self-sacrifice?—but a purely commercial code of ethics does not enable us to

cope with these all too many instances when circumstances conspire to ruin us, regardless of our virtuous practices. Life is unfair, and only a morality embedded in a transcendental religion can cope with that fact.[56]

Tod Lindberg took to the pages of *Commentary* to voice a different type of criticism of Gilder. Lindberg maintains that the morality of many of the specific capitalists celebrated by Gilder must be questioned because they often ignored their families in pursuit of profit. Missing from Gilder's capitalist heroes, Lindberg observes, are the bourgeois virtues that Kristol, Novak and others claim are crucial moral manifestations of capitalism.

> Successful entrepreneurs, as Gilder describes them, strive to compensate for their sense of personal alienation; they embrace great risks, going in the opposite direction from the crowd; although they fail frequently, they are undeterred; they bring new conceptions to bear on difficult problems, or on things never before regarded as problems; and they often realize their success in ways entirely unforeseen. What does any of this have to do with the bourgeois virtues, the Protestant ethic, or Benjamin Franklin's temperance, silence, order, resolution, and frugality? The very least one can say is that those virtues simply do not encompass all the qualities George Gilder has found in his entrepreneurs.[57]

Capitalism versus Totalitarianism

> The chief value of capitalism is not really its unequaled record of production and distribution of goods, but rather its guarantee of a private sector, a sector of society based upon property and income that is clearly distinguishable . . . from the power of the national state.[58]

Seymour Martin Lipset's point is integral to the neoconservative conception of capitalism. Believing capitalism to be a potent antidote to totalitarianism, the neoconservatives extend this argument in two directions. First, when people are concerned with profit, they will not want to divert their energy to war. This draws upon an old argument of political philosophy that holds that the best way to avoid belligerent conflict is to engage man into private pursuits that will distract him from the passions of public life.

However, most neoconservatives do not focus on this approach because they believe that the rational lures of commerce can be easily overcome by the human passions that have traditionally led men into battle. While this idea has excited many people throughout history, it has rarely fulfilled its promise. Irving Kristol characterizes it as "a dogmatic economic determinism [that] replaces a knowledge of history, political philosophy, and human nature."[59]

According to the neoconservatives, a better argument for the antitotalitarian power of capitalism is that it dissipates man's energies and allegiances. If people are concerned with their own businesses, jobs, and livelihoods, no one institution, such as the government, will be able to monopolize their attention. The diffusion of energy and money generated by a healthy free market system will create alternative centers of power to the government. As Paul Johnson notes, "Capitalism creates a multiplicity of power centers which rival the state."[60] By supporting several competing centers of power, society prohibits any one entity from acquiring the potency necessary for totalitarianism or oppression. With an infinite number of producers and consumers acting to advance their different definitions of self-interest, there is no way for an inordinate amount of power to amass in one place. The neoconservatives have stressed that this is especially important in modern times when the public sector is, for better or for worse, very large. Peter Berger explains, "The modern state has the innate tendency to project its power further and further into society, unless it meets up with institutionalized limits. Capitalism, by providing a social zone relatively independent of state control, facilitates this limit."[61]

The neoconservatives maintain that the dissipation of power generated by capitalism best suits man's imperfect nature. Capitalism does not demand a kind of individual that does not exist. As Irving Kristol points out, capitalism embodies the wisdom that "The lion shall lie down with the lamb, but not until the Second Coming."[62] Capitalist societies assume that people will be more concerned with the well-being of their families and communities than with larger social goals. If that is selfishness, so be it—the pursuit of that kind of selfishness leads to a more generous society because of the wealth it creates and the social bonds it nurtures. As Gertrude Himmelfarb writes,

> [Capitalism] takes people as they are and as they always have been, as human beings capable of being enlightened as well as selfish—enlightened precisely because they are selfish, because their "self" (properly understood, as Tocqueville would say) naturally embraces family and community, religion and tradition, interests and values.[63]

While capitalism does not demand altruistic individuals, it certainly does not deny them, either. People of extraordinary moral character can, in no small part because of the wealth created by regular people involved in the market, pursue their visions unencumbered by the need to supply a profitable good or service. No one is stopping the rare man from doing his selfless good work in a free economy. Just the same, the rare man who has little social conscience and few concerns outside himself can be domesticated by a capitalist system. While such people will not be righteous men, good citizens, or enlightened capitalists, at least they can be peaceful and even productive members of society. And, by producing a quality good or service at a low cost, they might inadvertently do some good.

Capitalism and Poverty

The neoconservatives maintain that capitalism is a moral system not only for what it prevents (totalitarianism) but for the positive virtues it inculcates. The neoconservatives disagree about whether capitalism produces or reflects morality. Irving Kristol, Paul Johnson, and Richard John Neuhaus believe that capitalism takes components of moral behavior and channels them effectively. Michael Novak and George Gilder contend that capitalism can help produce moral behavior as well as channel the morality that people bring from other sources.

Perhaps the most important moral justification of capitalism concerns how it handles the poorest citizens. As Novak has written, "A culture whose values spring from Judaism, Christianity, and a compassionate humanism cannot be satisfied unless the poor are well cared for."[64] Neoconservatives maintain that capitalism's remarkable production and efficiency serves the poor at least as well as it does the wealthy. While this is not a sufficient defense of capitalism standing alone, it is an important start. Novak asks, "If one keeps uppermost in mind the material needs of the poor, the hungry and the oppressed, rather than one's own state of feelings, one asks: What is the most effective, practical way of raising the wealth of nations?"[65] The answer, clearly to Novak, is democratic capitalism.

Because the only indispensable ingredients in capitalist success are bourgeois virtues, creativity, and hard work, the neoconservatives believe that the free market system allows everyone an opportunity to rise out of poverty. In such a system, government would play a generally passive role, ensuring that the free market can proceed to involve as many as possible in the circle of prosperity. Glazer describes a seminal moment in his intellectual development when he concluded, "It may be true that cutting fifty billion dollars from corporation income taxes may be doing more for the poor than distributing fifty billion to them."[66]

This is not just because corporate income is the ingredient necessary to produce private sector jobs to employ the poor (and everyone else)—although that is an important factor. Convinced by "the law of unintended consequences" that was so painstakingly developed in the early issues of *The Public Interest,* the neoconservatives believe that welfare programs often counter the message of the market by asserting that something can be received for nothing, thus sacrificing creativity and hard work on the altar of entitlement. The irony—and the paradox—of government programs is augmented when, as is apt to happen, government welfare programs are billed as "compassionate" in opposition to the hard-driving competitiveness of the market. Michael Novak notes,

> The man who said, "Patriotism is the last refuge of scoundrels" underestimated the possibilities of compassion. Under the beautiful intention of helping the poor, poverty is commonly made into a growth industry.[67]

Kristol agrees with Novak, and maintains that those who want to be compassionate ought to act compassionately—with their own time and money. Compassion is a trait that applies to individuals or small communities who make the decision to give significantly of themselves to understand and help others. Kristol explains,

> Compassion is authentic when it is directed at individuals. When you have compassion for an individual and really want to help him and you do something about it—that is authentic compassion. When you start organizing compassion into crusades, you get something that is not very compassionate. You tend to get a movement that really wants to push people around, remake their lives and sometimes even murder millions of people—all in the name of compassion. Compassion organized into a political movement is a very dangerous thing and, I think, a wicked thing. . . . When people start becoming bureaucrats of compassion and start making careers out of compassion—whether political, journalistic or public entertainment careers—then I must say I suspect their good faith.[68]

One of the nasty by-products of what Kristol calls "making careers out of compassion" is that a class of bureaucrats and professionals develops a vested interest in the perpetuation of poverty. First, armies of social workers, welfare bureaucrats, and other knowledge workers are employed by the government in order to deal with poverty problems. If poverty were to be eliminated, these people would be out of work. Thus, they have a professional investment in the maintenance of poverty, or at least in status quo methods of dealing with it.

Similarly, the most resonating case for socialism has been that capitalism creates a system that allows for, to paraphrase George Orwell, a fat man eating quails while children beg for bread.[69] The anticapitalist conviction would not be very effective if people are satisfied with their wealth or their potential to acquire it. This is especially so if it is clear that the source of the wealth is a free market unfettered by extensive regulation and confiscatory taxation.

Neoconservatives believe that those truly concerned with helping the poor now—as opposed to seeking a utopia in which everyone will be happy later—will want to liberate the untapped resources of creativity and ingenuity in the poor and allow them to blossom. The way to do this is by involving more people in the free market system, which rewards an infinite variety of talents, abilities, and of course, hard work—of which anyone is capable. The only other choice is creating a constituency for government programs, which do nothing for the self-esteem or long-term needs of the poor. Novak notes,

> The left sees the poor and the vulnerable as passive, awaiting the ministrations of the state. The right and the center see the poor as capable, creative, and active. The left clings to its appeals to action by the state; it becomes conservative in rhetoric, looking backward. The center and the right long for a new beginning, and sound positively radical in their demand for "civil society" rather than "state" as their main hope for the future.[70]

Most of the neoconservatives and especially Kristol have stressed the way in which the free market system has eliminated poverty, several times. Kristol and the other neoconservatives reason that the perpetuation of poverty is statistically guaranteed by the continual raising of the poverty rate. The neoconservatives maintain that if the poverty level at almost any time in our recent history were frozen, it would be clear that the poorest of our citizens have surpassed it many times over. Kristol suggests,

> Most of us would think that any society which made steady progress in improving the conditions of the poor, yet which resolutely kept denouncing itself for having failed to do so, is more than a little neurotic. Yet that is exactly the kind of society that many social critics today appear to regard as normal and desirable.[71]

To put poverty in human terms, a *First Things* editorial uses statistics from the Heritage Foundation to illustrate what is considered poverty in America.

> Thirty-eight percent of persons classified as poor own their own homes. The median value of these homes is $39,200, or 58% of the median value of all homes owned by Americans. Nearly half a million "poor" persons own homes worth over $100,000 and 36,000 "poor" persons own homes worth over $300,000. Sixty-two percent of "poor" households own a car, and 14% own two or more cars. Nearly half of all "poor" households have air conditioning, and 31% have microwave ovens. Poor people on average consume the same level of vitamins, minerals, and protein as do middle-class folk, and poor children actually eat more meat and protein than do

their middle-class peers. Poor adults are more likely to be overweight than those in the middle class.[72]

According to the neoconservatives, this gradual creeping of the poverty rate is not a statistical coincidence, but a direct consequence of principle—the principle of "the revolution of rising expectations." As Tocqueville predicted, this is a product of the modern state where the philosophy of egalitarianism leads people to constantly want more and more. From the early 1970s onward, the neoconservatives regarded this as a staple of American society. Kristol observes,

> To see something on television is to feel entitled to it; to be promised something by a politician is to feel immediately deprived of it. What is called "the revolution of rising expectations" has reached such grotesque dimensions that men take it as an insult when they are asked to be reasonable in their desires and demands.[73]

This revolution of rising expectations—the natural enemy of stability—is especially problematic in the United States because Americans often turn to the government to fulfill these expectations. The idea that people "deserve" certain things often does not accompany the proposition that they should work to receive them; the rights frequently overwhelm responsibility. And this makes things very difficult for a government attempting to prudently placate conflicting groups, foster economic growth, maintain fiscal responsibility, and keep people happy until the next election.

Capitalism and Virtue

The most important way in which capitalism inculcates morality is through its reliance on traditional bourgeois virtues. These values—diligence, humility, probity, punctuality, temperance, industry, frugality—are regarded by neoconservatives as essential components of a free, democratic, and capitalist society. An individual without these qualities will not have the discipline and the wherewithal to produce a quality good at a low price. Sacrificing for uncertain future gain, cooperation, attentiveness and kindness to customers and clients, and hours of tedious and unrewarded work are essential for prosperity in a capitalist system. Without a foundation of bourgeois virtues—whether they stem from a desire to be good or a realization that they are necessary to make money—capitalism will fail. Irving Kristol and Paul Weaver declare,

> The rules only work when the kinds of people to whom they apply want to see them work. A free market economy will not survive unless people are willing to respect the law of contract; if everyone tries to cheat, and if all contracts have to be enforced by the courts and the police, the system will collapse.[74]

Moreover, it is the public display of these values in the entrepreneur that morally legitimates capitalism to ordinary Americans by providing capitalism with a visible moral framework all can identify and admire. When people see capitalism reflecting the virtues they recognize to be morally worthy as opposed to just functionally efficient, they will be less prone to be tempted by socialism. In a 1974 *Wall Street Journal* column, Kristol elaborated on the praise he bestowed upon Horatio Alger in a 1957 *Commentary* essay, holding Alger's novels the model for a bourgeois capitalist society deserving of the respect and support of the citizenry.[75]

The neoconservatives maintain that capitalism elicits another important moral quality that is not generally included in a traditional list of bourgeois virtues, creativity. In *The Catholic Ethic and the Spirit of Capitalism*, Novak concluded, "The true moral strength of capitalism, however, lies in its promotion of human creativity."[76] Novak and the other neoconservatives have stressed that the entrepreneur must have a broad imagination that can conceive of numerous possibilities that challenge boundaries and expand new horizons. Herein lies a major component of the morality of capitalism. In a 1989 *Commentary* essay, Novak explained that the creativity inherent in capitalist success comes not only in the burst of an idea, but in the ability to put in long hours to translate that idea into a marketable product.

Capitalism, Democracy, and Freedom

Just as the neoconservatives claim that capitalism promotes morality through the reinforcement of traditional values, they believe that the free market is a prerequisite for political freedom. The presence of a free market is a necessary prerequisite for, though not a guarantee of, political democracy.[77] In 1978, Kristol offered proof.

> Never in human history has one seen a society of political liberty that was not based on a free economic system—i.e., a system based on private property, where normal economic activity consisted of commercial transactions between consenting adults. Never, never, never. No exceptions.[78]

Though capitalism can exist without political freedom, the neoconservatives maintain that they are, in the end, inextricably linked. How so? First, capitalism creates a middle class. In time, the opportunities opened to the middle class by mass education, modern communication, and a greater sense of social equality will lead people to demand political democracy. Middle-class people will not want to live under an aristocratic or authoritarian regime that denies the personal freedom that democracies allow; a prosperous people will usually demand political freedom. Moreover, as Michael Novak points out, only the political liberty engendered by democracy can guarantee the social stability necessary for the perpetuation for capitalism.[79]

The Cultural Contradictions of Capitalism

Just as capitalism can have positive cultural ramifications, such as in perpetuating democracy, neoconservatives contend that it can also breed internal contradictions. Perhaps the most obvious example of this is hard work. The story of an indolent son running his father's business into the ground is a common story because the corrupting influence of wealth is so familiar. According to the neoconservatives, the degeneracy bred by affluence in this story can be applied to wealthy societies as well as wealthy individuals. Thus, it is the responsibility—indeed, the requirement—

for a democratic state and a healthy culture to regulate or censure some of the more unfortunate cultural outgrowths of capitalism. These could include pornography, prostitution, gangsta rap music, and other potential economic goods that often serve to undermine the bourgeois values upon which capitalism relies. While many would ask what something like music has to do with the free market economy, the neoconservatives respond: a lot.[80] Capitalism depends on an ethic of sobriety, self-restraint, diligence—in short, the bourgeois virtues. Without a traditional culture sustaining these values, capitalism cannot survive in the long term. Capitalism is an integral part of a diverse social system with many components and as many ethical supports, which it depends on for its lifeblood.

Traditional human failings and temptations exist in capitalist societies as in any other, and the wealth generated by the free market allows people more time and energy to practice these vices. In premodern days, even people who might have been so inclined did not have the luxury to experiment with dramatically untraditional lifestyles or forms of amusement. When the cows had to be milked, one had to be up early to milk them. This was not so with late capitalism; the free market liberated people from the social and behavioral restraints imposed by the traditional economy.[81] Moreover, it provided the money, leisure time, and goods that allowed people to partake in what have long been regarded as deviant behaviors. The freedom that is such a wonderful outgrowth of capitalism spawns a special responsibility to steer that freedom toward virtue and away from vice. George Gilder remarked,

> The value of a society's goods always derives from the values of its people. A democratic society that is unwilling to bar *Hustler* from public newsstands or ban billboards from beautiful views cannot justly blame capitalism for these offenses. It is up to the political, judicial, and religious institutions of the society, not other businesses, to eliminate such opportunities for ugly profit.[82]

As Gilder suggests, the neoconservatives are explicit that their celebration of choice in the market system does not imply that all choices are equal or acceptable. While it may be good to be able to choose between a wide selection of porcelain or parrots, this same paradigm should not extend to prostitutes. In his 1971 *New York Times Magazine* essay, "Pornography, Obscenity and the Case for Censorship," Irving Kristol argues that pornography should be criminalized because it rends the moral fabric of society upon which both capitalism and political democracy depend. Just as art can be spiritually uplifting, it can be morally degenerate—and no democratic society concerned with its longevity can be blind to that. Not only can a liberal be for censorship, Kristol claims, but "unless one assumes that being a liberal must mean being indifferent to the quality of American life, then the answer has to be yes, a liberal can be for censorship—but he ought to favor a liberal kind of censorship."[83] The neoconservatives regard culture as more important than both politics and economics, for the latter two must exist in an environment conditioned by culture.

That is why such respect is accorded Daniel Bell's theory of the cultural contradictions of capitalism, even among neoconservatives who disagree with it. According to this theory, the innovation and attentiveness to tastes and fads in the economic sphere leads to a free market in morals as well. Consequently, the restraints of tradition, piety, custom, and class are hit hard as advertisers exhort consumers, in the words of a 1995 Nike commercial, to "jump up and down and scream until we get it." All of the neoconservatives are concerned with the implications of this argument, though several—especially Novak and Gilder—believe that the positive cultural aspects of capitalism largely domesticate or eliminate it.

After Bell, Kristol is the neoconservative whose writings indicate the most concern with the cultural contradictions of capitalism. Kristol has written that capitalism can feed a revolution in rising expectations, where the boon in material goods will lead people to want more and more. In this chase to acquire, the fundamental values of free enterprise—the values of Horatio Alger—may be sacrificed as people use their newly found freedom to "explore" different lifestyles and modes of behavior which were simply unaffordable in less wealthy times. The upshot:

> [As] societies become more affluent as a result of adhering to Smithian economics, they seem to breed all sorts of new social pathologies and dis-

> contents, so that the Smithian conception of the best economy no longer seems to have any connection, in the minds of the citizenry, with the best polity. Crime and all kinds of delinquency increase with increasing prosperity. Alcoholism and drug addiction also increase. Civic-mindedness and public-spiritedness are corroded by cynicism. . . . The emphasis is placed on the pleasures of consumption rather than on the virtues of work. The ability to defer gratification . . . is scorned; "fly now, pay later," becomes, not merely an advertising slogan, but also a popular philosophy of life.[84]

Kristol maintains that the same effect could take place in the polity. The bounty and the opportunities produced by capitalism erode the crucial conservative sensibility of satisfaction. As a result, people demand more and more—fueling the revolution of rising expectations. To fulfill these expectations, they often look to the government. The demands on the government may be virtually unlimited, but this is of no concern to a people spoiled by the cultural ramifications of capitalism unmanned by a virtuous citizenry. Aaron Wildavsky makes this point in his seminal 1973 *Commentary* essay, "Government and the People."[85] He writes that the perceived inability of government to solve social problems is not, as commonly claimed, a function of incompetence, but rather of unrealistic expectations. No government could possibly solve the problems Americans expect theirs to solve, and yet Americans become upset when the government fails to do so. Because Americans are fraught with a sense of continually rising expectations, we are not chastened by these failures; instead, we ask government to do more as we trust it less.

While Daniel Bell coined the term "cultural contradictions of capitalism," and Irving Kristol helped to develop it, its true genesis lay in Joseph Schumpeter's admonitions of the "creative destruction" of capitalism. Karl Marx said that capitalism would be destroyed by its failures. Schumpeter agreed that capitalism would be destroyed, but said that it would be done in by its successes. The constant processes of destruction and construction that capitalism brings would eventually attack the free market system itself.

> Capitalism creates a critical frame of mind which, after having destroyed the moral authority of so many other institutions, in the end turns against its own; the bourgeois finds to his amazement that the rationalist attitude

> does not stop at the credentials of kings and popes but goes on to attack private property and the whole scheme of bourgeois values.[86]

Schumpeter claims that intellectuals will be the ushers of the creative destruction of capitalism. He maintains that capitalism has generated the wealth to fund a system of higher education that includes more people than ever before. This can be dangerous; college graduates will not consider jobs that entail manual labor and, being trained to do nothing in particular, may not be suited for professional work, either. Schumpeter concludes that many of these outcasts from the capitalist system will become intellectuals—a vocation that requires some brains but no practical skills. The intellectual, resentful of the fact that capitalism does not reward his talents, will thus have a very good reason to attempt to destroy capitalism.

Realizing that the free market cannot be destroyed from the ivory tower, the intellectual will descend to work among ordinary people. However, ordinary people, whom Schumpeter refers to as "labor," do not necessarily have anything against capitalism and may very well want nothing to do with the intellectuals, whose craft they will not necessarily appreciate. As a result, the intellectuals must take advantage of their special skill—the crafting of words and phrases—to convince labor to listen to them. Consequently,

> Having no genuine authority and feeling always in danger of being unceremoniously told to mind his own business, [the intellectual] must flatter, promise and incite, nurse left wings and scowling minorities, sponsor doubtful or submarginal cases, appeal to fringe ends, profess himself ready to obey. . . .[87]

The New Class

Schumpeter's discussion of intellectuals resonates for the neoconservatives, and they constructed many of their arguments regarding the cultural contradictions of capitalism around his ideas. Like Schumpeter, the neoconservatives believe that resentful intellectuals are the driving force behind the anticapitalist sentiment in America—especially concerning his description of the role of anticapitalist intellectuals in politics. The neoconservatives referred to these intellectuals as "the new class," borrowing a term from the Yugoslavian writer Milovan Djilas to describe Communist elites in Eastern Europe. Irving Kristol had been writing about the new class—before it was called that—as early as 1963.

> The liberal community—i.e., the teachers, the journalists, the civil servants, the trade unionists, the leaders of minority groups, etc.—envisages the welfare state as the one institution through which it can exercise a power and authority over the nation's affairs which it does not otherwise possess.[88]

Like Schumpeter before them, the neoconservatives write that "the new class" is a unique product of capitalist wealth. Paradoxically, capitalism has generated the resources to employ a host of intellectuals in universities and government agencies whose calling is not only to criticize capitalism but to work actively against it from within government. The new class rose to the pinnacle of its power in the days of the Great Society as the economy blossomed, generating the wealth needed for a large public sector. Though the new class speaks of environmentalism or public health or city planning, the neoconservatives warn that their true motivations are simple to discern. As Kristol wrote in 1975,

> they are acting upon a hidden agenda: to propel the nation from that modified version of capitalism we call "the welfare state" toward an economic system so stringently regulated in detail as to fulfill many of the traditional anti-capitalist aspirations of the left.[89]

As Kristol suggests, the political philosophy of the new class is anticapitalist meliorism. Better educated than most, the members of the new class are disgusted by the chaotic and uncontrollable nature of capitalism. David Bazelon, one of the first American intellectuals to address the new class, noted, "it strikes me as distinctly possible that *all* the education of all the members of the New Class has a common denominator—namely, to plan something."[90]

When considering the neoconservative discussion of the new class, it cannot be stressed enough that the idea of the new class applies strictly to anticapitalist intellectuals or bureaucrats. Some of the harshest criticism directed against neoconservatives comes from those who consider the neoconservative condemnation of the new class hypocritical. In an essay in *The New York Review of Books* in 1979, the distinguished liberal thinker Michael Walzer refers to the "virtually incoherent [neoconservative] doctrine of the 'new class.' "[91] Gary Dorrien, author of *The Neoconservative Mind: Politics, Culture and the War of Ideology*, writes of Kristol, "The supreme irony of his attacks on the self-promoting opportunism of the New Class intellectuals was that they were most convincing as descriptions of the career he knew best."[92]

Unless one appreciates that the term new class refers to a politically specific group of thinkers and bureaucrats, the concept of the new class might be, as Walzer charges, virtually incoherent. Obviously, the neoconservatives did not want to indict themselves; nor does consistency demand that they must. They have merely criticized a group that accepted positions and power generated by the capitalist system and used their leverage to question the legitimacy of the system itself. While some neoconservatives hold similar jobs as the new class, they hold different ideas—and therein lies the crucial difference.

Case in point: the philosophical case against government regulation that is so prevalent today is evident in neoconservative writings on the new class starting in the 1970s. They noted early on that many such government initiatives stemmed from new class bureaucrats intent on radically transforming capitalism. In a 1979 essay, *Wall Street Journal* editor Robert Bartley cites the example of the Occupational Safety and Health Administration (OSHA).

> Founded in 1971, OSHA promptly set about decreeing the proper heights of fire extinguishers, worrying about the placement of exit signs, requiring coat hooks in toilet stalls, and issuing booklets warning farmers that manure is slippery and may cause falls.[93]

In a 1974 piece entitled "The Environmental Crusade," Kristol illustrates the anticapitalist ethos of the new class with the example of the Environmental Protection Agency (EPA) closing down a New York City tenement for "noise pollution." Kristol exclaims,

"Noise pollution in a New York slum! People are being mugged right and left, children are being bitten by rats, junkies are ripping out the plumbing of decaying tenements—and the EPA is worried about noise pollution!"[94]

This essay from the 1970s was prescient in another respect; it provides a window on the neoconservative perception of the environmental movement which grew rapidly in the 1970s and 1980s. As "The Environmental Crusade" suggests, neoconservatives regard environmentalism as the socialism of post-Communist left-wing intellectuals. Still disgusted with capitalism but lacking socialism as a viable alternative, the left turned to environmentalism which, through language and goals that sound unarguably laudable, damages capitalism as much as excessive taxation. In 1991, Michael Novak wrote, "One can predict with some certainty that environmentalism is likely to replace Marxism as the main carrier of gnosticism (and anti-capitalism) in the near future."[95] A year before, Richard John Neuhaus explained that Novak's prudence was unnecessary. "After the demise of Marxism as an ideological force, and the severe body blows dealt to schemes of socialist 'third ways' propounded by 'prophetic' religion, the banner of choice is currently THE ENVIRONMENT."[96] Like socialism, environmentalism embodied not only anticapitalism but a quasi-religious commitment. In 1970, Norman Podhoretz characterized the first celebration of Earth Day as pagan.[97] The neoconservatives considered environmentalism an especially potent adversary, considering that it would have an easy time winning the battle of rhetoric, the most important in politics. While few would rally to the cause of "workers of the world, unite!" not many would object to "save the earth!" and no one would object to clean water for children.

Though the neoconservative critique of the new class was developed in the 1970s, Gertrude Himmelfarb writes in 1995 that it is as relevant as ever—even if the appellation "new" should now be dropped. The new class is, she maintains, "the mirror image of the underclass." Both—for different reasons and with different consequences—reject the bourgeois virtues and the Puritan ethic that is accepted by the working and middle classes.[98]

Why Leave Romance to the Socialists?

While the neoconservatives view capitalism as a morally enriching and extraordinarily productive system, they do not contend that capitalists always live up to the ideals of capitalism. Within neoconservatism exists a diversity of viewpoints about which types of capitalism should be considered praiseworthy. Irving Kristol's views are the most complex, but they stress the importance of bourgeois morality and the worldly asceticism of Max Weber's *The Protestant Ethic and the Spirit of Capitalism* as the backbone of free enterprise. Jude Wanniski refers to big business with no more respect than big government. "My interest is in entrepreneurial capitalism, the unborn business. Even the small businesses have lobbyists."[99] Michael Novak, on the other hand, has written theologies of corporations, which he considers to be invaluable mediating structures.

Richard John Neuhaus does not believe that capitalism is worthy of theologizing; he asserts that the free market can spawn as many vices as it can virtues. He maintains that it is crucially important to define specifically what is meant by capitalism before analyzing it because capitalism can take any number of forms.

> Michael [Novak] so richly and with such nuance construes what he means by capitalism in a moral, cultural, virtue oriented capitalism. Then you have to say, why yes, if that's what you mean by capitalism, then it is this thing to make a religious or at least quasi-religious commitment to. But if by capitalism one simply means exchanges between consenting adults, why that's as riddled with moral ambiguity as anything else.[100]

Responding to this criticism, Novak cites the example of Poland.

> I believe that Father Neuhaus, Paul Johnson and Peter Berger . . . tend to neglect that people have to practice capitalism with a moral character to make this modern version of capitalism take off. Look at Poland and Russia today. You can have markets, you can have private property, you can have exchange, but will you get dynamic entrepreneurship? So the question is, when Poland has private property and markets—what's going to happen? Are Poles so inured to socialism that they're just going to sit there and wait for the state to do something else? . . . There were 500,000 businesses

> formed in the first year, and now Poland is buzzing with activity. . . . I don't think it is romantic to call attention to it. I think you need a little romance to celebrate these businesses, because that's what leads people to aspire to them. Why should we leave romance to the socialists?[101]

The neoconservatives have not been content to stand aside while they saw capitalism heading down a path of self-destruction. But, in the politically polarized atmosphere of modern America, this happens often. Neoconservatives consider the first fault of capitalists to be their reluctance to defend themselves. Just as the neoconservatives excoriated liberals for failing to defend liberalism, they have excoriated capitalists for failing to defend capitalism.

The most revealing example of this concerns the relationship between capitalists and Communism. The fear among neoconservatives was, to paraphrase George Will, that capitalists love commerce more than they loathe Communism. When the choice is between making money or taking a stand against Communists, many businessmen choose the former. The tendency of business to discard ideology when it was profitable to do so and agree to sell critical goods to the Soviets constituted a major problem for the neoconservatives.

Neoconservatives have pointed out that the willingness of businessmen to surrender ideology for profit extended beyond Communism and into some purely economic issues, like free trade. *Commentary* articles throughout the 1970s and 1980s maintained that while businessmen are free traders in theory, they would abandon this belief when it came to protecting their own industry or receiving a government handout. Penn Kemble, a neoconservative with a special interest in human rights, explores these themes in *Commentary*.

> A capitalist is for the free market up to a point—the point at which he discovers some method for bringing the market under control in order to enhance his own position. The same general rule applies to his concern for the situation of the "free world." He may be a staunch cold warrior, but when his company is offered a grain-export contract, a Siberian natural-gas concession, or a bid on its new model computer, in all likelihood he will experience a "conceptual break-through." Suddenly he will realize that trade is the cornerstone of peace, and that support for Soviet dissidents and

a concern for our military "sufficiency" cannot be allowed to interfere with the higher purposes of commerce.[102]

A similar neoconservative criticism of capitalists has been the willingness of businessmen to seek and take advantage of government support, through anything from tariffs to direct subsidies, whenever possible. As James Q. Wilson concedes,

> I don't feel very comfortable before business audiences because I know that in many ways they are part of the problem. Given a large government they will attempt to seize control of some of its parts to use for their own advantage.[103]

Just as businessmen are willing to aid public sector anti capitalists, they see no problem with buttressing the cultural enemies of the free market. Kristol explains,

> Large corporations today happily publish books and magazines, or press and sell records, or make and distribute movies, or sponsor television shows which celebrate pornography, denounce the institution of the family, revile the "ethics of acquisitiveness," justify civil insurrection and generally argue in favor of the expropriation of private industry and the "liquidation" of private industrialists. . . . Our capitalists promote the ethos of the New Left for only one reason: they cannot think of any reason why they should not.[104]

The neoconservatives set out to show the capitalists why they should not. During the late 1970s, Michael Novak, Irving Kristol, Robert Goldwin, and Ben Wattenberg conducted seminars at the American Enterprise Institute to discuss the relationships between ideas and economics with corporate executives. The neoconservatives wanted to teach businessmen that capitalism was a precarious economic system that could collapse under ideological pressure unless defended effectively. It was no longer acceptable, Robert Bartley wrote, for Macy's to consider its primary enemy Gimbels; the new class was the enemy. Regulation of Gimbels does not help Macy's—it hurts the capitalist system upon which both depend.[105] Businessmen must, Norman Podhoretz exhorted, show the confidence in their calling that General Motors CEO Charles Wilson did when appointed secretary of the treasury by

President Eisenhower—Wilson said that what is good for General Motors is good for America.[106] Even if businessmen believe in the morality of their work and the virtue of capitalism, it does not necessarily come through. Irving Kristol notes, "Whatever they [businessmen] think, they don't think it very deeply."[107] The neoconservatives were determined to deepen that thought.

Irving Kristol took the lead. Serving as an ombudsman between the conservative intellectual and corporate communities, Kristol tried to show the two groups that they had common goals and interests that could be best served through a close relationship with each group doing what it does best. The intellectuals could serve as ideological soldiers for capitalism, so long as businessmen provided the requisite financial weaponry. Kristol did not intend to teach the corporate community to fight the counterculture; he simply provided businessmen with directions on where to find people who could fight its intellectual battles.

On the op-ed page of the *Wall Street Journal* where he wrote every month, Kristol has tirelessly explained that businessmen and intellectuals operate from two different conceptual frameworks. Kristol's major theme has been that that the left "thinks politically," and businessmen "think economically." Businessmen operate from a framework of profits and losses, employment, quarter earnings, and—on a more theoretical level—the best way to provide goods and services for all citizens. Unable to identify with those who oppose what Kristol has called "a liberal civilization which is given shape through the interaction of a countless sum of individual preferences,"[108] businessmen constantly lost intellectual battles with the New Left.

Kristol's criticism extends well beyond the large corporation and impugns ordinary Americans for failing to appreciate the destructiveness of the New Left and in turn for helping it to prosper. Sometimes, this takes the form of selling to the adversary culture; other times, it is more subtle. Kristol asks,

> How many businessmen walked out indignantly from a movie like *The Graduate*, which displayed them (and their wives) as hollow men and women, worthy of nothing but contempt? Not many, I would think. The

> capacity for indignation withers along with self-respect. How many businessmen refuse, as a matter of honor and of principle, to advertise in a publication such as *The Rolling Stone* or even *Playboy,* publications which make a mockery of their industry, their integrity, their fidelity, the very quality of their lives? The question answers itself.[109]

Novak extends this point to television shows, maintaining that "the villain in virtually every television plot is a businessman."[110] Businessmen are portrayed as greedy and selfish, and often downright sleazy and corrupt. But how often do companies refuse to advertise on anticapitalist television programs?

Capitalists further help the adversary culture directly through their philanthropy projects. Not "thinking politically," businessmen give money to cultural institutions—especially universities and foundations that promulgate anticapitalist ideas. In the name of "academic freedom," university presidents have often acted as through they have a right to corporate money, regardless of what they do with it. The neoconservatives have argued that those who donate money to cultural institutions ought to be concerned with how the money is spent, and without apology. Kristol notes, "that's the way it's supposed to be in a free society where philanthropy is just as free as speech."[111] If businessmen have trouble identifying which institutions are hostile to their way of life and which are supportive, Kristol maintains in another article, they should know what to do.

> "How can we identify such people, and discriminate intelligently among them?" corporate executives always inquire plaintively. Well, if you decide to go exploring for oil, you find a competent geologist. Similarly, if you wish to make a productive investment in the intellectual and education worlds, you find competent intellectuals and scholars. . . .

Just as "thinking politically" requires that businesses contribute to a culture more accepting of the free market, it requires corporations to make themselves forthrightly worthy of this support. When Kristol articulated this view in the mid-1970s, what he called "certain high-minded people" interpreted this to mean that corporations should give more to charities and cultural institutions.[112] Kristol emphatically denied this, maintaining that corporate philanthropy is often part of the problem; corporations have enough trouble doing what they are supposed to do—supplying quality goods at competitive prices. They need not assume added responsibilities.

According to Kristol, corporations should not try to solve social problems directly, but should instead concentrate on working to create a climate friendly to capitalism itself. Corporations should stress that their daily activity and functioning is morally beneficial and socially worthwhile. To do this, it is essential for companies to provide convincing reasons why their enterprise is morally worthy. Buying and selling are amoral acts considered in isolation, and no human system—especially an economic system—can sustain itself without a moral foundation. This is especially so with modern capitalism, whose prosaic and rationalistic accomplishments have to contend with the powerful themes of equality, fairness, and community that emanate from the left.

Thus Kristol maintains that corporations must return to the ethos of Horatio Alger's characters, who demonstrated for all to see that profits—especially large profits—are the product of self-evidently virtuous living. Not all capitalist acts are created equal, but unless businessmen are vigilant, the left will link bourgeois entrepreneurs with speculators and hard-earned purchases with installment buying.[113] Because of the way businessmen have presented themselves—or have not presented themselves—it is simple for the left to define capitalists. Kristol holds,

> Not only don't we know who the chairman of General Motors is; we know so little about the kind of person who holds such a position that we haven't the faintest idea as to whether or not we want our children to grow up like him. Horatio Alger, writing in the era of pre-corporate capitalism, had no such problems. And there is something decidedly odd about a society in which a whole class of Very Important People is not automatically held up as one possible model of emulation for the young, and cannot be so held up because they are, as persons, close to invisible.[114]

Yet corporate executives are very powerful people in a crucial sector of America society, who, because of who they are, cannot afford to remain anonymous. While they should not be held accountable in the same way as politicians, they are by no means free to discard public opinion. In a democratic age of large government and uncontrolled regulation, everyone must work within the public interest, and do so forthrightly.

During the oil shock in the 1970s, Kristol used oil companies as an example of how free market ideology suffers a blow when companies operate without concern for the public interest—or even the perception of acting in the public interest. While the oil shock forced numerous Americans to alter significantly their lifestyles, oil companies amassed record profits. Naturally, profiting from hardship is not conducive to attracting public support. Kristol suggests that if the companies were "thinking politically," they might have cut oil prices to obtain only a 15 or 20 percent increase in profits or declared that they would not increase dividends or executive salaries. They should certainly have done something to appear as though they share a common fate with ordinary Americans and are working to solve a common problem. However, the companies, oblivious to or unconcerned with the cultural ramifications of profiting from the oil crisis, did nothing—they did not even account for inflation when calculating their massive profits. And these companies had no coherent response to the criticism that they were making money off the suffering of everyone else.[115] Working in the public interest? The businessmen failed to show that they were not working against it.

Neither Serfdom nor Utopia: Neoconservatives and the Welfare State

While the neoconservatives contend that a free market is essential to political freedom, they do not believe there is a contradiction between vibrant capitalism and a welfare state. First, neoconservatives accept the traditional conservative arguments of Metternich and Disraeli that a welfare state could serve as a buttress against the painful dislocations generated by capitalism. With a safety net or trampoline in place, the false security of socialism would be less tempting. This notion is not questioned in neoconservatism, as it is by libertarians and, to a lesser extent, *National Review* conservatives. As Gertrude Himmelfarb says, "We are children of the Depression, and are committed to the New Deal kind of welfare state—by present terms, a very minimal welfare state. Nevertheless, Social Security is something we regard as a very good thing."[116]

Second, neoconservatives realize that a welfare state is here to stay, for better or for worse. Neoconservatives maintain that conservative opponents of a welfare state ought to realize that there is absolutely no way their utopia will be enacted. Neoconservatives are impatient with libertarian arguments to eliminate Social Security or the income tax or to privatize sidewalks. As Kristol writes,

> There is no more chance today of returning to a society of "free enterprise" and enfeebled government than there was, in the 16th century, of returning to a Rome-centered Christendom.[117]

Concerning the welfare state, Kristol has written, conservatives have two choices. They can put forth their vision for a limited, energetic public sector or they can dream of laissez-faire utopias while the left creates a massive welfare state.[118] For several decades, Kristol has gradually constructed a vision (not a program) for a conservative welfare state. Kristol believes that the primary component of a conservative welfare state is insurance against the most drastic vicissitudes of modern life, such as medical catastrophes, natural disasters, unemployment, poverty among the elderly, and so forth. Government welfare policies should be broadly based, excluding no one. Welfare programs should not be directed at one particular group, such as the poor. Because there is no objective—or even close to objective—way of determining who is poor and who is not, the classification "needy" is meaningless and only alienates those who are designated as such. Instead, government programs should model themselves after public education and Social Security: they are open to all citizens of every socioeconomic group. Such a system would avoid enforcing the pathologies of the current welfare system because destructive behavior—such as teenage pregnancy—would no longer be subsidized.

Michael Novak, writing in *Crisis*, articulates the principles that would guide a neoconservative welfare state: "use state resources only indirectly; strengthen civil society; and keep natural, organic human institutions (especially the family) as vital and active as possible."[119] Along these lines, Kristol proposes that the government permit people to tax-deduct their medical insurance and be allowed to make additional tax-free contributions to Social Security and pension funds. Such policies would generate public support while limiting bureaucracy, maximizing individual autonomy, and serving the larger public goal of retirement security.[120]

In order for a government program to work, the individual being helped must be responsible, ambitious, directed, and motivated. Government programs can only be successful if they supply the means for an individual to reach an end that he desires and is willing to work toward. They can work very well when they remove obstacles or create opportunities for individuals to flourish in the free market. And they must deal with man as the complex, imperfect animal he is. As Kristol wrote in 1978, "What we call the 'neoconservative' impulse today . . . is basically a disillusionment with, and disengagement from, the strategy of environmental reform."[121]

Kristol writes that the government program which best illustrates these principles is night school (which, tellingly, does not have to be, and often is not, a government program). Night schools can be used by anybody, but are more likely to be frequented by aspiring blue-collar workers than by Wall Street lawyers. They attract people who are hard working, willing to sacrifice for future gain, and actively seek to help themselves. If people drop out, that is too bad, but it does not generate any negative unintended consequences like illegitimacy or drug abuse.[122]

Neoconservatives and Libertarians

By telling the Republican Party to accept a welfare state and work to shape it along conservative lines, Kristol, Novak, and other neoconservatives not only leave behind Republicans, but other conservative intellectuals as well. The one remaining significant source of ideological disagreement between the neoconservatives and the *National Review* conservatives concerns the welfare state. While the neoconservatives advocate a limited and conservative welfare state, *National Review* conservatives generally stick to the same arguments they have had since the New Deal. Buckley says,

> We accept [the welfare state] not because we approve of it. We accept it because it is simply apparently immutable. If tomorrow we could rewrite the Social Security Law, for instance, we most certainly would. And, in my judgment, it would be a better law. And, by the way, I am not a bit sure that Irving Kristol would agree with the reforms we would advocate.[123]

Neoconservatives regard the libertarian philosophy of economic determinism as being naively oblivious of the central issue of culture. Libertarians often concede that they are economic determinists; Jude Wanniski, for instance, maintains that he is still a Marxist in the sense that he is still an economic determinist.[124] Unlike Wanniski, the neoconservatives maintain that the free market is only one part of the equation of a just society, and that culture is far more important. Novak writes,

> The typical mistake of classic thinkers on this subject [economics] is to have laid too small a foundation to support the lived world of a democratic capitalist society as we have experienced it. They have too chastely considered the economic system in abstraction from the real world, in which the political system and the moral-cultural system also shape the texture of daily life.[125]

As Novak suggests, the neoconservatives divide society into three related parts: the economic sector, the political sector, and the moral/cultural sector. They believe that all sectors have to reinforce each other through the pursuit of the same goals and must be informed by the same values. The neoconservatives consider it dangerous to give too much emphasis to the political sector, as collectivists do; too much emphasis to the moral/cultural sector as the Old Right and New Left do; or too much power to the economic sector, as libertarians do. A system like capitalism, which is inherently uninspiring, is especially dependent on outside virtues to provide moral sustenance. Novak explains,

> Capitalist systems also have deep roots in specific moral-cultural soils, which supported moral and intellectual virtues, indispensable to their

growth. Capitalism historically embedded in the democratic republic and simulated by Jewish-Christian-humanistic energies is a far richer and more complex social reality than any mere dictionary definition suggests.[126]

While capitalism allows for great amounts of leisure time and freedom, what people do in that time and with that freedom is crucial. The fact that such decisions are left to individual discretion and that an individual generally has the freedom to be wrong should not detract from the grave moral consequences of being wrong. The choices people make shed light on how people view themselves, their place in the world, and what kind of society, government, or economy they desire. The neoconservatives maintain that the indispensable source of sustenance in a free market economy is religion, because it provides meaning to otherwise empty lives and answers to the ultimate questions that economics does not address.

While the neoconservatives had fought their battles against the left, whom they perceived to be substituting causes like environmentalism, consumerism, feminism, and socialism for Judeo-Christianity, neoconservatives have had to wage a similar war with certain elements on the right. Just as the neoconservatives told the left that capitalism is essential to freedom and economic and moral prosperity, they told the libertarian right that a culture grounded in Judeo-Christian values is essential for the healthy functioning of a free market.

Irving Kristol has written that Adam Smith had two intellectual offspring—bourgeois capitalists and libertarians. While the bourgeois capitalist model is embodied in Horatio Alger, the libertarian perspective is summarized by the subtitle of an eighteenth-century book by Bernard de Mandeville, *Fable of the Bees: Private Vices, Publick Benefits*. Whereas both the bourgeois and the libertarian philosophies inculcate the belief that an economic system should be driven by self-interest rather than a priori conceptions of the good life, libertarians take the idea of self-interest to an extreme. While bourgeois capitalists believe that self-interest has a role in the economic realm, libertarians contend that the sum total of everyone's individual pursuit of self-interest will lead to the common good. While the bourgeois capitalist needs to supplant the pursuit of self-interest with religion-based morality in the private realm, the libertarian has no such requirement. George Will deftly captures the libertarian view as "the Cuisinart theory of justice."[127]

Irving Kristol regards libertarians in Niebuhrian terms. Kristol believes that the libertarian conception of vice not only is nihilistic, but indicates a dangerously sanguine attitude toward the potential destructiveness of the dark side of humanity. Children of the light themselves, libertarians have a remarkably naive view of the children of darkness. Kristol writes that libertarians,

> simply [have] too limited an imagination when it came to vice. It [what Kristol called the "secular, 'libertarian' tradition of capitalism"] never really could believe that self-destructive nihilism was an authentic and permanent possibility that any society had to guard against. It could refute Marx effectively, but it never thought it would be called upon to refute the Marquis de Sade and Nietzche. It . . . could not demonstrate that . . . our New Left was wrong. It was, in its own negligent way, very much a bourgeois tradition in that, while ignoring the bourgeois virtues, it could summon openly a bourgeois version of vice.[128]

Kristol has maintained that libertarians cannot effectively challenge anticapitalists because libertarians have nothing with which to legitimate their support for the free market. There is no transcendent vision of justice upon which libertarian philosophy depends. Kristol suggests that the libertarian conception of society is the moral equivalent of paganism—instead of using economics as a means to a larger conception of justice, libertarians see nothing more important than the goods and services produced by capitalism.[129]

According to Kristol and other neoconservatives, the laissez-faire philosophy of the libertarians is most destructive when applied to the culture. Kristol maintains that a sharp distinction must be made between "a *capitalist, republican community* with shared values and a quite unambiguous claim to the title of a just order" and "a *free, democratic society* where the will to success and privilege was severed from its moral moorings."[130] The first society can last; the second will perish.

Neoconservatives and the Republican Party

While most neoconservatives voted for Ronald Reagan and many worked for him, most did not become Republicans. Some of their reasons for remaining in the Democratic Party are principled, others are idiosyncratic. For some, like Martin Peretz, registering Republican was not spiritually possible, let alone politically feasible. "I find it hard to vote Republican. The Psalmist says, 'if I pull the Republican lever, let my right hand wither.' And worse, 'Let my tongue cleave to the roof of my mouth.' "[131] Peretz expanded upon this sentiment in a 1994 interview. "There is a big social gulch between the current Republican Party and Jews and intellectuals. The Republican party is a pretty vulgar configuration."[132]

Regardless of party affiliation, most neoconservatives voted for Ronald Reagan twice and for George Bush in 1988. Many neoconservatives, including Joshua Muravchik, Aaron Wildavsky, Ben Wattenberg, Richard Schifter, Martin Peretz, Penn Kemble, and Peter Rosenblatt, endorsed Bill Clinton in 1992 because of President Bush's ambivalence toward Israel and the lack of leadership that he provided on domestic issues. In a statement emblematic of the neoconservative distress with Bush, Michael Novak writes,

> He [Bush] tried to govern without providing meaning. He was a good man and even exhibited, in the Gulf War preeminently, touches of greatness. But he eschewed meaning. He was averse to vision and people of vision—and ultimately, this was the flaw that did him in. He misunderstood the presidential office.[133]

Nevertheless, most of the neoconservatives voted for Bush begrudgingly. This leads to an inevitable question: why have the neoconservatives not joined the Republican Party? Certainly, the Republican Party is more receptive to their ideas. Many neoconservatives—William Kristol, William Bennett, Chester Finn, Richard Pipes, Lynne Cheney, Elliott Abrams, and others—served in high positions in the Reagan and Bush administrations. Until very recently, the neoconservatives have been doubtful that the Republican Party has an interest in ideas, let alone their ideas concerning a limited, yet energetic government.

The neoconservatives began the 1980s hoping that Reagan would be the president they had been waiting for, and left with mixed feelings. On the positive side, the neoconservatives believe that Reagan was, like them, an ideological determinist. They credit Reagan's stress on the primacy of ideas with the defeat of Communism and with the self-confidence that he revived in America. What he said was as important as what he did.[134] Moreover, they credit Reagan with maintaining an unwavering ideological opposition to Communism that resulted in its collapse. While other intellectuals derided Reagan for castigating the "evil empire" and desiring to throw Communism into "the dustbin of history," the neoconservatives believed that Reagan was articulating crucial ideas that could have magnificent consequences. And sure enough, they did. All of the neoconservative contributors to a 1990 *Commentary* symposium, "The American 80's: Disaster or Triumph"—Jeanne Kirkpatrick, Joseph Epstein, Michael Novak, James Nuechterlein, Richard John Neuhaus, and Hilton Kramer—asserted that Reagan was largely responsible for the collapse of the Communist empire. The neoconservatives in this symposium considered this a self-evident truth with which only the most unrepentant leftists would disagree; as *First Things* editor James Nuechterlein declared, "those who believe that the revolution of 1989 in Eastern Europe had little or nothing to do with the policies of the Reagan administration might as readily believe in the ministrations of the tooth fairy."[135]

The neoconservative problem with Reagan concerns not what he thought and said, but what he did—or, more accurately, what he did not do. Neoconservatives supported Reagan's tax cuts, but regretted the fact that domestic spending increased dramatically on his watch. In addition, Reagan did not have much impact on important moral issues; to the dismay of many neoconservatives, he did not even eliminate quotas in the federal government.[136] Several neoconservatives, while supporting Reagan's arms buildup and his rhetorical posture toward the Soviet Union, maintained that he demonstrated striking foreign policy weaknesses at crucial moments. One such example concerned the

Communist crackdown in Poland. In a 1982 *New York Times Magazine* article, Norman Podhoretz argued that the administration should have taken a few relatively easy steps that did not involve a threat of war with the Soviet Union, such as an embargo, a cessation of economic aid, a termination of grain credits, and an all-out effort to have western European countries halt the construction of the natural gas pipeline from Siberia to western Europe.[137]

The neoconservatives' disappointment with Ronald Reagan certainly does not explain their reluctance to join the Republican Party, for they believe that he was a far better president than Jimmy Carter was or Walter Mondale would have been. More to the point was that the Republican Party did not offer them very much in the way of ideas or vision that would lead them to change their affiliation. For those passionate about and involved with politics, party affiliation can be an important source of personal identity. As the neoconservatives have shown in other contexts, it is very difficult to shed an important part of identity, even if it has serious flaws. Most people do not confront the choice of political parties as they would treats in a bakery, selecting whichever looks more appealing at the moment. Party affiliation is often inherited from one's family and, like all tradition, embodies a certain mysticism that sometimes defies pure reason. The burden of proof is on the new party, not the old, and this burden is one that the Republicans largely not meet for the neoconservatives in the 1980s.

Why did the Republican Party fail to meet the burden of proof for the neoconservatives? The reason is best articulated by Jeanne Kirkpatrick (she has since become a Republican) in a 1979 article, "Why I Am Not a Republican," published in *Common Sense*, then the official journal of the Republican Party. After providing passionate reasons why she is a conservative and has no use for the Democratic Party, Kirkpatrick nevertheless concludes that she cannot bring herself to switch parties.

> The problem is that the Republican Party has not articulated any inclusive vision of the public good that reflects concern for the well-being of the whole community. During the past half-century or so, Republican spokes-

> men have consistently emphasized private concerns such as self-discipline and self-reliance and either have not had, or have not communicated, a persuasive conception of the public good. It has been left to the Democratic Party to make clear that in a civilized society people must look out for one another, and devise, however ineptly, the mechanisms for doing so.[138]

Irving Kristol, a Republican, wrote several essays in the 1970s pointing out similar weaknesses in the Republican Party. Borrowing from John Stuart Mill's condemnation of the Conservative Party in his day, Kristol calls the Republican Party "the stupid party." They are stupid because they refuse to "think politically" when confronted with Democrats who do. Not accepting the inevitability of a welfare state, the Republicans have no vision for the way the nation should be governed, at least with regard to domestic politics. Instead, Republicans tend to worry about the punctuation rather than the poetry of politics. Democrats generally do not worry about the bottom line as they present a vision for a liberal welfare state and thus not only set the agenda not only for government programs, but for the terms for the debate about these programs. Republicans are relegated to the task of balancing Democratic budgets, a calling that is less than inspiring.[139] Michael Novak wrote in 1994, "The Republican motto for two generations seemed to be: 'Not yet! Not so fast! A little less.' . . . I used to think of it as 'the GOP school of dentistry,' whose motto was, 'It isn't good for you unless it hurts.' "[140]

Politics and Principles

Underlying much of the discussion of party affiliation and neoconservatism is the relationship between politics and ideas. Neoconservatives have criticized the Democrats and liberals for having bad ideas and the Republicans and conservatives for not having ideas. This is not to say that the neoconservatives' threshold for political acceptability is very high. They appreciate the limits that democracy places on the ability of ideas to become policy, and do not seek anything more than is possible in this regard. Their expectations are not high; neoconservatives do not believe that American politics fulfills its relatively low potential to incorporate ideas into the workings and doings of government.

Perhaps unique for a group of intellectuals so intensely committed to the importance of ideas, neoconservatives have stressed that compromise—which mandates the dilution of ideas—is an essential component of politics. According to the neoconservatives, compromise is morally neutral; it is a fact of life from which even the most principled of politicians should not shirk. Irving Kristol writes,

> Life is too complicated to be encompassed by the human intellect, with the result that there are moments when it is wrong to do the right thing. The reason is that the right thing is defined by a set of abstract principles that serve as a guide to behavior, while there are times when these principles collide so brazenly with reality that it is sensible to permit circumstances to trump principles. In politics, unfortunately, such times are not infrequent.[141]

Just the same, it is important that politicians have something *to* compromise. If it is clear what is being conceded, the politician will know what he can relinquish safely while maintaining he integrity of his fundamental principle or ultimate goal. Kristol explains that "compromise should be presented candidly to the public for what it is—compromise—not victory. It also means that prior to any compromise the issues should be defined in a clear-cut way, not fudged."[142]

Norman Podhoretz has maintained that the natural duty of the politician to compromise is at odds with the duty of the intellectual to seek the truth at all costs. This is not to say that intellectuals and politicians can have no relationship; to the contrary, intellectuals supply the principles that the politicians compromise. However, it is usually a disaster when intellectuals enter politics because their callings are so different. Politicians cannot be faithful to ideas; compromise is too much a part of their job. It is for this reason that Podhoretz will not publish essays by people in public office.[143] He comments,

> Democratic politics involves compromise, it involves coalitions. It is very hard to get elected unless you can appeal to different constituencies. The

> art of being a democratic politician is, at least in this country—with the kind of system that we have (it is not necessarily so with a parliamentary system)—the democratic politician has to avoid making enemies. And that means he cannot do what intellectuals do—seek clarity—for that is polarizing. A politician likes to fudge differences, likes to square the circle, likes to get you to vote for him without alienating the other guy.[144]

The Road to Culture

By the late 1980s, the neoconservatives looked at their situation in relationship to the larger political and cultural world and were quite dissatisfied. The Democrats had abandoned the traditional liberal principles of Roosevelt, Kennedy, and Truman, and the neoconservatives hoped they would find a home in the Republican Party. While the Reagan administration certainly was receptive to the ideas of Norman Podhoretz, Elliot Abrams, Jeanne Kirkpatrick, and others in the beginning, it did not fulfill their hopes. From quotas to détente to runaway social spending, the neoconservatives found numerous policies of the Reagan administration woefully inadequate or downright wrong. Though the neoconservatives never envisioned a Republican administration run by *Public Interest* contributors responding to the latest issue of *Commentary*, they did hope for a government willing to advance an energetic, activist, thoughtful conservatism. They did not find this under Reagan and things got only worse under Bush, who, through his rhetoric and support for a massive expansion of federal regulations, advanced the liberal agenda better than any self-proclaimed liberal could have.

The neoconservatives had similar problems in the intellectual world, especially concerning capitalism. As almost everyone (and every neoconservative) has recognized, the idea of socialism had been dead for a long time—but this did not mean that capitalism was triumphant. The nature of ideas is much more complicated than that; the death, even the earth-shattering, crashing demise, of a particular idea does not mean the triumph of its presumed opposite. Keepers of the dead idea do not always die along with it, nor do the methods of reasoning or ways of approaching political questions that culminated in the dead idea. Dead ideas may be transformed, perhaps channeled toward different ends, but their souls are eternal. Thus, while no one speaks about dictatorship of the proletariat and only a few true believers consigned to irrelevancy blatantly advocate redistribution of wealth, many of these people found a home in environmentalism or excessive regulation of industry. In short, anticapitalism would not die, and capitalism needed supporters as much as ever. Bashed by anticapitalists of numerous stripes, capitalism received little defense from libertarians, who did not appreciate its moral roots in the bourgeois ethic or from businessmen, who largely did not appreciate the importance of ideas.

With the adversary culture opposed to bourgeois capitalism and with the business community eager to profit from the adversary culture's need for material goods, the neoconservatives were in a precarious position. How would they explain to a deaf culture that capitalism was valuable, indeed, a great economic system, but only if sustained by moral values which the ordinary American could recognize, support, and strive to manifest? This was very difficult, indeed, and the neoconservatives saw that it could not be done without a culture predisposed to nourish the values that sustain not only capitalism, but the Judeo-Christian society in which Western capitalism is embedded.

In short, the cultural climate of the 1980s impressed upon neoconservatives once again the necessity of thinking systematically. Thus, Michael Novak's seminal book on capitalism is entitled *The Spirit of Democratic Capitalism*. No society, according to Novak and the other neoconservatives, can be morally satisfying and financially prosperous without a free economy, a democratic polity, and a moral/cultural system anchored in traditional and ethical values. Capitalism can exist for a short time without democracy or without a solid moral/cultural system, but it needs both to sustain itself. Though capitalism has enormous moral capital and history from which it can draw, that capital is not limitless and may expire precipitously. As Irving Kristol explained in a 1974 *New York Times Magazine* essay,

> [People] will accept or tolerate or even praise institutions which, suddenly, will be experienced as intolerable and unworthy. Institutions, like worm-

> eaten trees, can look healthy and imposing, until they crumble overnight into dust . . . abrupt eruptions of profound discontent . . . are characteristic of a society whose institutions . . . are being drained of their legitimacy, that is to say, of their moral acceptance.[145]

For the neoconservatives, the first sign of a breakdown in the moral legitimacy of any institution is the transformation of the language it uses to describe itself, its principles and its goals. Rhetoric and language have always meant much more than their dictionary definitions to neoconservatives; they signify the way a society understands and evaluates itself. Just as the Communist expropriation of Western ideals leads to a grossly inaccurate and unjust portrayal of reality, the inability of bourgeois capitalist society to defend itself leaves the culture in a state of moral disarray. As almost all the neoconservatives have stressed, the language that the right and the left use to discuss capitalism is woefully inadequate. Both sides regard capitalism as dependent on "self-interest," "individualism," "rationality," and so on. However, both libertarians and leftists often miss the point Irving Kristol made in 1958: "[Being] selfish is not the same as being rational."[146] How, for instance, can the ordinary language and logic of economics explain the monumental self-sacrifice that most Americans make for their family, and many make for their communities? These ordinary acts of heroism cannot be explained by the economist's equation of self-interest with rationality; there must be something else at work here.

According to the neoconservatives, that something else is bourgeois values, the indispensable component of a society that cherishes both freedom and order. The brakes of bourgeois morality must be applied to the seemingly perpetual motion of the free market. The essential question "Are we living a good life?" is asked in every human society, no matter how wealthy. And if it cannot be answered in the affirmative, any economic or social system is in trouble.

And, in the aftermath of the counterculture, it seems as though Americans have lost the ability to define what they mean by the good life and how they hope to get there. Unaware of how to articulate that freedom is dependent on a moral order, Americans often cannot defend what they know to be true. As Irving Kristol wrote in 1970 of drug legalization,

> Today . . . [there] is an overwhelming majority who believe that the drug habit is bad [and] seem incapable of giving the reasons why. I mean the real reasons why [drugs should be criminalized], which have to do with the reasons why it is desirable to function as autonomous and self-reliant citizens in our urban, democratic society, rather than to drift through life in a pleasant but enervating haze. The moral code for all civilizations must, at one time or another, be prepared to face the ultimate subversive question: "Why not?" Our civilization is now facing that very question in the form of the drug problem, and, apparently, it can only respond with tedious, and in the end ineffectual, medical reports.[147]

The neoconservatives—seeing America becoming less and less able to answer Kristol's question, "Why not?"—devoted themselves to telling the country how to do so. Rejecting permissiveness and authoritarianism, the neoconservatives sought to establish moral authority, which, as Kristol maintains, "means the exercise of power toward some morally affirmed end and in such a reasonable way as to secure popular acceptance and sanction."[148]

To return to a society that combines order and freedom well within the poles of permissiveness and authoritarianism, the neoconservatives returned to the first things—those basic moral qualities that keep a society wealthy, virtuous, and happy. The importance of virtuous individuals peopling the just institutions about which Kristol wrote became a major neoconservative concern after the aftermath of the counterculture and the acquiescent response to it. Bourgeois society needed confidence, and its institutions needed to regain their moral bearings in a confusing world. And for that, the neoconservatives looked intensively to the culture. But the culture is a large thing; what in the culture could supply the moral basis for the societal transformation the neoconservatives advocated? In what province would the ingredients for America's needed spiritual reinvigoration—and new self-understanding—be found? Kristol suggests,

> The truth, which we are in danger of forgetting, is that a "civil religion" both engenders and requires a moral endorsement of a regime, not simply a utilitarian one. It is such a moral endorsement that has always led Ameri-

> cans to believe that their constitutional order is not only efficient and workable, but also just. For such an endorsement to prevail, the "civil religion" must be at least minimally nourished by its religious roots . . . A "covenant" is meaningless unless it is based on moral truths which, if not indisputable in the abstract, are not widely disputed in practice. The source of such moral truths has always been a religious tradition or a composite of religious traditions. Science cannot provide such moral truths, neither can philosophy; both can only offer us reasons for skepticism about them. But a "way of life" involves commitment, and only a religious attachment, however superficial, can provide that.[149]

It was the consideration of these moral truths enforced by religious attachment that composed the last great project of neoconservatism.

Notes

1. Alan Wolfe, "Why the Neocons Are Losing Out," *Nation* (September 28, 1985) p. 281.
2. Michael Novak, "Seven Theological Facts," *Capitalism and Socialism: A Theological Inquiry.* (Washington: American Enterprise Institute, 1979) p. 109.
3. Adam Meyerson, "Welfare State Conservatism: Jeanne Kirkpatrick Speaks about Her Domestic Policy Views," *Policy Review* (Spring 1988) p. 5.
4. Interview with Midge Decter, November 27, 1993.
5. Irving Kristol, "An Odd Lot," *Encounter* (December 1960) pp. 62–63.
6. The review of *The Affluent Society* is "Our Boondoggling Democracy," *Commentary* (August 1958) pp. 176–78. The review of *The Constitution of Liberty* is "Last of the Whigs," *Commentary* (April 1960) pp. 353–54.
7. Irving Kristol, "Keeping Up with Ourselves," *The Yale Review* (June 1960) p. 515.
8. Irving Kristol, "Taxes and Foundations," letter to *The New Republic* (February 15, 1964) p. 39.
9. Irving Kristol, "Class and Sociology: 'The Shadow of Marxism,'" *Commentary* (October 1957) p. 353.
10. As it turns out, Laffer's prediction was very close to the correct figure, which was $1.32 trillion.
11. Sidney Blumental, *The Counter-Establishment: From Conservative Ideology to Political Power* (New York: Times Books, 1986) p. 182.
12. David Stockman, *The Triumph of Politics: Why the Reagan Revolution Failed* (New York: Harper and Row, 1986) p. 39.
13. Interview with Jude Wanniski, December 29, 1993.
14. *The Rise of the Counter-Establishment: From Conservative Ideology to Political Power,* p. 193.

15. Irving Kristol, "The Economics of Growth," *Wall Street Journal* (November 16, 1978) p. 24.

16. *The Rise of the Counter-Establishment: From Conservative Ideology to Political Power,* p. 130.

17. George Gilder, *Wealth and Poverty* (San Francisco: Institute for Contemporary Studies, 1993) p. xii (originally published by Basic Books, 1981).

18. Joseph Epstein, "The Education of an Anti-Capitalist," *Commentary* (August 1983) p. 51.

19. William Barrett, quoted in Norman Podhoretz, "The New Defenders of Capitalism," *Harvard Business Review* (March/April 1981) p. 103.

20. Irving Kristol, " 'When virtue loses all her loveliness'—some reflections on capitalism and 'the free society,' " *The Public Interest* (Fall 1970) p. 3.

21. Daniel Bell, quoted in George Gilder, *Wealth and Poverty,* p. 4

22. Irving Kristol, quoted in Joseph Epstein, "Education of an Anti-Capitalist," p. 54.

23. Irving Kristol, " 'When virtue loses all her loveliness'—some reflections on capitalism and 'the free society,' " p. 8.

24. Irving Kristol, "From the Land of the Free to the Big PX," *New York Times Magazine* (December 20, 1964) p. 32.

25. Irving Kristol, "Horatio Alger and Profits," *Wall Street Journal* (July 11, 1974) p. 8.

26. Peter Berger, *The Capitalist Revolution: Fifty Propositions about Prosperity, Equality, and Liberty* (New York: Basic Books, 1986) p. 208.

27. Irving Kristol wrote in 1978, "There have been . . . two great economists who offered economic growth that are perfectly congruent with our historic and personal experience. They are Adam Smith in the 18th Century and Joseph Schumpeter in the 20th" ("The Economics of Growth," p. 24).

28. Joseph Schumpeter, *Capitalism, Socialism, and Democracy* (New York: Harper Torchbooks, 1975) p. 127 (originally published by Harper and Row, 1942).

29. Richard John Neuhaus, *Doing Well and Doing Good: The Challenge to the Christian Capitalist* (New York: Doubleday, 1992) p. 20.

30. In his introduction to George Orwell's *Homage to Catalonia,* Trilling refers to this expression as "the old, reactionary Anglican phrase that used to drive people of democratic leanings quite wild with rage," precisely because it is so illiberal.

31. Midge Decter, contribution to *Commentary* symposium, "Who Is a Liberal—What Is a Conservative?" *Commentary* (September 1976) p. 50.

32. Irving Kristol, "People Who Are S-S-ST," *Wall Street Journal* (July 24, 1978) p. 10.

33. Irving Kristol, "Adam Smith and the Spirit of Capitalism," from *The Great Ideas Today* (Chicago: Encyclopedia Britannica, 1976) Reprinted in *Reflections of a Neoconservative* (New York: Basic Books, 1983) p. 172.

34. *Wealth and Poverty,* p. 10.

35. Michael Novak, "Boredom, Virtue and Democratic Capitalism," *Commentary* (September 1989) p. 34.

36. Michael Novak, *The Spirit of Democratic Capitalism* (Lanham, Md.: Madison Books, 1991) p. 107 (originally published by Simon and Schuster, 1982).

37. Interview with Michael Novak, January 26, 1994.

38. Nathan Glazer, contribution to "Neoconservatism, Pro and Con," *Partisan Review* (Vol. 4, 1980) p. 501.

39. Irving Kristol, "The Credibility of Corporations," *Wall Street Journal* (January 17, 1974) p. 16.

40. *The Spirit of Democratic Capitalism*, p. 175.

41. See Irving Kristol, "No Cheers for the Profit Motive," *Wall Street Journal* (February 20, 1979) p. 16.

42. Michael Novak, "Social Policy and the Poor: The New Plantation," *Public Welfare* (Fall 1980) p. 32.

43. Michael Novak, "In Praise of Bourgeois Virtues," *Society* (January/February 1981) p. 62.

44. Michael Novak, "A Theology of the Corporation," in Michael Novak and John Cooper, eds., *The Corporation: A Theological Inquiry* (Washington: American Enterprise Institute, 1981) p. 211.

45. Michael Novak, "The Virtue of Enterprise: The Pope's Discovery of a 'Right to Economic Initiative' Could Revolutionize Catholic Social Thought," *Crisis* (May 1989) p. 24.

46. Donald McCloskey, "Bourgeois Virtue," *The American Scholar* (Spring 1994) p. 182.

47. Gertrude Himmelfarb, "Victorian Values/Jewish Values," *Commentary* (February 1989) p. 31.

48. *The Spirit of Democratic Capitalism*, p. 140.

49. *Doing Well and Doing Good: The Challenge to the Christian Capitalist*, p. 47.

50. George Gilder, *Recapturing the Spirit of Enterprise* (San Francisco: Institute for Contemporary Studies Press, 1992) p. 5.

51. *Recapturing the Spirit of Enterprise*, p. 6.

52. See George Gilder, "In Defense of Capitalists," *Commentary* (December 1980) pp. 42–45.

53. George Gilder, "The Moral Sources of Capitalism," *Society* (September/October 1981) p. 24.

54. "The Moral Sources of Capitalism," p. 27.

55. *Wealth and Poverty*, p. xx.

56. Irving Kristol, "A New Look at Capitalism," *National Review* (April 17, 1981) p. 414.

57. Tod Lindberg, "Four Cheers for Capitalism," *Commentary* (April 1985) p. 67.

58. Seymour Martin Lipset, contribution to *Commentary* symposium, "Capitalism, Socialism and Democracy," *Commentary* (April 1978) p. 62.

59. Irving Kristol, "A Transatlantic 'Misunderstanding': The Case of Central America," *Encounter* p. 11

60. Paul Johnson, "Is There a Moral Basis for Capitalism?" in Michael Novak, ed., *Democracy and Mediating Structures* (Washington: American Enterprise Institute, 1979) p. 56.

61. *The Capitalist Revolution*, p. 79.

62. Irving Kristol, "Christianity, Judaism and Socialism," *Capitalism and Socialism: A Theological Inquiry*, p. 320.

63. "Victorian Values/Jewish Values," p. 31.

64. Michael Novak, "The Rich, the Poor and Reaganomics," *First Things* (April 1991) p. 50.

65. *The Spirit of Democratic Capitalism*, p. 26.

66. Nathan Glazer, "Neoconservatism: Pro and Con," p. 509.

67. "Social Policy and the Poor: The New Plantation," p. 31.

68. Quoted in Robert Glasgow, "An Interview with Irving Kristol," *Psychology Today* (February 1974) p. 80.

69. George Orwell, *Homage to Catalonia* (New York: Harcourt Brace Jovanovich, 1980) p. 115 (originally published in 1938).

70. Michael Novak, *The Catholic Ethic and the Spirit of Capitalism* (New York: Free Press, 1993) p. 142.

71. Irving Kristol, "Taxes, Poverty and Equality," *The Public Interest* (Fall 1974) p. 22.

72. Editorial, "What Shall We Do about the Poor?" *First Things* (April 1992) p. 7.

73. Irving Kristol, "The Shaking of the Foundations," *Fortune* (July 1968)

74. Irving Kristol and Paul Weaver, "Introduction," in Irving Kristol and Paul Weaver, eds., *The Americans: 1976* (Lexington, Ky.: Lexington Books) p. xix.

75. "Horatio Alger and Profits," p. 8.

76. Michael Novak, "The Creative Person," *Journal of Business Ethics* (December 1993) p. 977.

77. See Peter Berger, "Capitalism: The Continuing Revolution," *First Things* (August/September 1991) p. 25.

78. Irving Kristol, contribution to *Commentary* Symposium, "Capitalism, Socialism, Democracy," *Commentary* (April 1978) p. 53.

79. *The Spirit of Democratic Capitalism*, p. 15.

80. See Kristol and Weaver, "Introduction," p. xix.

81. The free market has also, unfortunately, liberated people from appreciating the incredible work that goes into producing everyday goods. See "A Well-Kept Secret," a My Turn essay by a farmer's wife, Bonnie Hellum Brechbill, on page 21 of the February 20, 1995 issue of *Newsweek*. Visiting New York, she recounts a conversation between her husband and a city salesman. "'Do your cows have to be milked every day?' he asked. 'Twice every day,'. . . I'd have added, 'That means Sundays, birthdays and school-concert days. Meditate on

that the next time you think the price of milk, cheese, or ice cream is too high." Perhaps the lack of appreciation that Mrs. Brechbill points out contributes to, or is a symptom of, the revolution of rising expectations the neoconservatives write about.

82. *Recapturing the Spirit of Enterprise*, p. 93.

83. Irving Kristol, "Pornography, Obscenity and the Case for Censorship." *New York Times Magazine* (March 28, 1971) p. 114.

84. Irving Kristol, "Adam Smith and the Spirit of Capitalism,"p. 175.

85. Aaron Wildavsky, "Government and the People," *Commentary* (August 1973) p. 25–32.

86. *Capitalism, Socialism, and Democracy*, p. 14.

87. *Capitalism, Socialism, and Democracy*, p. 154.

88. Irving Kristol, "Is the Welfare State Obsolete?" *Harper's* (May 1963) p. 39.

89. Irving Kristol, "Corporate Capitalism in America," *The Public Interest* (Fall 1975) p. 134.

90. David Bazelon, quoted in B. Bruce Briggs, "An Introduction to the Idea of the New Class," from *The New Class?* p. 7.

91. Michael Walzer, "Nervous Liberals," review of *The Neoconservatives: The Men Who Are Changing American Politics* by Peter Steinfels, *New York Review of Books* (October 11, 1979) p. 7.

92. Gary Dorrien, *The Neoconservative Mind: Politics, Culture and the War of Ideology* (Philadelphia: Temple University Press, 1993) p. 102.

93. Robert Bartley, "Business and the New Class," from *The New Class*? p. 62.

94. Irving Kristol, "The Environmentalist Crusade," *Wall Street Journal* (December 16, 1974) p. 14.

95. Michael Novak, "Democratic Capitalism: Moral, or Not at All," *Freedom Review* (May/June 1991) p. 12.

96. Richard John Neuhaus, "The Many Causes of Environmentalism," *First Things* (August/September 1990) p. 67. "THE ENVIRONMENT" was capitalized in Neuhaus's work.

97. Norman Podhoretz, "Reflections on Earth Day," *Commentary* (June 1970) p. 26–28.

98. Gertrude Himmelfarb, *The Demoralization of Society: From Victorian Virtues to Modern Values* (New York: Knopf, 1995) p. 244.

99. Interview with Jude Wanniski, December 29, 1993.

100. Interview with Richard John Neuhaus, January 10, 1994.

101. Interview with Michael Novak, January 26, 1994.

102. Penn Kemble, contribution to "Capitalism, Socialism and Democracy," *Commentary* p. 51.

103. James Q. Wilson, Contribution to "Neoconservatism: Pro and Con," *Partisan Review* (Number 4, 1980) p. 510.

104. Irving Kristol, "Capitalism, Socialism and Nihilism," *The Public Interest* (Spring 1973) p. 12–13.

105. Robert Bartley, "Business and the New Class," p. 65.
106. Norman Podhoretz, "The New Defenders of Capitalism," p. 105.
107. Interview with Irving Kristol, January 26, 1994.
108. "Capitalism, Socialism and Nihilism," p. 8.
109. "Horatio Alger and Profit," p. 8,
110. *The Spirit of Democratic Capitalism*, p. 125.
111. Irving Kristol, "On Corporate Philanthropy," *Wall Street Journal* (March 21, 1977) p. 18
112. Irving Kristol, "The Credibility of the Corporation," p. 16.
113. See Irving Kristol, "Capitalism, Socialism and Nihilism," and "Utopianism, Ancient and Modern," from *Imprimus* (April 1973) or *Vital Speeches* (June 1, 1973).
114. Irving Kristol, "On Corporate Capitalism in America." p. 19.
115. See Irving Kristol, "The Corporation and the Dinosaur," *Wall Street Journal* (February 14, 1974) p. 20.
116. Interview with Gertrude Himmelfarb, March 24, 1994.
117. Irving Kristol, "Reforming the Welfare State," *Wall Street Journal* (October 25, 1976) p. 14. The theme of nostalgia as a destructive instrument has been a consistent theme in the work of Irving Kristol. As early as 1959, Kristol warned that "fascism is distinctively the politics of nostalgia" ("A Cool Sociological Eye." Review of *Political Man: The Social Basis of Politics* by Seymour Martin Lipset. *Reporter*, February 4, 1960, p.142). In 1964, Kristol added, "Nostalgia is one of the most legitimate, and certainly one of the most enduring of human emotions; but the politics of nostalgia is at best distracting, at worst pernicious" ("From the Land of the Free to the Big PX," p. 7). Kristol thinks that nostalgia has its place in romantic poetry, where many of the greatest poets of the modern era—Yeats, Larkin, Eliot, Pound—have been reactionaries. Brigette and Peter Berger make a similar point in "Our Conservatism and Theirs." *Commentary* (October 1986) p. 64.
118. Irving Kristol, "A Conservative Welfare State," *Wall Street Journal* (June 14, 1993) p. 14.
119. Michael Novak, "The Crisis of the Welfare State," *Crisis* (July-August 1993) pp. 6–7.
120. Irving Kristol, "The Republican Future," *Wall Street Journal* (May 14, 1976) p. 18.
121. Irving Kristol, "Human Nature and Social Reform," *Wall Street Journal* (September 18, 1978) p. 22.
122. "Human Nature and Social Reform," p. 22.
123. Interview with William Buckley, January 18, 1994.
124. Interview with Jude Wanniski, December 29, 1993.
125. *The Spirit of Democratic Capitalism*, p. 36.
126. *The Spirit of Democratic Capitalism*, p. 432.
127. George Will, *Statecraft as Soulcraft* (New York: Simon and Schuster, 1983) p. 35.

128. Irving Kristol, "Capitalism, Socialism and Nihilism," p. 14.

129. Irving Kristol, "No Cheers for the Profit Motive," p. 16.

130. " 'When virtue loses all her loveliness'—some reflections on capitalism and 'the free society'," pp. 3–15.

131. Martin Peretz, quoted in *Second Thoughts: Former Radicals Look Back at the Sixties*, p. 170. Peretz's move from radicalism to conservatism (in several ways) was marked by a sort of spiritual progression. Someone who attended his Passover seders in the mid-1970s relates a humorous story regarding Peretz's switch. During the seder, Jews recline to the left at certain points. However, one year, Peretz said, "Normally, we recline to the left. Why is this so? I am not sure. Let us assume that Jews have traditionally leaned to the left because that is where they felt most comfortable; the left represented freedom, liberty and all that made us comfortable in this land. These days, I am not so sure that those reasons still hold. So let's wiggle around."

132. Interview with Martin Peretz, April 25, 1994.

133. Michael Novak, "The Conservative Mood," *Society* (January/February 1994) p. 13.

134. See Joseph Epstein, contribution to *Commentary* symposium "The American 80s: Disaster or Triumph?" p. 25.

135. James Nuechterlein, contribution to, "The American 80s: Disaster or Triumph?" *Commentary* (September 1980) p. 41.

136. See Chester Finn, "Affirmative Action under Reagan," *Commentary* (April 1982) p. 17–28. and Chester Finn, "Quotas and the Bush Administration," *Commentary* (November 1991) p. 17–23.

137. Norman Podhoretz, "The Neo-Conservative Anguish over Reagan's Foreign Policy," *New York Times Magazine* (May 2, 1982) p. 88. See also Norman Podhoretz, "The Reagan Road to Détente," *Foreign Affairs* (Issue #3, 1985) pp. 447–64.

138. Jeanne Kirkpatrick, "Why I Am Not a Republican," *Common Sense* (Fall 1979) p. 34.

139. Kristol's views on the Republican party are discussed in "The Republican Future" (May 14, 1976) p. 18, and "The Stupid Party," *Wall Street Journal* (January 15, 1976) p. 12.

140. Michael Novak, "The Conservative Mood," p. 13.

141. Irving Kristol, "When It's Wrong to Be Right," *Wall Street Journal* (March 24, 1993) p. 14.

142. Irving Kristol, "Running Like a Dry Creek?" *Wall Street Journal* (October 6, 1983) p. 30.

143. Interview with Midge Decter, November 27, 1993.

144. Interview with Norman Podhoretz, January 11, 1994.

145. Irving Kristol, "Thoughts on reading about a summer-camp cabin covered with garbage," *The New York Times Magazine* (November 17, 1974) p. 132.

146. Irving Kristol, "Class and Sociology: 'The Shadow of Marxism,' " *Commentary* (October 1958) p. 362.

147. Irving Kristol, "Urban Civilization and Its Discontents," *Commentary* (January 1970) p. 35.
148. Irving Kristol, "Thoughts on reading about a summer-camp cabin covered with garbage," p. 137.
149. Irving Kristol, "The Spirit of '87," *The Public Interest* (Spring 1987) pp. 8, 9.

6

Of Pyrrhic Victories and Culture Wars: Neoconservatism after Communism

> There is a great deal that is public but not in the ordinary sense of the term political. Family life, work, learning and entertainment all have public dimensions of interaction, not only interaction with other individuals but also with other communities. For those of us who are not professional politicians or political junkies, what matters to us most does not take place in the political arena as such. The things that matter most happen in the "mediating structures" of our personal and communal existence. These structures—family, neighborhood, church, voluntary association—are the people-sized, face to face institutions where we work day by day at our felicities and our fears. The public square is not limited to Government Square.—Richard John Neuhaus, 1984

> Moreover, it can often seem as if our cultural moment demands uncompromising confrontation rather than polite dialogue. When unborn children have less legal standing than an endangered species of bird in a national forest; when any conceivable configuration of consenting adults sharing body parts is considered in enlightened circles to constitute a "marriage"; when senior United States Senators bloviate about "sexual harassment" in kindergarten while national illegitimacy rates approach 30 percent of all births: one is reminded of Orwell's observation, two generations ago, that "we have now sunk to a depth at which the restatement of the obvious is the first duty of intelligent men."—George Weigel, 1994

This Simple Fact

> Don't ever be right too often. The fact is that we were right about the 1980s, we were right about the Soviet Union, we were right about Central America and we have been more right than wrong about domestic issues. It is not easy for people to take.[1]

So admonishes George Weigel, articulating the neoconservatives' belief that many of their major political battles were won decisively by 1990. Two generations of neoconservatives and neoconservative precursors had fought the ideological battles against Communism and its sympathizers and witnessed a victory they never thought they would see. And yet, in 1989, Communism began to collapse, a process that was much quicker and more peaceful than anyone imagined. After their liberation, formerly Communist nations had no doubt that they favored a free market in economics. But this capitalist revolution was not limited to these countries; the revolution in economic thought in the Vatican has been just as profound. Traditionally a bastion of premodern, anticapitalist and antisocialist economics, the Catholic Church has come around to an acceptance of capitalism, some say directly due to the work of Michael Novak.[2] Domestically, even former liberal Democrats are now seeing the failings of the welfare state and the counterculture about which the neoconservatives have been writing for three decades.

Instead of gloating, the neoconservatives have looked at the United States, now freed from the threat of Communist totalitarianism, and have wondered, "We have won . . . for what?" Neoconservatives contend that Communism did not carry the idea of collectivism to the grave, nor did economic liberty, bourgeois values, and community solidarity emerge culturally triumphant. True, Ronald Reagan had won twice, but he won elections, which have little to do with the culture. Those peopling the media, the academy, the arts, the literary and publishing worlds, the entertainment industry, and the Democratic Party did not vote for Ronald Reagan. Dan Quayle, influenced by his chief of staff, William Kristol, termed these people "the cultural elite"; Michael Novak referred to them as the "Lords Spiritual of Opinion."[3] Whatever they were called, they are powerful allies of, or appendages to, the new class which, as the neoconservatives demonstrate, rejects and works against bourgeois morality and institutions. Robert Bork writes, "So pervasive is the influence of those who occupy the commanding heights of our culture that it is not entirely accurate to call the United States a majoritarian democracy."[4]

Few in number and not Reagan voters, the cultural elite is, the neoconservatives maintain, very powerful. Newt Gingrich, Bork points out, cannot do anything about political correctness and multiculturalism—which are ultimately more important than the budget.[5] It is the culture, neoconservatives contend, that drives and informs all other sectors of American life. John Podhoretz explains, "most of us, even those with a passion for politics, experience life culturally, not politically. We listen to music, go to the movies, watch TV; and these pastimes give us more of a sense of our country than anything else."[6] Irving Kristol maintains that even the questions that appear to be the most political are, at their roots, cultural.

> The plain truth is that if we are ever going to cope with the deficit and the social programs that inflate it, we are going to have to begin with a very different view of human nature and human responsibility in relation to such issues as criminality, sexuality, welfare dependency, even medical insurance. Only to the degree that such a new—actually very old—way of looking at ourselves and our fellow citizens emerges can a public opinion be shaped that will candidly confront the fiscal crisis of the welfare state. Presidential calls for "sacrifice," meaning a willingness to pay higher taxes, are a liberal cop-out. Why don't we hear something about self-control and self-reliance? It's the traditional spiritual values that we as individuals need, not newly invented, trendy ones.[7]

The neoconservatives maintain that many of our political problems can be traced to a sick culture. As Hilton Kramer said, "We are still living in the aftermath of the insidious assault on the mind that is one of the most repulsive features of the radical movement of the 1960s."[8] Robert Bork agrees, maintaining, "What we are seeing in modern liberalism is the ultimate triumph of the New Left of the 1960."[9] Michael Novak elaborated in a 1993 article.

> In the ecology of our culture, the moral ecology, who could possible say that the air is fresh and clean? Even at the primary levels of the public schools, textbooks are increasingly filled with scurrilous materials being forced upon unwilling or reluctant parents. Even the most innocent forms of religious observance in the schools—ecumenical, generous, and open-minded—are rejected by the courts as "unconstitutional." Producers of motion pictures compete with one another to see how often they can insult their audiences by repetitive use of the "F" word—one movie was clocked at once every thirty-nine seconds. When manners deteriorate, so does respect for common decencies. And so does respect for life.[10]

The neoconservatives have extrapolated their admonitions to businessmen who fund anticapitalist causes to the culture at large. While neoconservatives do not respect the intelligence of movie stars or the social value of sitcoms, these forms of amusement nonetheless have a significant influence on the way people view the world and understand their place in it. Entertainment, according to the neoconservatives, is much more than personalized enjoyment. The way a society entertains itself is a window into how it views itself and what it is striving for. Is it nihilistic or visionary, hopeful or helpless? One who does not ponder these questions should not be surprised when social decay and moral decadence follow from what are sometimes regarded by the philistine bourgeois mentality as plain fun. Neoconservatives decry the adversarial posture that much of popular culture strikes toward traditional American life. They believe that such entertainment has a role in the decline of bourgeois virtues, which largely accounts for social pathologies such as illegitimate births. Irving Kristol writes,

> The percentage of illegitimate births has increased to a startling degree since World War II. . . . Girls today are far more "sexually active" . . . than was formerly the case. Why this increase in sexual activity? Well, the popular culture surely encourages it. You can't expect modesty (to say nothing of chastity) from girls who worship Madonna.[11]

Neoconservatives wish that marital love, family responsibility, and piety were more celebrated in the popular culture instead of the values of the adversary culture. Michael Novak contends,

> To develop sound and habits and attitudes is crucial for success in every walk of life. If the nation's media—its rock stars, popular entertainers, and commentators on morals—sounded a drumbeat of hard work, responsibility, and a sound family life, parents' efforts to teach their children the basics of self-reliance would be greatly strengthened.[12]

The neoconservative critique of American culture is broad and extensive. However, its essence is encapsulated in one Irving Kristol line: "[In America] an 18-year-old girl has the right to public fornication in a pornographic movie—but only if she is paid the minimum wage."[13] Norman Podhoretz extended this argument in a 1979 essay:

> The ascendant ethic preached in the public schools, in the mass media, and even in comic books and pornographic magazines now seems to be that nothing—not wives, not husbands, not children, and certainly not the state—must stand in the way of the individual's right to self-fulfillment and self-expression in the realm of morals, sex, and personal relations (which was, of course, the adversary culture's traditional version of individualism as well as its answer to middle-class or bourgeois values). But where economic enterprise was concerned, the opposite view prevailed: there everything must be put in the way of "rugged individualism" and the more state control the better.[14]

If one does accept the popular culture, one cannot—as the left and libertarian right often maintain—simply ignore it. Man is a social animal—and society is conditioned by the values that pervade it and the works that entertain it. If individual X ignores a sick popular culture, individual Y may not—and individual X may meet individual Y in the workplace, at a Little League game, or at his own dinner table. As Michael Medved, a conservative movie critic, points out, "To say that if you don't like the popular culture then turn it off, is like saying, if you don't like the smog, stop breathing."[15]

According to the neoconservatives, the liberal conception of freedom unrestrained by virtue is ultimately destructive. This idea was at the crux of the neoconservative critique of libertarianism, and it extended into the libertine ethic pervading the culture. As Michael Novak notes, "Liberty is the outcome of reflection, deliberate choice, and commitment to taking responsibility for consequences . . . liberty is not acting on a whim, unreflectively, or by idle preference. . . . To be free is to be responsible."[16]

The neoconservatives never celebrate expression, speech, or activism for its own sake. To the contrary, Richard John Neuhaus maintains, "Adults who demand attention for their self-expression assume, usually without warrant, that they have very interesting selves to express."[17] There is nothing good about realizing oneself unless that self is worth realizing. And because there are good and bad qualities and good and bad people, it is wrong to make a blanket statement that "self-realization" is good. Is it good to realize a bad self? Certainly not—although such a statement requires an admission that there can be bad selves.

What is needed, neoconservatives maintain, is a resurrection of the distinction between liberty and license. They are not, as modern liberalism suggests, semantic siblings, but dead opposites and bitter enemies. Gertrude Himmelfarb explains,

> Absolute liberty also tends to corrupt absolutely. A liberty that is divorced from tradition and convention, from morality and religion, that makes the individual the sole repository and arbiter of all values and puts him in an adversarial relationship to society and the state—such a liberty is a grave peril to liberalism itself. For when that liberty is found wanting, when it violates the moral sense of the community or is incompatible with the legitimate demands of society, there is no moderating principle to take its place, no resting place between the wild gyrations of libertarianism and paternalism.[18]

A symptom of this illness is the common way of thinking of American social and political questions as a debate between the individual and the state. That leaves little room for those who are neither libertarians nor statists—in short, it excludes the best of the American tradition. Novak explains,

> What is the movement coming in behind that seems to have the most staying power? It is called neoconservative. One characteristic of neoconservative thought that is understated—because people interpret it politically—is the degree to which it is fundamentally an ethical and religious movement. It is characteristic of all the neoconservatives that they have regained a religious sensibility and think religion is terribly important. Moreover, they turn to the English tradition. Neoconservatives are really old liberals, but they are old liberals in a Burkean sense: they believe in the importance of liturgy, community, ethnicity, and roots, not atomic individuals. They have a sense of community, prayer, religion. . . .[19]

In the 1980s and 1990s, the neoconservatives found themselves aligned against the dominant media elites, the academic elites, even the business elites. It may seem strange, or at least historically unusual, that conservatives are aligned to fight against the establishment. Aren't conservatives supposed to conserve? To support order and fear change? These are all very real questions; indeed puzzling ones when applied to a group of forthrightly conservative intellectuals vigorously opposing an establishment and demanding significant change. Andrew Ferguson provides a telling answer to this dilemma.

> A conservative in late-20th century America is a walking paradox. By definition, he cherishes order, plays by the rules, takes comfort in orthodoxy. But nowadays the conservative disposition puts you at odds with the rulemakers, the wised-up boys and girls who write the news, teach the kids, publish the books, and produce our entertainments. When the guardians of the new orthodoxy celebrated the unorthodox, as they do, and when the rulemakers discard the old rules, as they have, the conservative, against his better judgment and contrary to his every tendency, becomes a trouble-maker.[20]

In a sense, the neoconservatives see themselves in a position paradoxically manned by conservatives for much of modern American intellectual history. Like William Buckley and *National Review* in the 1950s, the neoconservatives are aligned against a common culture they want to change drastically. As Buckley described his situation in 1955, the neoconservatives, too, have been standing athwart history and yelling stop! An odd place for conservatives to be, but one that seems to be inevitable for Americans of that persuasion.

Why are conservative intellectuals on the defensive in a conservative country? In a *National Review* essay adapted from a speech at the Heritage Foundation and in a *Society* essay, Samuel Lipman suggests an answer. Consistent with the neoconservative critiques of businessmen, Lipman argues that many people in the natural conservative constituency are simply philistines. Focusing on the important tasks of electing presidents, fighting Communism, and running businesses, conservatives often leave the province of culture to the left. Lipman maintains, "Culture shapes our lives and affects every action we take. The Left knows this simple fact; we seem not to know it, and as a result we are content to leave the Left in control of culture."[21]

Conservative opposition to outrageous grants by the National Endowment of the Arts (NEA) reflects this intellectual poverty. Lipman writes that conservative politicians such as Jesse Helms and Dana Rohrabacher have erred in condemning only the source of funding for obscene art. Lipman and the other neoconservatives contend that such products of the adversary culture are destructive regardless of who pays for them. Funding is an incidental part of the so-called art; the real concern is the quality of culture. Lipman suggests,

> [The NEA grants are] part of a much larger social discussion involving the limitations of social behavior and whether or not we, as a society, are ready to pull back and redefine those limitations which have expanded so much over the last 25 years. . . . It is one of how we wish to live. Those who support art must refuse to fund work they find morally wrong, making it clear why they are not supporting it. They must use their power to promote morally responsible visions, not irresponsible ones.[22]

The neoconservatives consider the conservative stress on funding as the major issue concerning art to be a manifestation of the lack of appreciation for culture that pervades the Republican Party. In reducing the debate over obscene art to a matter of funding, conservatives automatically concede the legitimacy of the art—and lose most of the battle right there. Culturally destructive art is not acceptable, funded privately or publicly. Far more cognizant of the importance of culture in shaping the world than the right, the left knows that the moral dimension of the art is far more important than who funds it. Lipman again:

> The Left, in and out of government, knows full well that he who controls culture controls not just how people live but how they perceive themselves. We are all aware of the Left's cultural agenda: primitivism, feminism, racialism, multiculturalism, and sexual radicalism. The Left wishes to use culture to remold man and society on radical lines, with destruction of individual autonomy and reason followed by the destruction of every traditional social habit and institution, including churches and ending with the family.[23]

It will take a lot more than success in the free market or disengagement of government funding of the arts to stop that.

Law, Morality, and Liberal Authoritarianism

Ideas meet politics, Lionel Trilling wrote, at the bloody crossroads. And few crossroads in American politics have been as bloody as the Supreme Court. While neoconservatives differ on the abortion question (their positions are explored later in this chapter), all neoconservatives agree that the Constitution says nothing about it and that the state can prohibit or regulate it. Even the neoconservatives who would not vote to criminalize abortion were they in a legislature consider *Roe v. Wade* a travesty in its trammeling of community standards in the name of an authoritarian, antidemocratic brand of liberalism. As Richard John Neuhaus has noted, "The logic and the consequences of this decision drive to the heart of the American social and political experiment."[24] *Roe* is emblematic of a way of thinking—a liberal elitism that flaunts the democratic will in favor of absolute freedom unleashed from virtue or community.

According to the neoconservatives, the promiscuous use of the judiciary to obtain political ends (of which abortion is just one example) is emblematic of the liberal contempt for democracy. And this contempt contaminates spheres other than the law and the polity. Neoconservatives claim that such judicial arrogance has, most importantly, crippled the culture. Culture depends on community, community depends on consensus, and consensus is the consequence of shared moral understanding. By imposing its will on the democratic majority, the Court has denied communities the chance to develop and act on such an understanding.

This is not to say that the culture follows the Court; culture is too broad a phenomenon to follow anything directly. But the courts validate the culture, influence it, and automatically lend legitimacy to whatever ideas it endorses. Neoconservatives claim that perhaps the most dangerous by-product of this union is the impoverishment of political discourse. While political philosophy has always dealt with the eternal conflicts between community and individual and order and freedom, neoconservatives charge that the radical individualism of the left has reduced those discussions to questions of rights. These rights are often not unaccompanied by responsibilities; they are claims by individuals against the will or ethos of the majority. And the majority has no language with which to respond.

Mary Ann Glendon offers an instructive example of this in her 1992 book, *Rights Talk*. On the day after the Supreme Court ruled that flag burning was a constitutional right in 1989, a spokesman for the American Legion went on the *Today* show to articulate an opposing view. Jane Pauley asked her guest what the flag meant to the nation's veterans. He replied, "The flag is the symbol of our country, the land of the free and the home of the brave." Pauley pressed, asking "what exactly does it symbolize?" The man responded: "It stands for the fact that this is a country where we have the right to do what we want."[25]

As Glendon suggests, this is the perfect example of the domination of the rhetoric of "rights" in American democratic discourse. This Legionnaire simply had no political language to express the values of community solidarity, shared sacrifice, social order, reverence for the sacred, and historical memory that he obviously felt so strongly. As a result, he was consigned to sounding like a vulgar individualist using the reductionist and dessicated language of who is taking away whose rights. Thus, it has been a primary neoconservative project to inject American democratic discourse with a different language, one that accounts for responsibilities as well as rights, obligations as well as payments due.

Just as language of rights is explicit in cultural discourse and court decisions, the neoconservatives claim that its effect has thoroughly infiltrated almost all public policy decisions. Liberals often assert the primacy of rights through a variation on the line "we cannot legislate morality." The neoconservatives strongly dissent, holding that the state's capacity as a repository of moral consensus is especially important in a republic of diverse individuals such as that of the United States, where government can be a rare unifying factor in a society of different religions, ethnic backgrounds, and even languages. Glendon writes,

> Law, for better or worse, now penetrates deeply into every aspect of life. Government, whether pursuant to a constitutional obligation or not, plays an even greater role in the lives of individuals as a source of support and security. Under these conditions, law becomes increasingly identified with legitimacy in the minds of citizens, whether it was meant to or not. Americans today, rightly or wrongly, regard many legal norms, especially those of criminal, family and constitutional law, as expressions of minimal common values. They are disconcerted by legal norms that seem to be radically at odds with common understandings. In such circumstances, the silences of law can begin to speak.[26]

Neoconservatives believe that legislating morality is not only inevitable, but desirable when done thoughtfully. Law inherently embodies some sort of morality, regardless of whether legislators intend it. For instance, the law against rape is based on the premise that rape is immoral. And behind that claim are several more fundamental moral claims—that sex should never be coerced, that might does not make right, that society should protect its physically weaker members, etc. The neoconservatives apply the same reasoning to laws governing everything from murder to insider trading to civil rights legislation, which, for instance, is based on the premise that discrimination on the basis of race is immoral and should therefore be illegal. Neoconservatives maintain that unless liberals are willing to abandon civil rights laws, they have no basis from which to object to legislating morality. James Buckley suggests in *First Things*,

> Nor have we, in this "enlightened" age, ceased to legislate morality. How, for example, are we to describe the civil rights laws of the past generation except as the codification of a moral imperative? And what about our various social welfare laws? Are they not expressions of a corporate responsibility for the old, the sick, and the poor among us?[27]

People may object to the specific manifestation of morality being legislated—and that is fine; after all that is what legislative debate is all about!—but the debate should not be conducted as if the very enterprise of legislating morality were illegitimate. While the notion of moral responsibility cannot be articulated in rights talk, it is nevertheless incorporated into each piece of legislation. And the neoconservatives have claimed that it is better to discuss in the open exactly how morality should be legislated than to do it unwittingly.

While neoconservatives believe that the state should have no compunction about legislating morality, serious moral questions can only be touched ever so lightly by legislation. Not recognizing a constitutional "right to privacy," neoconservatives have nonetheless argued that there should be a wide zone of individual behavior off limits to the government. The risks of totalitarianism, or at least creeping totalitarianism, are too great for government to become too involved in the strictly personal affairs and actions of individuals. Neoconservatives have not offered a simple formula for determining when the government should involve itself in issues of morality and when it should not; they neither subscribe to the liberal dictum "You have the right to swing your fist until it hits my nose" nor substitute another. The level of direct government intervention into issues of morality depends on the needs and mores of a particular community, which inherently elude universal classification. Neoconservatives realize that New York and Salt Lake City are going to enact laws that inculcate different types of morality, and find nothing inherently wrong with that.

Neoconservatives believe that the culture must enforce its moral standards independent of the law. The culture can—and should—go places the law cannot and should not. As Richard John Neuhaus states, "Civilization depends upon obedience to the unenforceable."[28] It is the duty of free citizens to establish community standards and to hold individuals to them without resorting to the coercive powers of the state. In a 1989 essay, Gertrude Himmelfarb explained that the need for coercive laws declines in direct proportion to the level of morality inculcated in the people. If the left would relent from its philosophy of radical individualism, the coerced moral standards that it so dreads might become less necessary. Community standards could domesticate individual freedom, and individual freedom could soften community standards.[29]

The Virtue of Mediating Structures

> Liberalism has no real message for private life. Its attitude toward private life is, essentially, that it should be left alone, for the individual to manage as best he can. While this attitude has of late been in some tension with the "statist" trend, it is still quite vital. Liberals continue to have a serious commitment to the protection of private freedoms against encroachment by large public institutions. Now, this laissez-faire attitude works well as long as private life is given structure and meaning from other sources—religion, the family, folk or ethnic subcultures, and the like. The crisis of modernity, however, is precisely the fact that these other sources are in

> danger of drying up. The liberal political order itself depends upon the continuing viability of these other structures—yet these are structures that liberalism has tended to be uninterested in and, in some instances, has even intended to oppose as narrow or "backward."[30]

Peter Berger's words articulate one of the most important neoconservative projects: mediating structures. Mediating structures are private, voluntary organizations such as unions, churches and synagogues, veterans' groups, families, schools, charitable associations, trade groups—all manner of associations that provide meaning, sustenance, and comfort to individuals outside government. People give of their time, effort, and money to these organizations that work toward a common purpose or a common goal. The abstract sacrifice and empathy necessary for communal action is not the only way in which morality is served by these groups, which often provide support services and tangible aid to members in need. While these groups start locally, they nourish the qualities that are necessary for people to participate in larger communities, culminating in the state.

Mediating structures serve two major purposes; they nurse and inculcate virtue in the people who are involved with them, and they play direct and important roles in the community. The work of mediating institutions starts very soon after someone is born. James Q. Wilson explains,

> The fraction of children who fail morally is probably far smaller than the fraction of automobiles that fail mechanically. Part of the reason, of course, is that society doesn't leave matters entirely in familial hands; it has self-protection and control mechanisms. . . .[31]

Neoconservatives have argued that mediating structures serve the needs of social welfare far better than government. While government programs generally give people things (such as welfare checks, child care, public housing, food stamps, or job training), it has a very difficult time holding people accountable for their actions and making sure that there is a return on the investment of the taxpayers. Because government aid is generally dispensed from Washington or a state capital, the recipient usually has little connection with those who are providing the aid. There is generally little sense of commitment or solidarity between the producers and the recipients. Often, the recipient of welfare will not be influenced by the work ethic and values of productive members of society—the taxpayers—but will have dysfunctional values enforced by other members of the underclass. And without a mutual exchange of aid and responsibility, the condition of the recipient will likely be worsened. Irving Kristol explains, "obligation is not only a right but a need—people upon whom no obligations are imposed will experience an acute sense of deprivation." Institutions that do not place moral demands on people will rapidly fall into disrepute, as the citizenry loses respect for institutions that lose respect for themselves.[32]

Richard John Neuhaus maintains that institutions can best make these moral demands when they are closest to the people being served. Because smaller groups and more contained communities are closer to the individual, they can be more sensitive to his concerns, needs, background, and abilities than can larger and more impersonal groups. Hence, mediating structures often serve the social function of government more effectively than does the state. The closer an institution, whether a government or a mediating institution, is to the people it needs to help, the better. Neuhaus suggests that mediating structures are excellent manifestations of the Catholic idea of subsidiary.

> A community of a higher order should not interfere in the internal life of a community of a lower order, depriving the latter of its functions, but rather should support it in case of need and help to coordinate its activity with the activities of the rest of society, always with a view to the common good.[33]

Like capitalism, mediating structures are considered by neoconservatives to be indispensable antidotes to totalitarianism. And they operate best when the government does not co-opt social responsibility—and thus the role of mediating institutions. Michael Novak says simply, "When Leviathan falters, civil society stirs. When Leviathan relaxes, civil society expands."[34] If people are sufficiently concerned and involved with the mediating structures toward which they have allegiance, it will be difficult for a central government to obtain an inordinate amount of power. Just as the free market helps to disperse power by providing economic diversity, mediating structures scatter power among social institutions. When a citizenry has a large spiritual and financial investment in mediating structures, people will be too concerned with the work of their church, school, neighborhood, etc., to allow government to monopolize those functions. Agreeing with Novak's point, George Will has suggested that the state should set up barriers to its own power by aiding mediating institutions.

> An aim of prudent statecraft is to limit the state by delegating many of its chores to intermediary institutions. Government can become, to a dangerous degree, an interest group, as self-interested as any other, and more abusive than most. But government can apply to itself a kind of antitrust policy. With all its dimensions, from law through rhetoric, government can encourage strength in private institutions just as surely as totalitarian regimes work to enfeeble such institutions. . . . The institutions that once were most directly responsible for tempering individualism—family, church, voluntary associations, town governments—with collective concerns have come to seem more peripheral. Using government discriminatingly but energetically to strengthen these institutions is a part of the natural program of conservatives.[35]

Judeo-Christian Morality and Public Virtue

In order to fully understand and appreciate the potential of mediating structures, the neoconservatives argue that it is essential to analyze the source of the virtue and morality that makes mediating structures so worthy. Mediating structures cannot produce virtue by themselves, but they can help to nurture and channel existing moral qualities into healthy and productive avenues. Where does this virtue come from?

The neoconservatives believe that morality is derived primarily from Judaism and Christianity. The importance of Judeo-Christian values in neoconservative thought cannot be underestimated; neoconservatives believe that values influence everything, and that Judeo-Christian values should influence everything. As Neuhaus writes, "politics is chiefly a function of culture, at the heart of culture is morality, and at the heart of morality is religion."[36]

In *The Neoconservative Mind: Politics, Culture and the War of Ideology*, Gary Dorrien writes,

> [Neoconservatives] found more difficulty, however, making constructive religious claims beyond these carefully chosen [values] themes. The neoconservatives were too theologically diverse to make the common theologically based arguments and too utilitarian to make the effort . . . they did not agree, however, on the role that religious institutions should play in society or on what theological basis they should act. . . .[37]

An understanding of the neoconservative vantage point on religion can begin by taking Dorrien's statement and inverting it. Neoconservatives believe that Judaism and Christianity provide individuals and society with the moral foundation they require. The neoconservative progenitor Reinhold Niebuhr put it best: "Religious ideas and traditions . . . are the ultimate sources of the moral standards from which political principles are derived. In any case both the foundation and the pinnacle of any cultural structure are religious. . . ."[38]

Before probing neoconservative extrapolations of Niebuhr's principle, it is useful to investigate the strange relationship between intellectuals and religion. Much of neoconservative thought on this issue responds to the intellectuals and cultural leaders with whom they disagree. Speaking very generally, intellectuals at home in the tradition of philosophy (and this includes most of them) believe in apprehending truth through the use of their reason and mental facilities, often unassisted by the absolute truths posited by religion. Intellectual support for religion often takes a utilitarian form; as Werner Dannhauser wrote in a 1985 *Commentary* article, "Exaggerating considerably, one may say that the whole tradition of philosophy is strong in praising the utility of religion and weak in claiming truth for it."[39]

The utilitarian view of religion was incisively articulated by Dostoevsky. "Man must worship something; if he does not worship God, he will worship an idol made of wood, or of gold, or of ideas."[40] Because belief in a Jewish or Christian God requires ethical conduct, as articulated in the Ten Commandments and the whole array of other lessons and teachings of the two religions, intellectuals have traditionally encouraged religion among others if not always among themselves. Voltaire, voicing a sentiment with which many secular intellectuals have identified, said, "I want my attorney, my tailor, my servants, even my wife to believe in God because then I shall be robbed and cuckolded less often."[41]

A remarkable debate between intellectuals which brings to the fore the necessary points regarding this was carried on between Sidney Hook and Ernest van den Haag in *Partisan Review* in 1952. In the second installment of an important *Partisan Review* symposium, "Religion and the Intellectuals," the secularist Hook wrote an essay castigating religion as irrational and nonbelieving intellectual supporters of religion: "[It] still remains true that as a set of cognitive beliefs, religion is a speculative hypothesis of an extremely low order of probability." Religion is not necessary to provide a sense of humility and appreciation of the greatness of the world. "Why should the world appear less wonderful or awesome if some day we step from one planet to another, synthesize protoplasm, or lift the darkness from the minds of the insane?" To accord intellectual credence to religion is not only logically incoherent but dangerous to the all-important task of fighting Communism.

> A sure way to lose the struggle for the democratic world is to permit the Pope to take the lead in a crusade against Bolshevism. The struggle of the unfettered intelligence against institutional orthodoxy must continue despite the fact that conflicting orthodoxies, in the interest of their own religious freedom, find themselves allied for the moment against the super-orthodoxy that will brook no dissent, not even that of silence.[42]

In the next issue, in "An Open Letter to Sidney Hook," van den Haag admitted having no more religious faith than Hook. However, van den Haag wrote, "You have convincingly shown that religious beliefs cannot be logically justified. . . . You believe that most men, if left alone, are as reasonable as you are. This is admirable but also dangerously wrong." Van den Haag writes that Hook's condemnation of religion as false and irrational is irrelevant because "it is socially and politically not important whether religious doctrines are true . . . religion is a useful, even a necessary opiate—a sedative protecting us from excessive anxiety and agitation." And Hook ought to realize that

> Religious sanction is required—just as the police force is—for any society which wishes to be stable without being totalitarian. It is required for ours not logically, but psychologically. (Surely you know that few people hold any belief—right or wrong—for sufficient reasons. Beliefs are held because of more or less institutionalized myths.)[43]

Hook was not impressed by van den Haag's response. In "A Rejoinder to Mr. van den Haag," Hook reiterates many of the same points from his original article, asserting, "To defend, as you do, organized irrationalism in behalf of human freedom is an intellectual absurdity—a cruel paradox which requires that we forget whatever we know about history, social institutions and human beings."[44]

Neoconservatives believe in the utility of religion, and most (unlike Ernest van den Haag) value religious truth as well. The Christian neoconservatives emphatically contend that the former without the latter is a grossly insufficient. Richard John Neuhaus says, "religion is essential to public virtue, public virtue is essential to our being a free and democratic society, therefore that we should all be included in religion. Now, in so far as that goes, it's true. But it doesn't go very far."[45] Neuhaus, once a Lutheran pastor and now a Catholic priest, Michael Novak, and George Weigel are all devout Catholics.

The Podhoretzes and the Kristols are Jewish. Irving Kristol's position on religion has drawn criticism—always polite criticism, to be sure—from some of the other neoconservatives. Kristol declares that he is a "neo-orthodox Jew," explaining, "I am nonpracticing—or nonobservant as we say—but in principle, very sympathetic to the spirit of orthodoxy."[46] Several neoconservatives have criticized Kristol for holding a strictly instrumental view of religion in the mode of van den Haag. Richard John Neuhaus, for instance, states, "Irving, God bless him, has a very different understanding of religion than I do. We agree on many things, but his [view on religion], how should I put it accurately, is more of an instrumental view. . . ."[47] George Weigel advances a similar sentiment, maintaining,

> Irving is a very special case. Irving has an instrumental view of religion here because he—as he would admit—is tone-deaf to religious sensibilities. This

> is not music that makes his heart sing. Yet, he is smart enough an observer of the human condition to understand that he should not take a Kantian imperative here.[48]

Both Irving Kristol and William Kristol assert that this criticism misses the point. William Kristol maintains,

> My father is obviously talking about religion in the public sphere. And obviously when one talks about religion that way, one talks about it instrumentally. I think there has been too much made of this notion that my father likes religion for these reasons. How else would one discuss religion in this secular, worldly context?[49]

While most neoconservatives are Jewish or Catholic, they do not focus on their theological differences in their writings on religion. They respect—revere, actually—the other religions and have made no known attempts to convert one another. The neoconservatives believe that individuals should be strong in their own faiths. As *First Things* editorializes,

> To say that ours is a Christian-Jewish enterprise does not mean that it is some hybrid "third way" called Christian-Jewish, distinct from the ways of Judaism and Christianity. As we understand it, the Christian-Jewish partnership requires that Jews be Jews and Christians be Christians.[50]

The alliance between Christian and Jewish neoconservatives on religious issues is based on a genuine respect for the other religion. Theological differences are neither denied nor stressed in public debate. While the Jewish neoconservatives genuinely like Christianity and the Christian neoconservatives genuinely like Judaism, the theological differences between Jewish and Christian neoconservatives remain, even if they are muted in public arguments. Questions of theology are more complicated than political issues, and the theological differences between Christianity and Judaism are quite significant. Richard John Neuhaus is a great philo-Semite, having written since his days as a radical in the 1960s of his reverence for the Jewish people and for Judaism. Yet he writes in *The Naked Public Square*, "One day every knee will bow and every tongue confess that Jesus Christ is Lord."[51] The Podhoretzes and the Kristols surely disagree, but this major theological difference in no way interferes with the vast areas of agreement that they share with Neuhaus concerning issues of morality, virtue, and religion in the public square.

An important reason for the neoconservative support for Judeo-Christianity is that the shared tenets of Judaism and Christianity have provided a ground from which to align against the cultural left. As Matthew Berke asserts in *First Things*, "Whatever may separate Jew and Christian, they are united against the creeping nihilism of modern culture and in their common hope for a redemption of the world."[52] Similarly, Michael Novak writes that while Jews and Christians have significant theological differences, their basic moral structures are virtually identical and serve as a common basis for living ethically in the public square. He writes, "The two [Judaism and Christianity] share an astonishing number of convictions, aims, expectations, perspectives, and criteria of goodness. It is hard to exaggerate how much they have in common."[53] James Q. Wilson elaborates in 1995 *Crisis* article.

> Religions that make you aware of the dark forces within you, equip you with the recognition that you need help to manage those forces, supply you with a conviction that such help is available from Somebody or Something provided you submit to Him or It, and lead you to act in accord with natural law . . . are great religions. As countless others have observed, viewed in these terms there is not much difference among the great religions.[54]

Neoconservatives perceive the cultural left as largely secular and often hostile to the values that are shared by Judaism and Christianity. Only a transcendent moral structure provided by Judeo-Christianity can compete with the grand visions presented by left-wing utopians, who are really brandishing their own kind of secular religion. In such a climate, the secularists must be fought—and on the ground shared by Judaism and Christianity. Rabbi David Novak explains,

> secularity has threatened them [Jews and Christians] both quite similarly. A common threat has created a new common situation. It is thus inevitable that historically perceptive Jews and Christians should be rediscovering one another. As Jakob J. Petuchowski put it so well, "Neither Jews nor Chris-

tians can really afford to be isolationists. In this pagan world of ours, we together are the minority 'people of God.' "[55]

Neoconservatives also believe that traditional Jews and traditional Christians should align themselves culturally and politically because they share the same values. There is agreement among these groups concerning the importance of family, community, religion, diligence, respect for elders, honesty, probity—in short, the Judeo-Christian and bourgeois virtues that stem from the Ten Commandments and the Bible. Although they are not always separated, the question of whether Jesus Christ is the Savior is different from the question of which morals should guide society. While Jews and Christians will (according to Judaism) or may (according to Christianity) never reach agreement on the former issue, they can certainly agree on the latter. President Eisenhower, voicing a theme that would be later developed by the neoconservatives, stated, "Our government makes no sense unless it is founded in a deeply felt religious faith—and I don't care what it is."[56] According to the neoconservatives, the morality inculcated by religion is at least as important as its theology.

The neoconservatives have a theory of the role of religion in public life, and like most of neoconservatism, it starts in opposition to the left. Because the debate over religion in the United States so often revolves around "the separation of church and state," the neoconservatives have written extensively about this issue. They argue that this phrase—which appears neither in the Constitution nor in any of the founding documents—is a gross misnomer. The First Amendment reads, "Congress shall make no law respecting an establishment of religion, or prohibiting the free exercise thereof. . . ." Neoconservatives maintain that the "establishment" part of the religion clause was meant to service the free exercise part. To demonstrate this argument, the neoconservatives turn to the Constitution and to the intent of the Founders in drafting the religion clause. In this sense, they are like the British socialist Harold Lasky. Disputing a colleague on a fine point of Marxist thought, Lasky replied, "You interpret [Marx] your way, I'll interpret him in His [*sic*]."[57]

According to the neoconservatives, the gravity and import of the free exercise part of the religion clause is self-evident. The Founders believed religion to be essential to public virtue, and wanted to make sure that everyone is given the opportunity to practice a religion that will foster the private morality that leads to public virtue. The "no establishment" portion of the religion clause is open to greater controversy. While the Founders' contention that free exercise of religion is a requirement for public virtue is clear, what about "no establishment"? An established church might imply that the state has the power to coerce people to join that church, thus denying people the free exercise of their religion.

Perhaps even more important than the negative effects that an established church could have on the state are the negative effects the state could have on religion. According to the neoconservatives, the establishment part of the religion clause is just as geared toward protecting the church as it is toward protecting the state. Rebounding from a tyrannical monarchy, the Founders realized how corrupting the power of the state could be when placed in the wrong hands. With strong churches, there is only so much that a tyrannical ruler could do. Whatever power he amassed would be checked by that of the churches. A clergyman could probably command more allegiance from his parishioners than a tyrant could from his citizens. While a government could fall into bad hands, society would survive as long as the government was denied the opportunity to infiltrate and manipulate the leadership of the churches. In his famous "Memorial and Remonstrance" James Madison demonstrates the fear of the Founders that the state could corrupt religion.

> Before any man can be considered a member of civil society, he must be considered as a subject of the governor of the universe; and if a member of civil society, who enters into any subordinate association must always do it with a reservation of his duty to the general authority, much more must every man who becomes a member of any particular civil society do it with the saving his allegiance to the universal sovereign. We maintain, therefore, that in matters of religion no man's right is abridged by the institution of civil society.[58]

According to the neoconservatives, the establishment part of the religion clause has no independent value. The Founders thought that an establishment of religion would hamper the free exercise of religion either directly by denying religious liberty to believers in a nonestablished faith or indirectly by corrupting the churches where people freely choose to worship. The Founders did not specifically mention the master-servant relationship between the free exercise and establishment parts of the clause because it needed no explaining at the time. Richard John Neuhaus cites Thomas Jefferson on this point.

> We the General Assembly of Virginia do enact that no man shall be compelled to frequent or support any religious worship, place, or ministry whatsoever, nor shall be enforced, restrained, molested, or burthened in his body or goods, nor shall otherwise suffer, on account of his religious opinions or beliefs; but that all men shall be free to profess, and by argument to maintain, their opinion in matters of religion, and that the same shall in no wise diminish, enlarge, or affect their civil capacities.[59]

This is, more or less, an elaboration of the religion clause. Jefferson states that the General Assembly may not establish religion nor prohibit its free exercise. Neuhaus points out that the key phrase in this statement is "but that."

> The "but that" immediately after the semicolon sums up the entirety . . . [of the servant-master relationship]. What follows "but that" is the statement of the end. The very limited "no establishment" provisions preceding it are means in the service of that end.[60]

Neoconservatives believe that the doctrine of strict separationism (the divorce of religious symbols and the public square through the establishment section of the religion clause) has altered the original framework of state and religion and greatly damaged moral discourse. In their hostility to religion, liberals have interpreted the First Amendment to ban religious symbols from public lands and to purge religious references from public events such as high school graduations. Along the same lines, religious themes have become, if not illegitimate, at least highly suspect when used in public debate.

Neoconservatives argue that when public debate is robbed of its religious references and grounding, it cannot be informed by religion's child, morality. This is detrimental to the polity and the culture, which operates from either a moral or an immoral—not a morally neutral—foundation. And even the most commited of liberals once recognized the importance of Judeo-Christianity in this. As James Q. Wilson points out,

> Suppose this were 1944, not 1994, and lynchings were commonplace in certain parts of the country. People were then "deeply divided" over what respect, if any, was due to the life of a black man. Some people genuinely believed that only vigilante justice could maintain a society based on the [to them] necessary principle of white supremacy. Should people who disagreed with this view—who felt that the life of a black man was entitled to as much respect as the life of a white one—have been forbidden from enacting their views into law because to do so would have violated the separation of church and state?[61]

Furthermore, when religion is confined to the private sphere, numerous citizens are denied their right to influence the polity and the culture through mediating structures. Religious institutions are voluntary associations of free individuals solidified by a common belief structure, culture, or heritage. People form, develop, and act on moral convictions through religious mediating institutions. Neuhaus argues,

> Religious institutions may understand themselves to be brought into being by God, but for the purposes of this democratic polity they are free associations of citizens. As such, they are guaranteed the same access to the public square as are the citizens who comprise them. It matters not at all that their purpose is to advance religion, any more than it matters that other associations would advance the interests of business or labor or radical feminism or animal rights or whatever.[62]

Religion in the Public Square

Neoconservatives maintain that—even aside from the destructive cultural impact of strict separationism—liberals distort the First Amendment conception of the relationship between government and religious liberty. In contending that crèches at Town Hall, school prayer, and mentions of God at graduation ceremonies are unconstitutional, liberals maintain that the state violates the establishment part of the religion clause by indirectly establishing Christianity or Judeo-Christianity. Neoconservatives respond that crèches and prayers at graduations could only be unconstitutional if it were proved that they denied nonbelievers the right to freely practice their religions. Finding no indication that a manger at Town Hall on Christmas Eve prohibits Jews from worshiping in synagogue or Muslims from going to the mosque, the neoconservatives see no way that the liberal view is consistent with the Constitution. Liberals generally come back and claim that a crèche de facto establishes Christianity by making non-Christians feel "uncomfortable" or as "outsiders" when they pass a crèche. Neoconservatives question the strength of a religious faith that is threatened by such a symbol. As is evidenced by the lack of interest among Orthodox Jews regarding Christian symbols in the public square, those who are truly secure in their faith are not concerned when symbols of a different religion are placed in public. Their children will not have a crisis of faith at the sight of the likenesses of Mary and Jesus in front of a courthouse.

According to the neoconservatives, the strict separationist view of the left not only violates the intent of the Founding Fathers regarding religion, but runs contrary to their vision of a free and virtuous republic. Neoconservatives stress that the Founders thought that religion should play a significant role in the lives of the citizenry and that Judeo-Christian morality is the basis upon which public debate should be conducted. Thus, while church can—and must—be separated from state, religion must never be separated from politics.[63] Irving Kristol explains,

> One of the functions of a liberal government was to see that religious institutions prospered. That is a very important point. Regardless of what the Constitution says about separating church and state, it does not separate state and religion. . . . The state in Anglo-Saxon liberal thought had a positive responsibility to encourage established religions, because those established religions supplied what a liberal philosophy could not by itself supply, namely, a sense of moral responsibility.[64]

In a 1990 *First Things* essay, Michael McConnell, a University of Chicago Law School professor, maintains that the liberal reading of the First Amendment swallows itself. The seminal Supreme

Court ruling in establishment clause jurisprudence is *Lemon v. Kurtzman* (1971). In that decision, the Court determined that government actions violate the establishment clause if they lack a secular purpose, "advance" religion, or threaten to "entangle" government with religion. This decision is an excellent example of strict separationism; virtually all contact between government and religion is prohibited by the *Lemon* standard. However—if the *Lemon* standard is taken seriously—the free exercise part of the religion clause must be declared unconstitutional. McConnell explains, "a vigorous defense of the free exercise of religion is non-secular, advances religion, and often embroils government in issues of religion."[65]

To the neoconservatives, free exercise of religion can and should be forthright. Diluted secularist religion is dishonest, even—and perhaps especially—in the public square. Judaism and Christianity do not have to give of themselves to be tolerant of other faiths; they are untrue to the message of God if they are intolerant. This proud affirmation of a particular religion while demonstrating at least tolerance if not reverence for other religions is the product of religious conviction itself. In short, religious tolerance comes from religion. Neuhaus suggests, "Americans believe that it is the will of God that we be tolerant of those who disagree with us about the will of God."[66]

Indians and Swedes

Neoconservatives maintain that the central void separating the cultural elite and the mass of American people is religious. Michael Novak calls the cultural elite "Christophobic," and maintains that the cultural elite has set the agenda for liberalism so that a militant secularism is broadcast in movies, newspapers, television programs, and contemporary music. While the American people may be incorrigibly religious, the cultural elite does its best to call into question the moral legitimacy of acting following religious commands. Novak states,

> Those who work in the movies, rock music, television, the law schools, some leaders of the feminist movement, some leaders of the gay rights

movement, and many in journalism who worry about protecting their progressive credentials are together waging a form of total warfare to destroy every vestige of cultural support for . . . Christian faith and morals.[67]

Contrast this, Weigel suggests, to the religious beliefs of the American people.

90% of the American people believe in God; 86% believe that the Bible is "the inspired word of God"; 60% pray daily and 75% weekly; 57% are formal members of a religious organization; 45% attend religious services weekly; and 25% do regular voluntary work for a religious organization.[68]

In another essay, Weigel ties this phenomenon in a neat knot.

Put in the simplest symbolic terms, the people who produce the "CBS Evening News" do not necessarily share the broader cultural and more specifically religious sensibilities of the people who watch the "CBS Evening News."[69]

Neoconservatives maintain that the lack of religious faith on the part of the cultural elite is reinforced by its contempt for people who have religious faith. Members of the cultural elite do not share even the beliefs of Ernest van den Haag; they have no faith themselves and despise it in others. George Weigel again:

the broader inclination of elite Western opinion to view religion as an irrational, premodern phenomenon, a throwback to the dark centuries before the Enlightenment taught the virtues of rationality and decency and bent human energies to constructive, rather than destructive, purposes. Nor should it be considered a secret that this elite Western suspicion of religion frequently involves a caricature of religious conviction.[70]

Neoconservatives concede that the secular cultural elite has a small membership, but assert that its numbers do not reflect its influence. However, this elite is located in important opinion-making sectors in American life; the church-going folk who comprise the bulk of the country by and large do not produce movies, write books, or act in television shows. Peter Berger explains this situation by stating that while India is the most religious country in the world and Sweden is the most secular, America is a nation of Indians ruled by Swedes.[71]

The neoconservatives believe that the combination of a secular polity and culture with a religious people is not a mere anomaly, but a destructive inconsistency. To begin with, confining religion to the private sphere denies the very nature of religion. Religion is a public enterprise, practiced in a community of faith. Religion brings people together spiritually and socially and requires that they pray and work together. The lessons that religion teaches concerning how to live the good life apply to communities far more than to isolated individuals; individuals are instructed by religion how to act in relation to others.

Therefore, communities of faith that are formed from religion must be nourished by the common culture. A culture that consistently derides society's basis for morality and community cannot be healthy. People cannot think one way at home and another way in the street—and should not have to—though this is often required by the distinction between the culture and the polity in contemporary America. As Richard John Neuhaus states,

> While the society is incorrigibly religious, the state is secular. But such a disjunction between society and state is a formula for government delegitimation. In a democratic society, state and society must draw from the same moral well.[72]

Peter Berger maintains that this discrepancy between a militantly secular state and an incorrigibly religious people has contributed to a lack of confidence in the nation's social institutions. He writes, "every society, and a democratically governed society more than others, requires legitimization. It requires the belief that it is morally justified." And when the lessons of America's moral messenger—religion—are contradicted by a doctrine like strict separation, a sense of confusion fueling an institutional insecurity is inevitable.[73]

The neoconservatives are not content to limit their concern with religion in the public sphere to crèches, school prayer, and Supreme Court decisions. The state has a role to play—or not to play—in religious issues, but this role is secondary. Neoconservatives are most concerned with the effect that religion has on the culture. Neoconservatives believe that healthy political debate and cultural discourse must rest upon a foundation of Judeo-Christian values. To deny society access to this heritage is to rob democracy—already a delicate political system of compromise and relativity—of access to certain truths and accepted articles of wisdom from which to base public policy and cultural norms. Neuhaus writes,

> Without a transcendent or religious point of reference, conflicts of values cannot be resolved; there can only be procedures for their temporary accommodation. Conflicts over values are viewed not as conflicts between contending truths but as conflicts between contending interests. If one person believes that incest is wrong and should be outlawed while another person believes incest is essential for sexual liberation the question in a thoroughly secularized society is how these conflicting "interests" might be accommodated.[74]

The Challenge from Paganism: The de facto Established Religion

The neoconservatives write that the liberal attempt to purge Judeo-Christianity from public debate is an enterprise inevitably bound for unintended consequences that could be quite devastating. In a major 1991 *Commentary* essay, "The Future of American Jewry," Irving Kristol maintained that those who attempt to purge religion from the public square are not harmless advocates of reason but clergymen in the church of secular humanism. According to Kristol,

> [Secular humanism] can be summed up in one phrase: "Man makes himself." That is to say, the universe is bereft of transcendental meaning, it has no inherent teleology, and it is within the power of humanity to comprehend natural phenomena and to control and manipulate them so as to improve the human estate.

While its practitioners deny that it is a religion, Kristol maintains that it is.

> Merely because it incorporates the word "secular" in its self-identification does not mean that it cannot be seriously viewed as a competitive reli-

> gion—though its adherents resent and resist any such ascription . . . secular humanism is more than science, because it proceeds to make all kinds of inferences about the human condition and human possibilities that are not, in any authentic sense, scientific. Those inferences are metaphysical, and in the end theological.[75]

Such a religion, which may sound appealing to those who are more concerned with abortion rights than the afterlife, is bound to fail because it does not appeal to man's need for a special place in a transcendent universe. Kristol writes,

> It is crucial to the lives of all our citizens, as of all human beings at all times, that they encounter a world that possesses a transcendent meaning, in which the human experience makes sense. Nothing, absolutely nothing, is more dehumanizing, more certain to generate a crisis, than experiencing one's life as a meaningless event in a meaningless world.[76]

Because secular humanism cannot generate a moral structure or infuse a community with anything other than interest and preference, it will falter. And when it falters, or as it falters, people will worship something, and not necessarily the God of Judaism and Christianity. In a statement that encapsulates the belief of many neoconservatives on religion, T. S. Eliot warned, "If you will not have God—and he is a jealous God—then you should pay your respects to Hitler or Stalin."[77]

The focus of "The Future of American Jewry" and much of the recent work of the Jewish neoconservatives concerns the political and social views of American Jewry. While almost all other immigrant groups have abandoned the monolithic attachment to the Democratic Party and liberalism their forebears had, Jews have not. Years after discrimination against Jews became a bad memory, the blatant anti-Semitism of liberals such as Andrew Young and Jesse Jackson, and liberal institutions such as the United Nations and socialist governments, and after Jews have risen to the top of the nation's economic strata, Jews remain unrepentant Democrats. As Jay Lefkowitz writes in *Commentary*,

> Jews have shown a virtually congenital proclivity to pull the Democratic lever. With the exception of blacks, there is no group in America—

including even union members and welfare recipients—more loyal to the Democratic Party.[78]

Milton Himmelfarb has exhaustively studied the statistics on Jews and politics and has come to one conclusion—Jews are die-hard conservatives.[79] In light of the dramatic transformation of liberalism from equal opportunity to quotas and from support for Israel to allegiance to the Palestinians, Jews simply refuse to change. In another descriptive analogy, Himmelfarb compares Jewish voting to compulsive smoking. "Compulsive smokers know that smoking is not good for them but they keep smoking. Most Jews are compulsive Democratic voters."[80]

Jewish neoconservatives contend that the Jewish allegiance to liberalism is destructive—indeed, potentially deadly to the survival of the Jewish people—for several reasons. The first concerns Israel. As the neoconservatives have discussed since the 1970s, large segments of the left changed their allegiance from Israel to the new "victims," the Arabs, and, more specifically, the Palestinians after the 1967 war. Neoconservatives maintain that this change was so pronounced and often so obnoxious—as in the case of the U.N. resolutions in the 1970s—that any Jew whose liberalism was not a bit chastened by it must have a quasi-religious faith in liberalism.

The neoconservatives claim that Jewish liberalism is self-destructive in ways beyond the salient example of left-wing anti-Semitism. For instance, consider the American defense budget. Throughout the 1970s and 1980s, the neoconservatives claimed that smaller United States defense budgets would be devastating to Israel. Throughout the Cold War and after, Israel depended on American weaponry and technology to stay even with their well-equipped Arab enemies. However, many liberal Jews stayed true to liberalism in their opposition to defense spending. It was as though they did not consider that Israel could not benefit from weapons that did not exist. As Martin Peretz characterizes pro-Israel Democrats, "It means the eagerness of Democrats to provide weapons to Israel which these Democrats don't think the United States should build at all."[81]

Most of the arguments concerning the defense budget and Israel surfaced in the 1970s and 1980s. More recently, the neoconservatives have focused on what they believe to be the destructive results of Jewish views of Christianity and religion. It is no secret that Jews have been at the forefront of the effort to promulgate the secularization against which the neoconservatives have fought. In a long essay published by the American Jewish Committee, Naomi Cohen quotes a "prominent rabbi" as saying, "When I hear the words 'Christian America,' I see barbed wire."[82] According to this rabbi and others, the less Christian Christians are, the better. The sentiment of the rabbi is far from isolated or idiosyncratic, and the Jewish neoconservatives are chagrined by it—and not just because some of their best friends are religious Christians.

Most of the neoconservatives believe that Jews are safer and Judaism is more secure in a forthrightly Christian society than in a secular society that relegates religion to the private sphere. They contend that an unabashedly Christian society can have strong, religiously based barriers against anti-Semitism that a secular humanist order will have no overarching reason to erect. In a secular humanist society, which cannot inculcate a transcendent moral structure, there can be no objection to anti-Semitism grounded in ineluctable principle. Secular humanists are not going to believe that anti-Semitism is a sin against God that must be fought at all costs, as many Christians do. As Midge Decter maintains,

> Whatever unease Jews felt in an American culture dominated by Christianity ain't nothin' compared with the anxiety for Jews and everybody else in a culture dominated by raving atheists (sometimes mistakenly called "humanists"), including, be it noted, for the atheists themselves.[83]

The neoconservatives point out that the societies that have been least hospitable to Jews have not been Christian societies, but have rather been paganist. Neuhaus holds,

> The case can be made that the great social and political devastations of our century have been perpetrated by regimes of militant secularism, notably those of Hitler, Stalin and Mao. This is true, and it suggests that the naked public square is a dangerous place. When religious transcendence is excluded, when the public square has been swept clean of divisive sectarian-

> ism, the space is opened to seven demons aspiring to transcendent authority.[84]

Irving Kristol makes a similar point in "The Future of American Jewry," adding that it is imperative that Jews especially should be aware of the dangers of radical secularization. He writes, "American Jews, alert to Christian anti-Semitism, are in danger of forgetting that it was the pagans—the Babylonians and the Romans—who destroyed the temples and twice imposed exile on the Jewish people."[85] Milton Himmelfarb has suggested that paganism has once again come upon us, as the storm of secular humanism has swept away traditional religious allegiances and codes of behavior. He writes, "The trouble is not that religion in general has too small a role in American public life or American life simply. The trouble is that a particular religion has too great a role—paganism, the de facto established religion."[86]

Jews, Christianity, and Judaism

The neoconservatives write that the best friends of Israel have consistently been evangelical southern Protestants. While Jerry Falwell may not have won the support of liberal American Jewry, he was a close friend and ally of Israeli Likud party leaders Menachim Begin and Yitzhak Shamir. Begin explained, "What fundamentalists believe about the conversion of Jews is something in the future, maybe a thousand years from now. Israel needs all the friends it can get right now."[87]

Instead of focusing on the support for Israel among evangelical Protestants, many Jews ignored Begin's advice and concentrated on the theology of the evangelicals. These liberal Jews especially concentrated on an infamous line from 1980 by Dr. Bailey Smith, president of the 13-million-member Southern Baptist Convention. "With all due respect to those dear people, my friends, God Almighty does not hear the prayer of a Jew, for how in the world can God hear the prayer of a man who says that Jesus Christ is not the true Messiah?"[88]

In 1984, Irving Kristol and Lucy Dawidowicz, the renowned

historian of the Holocaust, wrote essays in *Commentary* discussing this statement and the reaction it spawned. Dawidowicz suggested that the comment may not be anti-Semitic; the same exclusive sentiment can be found in some Orthodox synagogues. Furthermore, both she and Kristol questioned, why should Jews care what Smith says about theology, anyway? Kristol asks,

> Why should Jews care about the theology of a fundamentalist preacher when they do not for a moment believe that he speaks with any authority on the question of God's attentiveness to human prayer? And what do such theological abstractions matter as against the mundane fact that this same preacher is vigorously pro-Israel?[89]

Dawidowicz writes in a similar vein as Kristol, maintaining that Jews have no business concerning themselves with whomever Bailey Smith thinks God listens to when Israel's security is constantly under siege.

> In our time, [the evangelicals'] friendship and political support for Israel have been genuine and substantial. Rationalist liberals ridicule this support because they think it is premised entirely on Christian millennial expectations. But evangelical support for Israel is derived from the Bible, from God's promise to Abraham to bless those who bless Israel and curse those who curse it. And even if the evangelicals did support Israel only for ulterior and religious ends, better such support now than the hostility which distinguished their politicized brethren in the National Council of Churches.[90]

Kristol expands on the relationship between liberal Jewry and the moral majority in his response to letters to *Commentary* concerning that 1984 article. This statement encapsulates the beliefs of Kristol and many of the Jewish neoconservatives on the relationship between American Jewry and conservative Christianity, and warrants recapitulation:

> The fact that the Moral Majority is pro-Israel for theological reasons that flow from Christian belief is hardly a reason for Jews to distance themselves from it. Why would it be a problem for us? It is their theology, but it is our Israel.
>
> One would think that Jewish leaders would be interested in exploring the possibility of some degree of cooperation with this group. But they shy

nervously away from the prospect. This is not so much because the Moral Majority is Christian, as because it is conservative. (Jewish leaders, for years now, have found it possible to work with politically liberal Christians.) In other words, it is not Judaism or Christianity that causes Jews to keep a political distance from the Moral Majority, but the Jewish commitment to the secular, political religion—a fair description, I think—of the "politics of compassion," which the Moral Majority does not share. It is revealing to note that Orthodox Jews seem to have no such problem in establishing cordial, if less than completely harmonious relations, with the Moral Majority.

Yet, there are important issues that separate the Moral Majority from the majority of the Jewish community. But are they all non-negotiable? Some may be (e.g., abortion). Others, in my opinion, ought not to be. One such issue is school prayer. When I attended the public schools of New York City, every weekly assembly was opened by principal's reading of a Psalm while we stood in silent attention. It strikes me in retrospect as a pretty good way of instilling a minimum of reverence in young people for the religious roots of Western civilization. In addition, we all became familiar with the Psalms, which is a good thing in its own right. . . .

Jewish organizations (most of them, anyway) have been so dedicated to this task that, by now, they are absolutely convinced that such a rigid wall is constitutionally prescribed—which, for almost two centuries, it was not thought to be. Indeed, their dedication is so extreme that they can simply shrug off their absurd paradoxes that their views lead to. Do we Jews really wish to argue that it is permissible for high-school students to use a schoolroom, after hours, to study *Das Kapital* but not to study the Bible? That is exactly the position we have maneuvered ourselves into.[91]

Just as almost all the neoconservatives have written against the removal of religion from the public square, Jewish neoconservatives have specifically challenged Jews to account for their overwhelming support for strict separation. Neoconservatives have maintained that Jews should not object to public displays of Christianity because the symbols makes them feel "different" or like "outsiders." Why? Because Jews are different and they are outsiders. There is no reason to be ashamed of this; if Jews were not different and outsiders, they would not be Jews. And, given the astronomical rates of intermarriage, American Jews could use a special reminder of their religion. Neoconservatives believe that it is ironic that many of the same liberal Jews who most vociferously object when Christian symbols or references are interjected into public debate placidly watch their children marry Christians.

Irving Kristol suggests, "One does not get the impression that many American Jews would rather see Judaism vanish through intermarriage than hear the President say something nice about Jesus Christ."[92]

Irving Kristol maintains that the only way that intermarriage will abate is if Christians become more Christian and insist on marrying within their faiths. Much of what liberal Jews claim makes them feel "different" or like an "outsider" is probably good if it really does that. He recounts,

> People say, "What are you trying to do, ghettoize the Jews?" And I say, "Yes—as you must—if you care about the survival of the Jews." The only thing that is going to stop intermarriage is if American Christians become more Christian, and Jews don't want that. They fear they'll become anti-Semitic. It's a trap.

In one sense, Kristol believes that Jews would be better off if they were more like Mormons. Jews and Mormons each compose around two percent of the population, have strong family values, and do far better on social indices than any other groups. And yet, most Mormons, who maintain a base in Utah while being scattered throughout the country, do not intermarry as Jews do.[93] Jay Lefkowitz takes Kristol's reasoning one step further, maintaining, "A little anti-Semitism is a good thing for the Jews. It reminds us who we are."[94]

Like Irving Kristol, Elliot Abrams defends a far greater role for Christianity in the public square. Abrams hearkens back to the days when religion was a crucial part of one's identity in the home and in the public sphere—when people were either Protestant, Catholic, or Jewish. His reasons concern the survival of the Jews.

> There was a time . . . when Jews were one-half of America or one-third of America. It was Judeo-Christian or Protestant-Catholic-Jew. Well, we're against that, right, the Jewish community is against all that. We want militant secularization. We want our separatism. . . . Now we have a public square where we have driven out all references to religion. So what are Jews? From 50% or 33$^1/_3$%, we are 1.8%. Can our influence be maintained? Forget it! We have driven the nail into our own coffin.[95]

Abrams believes that religion in the public square should go beyond nativity scenes at Christmas. He points out that Reform

Jews intermarry more than Conservative Jews, who intermarry more than the Orthodox. Those who grow up in a kosher home and attend Jewish day school and synagogue on the Sabbath intermarry less than those who do not. The correlations are basically what common sense would dictate; those who are brought up in religious homes are more likely to have Jewish homes themselves than those who are raised in secular homes.

Clearly, there is nothing government can or should do about how religious a particular home is. However, Jews who are concerned about the survival of their people should support the Jewish day school movement, which does an excellent job perpetuating the faith. And support for the Jewish day school movement implies support for private school vouchers, which would allow Jews without means to take advantage of the opportunities these parochial schools offer. Would that mean also using the government to help Christian children to attend Christian schools? Of course it would, but that would only lead to a more religious society, which is good for the Jews because it might help stem the rate of intermarriage.

What about the argument advanced by liberal Jews that encouraging Christianity will foster anti-Semitism? The neoconservatives answer first that it will not happen; an individual's conversion to Christianity or transformation to devout Christianity in no way implies anti-Semitism. Furthermore, while Christian anti-Semitism exists, it is a relatively minor problem, in light of the other—many self-inflicted—threats to the Jews. Kristol writes,

> [There is no] "resurgent anti-Semitism," as some major Jewish organizations claim. . . . What anti-Semitism still prevails in the larger society is primarily social, a reluctance to assimilate Jews into social life and social activities of the non-Jewish community. Such discrimination has some nasty side-effects at the occupational and professional level, though on the whole American Jews seem to manage to evade those effects. In any case, as a Jew who is not particularly interested in participating in such an assimilation, I can live with it. . . .[96]

In other words, Kristol stated at another time, Jews should stop worrying about Christians persecuting them and start worrying about Christians marrying them.[97]

Even from a strictly pragmatic and political standpoint, Jewish neoconservatives argue that Jewish support for strict separationism is counterproductive. First, it is probably not a great strategy to ask the American people, who are overwhelmingly Christian, to support Israel while trying to purge Christian symbols and references from the public square. If Christians can send money and weapons to Israel, Jews can tolerate crèches. This is not only a needed compromise; neoconservatives argue that it is consistent with the teachings of Judaism. Accommodation of and respect for one's neighbor is a Judaic principle that neoconservatives contend should be applied in the case of Christian influences on the public square. Jacob Petuchowski writes that Jews should abide by the Talmudic injunction *liphnim mishurat hadin*, "On occasion, it is preferable not to make use of the full extent to which the law, strictly interpreted, entitles one to go." An appropriate time to exercise this principle regards Christian symbols in the public square. These symbols do not prohibit Jews from worshiping in their tradition, and objecting to them only causes unnecessary trouble. Petuchowski asks,

> What are we to think of a "Judaism" so weak that it feels threatened by the display of a crèche at City Hall, or by the sound of a Christmas carol at a public-school assembly? Why not, then, show some generosity at a season when Christians celebrate the birth of the Jew in whose name they proclaim peace and good will to humankind?

And if Jews still do not want to tolerate the symbols? Petuchowski adds, "Even if the strict separationist were right on the legal issues, one would still be entitled to wonder what these organizations hope to gain by stirring up animosities every winter."[98]

In light of these arguments, why would Jews care so vehemently about Christian symbols in the public square? The neoconservatives provide an explanation. Many people who call themselves Jews practice the religion of secular humanism rather than Judaism. Ruth Wisse identifies this type of individual as a "non-Jewish Jew—that is, someone identifiably Jewish who underscores her disaffiliation from both the religious and the national content of Jewishness."[99] Some of these Jews interpret liberal politics as not only a religious imperative, but a sufficient expression of their faith. In 1980, when he was making the change from liberalism to neoconservatism, Joseph Epstein admitted that he had been satisfied to be more of a liberal than a Jew.

> I have been a better liberal than Jew, at least from the standpoint of observance of ritual. I have never kept kosher but I often argued for the efficacy of strong central government; at no time did I ever attend synagogue regularly, but I never doubted the value of welfare programs and foreign aid. What would this make me? A Reform Jew and an orthodox liberal? Funny, I hear someone saying, he doesn't look liberal.[100]

For further evidence of the allegiance of liberal Jews to liberalism rather than Judaism, the neoconservatives point to the pronouncements of several of the major Jewish groups. Whereas these groups—namely Hadassah and the National Council of Jewish Women—used to focus on Israel and other issues of Jewish concerns, they now spend a considerable amount of time, effort, and money lobbying for abortion rights. The neoconservatives cannot figure out why abortion is a Jewish concern. Irving Kristol points out that Jewish women are experts at birth control and rarely have out-of-wedlock births or abortions. Therefore, Kristol suggests, abortion should not be an issue for Jewish groups. Furthermore, abortion cannot be a Jewish issue because the Talmud prohibits it in all but a few cases. So in the name of what faith are these groups advocating abortion rights? Certainly not Judaism, so it must be liberalism.[101]

Milton Himmelfarb has written of how the substitution of liberalism for Judaism is destructive to Jewish interests while harming their political interests as well. He believes that Jewish support for abortion rights as Jews is not only inappropriate, but bad for the Jews.

> Really, what difference does it make in the actual availability of abortion if the Union of American Hebrew Congregations passes a resolution or does not pass a resolution or even testifies before a congressional subcommittee? What practical difference does it make? On the other hand, look at the practical benefit from not testifying. You do not [need to] irritate Catholics needlessly. You do not [need to] irritate an awful lot of Americans who

hate abortion. So shut up, organizations. Do not come out antiabortion. Just shut up.[102]

In his writings on Christianity, Norman Podhoretz (and *Commentary*) has primarily focused on Israel. As numerous *Commentary* essays suggest, conservatives, and especially evangelical Protestants, have been much better friends to Israel than most liberals, who are often loathe to dissociate themselves from those who call themselves victims (the Palestinians) or progressive and nonmilitaristic (the United Nations). With regard to issues relating to Israel and concerning other Jewish concerns, Podhoretz has found the left to be hospitable to anti-Semitism while the right has spurned it. Having believed this for years, Podhoretz writes in a 1986 *Commentary* article, "The Hate That Dare Not Speak Its Name," that two recent events have convinced him of its veracity.

Anti-Semitism Right and Left: The Cases of Joseph Sobran and Gore Vidal

The first incident discussed in "The Hate That Dare Not Speak Its Name" concerns Joseph Sobran, a conservative writer who was a senior editor at *National Review* through the mid-1980s and a protégé of William Buckley. While a gifted crafter of prose, Sobran, to put it gently, does not share Buckley's views about the Jews. Buckley characterizes Sobran's thinking on the Jewish question in holding that "it is only Israel and the Jews that seem to have him semi-permanently obsessed."[103] And this is not a good obsession. Sobran has concluded that the American raid on Libya was a Zionist plot inspired by *The New York Times*.

> On the issue of Libya, the *Times* sounds like *Soldier of Fortune* magazine . . . the *Times*, one of America's most ardently Zionist newspapers, understands that Israel has its own reasons for desiring to pit the United States against the whole Arab world.[104]

Sobran has never shown a great concern for the truth when it comes to Israel. At one point, he claimed,

> Israel is a deeply anti-Christian country; it has even eliminated the plus sign from math textbooks because the plus sign (yes, this: +) looks like a cross! Yet Israel depends on American Christians for tax money and tourism, so it has to mute this theme for foreign consumption.

Even if we put aside his ludicrous assertion that Israel is anti-Christian, plus signs were never banned from textbooks. Sobran also lied in stating that Thomas Friedman, a reporter with *The New York Times,* had been suppressed by his editors from writing "a path-breaking story describing the massive Israeli bombing of Beirut as 'indiscriminate.' " Friedman, in a discussion with William Buckley, denied it categorically. Moreover, Buckley charged Sobran with showing extraordinary carelessness in citing a discredited book as evidence that Israeli government officials were aware of the Syrian terrorist attack on American marines in Beirut before it happened. Furthermore, Sobran, never very concerned about South African apartheid, nevertheless championed the Palestinians for the same reasons he maintained were illegitimate to use in favor of South African blacks.[105]

The most invidious of Sobran's columns was surely that of May 8, 1986 which he dedicated to the viciously racist and anti-Semitic magazine *Instauration*. He writes,

> I know of only one magazine in America that faces the harder facts about race: a little magazine called *Instauration*. Its articles are unsigned, and the name of its editor, Wilmot Robertson, is apparently fictitious. *Instauration* is an often brilliant magazine, covering a beat nobody else will touch, and doing so with intelligence, wide-ranging observation, and bitter wit. . . . It is openly and almost unremittingly hostile to blacks, Jews, and Mexican and Oriental immigrants. It is also hostile to Nazism, which makes things confusing. Furthermore, it is hostile to Christianity.[106]

The neoconservatives had been disgusted with Sobran for years, and several of the *National Review* conservatives shared their sentiments. The neoconservatives could no longer tolerate Sobran after his columns about Libya and *Instauration*, and Midge Decter fired off a letter to Buckley charging that Sobran was a "crude and naked anti-Semite."[107] Buckley, while denying that Sobran was an anti-Semitic individual, admitted that his writings gave that impression. In a painful break for Buckley, Sobran was demoted from senior editor to critic-at-large with *National Review.* Buckley forbade him to write about Jews or Israel for *National Review.* Sobran has continued to complain about Jews in other forums, complaining in a 1994 column, "The older I get, the more I am impressed by this pervasive fear of the Jews—or rather, pervasive in some critical power centers, unfelt in other places. It is a huge factor, invisible and incalculable, in American culture and politics."[108]

Podhoretz compared the swift condemnation of Sobran's anti-Semitism by the right to a similar incident, involving the left-wing writer Gore Vidal and *The Nation*, in 1986. In the 120th Anniversary issue of *The Nation*, Gore Vidal contributed "The Empire Lovers Strike Back," a screed against Midge Decter and Norman Podhoretz (to whom he refers, for unexplained reasons, as "Poddy"). The article begins as a personal attack before veering sharply into the province of anti-Semitism. Vidal explains the Podhoretzes' efforts in the Cold War as follows,

> In order to get Treasury money for Israel (last year $3 billion), pro-Israel lobbyists must see to it that America's "the Russians are coming" squads are in place so that they can continue to frighten the American people into spending enormous sums for "defense," which also means the support of Israel in its never-ending wars against just about everyone.

Vidal becomes even more explicit later, characterizing the Arab-Israeli conflict with the sentence, "in the Middle East another predatory people is busy stealing other people's land in the name of an alien theocracy."[109] Vidal leveled the final blow by resurrecting the dual loyalty charge against the Podhoretzes, stating that while he likes his country just fine, he does not like the country of the Podhoretzes, Israel.

Podhoretz and Decter were shocked. Podhoretz wrote, "My own reaction on first reading this article was amazement: I could hardly believe my eyes." In response to the attack, Podhoretz had the managing editor of *Commentary*, Marion Magid, send a copy of Vidal's article to the twenty-eight respected figures who had written congratulatory letters to *The Nation* on their anniversary along with a cover letter that said,

> In connection with a projected article, we are asking a number of friends and supporters of *The Nation* whether they have seen fit to protest against the contribution by Gore Vidal to the 120th anniversary issue ("The Empire Lovers Strike Back"). Could you let us know whether you have made such a protest, either in private or in a letter for publication?[110]

The response was underwhelming. Including letters that were sent directly to the *Nation*, there were eleven replies. Five said they saw nothing wrong in the Vidal piece. Two (the sociologist Norman Birnbaum and columnist Tom Wicker of *The New York Times*) did not respond to the substance of Magid's letter; instead, they said that the *Commentary* response was inappropriate.[111] The journalist Roger Wilkins wrote a letter to the editor of *The Nation*, claiming that Vidal's piece was not anti-Israel, let alone anti-Semitic. After a few weeks and much publicity, Fred Friendly of the Columbia School of Journalism, the writer Elinor Langer, and Senator Paul Simon voiced their disapproval in private, but not in print. Comparing the response of the conservative community to Sobran and the liberal community to Vidal, Podhoretz writes,

> From Vidal's political friends on the Left, then, mainly denial, and from the editor of *The Nation*, stonewalling. From Sobran's political friends on the Right, mostly outrage, and from the editor of *National Review*, dissociation and repudiation of anti-Semitism.[112]

The Discontents and Their Civilization: The Paleoconservatives

Just as the neoconservatives have staked out principled ground between the left and the right since liberal anti-Communism, the Jewish question required them to do so again in the 1990s. The Rockford Institute is a paleoconservative organization based in Rockford, Illinois, that funds paleoconservative thinkers and institutions. In the mid-1980s, the institute had one neoconservative client, the Center on Religion and Society, an organization run by Richard John Neuhaus, which published the journal *This World*. The Rockford Institute was given some funding by various neoconservative foundations, such as the Bradley and Scaife

Foundations, with the sole purpose of channeling that money to Neuhaus. The other major journal that Rockford published is *Chronicles*, edited by Thomas Fleming.

In March 1989, *Chronicles* produced one of the most controversial issues of a journal in the history of American conservative journalism. The lead article, "The Real American Dilemma," by Thomas Fleming, was a diatribe against immigrants.

> Conservatives want to open the door to Cubans and Nicaraguans, while leftists give shelter to Salvadorans and South African blacks. What both groups are saying, in essence, is that they would like the United States to turn into Nicaragua or Haiti.[113]

The issue also contained three articles blasting the neoconservatives. In two of these articles, the vehicle for the attack on the neoconservatives was praise for Gore Vidal. "Gnawing Away at Vidal," by Bill Kauffman, praised Gore Vidal as the quintessential American conservative, "[an] embodiment of Ben Franklin's notion of Republican virtue." Part of Vidal's heroism stems from the enemies he has made, namely,

> all three pointy-heads of the regnant American political triangle: the Manhattan-Washington-based neo-conservatives, the Manhattan-Washington-based New Class conservatives, and the Manhattan-Washington-based corporate-state socialists. In short, the power elite.[114]

This was too much for the neoconservatives, who believed that Vidal's bigotry precluded him from becoming the epitome of republican virtue. Moreover, they did not appreciate the insinuation of conspiracy in Kauffman's article. Podhoretz sent a letter to Neuhaus declaring, "I know an enemy when I see one, and *Chronicles* has become just that so far as I am concerned," and suggested that Neuhaus dissociate himself from the Rockford Institute. George Weigel, too, wrote Neuhaus a letter expressing his anger with *Chronicles*.

> I find the March 1989 issue of *Chronicles* quite disturbing. . . . Tom Fleming's lead editorial is simply nativism shorn of a few of its more egregious Know-Nothing and American Protective Association excesses. . . . [Fleming's] idiosyncratic course [amounts to] the very kind of conservatism that

> Bill Buckley, chief among the brethren, has worked so hard to put beyond-the-pale: mean-spirited, nativist, anti-Semitic . . . obsessed with a mythical past.

Neuhaus had been arguing with Fleming about the treatment of Jews and other minorities in *Chronicles* for over a year. He wrote a memo to Fleming detailing his concern that *Chronicles* was becoming a place where bigots could voice their prejudice in thinly veiled language. Neuhaus explained,

> Anti-Semitism, any hint of anti-Semitism, is morally odious and absolutely intolerable. This concern has been raised by several issues of *Chronicles*. In issue after issue, the emphasis upon cultural rootedness has assumed the nature of a running polemic against those whom the reader is invited to view as rootless, deracinated and cosmopolitan elites. And, of course, the persistent reference to New York in that connection reinforces the impression that the reference is to the cultural influence of the Jews.[115]

Careful not to accuse Fleming and his colleagues of anti-Semitism, Neuhaus says, "They [*Chronicles*] were indifferent to what any serious intellectual should be able to recognize as the classic innuendoes and suggestions of anti-Semitic thought or toleration of anti-Semitic thought."[116] Neuhaus concluded that he could not be funded by the same patron as *Chronicles*, and he began talks with neoconservative foundations to ensure that his institute and journal would be funded after the split with Rockford.

When the people at Rockford heard that Neuhaus was speaking with the neoconservative foundations, they were furious. Paleoconservative author and promoter Paul Gottfried claims that the Rockford Institute was upset with Neuhaus for two reasons. First, "Neuhaus had spoken out against *Chronicles* at social gatherings," a charge to which Neuhaus pleads guilty.[117] Second, the Rockford Institute accused Neuhaus of secretly plotting to capture their funding, and actually threatened to sue the Bradley Foundation and others if they did not give them grants. Neuhaus and others found this absurd for several reasons. First, it is unheard of for a grantee to sue a foundation for not giving it money. Second, the money from these foundations was never intended for Rockford anyway, it was just given to them to funnel to Neuhaus.

Rockford did not see things that way. On May 5, 1989, at 9:20 a.m., Neuhaus arrived at his office to find his staff outside in the rain. "What is going on?" he asked. The Rockford Institute had sent thugs to lock the office doors and seal the files of the Center on Religion and Society. This incident was covered in the national press, and succeeded in rallying key foundations and individuals around Neuhaus and against Rockford. Neuhaus got his papers back and subsequently opened the Institute on Religion and Public Life, which publishes *First Things*.

While William Buckley had tried for years to bridge the *National Review* conservatives and the neoconservatives, taking sides in their disputes only when absolutely necessary, this incident proved to be too much. Neuhaus says, "Bill was really shocked by the Rockford incident in 1989. His immediate, powerful reaction was, '. . . what the heck is going on? You just don't deal that way.' "[118]

The decisive reaction of the conservatives to the anti-Semitism of Joseph Sobran and *Chronicles* would not last in its pristine form, prompting what Norman Podhoretz called "the conservative crack-up."[119] The conservative crackup occurred over Patrick Buchanan, the columnist and commentator who launched a primary challenge to George Bush in 1992.

Patrick Buchanan, the Jewish Question, and the Conservative Crackup

Before I discuss the case of Patrick Buchanan, it is important to provide some background to illustrate why this columnist could precipitate the conservative crackup. Until the 1980s, the neoconservatives and the paleoconservatives did not have much occasion to speak with one another. The descendants of Lionel Trilling and the descendants of Richard Weaver resided in completely different worlds. Their one mutual friend, William Buckley, felt no need to bring them together. Quite simply, the neoconservatives and the paleoconservatives traveled in different circles, and this, presumably, was acceptable to both groups.

In 1981, however, the two groups met. Ronald Reagan appointed M. E. Bradford, a paleoconservative stalwart, to head the National Endowment for the Humanities. The neoconservatives regarded this as a deplorable move; Bradford seemed to many conservatives to be hopelessly lost somewhere in the fourteenth century. His politics were no better; he opposed the Civil Rights Act of 1964 and twice endorsed George Wallace for president. Much of his scholarly work focused on how Abraham Lincoln contributed to the decline of the West. If Bradford went through Senate confirmation hearings, he would have been destroyed while embarrassing President Reagan.

Sensing this, several prominent conservatives rushed to Reagan's aid. Irving Kristol and Edwin Feulner, president of the Heritage Foundation, urged that Reagan withdraw Bradford's name and substitute that of William Bennett, the relatively unknown head of the National Humanities Center. Certain conservative senators, notably Strom Thurmond and John East, were concerned that Bennett might not be conservative enough, given that he was a Harvard Law School graduate and a registered Democrat.[120] But Kristol and Feulner verified Bennett's conservative credentials. William Buckley was initially caught in the middle, having friends in both the Bennett and the Bradford camps. After some consideration, Buckley sided with Feulner and Kristol, and Reagan took their advice. Feulner comments,

> you had, right after the election, Buckley and Kristol and Feulner all on the same wavelength—and supposedly, at this time, Feulner and Buckley had deserted their old buddy Mel Bradford to get Bennett the job. . . . It was a coalescing of the different parts of the movement on a whole different area—different than foreign policy—that showed that we could in fact work together, that we had common views.[121]

This coalescing of the conservative movement came at the expense of the paleoconservatives, and the paleoconservatives did not like it at all. They were upset with Buckley and Feulner, but reserved most of their hatred for the neoconservatives. The Spring 1986 issue of the paleoconservative journal, *The Intercollegiate Studies Review*, is composed of essays decrying the invasion of the conservative movement by neoconservatives. In a *National*

Review article that year, Jeffrey Hart did an excellent job in summarizing the ideas in *The Intercollegiate Review.* He distilled the paleoconservative complaints about the neoconservatives into four arguments.

> 1) [The neoconservatives] aren't religious enough. Professor George Panichas, of the University of Maryland, calls for "spiritual exercises" and a "spiritual and visionary conservatism." 2) [The neoconservatives] are "welfare-state Democrats" thinly disguised, who have captured media attention, dominate some conservative institutions, and have even invaded *National Review* (Paul Gottfried, formerly of Rockford College, now at the *Washington Times*). 3) [The neoconservatives] do not have formative experiences with real conservatives—e.g., the Goldwater movement—and use an alien vocabulary mostly drawn from the social sciences: "These refugees now speak in our name, but the language they speak is the same one they always spoke. . . . Our estate has been taken over by an impostor, just as we were about to inherit." (Clyde Wilson, University of South Carolina). 4) [The neoconservatives] have been alarmingly successful in getting jobs and establishing priorities within the Reagan Administration: The "Old Guard cannot help but catch in the wind from the Potomac a faint but unmistakable odor of opportunistic betrayal" (Clyde Wilson), and the Administration's "surviving reserves of conservatism" might as well be concentrated on judicial appointments (M. E. Bradford, University of Dallas).[122]

This issue of *The Intercollegiate Studies Review* was noticed by the neoconservatives, but it turned out to be just a prelude to the 1986 conference of the Philadelphia Society, an organization of all kinds of conservative intellectuals. According to Burton Yale Pines, former vice president of the Heritage Foundation in the mid-1980s, these meetings are generally "extraordinarily tame."[123] Not, however, at the 1986 meeting in Chicago, when Stephen Tonsor, a prominent paleoconservative, delivered a speech containing the following paragraph:

> It is splendid when the town whore gets religion and joins the church. Now and then she makes a good choir director, but when she begins to tell the minister what he ought to say in his Sunday sermons, matters have been carried too far. . . . [Had] Stalin spared Leon Trotsky and not had him murdered in Mexico, he would no doubt have spent his declining days in an office in Hoover Library writing his memoirs and contributing articles of a faintly neoconservative flavor to *Encounter* and *Commentary.*[124]

As later words suggested, Tonsor's church analogy was not merely rhetorical. He declared that conservatism's "world view is Roman or Anglo Catholic," in marked contrast to the "instantiation of modernity among secularized Jewish intellectuals."

Not surprisingly, this meeting did not end on a happy note, and all present agreed that conservatism had seen more pleasant days. Subsequently, however, the paleoconservatives persisted in their bitterness, often insisting that the neoconservatives were conservative only because of their loyalty to Israel. The doyen of the paleoconservatives, Russell Kirk, led this attack. Kirk said, "What really animates the neoconservatives, especially Irving Kristol, is the preservation of Israel. That lies in back of everything." Kirk reiterated this sentiment at a speech delivered at the Heritage Foundation, declaring that neoconservatives think that the capital of the United States is Tel Aviv.

The neoconservative-paleoconservative rift did not have significant ramifications on the conservative movement at the time because the paleoconservatives were as irrelevant as always. When asked to respond to the paleoconservative attacks, Irving Kristol demurred. "I won't say anything. Anything that I say is only going to throw fuel on the flames. I'll wait for it to pass. It'll pass." Norman Podhoretz concurred, adding, "I am embroiled in too many controversies about anti-Semitism. I am not looking for another fight."[125] Sure enough, Podhoretz did not publish any articles on the paleoconservatives in *Commentary*. The neoconservative response to the paleoconservatives came years after the event, in a *First Things* book review by James Nuechterlein of a work of Russell Kirk. In a powerful attack on Kirk, Nuechterlein writes of paleoconservatism, "It has very little to do with American reality, but for those of a reactionary bent who imagine themselves superior to that reality, it apparently provides a congenial home."[126] While most neoconservatives held their fire when the paleoconservatives attacked, this did not signal a permanent peace in conservatism. Tensions were high, as neoconservatives were reminded that Buckley had not succeeded in purging all of the anti-Semitic elements from the right.

This lesson became even clearer in the example of Buchanan. In the early 1990s, the neoconservatives cited many of Buchanan's statements that reveal systematic anti-Semitism transcending individual issues, which are chronicled in Joshua Muravchik's "Patrick J. Buchanan and the Jews," published in the January 1991 issue of *Commentary*. Buchanan's Jewish problem came to the fore in the Gulf War, which he opposed for isolationist reasons. He said that the only supporters of the Gulf War were the "Israeli Defense Forces and its Amen corner in the United States." Buchanan elaborated a few days later, stating that the war was largely the product of certain hawks—A. M. Rosenthal, Richard Perle, Charles Krauthammer, and Henry Kissinger, all of whom are Jewish. Soon after, Buchanan explained that those fighting the war engendered by these Jews would be "kids with names like McAllister, Murphy, Gonzales, and Leroy Brown."

Muravchik found Patrick Buchanan's fervent support for the Palestinians to be interesting. Buchanan said that the Palestinian intifada (holy war against Israel), "will be recorded in [the] history [of a coming Palestinian state] like the 'Boston Massacre' of 1770. . . . This time, the Palestinians did it right. . . ." On another occasion, Buchanan remarked that the Palestinians have a "God-given right to a homeland: If America stands for anything in this world it is the right of peoples everywhere to determine their own destiny." This, Muravchik notes, comes from a man who had declared in reference to those who commented on the idea that a white minority rule over the black majority in South Africa: "But where did we get that idea? The Founding Fathers did not believe this. . . . To elevate 'majority rule' to the level of divine revelation is a heresy of the American idea."[127]

Buchanan made another exception to his general rule to defend a particular position when it came to the issue of Nazi war criminals. Decrying "Holocaust Survivor Syndrome," he maintained that the gas chambers at Treblinka "[did] not emit enough carbon monoxide to kill anybody," a finding based on the gas produced from a train wreck in New York. In addition, he championed the case of Arthur Rudolf, a Nazi who had supervised slave labor and Hitler's V-2 rocket program.[128]

While the most thorough, Muravchik's attack in *Commentary* was just one of a long list of articles published by neoconservatives castigating Buchanan. A. M. Rosenthal entered into a full-fledged column war with Buchanan in the fall of 1990 which caught the attention of the national press. Charles Krauthammer wrote in a column about Buchanan, "With Communism defeated, Buchanan emerges, like a woolly mammoth frozen in the Siberian ice, as a perfectly preserved specimen of 1930s isolationism and nativism." Buchanan's beliefs about the Jews are only incidental to his larger philosophy. Krauthammer charges, "The real problem with Buchanan . . . is not that his instincts are anti-Semitic but that they are, in various and distinct ways, fascistic."[129] David Frum, then a *Wall Street Journal* editorial writer, published a long attack on Buchanan as an *American Spectator* cover story, declaring that

> [Buchanan's] real message is inseparable from his sly Jew-baiting and his not-so-sly queer-bashing, from his old record as a segregationist and his current maunderings about immigrants and the Japanese. And it's not a message that can be accommodated in any conservatism—Big Government or Small—that seriously hopes to govern a great and diverse country.[130]

On December 31, 1991, *National Review* ran an issue which had only one article, William Buckley's "In Search of Anti-Semitism." "In Search of Anti-Semitism," composed of personal reflections on his forty-year battle with anti-Semitism as well as an analysis of the four alleged cases of highly publicized anti-Semitism in recent years. One was Gore Vidal, whom Buckley easily showed to be anti-Semitic. Another was the conservative college paper, *The Dartmouth Review,* which Buckley (and Podhoretz, Jeffrey Hart—the paper's faculty adviser—and others) found to be the undeserving victim of politically motivated charges of anti-Semitism. The other cases investigated by Buckley were Joseph Sobran and Patrick Buchanan. While Buckley did not say that either Sobran or Buchanan is personally anti-Semitic, he conceded that a fair-minded individual might reasonably conclude that they are anti-Semitic on the basis of their work. Buckley's article generated a great deal of attention and responses from Irving Kristol, David Frum, Norman Podhoretz, Henry Hyde, Murray Rothbard, Joseph Sobran, and others, all published in a special supplement to *National Review* on March 4, 1991 and reprinted in a book, *In Search of Anti-Semitism.*

The lead essay in the February 1992 issue of *Commentary* was Norman Podhoretz's "What Is Anti-Semitism? An Open Letter to William F. Buckley, Jr.," a direct response to "In Search of Anti-Semitism." Despite a few minor disagreements, Podhoretz lauded the article on the whole as an example of Buckley's consistent efforts to combat anti-Semitism on the right.

> [By dissociating yourself from Buchanan] you have taken another step in the campaign you inaugurated some 35 years ago to rescue the conservative movement from those who would besmirch it by spreading anti-Semitism in its name. If the people who lead the left nowadays only had the decency and the courage to police their own ideological precincts in the same way and to the same degree, there would be little cause to worry as much as some of us do about the resurgence of anti-Semitism in this country. . . .[131]

The Buchanan problem came to a head when he entered the Republican primary in New Hampshire to challenge President Bush. While no branch of conservatism liked Bush, the neoconservatives believed that he was far superior to Buchanan. For all of Bush's faults, the neoconservatives reasoned, at least he was not a bigot. The editors at *National Review*, on the other hand, believed that Bush was so bad that Buchanan deserved their vote as a protest. On February 17, 1992, *National Review* ran an editorial advocating a temporary endorsement of Buchanan for president.

> Pat Buchanan, the challenger who did come forward, while trenchant and correct in most respects, has a number of serious flaws—a fondness for protectionism, a nostalgia for isolationism, a careless rhetoric which has given rise to suspicions of anti-Semitism. *NR* pointed out these flaws in anticipation of his announcement, and hoped he would remedy them. He has not yet done so. . . . Yet Buchanan's boners are not the whole, or even most, of his campaign. He has been hitting Bush in New Hampshire on the very tax pledge which allowed Bush to save his nomination four years ago. . . . *NR* therefore, while reserving its position for the later stages of the campaign, urges conservatives to cast a tactical vote for Buchanan in the New Hampshire. . . . A large Buchanan vote would show the country that George Bush is no longer one of us, and that there are a lot of us. Conceivably it might shock Mr. Bush into paying attention to the people, and perhaps even the principles, he has ignored for so long.[132]

John O'Sullivan, the editor in chief of *National Review*, took to the pages of his magazine a month later to elaborate on this position. The neoconservatives had reason to question if O'Sullivan shared Buckley's views on anti-Semitism and the Jews. O'Sullivan had not taken a forthright position on the *Chronicles* incident, commenting that "Tom [Fleming] knew he would be annoying Norman and Midge. He was tweaking their noses. He didn't realize it would be taken as something more serious."[133] Moreover, he disagreed with Buckley's conclusions in "In Search of Anti-Semitism," holding that Sobran and Buchanan were not anti-Semitic. He did not ingratiate himself any further with the neoconservatives by writing in *National Review* in March 1992, "My own preference would be to support Mr. Buchanan until a millisecond before he himself decides to support Mr. Bush, probably sometime in early April."[134]

National Review's endorsement was a clear cause for alarm among the neoconservatives. William Buckley had come close to admitting that Buchanan was a downright anti-Semite, but he and the other editors of his magazine endorsed Buchanan for president nonetheless. In a move that Buckley called "the major shock,"[135] thirteen Christian conservative intellectuals—Peter Berger, Walter Berns, Robert Bork, Terry Eastland, Patrick Glynn, Michael Joyce, Harvey Mansfield, Richard John Neuhaus, Michael Novak, James Nuechterlein, Thomas Pangle, R. Emmett Tyrrell, and George Weigel—many of whom are *National Review* contributors and some of whom serve on its editorial board, jointly wrote a letter to *National Review* castigating the editorial endorsing Buchanan.

> [We] deeply regret the editorial recommendation of *National Review* that conservatives should vote for Patrick Buchanan. Our objection is a moral one . . . it is not morally consistent for the editors to recommend that conservatives should vote for Patrick Buchanan, after Wm. F. Buckley Jr., in his courageous dissection of anti-Semitism, publicly admitted that he finds it "impossible to defend Patrick Buchanan from the charge that what he said and did . . . amounted to anti-Semitism. . . ." That recommendation, further, sets a bad moral precedent for the future of American politics and the conservative movement. It opens the door for others to make discriminatory remarks against other Americans. . . .[136]

The neoconservatives did not like Bush any more than the *National Review* conservatives did; in fact, some of them were so disgusted with Bush that they eventually voted for Bill Clinton. Nevertheless, they found *National Review*'s position to be repulsive in elevating issues—albeit important issues like quotas and high taxes—above Buchanan's anti-Semitism. With *National Review*'s endorsement of Buchanan, the twenty-year consensus between the neoconservatives and *National Review* conservatives was split apart—though, as it turns out, temporarily.

The Christian Neoconservatives and Their Left

Just as the Jewish neoconservatives have written extensively about the destructive relationship between Jews and liberalism, the Christian neoconservatives have waged the war for the political soul of their faith as well. While the Jewish neoconservatives had to fight only one enemy on the front of religion (the left), the Christian neoconservatives had to contend with their enemies on the right—Buchanan, Sobran, and the paleoconservatives—as well as the powerful Christian left.

The Christian and Jewish neoconservatives agree that the stakes are different for each faith with regard to both religious and political issues. While both are prevalent in certain sectors of American culture and are variants of the same bigotry, no neoconservative elevates anti-Christian beliefs to the level of anti-Semitism. History and demography draw the distinction. Just as the neoconservatives distinguished between despicable authoritarianism and intolerable Communism in the 1970s, they did the same with anti-Christian and anti-Semitic attitudes two decades later. *First Things* editorialized,

> given the numerical imbalance between Jews and Christians in this society, and given the still recent horrors experienced by Jews in other societies where the majority claimed to be Christian—it should not be necessary to persuade Christians that there is not a moral or consequential equivalence between anti-Semitism and anti-Christianism.[137]

One major difference in the arguments of Jewish and Christian neoconservatives concerns the issue of intermarriage. In short, the survival of Judaism may hinge upon it; the survival of Christianity does not. A similar dichotomy informs the differing importance of mutual respect between Jews and Christians. Christianity will survive if Jews do not like it; Israel, however, depends on substantial Christian moral and financial support. These two central qualitative differences have colored much of the neoconservative conversation regarding religion. And they are essential for understanding the differences between the Jewish neoconservative reaction to left-wing Jews and the Christian neoconservative reaction to left-wing Christians.

While the Jewish neoconservatives have criticized both Jews and organized non-Orthodox Jewry for being too liberal, the Christian neoconservatives have directed their attacks at the main institutions of Christianity. The official or semiofficial mainstream Christian organizations, mainly the Catholic Bishops and the Protestant National Council of Churches (NCC), are in many ways to the left of their Jewish counterparts—and have received appropriate neoconservative firepower. Through the 1980s and the 1990s, these groups regularly issued pronouncements advocating massive redistribution of wealth, unilateral disarmament, pacifism, affirmative action, and an extensive panoply of government welfare programs.

Writing in *This World* in 1984, James Hitchcock suggested why the political pronouncements of the Protestant and Catholic organizations are so similar and so far to the left. He argues that the interfaith dialogue inaugurated after the Second Vatican Council in 1966 led to a working relationship between traditional Catholics and mainstream Protestants. The Protestants, already left-wing, had a significant influence on the Catholics, who perceived the Protestants as being better adapted to the challenges of modernity.

Hitchcock also points out that left-wing church pronouncements are largely a product of the church bureaucracies (Catholic and Protestant), which are virtually interchangeable. These bureaucracies, staffed by typical members of the new class, are more concerned with left-wing politics than with religion, but nonetheless have had a decisive impact on the bishops and the Protestant clergy. Because the new class bureaucrats are not especially concerned with the theological distinctions between Catholicism and Protestantism and are united in their animus toward bourgeois capitalism, the U.S. military and the free market, the pronouncements from each religion on politics sound the same.[138]

The Christian neoconservatives have not only dissented from these pronouncements, but have questioned the legitimacy of official religious groups making authoritative political statements. They believe that official statements of public policy in writing or from the pulpit are grossly inappropriate. American religion has enough problems confronting a secular culture without alienating the faithful with political pronouncements that are bound to offend some. Neoconservatives stress that people go to church and synagogue for various reasons; learning whom to vote for is not one of them. According to Neuhaus, "the facile invocation of the deity can be dangerous to politics and can, at the same time, devalue the currency of moral discourse." When people use religion specifically to advance a partisan political agenda, they are, Neuhaus charges, practicing blasphemy "by any serious definition of the term."[139] George Weigel agrees, maintaining,

> The treasure of the Gospel has been entrusted to the earthen vessels of our humanity for the salvation of the world, not for the securing of partisan advantage. We debase the Gospel and we debase the Body of Christ (which witnesses in history to God's saving work in Christ) when we use the Gospel as a partisan trump card. . . . The suggestion that Christian orthodoxy yields a single answer to virtually every contested issue of public policy is an offense, not simply against political common sense, but against . . . Christian orthodoxy."[140]

Neuhaus has elaborated on the relationship between religion and political thinking. He writes, "[when] there are reasons we find compelling, reasons informed by Christian morality, for favoring policy X . . . [we should not be saying] that X is the Christian position." He provides an example to illustrate this point. When he was involved in the Vietnam War protest movement, there was a debate over whether to use as a slogan "God says, 'Stop!' " or "Stop! in the name of God." Neuhaus maintains that the latter is superior because "there is a difference between presuming to announce God's position on U.S. foreign policy and pleading—in the name of God but not necessarily on behalf of God—for a change of policy."[141]

Neoconservatives admit that the line between legitimate and illegitimate modes of religious discourse is often difficult to discern. This is especially so with issues of great moral weight, which often, by their very nature, have profound religious and political implications. Neoconservatives believe that religion should inform political decision and public policy; they do not believe that official church groups should take political positions unless they are absolutely essential to the church's teaching. Peter Berger explains,

> There are specific evils in society that Christian bishops could publicly condemn ("prophetically," if you will): racial oppression and anti-Semitism are clear candidates. But is it incumbent upon bishops of the Church to get into the details of policy alternatives? Would it not be more useful if they were to raise incisive moral questions and put them to *all* partisans?[142]

A primary neoconservative objection to the left-wing pronouncements of the Catholic Bishops and their Protestant counterparts concerns the lack of intellectual seriousness with which many of the ecclesiastical views are articulated. Often, the intellectual foundation of these views is not rigorous analysis or even factual grounding, but sheer cant. Dinesh D'Souza catalogued this ignorance in a 1985 *Policy Review* article. D'Souza interviewed many of the bishops who had signed letters and proclamations supporting redistribution of wealth, unilateral disarmament, and the rest of the left-wing agenda and found that many of them did not know the meaning of terms such as "marginal tax rate," "frictional unemployment," and "hard target kill capability," though they had signed authoritative pastoral letters offering detailed policy suggestions on such matters. In response to basic questions, several of the bishops responded with "So the rich get richer, the poor get poorer, and the rich start working with the military," while condemning the "big monsters," who are "putting the mom and pop stores out of business."[143]

Peter Berger, a Lutheran, has written that similar political ineptitude is found in the upper reaches of the Protestant hierarchy. He maintains that such mindless politicking is especially damaging when it finds its way into Sunday services, leaving many parishioners questioning why they came to church in the first place.

> When I go to church or read church publications, I'm irritated when confronted with statements that I consider to be empirically flawed. I don't go to church in order to hear vulgarized, pop versions of my own field. The irritation deepens when these terrible simplifications are proclaimed to me in tones of utter certitude and moral urgency. Bad analysis obviously makes for bad policy, and here I'm not just intellectually irritated but morally offended.[144]

The neoconservative dispute with the left-wing hierarchy of the Catholic Church and the National Council of Churches reached its fiercest point with the Gulf War in 1991. Both the Catholic bishops and the Protestant leadership came out against the war with proclamations that sounded like pure pacifism. The neoconservatives—especially Weigel and Neuhaus—attempted to engage them in dialogue and to demonstrate how the Gulf War fit into the traditional Christian theory of just war. But to no avail; the Christian hierarchy insisted on a pacifism that was not so much Christian as it was simply left-wing. Weigel took to the pages of *First Things* to excoriate them, maintaining that the churches are not operating from an intellectual respectable pacifism, but out of

> a profound alienation from the American experiment and in a deep conviction that American power cannot serve good ends in the world. . . . The deepest taproot of the politics of the religious left is its profound skepticism about the American experiment. A racist, imperialist, militarist, and . . . sexist America cannot act for good ends in the world. That is the orthodoxy of the NCC and the Catholic episcopate.[145]

In his contribution to a *Commentary* symposium in 1985—"Has the United States Met Its Major Challenges since 1945?"—Richard John Neuhaus attributed the left-wing politics of the Protestant mainline to a disgust with the United States. He maintains that the best way to understand the religious leadership of the Protestant hierarchy is to think back to the New Left in the 1960s. The apologetics for totalitarianism with the underlying assumption that the real nation to blame is the United States did not disappear with the 1960s; it simply moved into the home of the Christian left.

This reflective anti-Americanism reflected in the policy pronouncements of much of the Christian hierarchy did not start with the Gulf War. Rather, neoconservatives contend that it has been a staple of church pronouncements on defense issues for some time. In a 1984 *Commentary* article, Patrick Glynn writes of the utter lack of moral seriousness that composed much of the thought of church leaders on military issues. Referring to a condemnation of the arms race by an organization of bishops as "an act of aggression" against "the poor," Glynn counters, "So remote has public discussion in the West grown from the life and death realities of politics that we seem at times to have lost the capacity to differentiate between maintenance of peacetime defenses and the actual waging of war."[146]

Hilton Kramer wrote that the crackup of the Christian leadership on political issues threatens its role as one of the cornerstones of modern society and of Western civilization. He explains,

> Traditionally, we have thought of the Christian religion as being one of the foundations of Western civilization, and the cradle of a good deal of its culture, as well of its spiritual life. Turning to the question of Western civilization, dead or alive, we inevitably have to confront the extraordinary degree to which the Christian churches have become so politicized, have become so much a part of the revolutionary movement in the world, that the question has to be raised: can the churches any longer be said to be one of the cornerstones of Western civilization, or have they become a threat to it?[147]

Neoconservatives have argued that anti-Americanism of all stripes is rooted in anticapitalism, and this applied especially vividly to the Christian left. The first dispute—actually, it is an ongoing dispute—between the neoconservatives and the Christian left was over capitalism versus socialism, starting in the early 1980s. The neoconservative objection to the left-wing politicizing of the churches became combined with their celebration of capitalism. A major concern of the Christian neoconservatives has been the lack of support that their religious traditions provide the free market. Neoconservatives contend that—at least until a recent papal encyclical, *Centesimus Annus*—official Christian beliefs about economics are drawn from a precapitalist age when the abilities of capitalism to transcend a zero-sum economy were unknown. George Weigel asked,

> What about your daily activities: do you hear or read anything from the religious leadership of your church that could be construed as a moral, theological, and spiritual legitimization of your efforts to create wealth? Your entrepreneurial energies have made jobs available to others. Your success has meant success—in investments, in employment, in personal satisfaction—for thousands of employees and shareholders. Through the tax system, and through your philanthropic activities, you are making a significant contribution to the common good. What does your Catholicism have to say about all that? . . . If the truth be told, not much at all.[148]

Consequently, many of the neoconservative ideas on religion which were formulated and developed in the 1980s were directly informed and inspired by their problems with the religious left. Often writing of capitalism in theological terms—as the titles of several of their books, such as *The Theology of the Corporation*, *The Catholic Ethic and the Spirit of Capitalism* and *Doing Well and Doing Good: The Challenge to the Christian Capitalist* indicate—the neoconservatives sought to demonstrate that the free market economy was not only consistent with, but integral to Christianity. The neoconservatives saw anticapitalism at the core of the ideology of the religious left; it informed ideas not only about the free market, but about America in general, the use of military force, and the role of the state.

The debate over economics extended to other realms as well. In the early 1980s, when the Catholic bishops issued pacifist proclamations advocating unilateral disarmament, *National Review* gave an entire issue to Michael Novak to rebut the bishops. Inspired by Niebhurian imperatives regarding the need to confront totalitarianism through force, "Moral Clarity in the Nuclear Age" makes the neoconservative case for peace through strength. Invoking the theme of the culture of appeasement that Podhoretz wrote of in the 1970s, Novak warns, "The widespread pacifism in churches and universities during the 1930s helped convince Hitler and the Japanese that the West lacked the resolve to defend itself, and encouraged them to launch World War II."[149] The parallel for the Cold War was, according to Novak, stark indeed.

Novak called on the nation's religious leadership to move beyond left-wing cant and to confront the harsh realities and moral imperatives of the Cold War. When the National Conference of

Catholic Bishops issued a far-left pastoral letter in 1984, Novak and the businessman and philanthroper William Simon created the lay Commission on Catholic Social Teaching and the U.S. Economy. The commission's report, "Toward the Future: Catholic Social Thought and the U.S. Economy," presented the neoconservative case for capitalism as more conducive to the interests and goals of Catholics than the statism of the bishops. The neoconservatives provided the religious left with the first institutionalized opposition ready and willing to confront it on its own terms. The neoconservatives—especially Novak—were able to rebut the bishops not in the language of businessmen or an economists, but in the more powerful language of theologians.

The Anti-Semitism of the Liberals

While the neoconservatives contend that the general culture is hostile to religion, they believe that one religion receives the brunt of the antagonism—Catholicism. This sentiment is encapsulated by Peter Viereck: "Catholic-baiting is the anti-Semitism of the liberals." Catholic-baiting—which Viereck differentiates from serious theological differences between Catholics and Protestants—has taken numerous forms in the postwar years.[150] It has long been said, generally resting on incorrect presumptions about papal infallibility, that Catholic hierarchy and strictness of doctrine preclude Catholics from being liberal Democrats. At the same time, anti-Catholicism served as a rallying point for anti-anti-Communists, who have, at times, maintained that reactionary and oppressive popes are as bad as Communists.[151]

According to the neoconservatives, the end of the Cold War has done nothing to temper anti-Catholicism, despite the Church's steadfast opposition to Communism. If anything, the anti-Catholicism has become more and more virulent in the popular culture to the point where it is perhaps the only remaining socially acceptable bigotry. Ironically, this remains so despite the fact that Catholicism is the largest single religious denomination in the United States. George Weigel has written and spoken widely on this issue, contributing "The New Anti-Catholicism" to *Commentary* in June 1992.[152] Weigel says that he wishes there were a Catholic equivalent of the Jewish Anti-Defamation League, which carefully monitors anti-Semitism in America. However, he maintains that there will never be such a group until Catholics realize the source of animus to their faith, the sexual revolution. "The single largest institutional barrier to the unmitigated triumph of the sexual revolution is the Catholic Church, here and around the world. For people for whom that enterprise is the bottom line, we are the enemy."[153] While the cultural elite has embraced and legitimated abortion rights, homosexuality, and premarital sex, the Catholic Church has steadfastly refused to "modernize." It is, then, not surprising that the Church has such bitter enemies.

Abortion

The Catholic neoconservatives write passionately about many of these issues that relate to the sexual revolution. The most important of these issues is abortion, an especially important concern to Neuhaus, Novak, Weigel, and Mary Ann Glendon. Their primary objection to abortion is simple enough: they consider it murder. Because a fetus in a mother's womb has all the genetic characteristics of a human being, and if left alone will grow until maturity, there can be no doubt that abortion is the taking of a human life. Any line drawn during a pregnancy—whether by trimester or by month pregnant, is inherently arbitrary. How does a fetus go from being a mass of tissue to a human being in an instant? And at what instant does it do so? The Catholic neoconservatives argue that because these questions cannot be answered, society has a responsibility to protect the fetus.

However, their arguments on abortion do not end here. While they consider abortion crucially important as an issue unto itself, the Catholic neoconservatives also maintain that it is important symbolically as well. Neuhaus writes, "As important as the question of abortion is by itself, it is not by itself. The abortion controversy is [a] flashpoint." Neuhaus and his colleagues consider abortion to be the product of a culture that trivializes the sexual sentiment and reduces the sacred to the mere physical. They hold that the pro-choice philosophy manifests a disrespect for life which, Neuhaus maintains, clears the path to "infanticide to eliminating the inconvenient elderly to, perhaps, genocide."[154]

Neuhaus, who has written more than any other neoconservative on abortion, began his slow and gradual break with the left over this issue in 1967. In the June 30, 1967 issue of *Commonweal*, Neuhaus published an article entitled "The Dangerous Assumptions," blasting the burgeoning movement to "liberalize abortion," as it was then called. In that article, Neuhaus wrote,

> A healthy democracy is marked by its concern and respect for its weakest members, for the aged, the poor, the powerless, the disinherited. Is this not to be true, opponents of liberalized abortion ask, also for the pre-natal child? And, if not for the pre-natal child, then what about the post-natal child?[155]

The passion to protect the most defenseless citizens—unborn children—has been a staple of pro-life neoconservative writing. Weigel writes of a pro-life position as being the logical extension of the noble tradition of American liberalism, which has enfranchised previously excluded groups.

> [The] story of America is the story of the expansion of the community of the commonly protected—the communities for which we claim, as Americans, a common responsibility. The framers ended religious tests for public office, and thus opened political participation in the American experiment to Catholics, Jews, and evangelical Protestants. A Civil War was fought, among other reasons, to bring black slaves into the American commons. Women were enfranchised, social security and welfare schemes adopted, civil rights and voting rights legislation enacted, and public spaces made accessible to the handicapped—all in the name of the community of common protection and mutual responsibility. . . . The defenders of the rights of the unborn are the true inheritors of the American liberal tradition in its quest to draw more widely the boundaries of the American commons.[156]

In a 1994 *First Things* essay, "Christian Conviction and Democratic Etiquette," Weigel maintains that this may be the only way to articulate the pro-life position in the public square. Weigel's claim speaks to an important neoconservative argument regarding religious discourse in America. Neoconservatives have stressed the importance of translating religious beliefs into the secular vernacular before entering them into public discourse. As Neuhaus has written, "public assertive religious forces will have to learn that the remedy for the naked public square is not naked religion in public."[157] While religious beliefs should inform political decisions, it is essential that religious convictions be discussed in a language accessible to all in the public square. Religious claims made in theological terms sound exclusive, while the operating principle of the public square is universalism. In order to have religious beliefs accepted by nonbelievers, they must be articulated so that all can identify with them. This is especially so with abortion, where the pro-life views are often informed by religious teaching. Weigel writes,

> We best make our case by insisting that our defense of the right to life of the unborn is a defense of civil rights and of a generous, hospitable American democracy. We best make our case by insisting that abortion-on-demand gravely damages the American democratic experiment by drastically constricting the community of the commonly protected. We best make our case by arguing that the private use of lethal violence against an innocent is an assault on the moral foundations of any just society. In short, we best make our case for maximum feasible legal protection of the unborn by deploying natural law arguments that translate our Christian moral convictions into a public idiom more powerful than the idiom of autonomy.[158]

The Catholic neoconservatives have argued that legalized abortion does not empower women by providing them with a "right to choose," but rather leads to a deranged sexual sentiment whereby men are divorced from the full sexual experience. With abortion "a woman's choice," men are provided with a license to avoid the potential consequences of their promiscuity. Similarly, the availability of abortion sends a message to men that they are not an important part of the childbearing and rearing process. If abortion is solely a woman's choice, men are led to believe that the whole sexual enterprise also resides in the province of a woman. If a man does not have responsibility and cannot be held accountable for his sexual activities from the start, it is very difficult to determine when he is. And it is even harder to convince men of whatever artificial dichotomies are determined. Glendon elaborates,

> By making abortion a woman's prerogative, the Court has made it easier to treat it as a woman's problem. Since contraception and abortion are entirely within a woman's control, the argument runs, pregnancy, child-bearing, and child rearing are her responsibility. . . .[159]

The neoconservatives have strongly dissented from the pro-choice argument that abortion rights liberate women by providing them with more freedom. Abortion rights may liberate men by freeing them from the consequences of their actions, but women still have to deal with pregnancy one way or another. A coalition of thinkers and leaders from across the political spectrum organized by Neuhaus ran an advertisement in *The New York Times* and *First Things* declaring,

> Unfettered access to abortion on demand has addressed none of women's true needs; nor has it brought dignity to women. It has, in fact, done precisely the opposite. It has encouraged irresponsible or predatory men, who find abortion a convenient justification for their lack of commitment, and has vastly expanded the exploitation of women by the abortion industry.[160]

Congressman Barney Frank said on the floor of the House of Representatives, "Sure, they're pro-life. They believe that life begins at conception and ends at birth."[161] Catholic neoconservatives have worked hard to prove that wrong. They are attuned to the very difficult circumstances that often lead women to have an abortion and they want to use mediating institutions and the state to ameliorate that pain. They want institutions to be in place to lead women to feel comfortable having their child. Neuhaus cites the example of John Cardinal O'Connor, who has offered the full financial support of the Catholic Church to any pregnant woman and her child for two years. Neuhaus also cites the example of crisis pregnancy centers, which outnumber abortion clinics.[162]

The Jewish neoconservatives agree with most of the arguments of their pro-life colleagues, but are generally not willing to go as far and criminalize abortion. *Commentary* has not published many articles on abortion, through the lead article in the January 1994 issue was "On Abortion" by James Q. Wilson. While Wilson is a Catholic, he is more closely associated with the Jewish neoconservatives (he serves on the board of *The Public Interest* and is a regular contributor to *Commentary*) than with the Catholic neoconservatives.[163] Wilson advocates a position on abortion based on moral sentiments, which would allow a woman to decide whether her fetus is a human being when presented with pictures of unborn children at various stages of development. He rejects the contention that life begins at conception, but suggests that women considering an abortion should be given all of the available evidence—in the form of pictures—to determine when they think the fetus is a person. He writes that women considering an abortion should be told, "You are X weeks pregnant, as near as we can tell. The embryo now looks like this (pointing). In another week it will look like this (pointing). You should know this before you make a final decision."[164] He suggests that this plan will reduce the abortion rate, as women see that the fetus has many of the identifiable characteristics of a human being only a few weeks after conception. This article spawned a heated debate between Wilson and Hadley Arkes in the April and May 1994 issues of *First Things*.[165]

While the pro-choice neoconservatives are all opposed to abortion, most are hesitant to join the pro-life side or are silent on the political question of abortion. None are pro-choice for the reasons that pro-choice forces generally give. The pro-choice neoconservatives think that abortion is wrong and should be stringently regulated and discouraged, and have nothing but contempt for the feminist rhetoric—often phrased in "rights talk"—used in defense of abortion, such as "It's a woman's right to choose." The pro-choice neoconservatives generally start from a point of practicality, declaring that regardless of the merits of the argument, the country will never be able to criminalize abortion. In a column published shortly after the election of President Clinton, "The Debate Is Over," Charles Krauthammer maintains that the abortion debate is over (and decided in favor of the pro-choice side) because—with the election of Bill Clinton—all three branches of government came to the same position.[166] And he did not mourn how the debate turned out.

For Irving Kristol, the pro-life position is a manifestation of the politics of nostalgia. He claims that the culture is far too liberal for the idea of criminalized abortion to be seriously contemplated as a political possibility. Instead of proscribing abortion completely, Kristol believes that it should be discouraged by the culture and regulated, when possible, by the government. There are several ways to do this, such as waiting periods, parental consent, and spousal notification. He holds that a good model to follow with regard to abortion is Israel, where the Orthodox Jews, who are as against abortion as are fundamentalist Christians in the United States, try to discourage the practice indirectly by making more people Orthodox Jews. Anti-abortion Christians, Kristol maintains, should stop trying to criminalize abortion and should help society to cut the abortion rate by helping to make Christians more confident and forthright in their Christianity, which does not countenance abortions.[167]

Both Catholic and Jewish neoconservatives believe there is room for political compromise on the issue. While the pro-life neoconservatives do not relish the thought of compromising on abortion, they are content to save as many lives as is feasible. All of the neoconservatives believe that compromise between the extreme pro-life and extreme pro-choice positions is possible, for that is where most Americans fall. *First Things* editorialized,

> About 20 percent of Americans favor an unconditional right to abortion, about 20 percent favor an absolute prohibition, and the remaining 60 percent think abortion should be legal in certain circumstances. When those "certain circumstances" are specified, it becomes evident that 75 percent of the people think that more than 95 percent of the abortions done today should not be allowed by law.[168]

For instance, while the vast majority of Americans believe that a woman should be able to obtain an abortion in the case of incest, they do not believe she should be able to do so a week before she is scheduled to deliver her child. While pro-choice groups have effectively focused the debate on the "hard cases," the neoconservatives are ready—politically at least—to concede those cases and to concentrate on the vast majority of abortions which do not lend themselves to the sympathy and understanding that a victim of rape or incest does.

Education

In a 1957 *Yale Review* essay, Irving Kristol made an especially prescient prediction.

> [Most] of the liberal-conservative quarrel in the United States has hardly anything to do with politics, strictly speaking. The locus of this debate is primarily in the sphere of education; it involves above all the image of man into which we should like to see the child mature. It is a clash of visions, of philosophies of life, loyalty and death—just the sort of thing that one would expect from a collision of ideologies. And in such a collision, the old truths of political philosophy—and political philosophy itself as a disinterested contemplation of *la condition politique de l'homme*—are crushed.[169]

According to the neoconservatives in 1994, the old truths of political philosophy have been crushed. Ideological disputes are clearest in higher education, where Gertrude Himmelfarb, Roger Kimball, Allan Bloom, and Dinesh D'Souza have led the neoconservatives charge against multiculturalism, feminism, deconstructionism, and other staples of the academic left. Just as in the 1960s, the neoconservatives saw liberal professors collapse without a fight as their radical colleagues assailed time-honored facets of education—from academic standards to the curriculum—as racist, sexist, and homophobic. The very idea of truth (not a particular conception of truth) has been assailed by multiculturalists as inherently invidious.

The warnings that James Q. Wilson and Norman Podhoretz sounded in the early 1970s—that an illiberal, oppressive left-wing orthodoxy was taking hold in the universities—have become common in the 1990s. Throughout the 1990s, conservative magazines have cataloged endless examples of multicultural thought police enforcing the laws of political correctness with a vengeance. Such examples are well known, and do not need be repeated here. Multiculturalists have succeeded not only in instituting stringent quotas in admissions offices and in faculty hiring, but in drastically changing the curriculum to eliminate what they call (in more polite moods) its "Eurocentric" bias. Standards and accepted norms of what should be studied have been discarded in this romp. Like their predecessors in the New Left, multiculturalists could not care less about politics or economics; multiculturalism is a strictly cultural phenomenon whose leftism revolves around tribal associations and assorted left-wing causes like radical environmentalism and gender feminism. Gertrude Himmelfarb encapsulates the left-wing assault on traditional education in saying, "The situation in the universities is very simple. It could not be worse."[170]

Starting in opposition, the neoconservatives have portrayed their opponents as illiberal anti-intellectual charlatans. The neoconservatives have also constructed a vigorous defense of traditional education. Once again, closed questions have been opened, and the neoconservatives have found themselves defending the very idea of literature and the value of figures like Shakespeare and Milton. This, according to the neoconservatives, is a legacy of liberalism. A philosophy that does not take ideas seriously, that does not recognize evil, that is afraid of judgment and averse to making moral distinctions, is not equipped for the modern world. A liberalism in a world with Communism, student radicalism, or political correctness must have the intellectual fortitude at least to be intolerant of intolerance—and the current version of liberalism does not have that component. With such a liberalism, a liberalism where anything goes so long as it is not conservative, what will come next? No one knows, but it is assured that it will—as John Updike said of the 1960s radicalism—percolate down to everyone.

Gertrude Himmelfarb explained this at a 1989 conference of the Committee for the Free World, a neoconservative anti-Communist group headed by Midge Decter.

> One of the great things about our country, I am sure you will all agree, is how wonderfully democratic it is. And it is democratic in this respect [regarding education] as in others. What starts at Harvard and Yale appears in the Midwest or in the South or in the most remote parts of the country in three months. It is really quite remarkable how that happens.[171]

This has certainly applied to multiculturalism and to political correctness, which started in institutions of higher learning but have since infiltrated the common culture. Bill Clinton's declared objective to appoint a cabinet that "looks like America" is but a small step from the academic multiculturalists who value diversity as a function of biology rather than personality. Kristol warned in the 1970s that the lack of ideology among businessmen made them susceptible to the loudest, most antibourgeois members of the left. Sure enough, Fortune 500 companies hire "diversity consultants," hire by quota, hold sensitivity sessions, and fund the most strident activities of the adversary culture and the new class.

The true victims of this multicultural onslaught have been, according to the neoconservatives, those who most need to be incorporated into the common culture. As Gertrude Himmelfarb wrote, ideas trickle down—and those that trickled down from the universities have poisoned the most vulnerable members of society. Nathan Glazer wrote in *Affirmative Discrimination* that he would support quotas if they actually helped their intended beneficiaries, and some neoconservatives might say the same for multiculturalism. But, like Glazer with affirmative action, the neoconservatives believe that what Kristol calls "the tragedy of multiculturalism" is the lessons multiculturalism teaches (and does not teach) to poor, often black children. Kristol has written of multiculturalism,

> The question is: Do such trivial pursuits of worthy but relatively obscure racial ancestors really help black students? There is no evidence that it does. In theory, it is supposed to elevate their sense of "self-esteem," as individuals and as blacks. But genuine self-esteem comes from real-life experiences, not from the flattering attention of textbooks.[172]

In a 1991 *Commentary* article, Midge Decter explained how the multiculturalism in the universities has filtered down to grade schools to the detriment of the students.

> Little black kids are . . . [being] used as ideological cannon fodder. And just as black studies in universities have encouraged anxious, perhaps frightened, black students to back off and take themselves out of the game, multiculturalism is likely to put a lid on the little ones altogether. . . . For all the damage that has been done to them, black children are not fools. Perhaps more than any other children, they know a hustle when they see one. Tell them they are African, and that African civilization is superior to the one that surrounds them, and they will get your message: they have no Ameri-

can future, they are hopeless, fit for nothing but the mob scene of some Reverend Al Sharpton or other.[173]

Defining Deviancy Up and Down

In 1992 and 1993, two of the most important neoconservative reflections on the culture were published by Daniel Patrick Moynihan and Charles Krauthammer. Moynihan's essay, published in the Summer 1992 issue of *The American Scholar*, "Defining Deviancy Down,"[174] is about the changing ways in which American society considers acceptable and unacceptable behavior—and the implications that consideration has for the nation. Social pathologies such as crime and illegitimacy have reached such astounding proportions that Americans have changed their definition of deviancy to accept this sad situation. Whereas the St. Valentine's Day Massacre a half-century ago shocked the nation and is mentioned twice in the *World Book Encyclopedia*, the same number of people killed on that night in Chicago—Moynihan cites James Q. Wilson on this—are killed in Los Angeles every weekend. Similarly, when illegitimacy was once shameful, something to avoid at all costs, rates of out-of-wedlock birth were low. But now, almost a third of American children are the children of unmarried parents—an act that is, by powerful segments of our culture, not considered deviant. In order to maintain an appearance of normalcy, we have redefined deviancy so that a whole range of behavior that was once considered deviant is now "normal."

In a Bradley Lecture delivered at the American Enterprise Institute and later turned into a *New Republic* article, Charles Krauthammer agrees with Moynihan, and offers a complementary concept.[175] The assault on bourgeois notions of civilized society does not stop with considering deviant behavior normal; it considers normal behavior deviant. In this sense, deviancy is being defined up. The most powerful example Krauthammer raises concerns feminists and date rape. He cites the famous Mary Koss study published in *Ms.* magazine, which is cited by feminists groups at campuses all over the nation. Koss reports that 15 percent of college women are raped—an astounding figure until it becomes clear that 73 percent of the women she labeled as having been raped do not consider themselves raped, and 42 percent continue to have sexual relations with the "rapist." This discrepancy is explained in Koss's definition of deviancy: a woman is raped if, for instance, she is taken in by "a man's continual arguments and pressure." Or, as Professor Susan Estrich writes, "Many feminists would argue that so long as women are powerless relative to men, viewing 'yes' as a sign of true consent is misguided." Krauthammer asks: "But if 'yes' is not a sign of true consent, then what is? A notarized contract?" What was once seduction is now rape; the normal is now abnormal, and deviancy is defined up. With deviancy being defined up and down in an Orwellian nightmare, the reconstruction of the culture will be that much more difficult as we fight to establish as normal what everyone took for granted.

Culture and the Future

The project of religion and culture that the neoconservatives have addressed in recent years is likely to remain for a long time. James Q. Wilson writes, "We are engaged in a cultural war, a war about values. It is not a new war; it has been going on for centuries as part of a continuing struggle at national self-definition."[176] The neoconservatives are generally very pessimistic about the chances to win this war. Irving Kristol concedes,

> In his convention speech, Pat Buchanan referred to the "culture wars." I regret to inform him that those wars are over, and the left has won. Conservative cultural critics exist (I am one such) and we work hard, with occasional success, at damage control. But the left today completely dominates the education establishment, the entertainment industry, the universities, the media. One of these days the tide will turn.[177]

Will that tide turn, and will the neoconservatives win this war? They do not think so, but then again, they never thought they would win the Cold War so decisively, either.[178] In all likelihood, even if the neoconservatives win more battles in the culture wars than they expect, there will be no resounding defeat as in 1989.

In the Cold War, the United States had one objective—to defeat Communism. Everyone had ideas about how to do this, but at least there was a widespread general consensus about the final goal. Some wanted to do it by force, some by talks, some in a day, some in the indefinite future—but only a few on the very far left actively objected to the ultimate aim. Thus, when Communism fell, no one expected it, but everyone realized that their goal had been achieved and that the United States had won.[179]

The same will not be true with the culture wars. For the culture wars just as much fights over ends as over means. Diametrically different ideas concerning order and liberty, freedom and justice serve as the basis for fierce disagreements over issues such as religion, education, families, mediating structures, the role of the state, and the role of morality in politics and private life. Only when a broad agreement on these issues is reached can we address the means to achieve the ends. The neoconservatives—a small group of like-minded intellectuals—have reached that stage, but do not agree even among themselves on the means. Hence, it is sheer fantasy to imagine a state where enough people and groups in the United States can come to an agreement on the ends to begin working on the means. And for the whole country to agree on the means? Let us just say that this is a debate which will never end, and that neoconservative ideas on these issues will surely outlive the neoconservatives and probably generations after them.

Notes

1. Interview with George Weigel, January 25, 1994.

2. *The Spirit of Democratic Capitalism* has influenced Pope John Paul II, as it has the nation of Poland, where it was secretly translated in the early 1980s. There was a major argument within Solidarity in the 1980s over whether Communism was intrinsically bad or whether Poland was in a state of economic shambles and political repression because of the corrupt individual Communist leaders. *The Spirit of Democratic Capitalism* convinced Solidarity of the former, and they of course embarked on aggressive market reforms when given the opportunity. This move was backed by Pope John Paul II, whose 1992 encyclical, *Centesimus Annus*, accepts a morally based democratic capitalism. Parts of it read like *The Spirit of Democratic Capitalism*. Novak is exceedingly humble on the

relationship between his book and the pope's thinking, saying that his personal connection with Pope John Paul II is very slight if it exists at all. *National Review* editorializes differently: "Those close to Pope John Paul II leave no doubt that his encyclical (*Centesimus Annus*) on the free society and the free economy was significantly influenced by the work of Michael Novak" (April 4, 1994, p. 24). We know for sure that the book was circulated underground throughout Eastern Europe prior to the fall of Communism and has significantly influenced thinkers from Europe to Latin America to Asia, and now to China—where it is being legally distributed for the first time. For his work in the fields of theology and economics, Michael Novak was the recipient of the Templeton Prize in 1994.

3. Michael Novak, "Against 'Affirmative Action'." *Commonweal* (April 5, 1974) p. 102.

4. Robert Bork, "Culture and Kristol," in *The Neoconservative Imagination: Essays in Honor of Irving Kristol* (Washington: American Enterprise Institute, 1995) p. 141.

5. "Culture and Kristol." p. 146.

6. John Podhoretz, "Our Town," *National Review* (June 27, 1994) p. 64.

7. Irving Kristol, "The Coming 'Conservative Century'," *Wall Street Journal* (February 1, 1993) p. 18.

8. Jay Lefkowitz quoted in James Atlas, "The Changing World of New York Intellectuals," *New York Times Magazine* (August 25, 1985) p. 52.

9. "Culture and Kristol," p. 143.

10. Michael Novak, "The Conservative Mood." *Society* (January/February 1994) p. 20.

11. Irving Kristol, "'Family Values'—Not a Political Issue," *Wall Street Journal* (December 7, 1992) p. 14.

12. Michael Novak, "A Community of Self-Reliance," *Notre Dame Journal of Legislation* (Volume 6, No. 2, 1990) p. 173.

13. Irving Kristol, "On Conservatism and Capitalism," *Wall Street Journal* (September 11, 1975) p. 60. In the spirit of congenial borrowing that is characteristic of neoconservatism, Novak transforms this remark in *The Catholic Ethic and the Spirit of Capitalism*. He writes, "If an adult couple were to make love openly on the public stage, for him [the liberal], the only moral issue at stake would be whether they were being paid the minimum wage" (p. 97).

14. Norman Podhoretz, "The Adversary Culture and the New Class," in B. Bruce-Briggs, ed. *The New Class?* (New Brunswick, N.J.: Transaction Books, 1979) p. 28.

15. "Culture and Kristol," p. 140.

16. "The Conservative Mood," p. 19.

17. Richard John Neuhaus, *Doing Well and Doing Good: The Challenge to the Christian Capitalist* (New York: Doubleday, 1992) p. 83.

18. Gertrude Himmelfarb, "One Very Simple Principle," *The American Scholar* (Autumn 1993) p. 550.

19. Milton Himmelfarb and Richard John Neuhaus, eds. *Jews in Unsecular America* (Grand Rapids, Mich.: Eerdmans, 1987) p. 88.

20. Andrew Ferguson, review of *My Times: Adventures in the News Trade* by John Corry, *The American Spectator* (February 1994) p. 86.

21. Samuel Lipman, "Can We Save Culture?" *National Review* (August 26, 1991) p. 36.

22. Samuel Lipman, "Morality and Philanthropy," *Society* (September/October 1990) p. 4.

23. "Can We Save Culture?" p. 38.

24. Richard John Neuhaus, "Nihilism Without the Abyss: Law, Rights and Transcendent Good," *Journal of Law and Religion* (1987) p. 55.

25. Mary Ann Glendon, *Rights Talk* (New York: Free Press, 1992) p. 8

26. Mary Ann Glendon, *Rights Talk*, p. 100.

27. James Buckley, "The Catholic Public Servant," *First Things* (February 1992) p. 21.

28. Richard John Neuhaus, *America against Itself: Moral Vision and the Public Order* (South Bend, Ind.: University of Notre Dame Press, 1992) p. 171.

29. Gertrude Himmelfarb, "Victorian Values/Jewish Values," *Commentary* (February 1989) p. 31.

30. Peter Berger, "Ideologies, Myths and Moralities," from *The Americans: 1976* (Lexington, Ky.: Lexington Books, 1976) p. 346.

31. James Q. Wilson, *The Moral Sense* (New York: Free Press, 1993) p. 158.

32. Irving Kristol, "Thoughts on reading about a summer-camp cabin covered with garbage," p. 137.

33. *Doing Well and Doing Good: The Challenge to the Christian Capitalist*, p. 243.

34. "The Conservative Mood," p. 16.

35. George Will, *Statecraft as Soulcraft: What Government Does* (New York: Simon and Schuster, 1983) pp. 145, 151.

36. Richard John Neuhaus, "Combat Ready," *National Review* (May 2, 1994) p. 53. In 1991, George Weigel wrote, "Politics is a function of culture, and at the heart of culture is religion." ("Religion and Peace: An Argument Complexified," *The Washington Quarterly* (Spring 1991) p. 39.) Did Neuhaus plagiarize Weigel? In 1990, Neuhaus said at a conference for the Committee for the Free World, "politics is, for the most part, an expression of culture, that is, of the available ideas for the order of common life, and that at the heart of culture is religion." (Does the West Still Exist?, Conference of the Committee for the Free World Orwell Press, 1989, p. 67) Who said it first? It doesn't matter! This is neoconservatism.

37. Gary Dorrien, *The Neoconservative Mind* (Philadelphia: Temple University Press, 1993) p. 385.

38. Reinhold Niebuhr, *The Children of Light and the Children of Darkness: A Vindication of Democracy and a Critique of Its Traditional Defense* (New York: Charles Scribner's, 1943) p. 125.

39. Werner Dannhauser, "Religion and the Conservatives," *Commentary* (December 1985) p. 53.

40. Will Herberg, *From Marxism to Judaism*, ed. David Dallin (Wiener: New York, 1992) p. 133.

41. *The Moral Sense*, p. 219.

42. Sidney Hook, contribution to *Partisan Review* Symposium, "Religion and the Intellectuals," pp. 230, 228, 231.

43. Ernest van den Haag, "An Open Letter to Sidney Hook," *Partisan Review* (1952) pp. 607–9.

44. Sidney Hook, "A Rejoinder to Mr. van den Haag," *Partisan Review* (1952) p. 612.

45. Interview with Richard John Neuhaus, January 10, 1994.

46. Irving Kristol, "Christianity, Judaism and Socialism," from *Capitalism and Socialism: A Theological Inquiry* (Washington: American Enterprise Institute, 1979) p. 315.

47. Interview with Richard John Neuhaus, January 10, 1994.

48. Interview with George Weigel, January 25, 1994.

49. Interview with William Kristol, January 25, 1994.

50. "Christians, Jews and Anti-Semitism," Editorial, *First Things* (March 1992) p. 9.

51. Richard John Neuhaus, *The Naked Public Square: Religion and Democracy in America* (Grand Rapids: William B. Eerdmans, 1984) p. 117.

52. Matthew Berke, "Across the Gulf of Faith," *First Things* (May 1991) p. 62.

53. Michael Novak, "Maritain and the Jews," *First Things* (January 1993) p. 33.

54. James Q. Wilson, "Response" in *Crisis* symposium, "Thinking about Common Morality," *Crisis* (July/August 1995) p. 35.

55. David Novak, *Jewish-Christian Dialogue: A Jewish Justification* (New York: Oxford University Press, 1989) p. 9.

56. Quoted in Will Herberg, *Protestant-Catholic-Jew* (Garden City: Doubleday and Co., 1955) p. 97.

57. Quoted in Daniel Bell's contribution to an *Encounter* symposium, "Who's Left, What's Right," *Encounter* (February 1977) p. 10.

58. Cited from Sidney Mead, *The Nation with the Soul of a Church* (New York: Harper and Row, 1975) p. 68. Any decent collection of Madison's writings or discussions of religion will include "Memorial and Remonstrance." One is *The Writings of James Madison*, (New York: G.P. Putnam's Sons, 1901) pp. 183–91.

59. Thomas Jefferson quoted in Richard John Neuhaus, "Contending for the Future: Overcoming the Pferrian Inversion," *Journal of Law and Religion* (Vol 8 No. 1 1990) p. 123.

60. "Contending for the Future: Overcoming the Pferrian Inversion," p. 123.

61. James Q. Wilson, "On Abortion," *Commentary* (January 1994) p. 24.

62. Richard John Neuhaus, "A New Order of Religious Freedom," *First Things* (February 1992) p. 13.

63. This point is made by Peter Berger in "Religion in Post-Protestant America," *Commentary* (May 1986) p. 42.

64. Irving Kristol, "The Disaffection of Capitalism," from *Capitalism, Socialism and Democracy*, p. 31.

65. Michael McConnell, "Taking Religious Freedom Seriously," in Terry Eastland, ed., *Religious Liberty in the Supreme Court: The Cases that Define the Debate over Church and State* (Washington: Ethics and Public Policy Center, 1993) p. 501. Reprinted from the May 1990 issue of *First Things*.

66. Richard John Neuhaus quoted in Neal Kozodoy, "Religion and Tolerance," *Freedom Review* (January–February 1993) p. 72.

67. Michael Novak, "Abandoned in a Toxic Culture," *Crisis* (December 1992) p. 16.

68. George Weigel, "Secularism R.I.P.: Reclaiming the Catholic Intellectual Tradition Crisis," *Crisis* (October 1989) p. 22.

69. George Weigel, "Achieving Disagreement: From Indifference to Pluralism," (*Journal of Law and Religion* 1990) p. 180.

70. "Religion and Peace: An Argument Complexified." p. 27.

71. Peter Berger quoted in Ken Adelman, "True Believer: George Weigel Puts a Lot of Faith in the Way Washington Works," *The Washingtonian* (December 1993) p. 25. Berger's original formulation is, "[when] one looks at the United States as a whole, in terms of the subjective and objective indicators of religiosity, one sees a remarkable resemblance to India (the content, needless to say, being different). Yet if one moves around in the cultural centers of America, one breathes a remarkably Scandinavian air. (Could this be why there are so many Volvos on Ivy League campuses?) And thereby hangs a tale of great significance: when it comes to religion, America is an India, with a little Sweden superimposed." "Religion in Post-Protestant America," *Commentary*, May 1986, p. 45.

72. *The Naked Public Square*, p. 82.

73. "Religion in Post-Protestant America, p. 45.

74. *The Naked Public Square*, p. 110.

75. Irving Kristol, "The Future of American Jewry," *Commentary* (August 1991) pp. 23, 22.

76. Irving Kristol, "The Capitalist Future," The Francis Boyer Lecture at the American Enterprise Institute (December 4, 1991) page 20 of American Enterprise Institute transcript. Reprinted as "The Cultural Revolution and the Capitalist Future," *The American Enterprise* (March 1992).

77. Quoted in Russell Kirk, "Prescription, Authority and Ordered Freedom." in Frank Meyer, ed, *What Is Conservatism?* (New York: Holt, Rinehart and Winston, 1964) p. 24.

78. Jay Lefkowitz, "Jewish Voters and the Democrats," *Commentary* (April 1993) p. 38.

79. Milton Himmelfarb, "American Jews: Diehard Conservatives," *Commentary* (April 1989) pp. 44–49.

80. Milton Himmelfarb, contribution to *Commentary* Symposium, "Liberalism and the Jews." (January 1980) p. 45.

81. Martin Peretz, contribution to David Horowitz, *Second Thoughts: Former Radicals Look Back at the Sixties* (Lanham, Md: Madison Books, 1991) p. 170.

82. Naomi Cohen, "Natural Adversaries or Possible Allies? American Jews and the New Christian Right," (New York: American Jewish Committee, 1993) p. 12.

83. Midge Decter, contribution to *First Things* Symposium, "Judaism and American Public Life," *First Things* (March 1991) p. 28.

84. *The Naked Public Square*, p. 5.

85. "The Future of American Jewry," p. 26.

86. Milton Himmelfarb, contribution to "Judaism and American Public Life," p. 26.

87. *The Naked Public Square*, p. 108.

88. "Natural Adversaries or Possible Allies? American Jews and the New Christian Right," p. 8.

89. Irving Kristol, "The Political Dilemma of American Jewry," *Commentary* (July 1984) p. 25.

90. Lucy Dawidowicz, "Politics, the Jews and the '84 Election," *Commentary* (February 1984) p. 28.

91. Irving Kristol, "Irving Kristol Writes," *Commentary* (October 1984) p. 17. In response to letters concerning, "The Political Dilemma of American Jewry."

92. "The Future of American Jewry," p. 26.

93. Interview with Irving Kristol, January 26, 1994.

94. Quoted in James Atlas, "The Counter Counter Culture," *New York Times Magazine* (February 12, 1995) p. 38.

95. Interview with Elliott Abrams, March 24, 1994.

96. Irving Kristol, "Christmas, Christian, and Jews," *National Review* (December 30, 1988) pp. 26–27.

97. Quoted in Jay Lefkowitz, "Romancing the State." Review of *The Fatal Embrace: Jews and the State* by Benjamin Friedman. *Commentary* (January 1994) p. 63.

98. Jacob Petuchowski, contribution to David Dallin, ed., *American Jews and the Separationist Faith* (Washington: Ethic and Public Policy Center, 1993) pp. 103–4.

99. Ruth Wisse, contribution to "Judaism and American Public Life," *First Things* (March 1991) p. 26.

100. Joseph Epstein, contribution to *Commentary* Symposium, "Liberalism and the Jews," *Commentary* (January 1980) p. 32.

101. "The Future of American Jewry," p. 24.

102. *Jews in Unsecular America*, p. 86.

103. William Buckley, *In Search of Anti-Semitism* (New York: Continuum, 1992) p. 4.

104. Quoted in Norman Podhoretz, "The Hate that Dare Not Speak Its Name," *Commentary* (November 1986) p. 30.

105. *In Search of Anti-Semitism*, p. 20, 22, 20, 17.

106. Joseph Sobran, syndicated column, May 8, 1986.

107. Quoted in John Judis, "The Conservative Wars," *The New Republic* (August 11 and 18, 1986) p. 15.

108. Joseph Sobran, "The Great Fear," Quoted in Richard John Neuhaus, "Jews, Christians and 'The Great Fear.'" (*First Things* October 1994) p. 84.

109. Gore Vidal, "The Empire Lovers Strike Back," *Nation* (March 22, 1986) p. 353.

110. "The Hate that Dare Not Speak Its Name," p. 25.

111. It is safe to assume that Wicker was not too exercised over Vidal's article. The April 1994 issue of *Modern Maturity* contains an interview of Gore Vidal by Tom Wicker. Wicker does not ask Vidal a question relating to the charges of anti-Semitism.

112. "The Hate that Dare Not Speak Its Name," p. 32.

113. Thomas Fleming, "The Real American Dilemma," *Chronicles* (March 1989) p. 9.

114. Bill Kauffman, "Gnawing Away at Vidal," *Chronicles* (March 1989) p. 46.

115. Quoted in Robert Moynihan, "Thunder on the Right," *Thirty Days* (September 1989) Podhoretz, Weigel and Neuhaus quotes are from pages 69–70, 70, and 69 respectively.

116. Interview with Richard John Neuhaus, January 10, 1994.

117. Paul Gottfried, "The Conservative Crack-up Continued," *Society* (January/February 1994) p. 24. Neuhaus pleads guilt in a letter to author, February 9, 1994. "I confess that I feel not a tiny inch of contrition for criticizing the flagscow magazine of the paleos."

118. Interview with Richard John Neuhaus, January 10, 1994.

119. Norman Podhoretz, 'The Conservative Crack-up." *Commentary* (May 1993).

120. Interview with William Bennett, January 27, 1994.

121. Interview with Edwin Feulner, January 24, 1994.

122. Jeffrey Hart, "Gang Warfare in Chicago," *National Review* (June 6, 1986) p. 33.

123. "The Conservative Wars," p. 16.

124. Stephen J. Tonsor, "Why I Too Am Not a Neoconservative," *National Review* (June 20, 1986) p. 54. Condensed from speech at the Philadelphia Society in May of 1986.

125. "The Conservative Wars," p. 16, 16, 18.

126. James Nuechterlein, "The Paleo's Paleo," *First Things* (August/September 1991) p. 46.

127. All quotes in the paragraph are from Joshua Muravchik, "Patrick J. Buchanan and the Jews," *Commentary* (January 1991) p. 31.

128. "Patrick J. Buchanan and the Jews," p. 36, 35.

129. Charles Krauthammer, "Buchanan Explained," *Washington Post*, (March 1, 1992) p. C7.

130. David Frum, "The Conservative Bully Boy," *The American Spectator* (July 1991) p. 14.

131. Norman Podhoretz, "What is Anti-Semitism?: An Open Letter to William Buckley." *Commentary* (February 1992) p. 20.

132. Editorial, "Four More Years?" *National Review* (February 17, 1992) p. 14.

133. "Thunder on the Right," p. 69.

134. John O'Sullivan, "Mr. Buchanan and His Friends," *National Review* (March 16, 1992) p. 40.

135. *In Search of Anti-Semitism*, p. 170.

136. "Dissent on the Right," Letter to *National Review* (March 16, 1992) p. 5.

137. Editorial, "Christians, Jews and Anti-Semitism," *First Things* (March 1992) p. 10.

138. James Hitchcock, "The Catholic Bishops, Public Policy, and the New Class," *This World* (Fall 1984) pp. 54–65.

139. *The Naked Public Square*, p. 44, 43.

140. George Weigel, "Christian Conviction and Democratic Etiquette," *First Things* (March 1994) p. 31.

141. *The Naked Public Square*, p. 43.

142. Peter Berger, "Can the Bishops Help the Poor?" *Commentary* (February 1985) p. 35.

143. Dinesh D'Souza, "Whose Pawns are the Bishops?" *Policy Review* (Fall 1985) p. 51–52.

144. Peter Berger, quoted in Richard John Neuhaus, ed. *Confession, Conflict, and Community* (Grand Rapids, Michigan: William B. Eerdmans, 1986) p. 73–4.

145. George Weigel, "The Churches and the War in the Gulf," *First Things* (March 1991) p. 42.

146. Patrick Glynn, "Why an American Arms Build-Up Is Morally Necessary." *Commentary* (February 1984) p. 27.

147. Hilton Kramer, quoted in *Does the West Still Exist?* p. 66.

148. George Weigel, *Freedom and Its Discontents: Catholicism Confronts Modernity* (Washington: Ethics and Public Policy Center, 1991) p. 78.

149. Michael Novak, "Moral Clarity in the Nuclear Age," *National Review* (April 1, 1983) p. 364.

150. Peter Viereck, *Shame and Glory of the Intellectuals* (Boston: The Beacon Press, 1953) pp. 45, 228–31.

151. This point is made by Will Herberg, in "The Sectarian Conflict over Church and State: A Divisive Threat to Our Democracy." *Commentary* (November 1952) p. 460. See, for instance, Sidney Hook: "If the Catholic Church ever became dominant in America, it would without doubt, by virtue of its

concrete mission, transform American life and institutions. In the measure of its power and prudence, it would abolish religious liberty, the freedom of the press, divorce, and lay education." (Sidney Hook, "Rejoinder to Mr. van den Haag," p. 614).

152. George Weigel, "The New Anti-Catholicism," *Commentary* (June 1992) p. 25–31.

153. Interview with George Weigel, January 25, 1994.

154. "Nihilism Without the Abyss: Law, Rights and Transcendent Good," p. 55, 58.

155. Richard John Neuhaus, "The Dangerous Assumptions," *Commonweal* (June 30, 1967) p. 410.

156. George Weigel, "The Abortion Debate and the Hospitable Society," *Human Life Review* (Summer 1989) pp. 74–5.

157. "Nihilism Without the Abyss: Law, Rights and Transcendent Good," p. 62.

158. "Christian Conviction and Democratic Etiquette," p. 32.

159. *Rights Talk*, p. 66.

160. Declaration, "A New American Compact: Caring about Women, Caring about the Unborn," *First Things* (November 1992) p. 44. Prominent signers include Hadley Arkes, Hugh Carey, Robert Casey, Robert George, Mary Ann Glendon, Nat Hentoff, Leon Kass, Peter Lynch, Michael McConnell, Richard John Neuhaus, Eunice Kennedy Shriver, Sargent Shriver, William Simon, and George Weigel.

161. Quoted in Michael Barone and Grant Ujifusa, *The Almanac of American Politics* (Washington: *National Journal*, 1990) p. 564.

162. Kristin Daley and Mark Gerson, "An Interview with Richard John Neuhaus," *Williams Observer* (January 1993) p. 21.

163. With the exception of partaking in a debate spawned by his *Commentary* article on abortion, James Q. Wilson's contributions to *First Things* have consisted of a rather bitter series of exchanges with Hadley Arkes, one of the most articulate defenders of the pro-life cause. Wilson is far more skeptical of the relationship between morality and religion than are many neoconservatives. On page 220 of *The Moral Sense,* he writes, "Religion is for many a source of solace and for a few a means of redemption, but if everyday morality had depended on religious conviction, the human race would have been destroyed long ago." In a 1995 *Crisis* symposium on *The Moral Sense*—and specifically the religious (or lack of religious aspects) of the book—Wilson wrote, "I am struck by how easy it is for so many people to speak confidently about the relationship between religion and morality, either by declaring that morality requires religion for its support or that morality depends not at all on 'superstition' " ("Response," p. 34).

164. James Q. Wilson, "On Abortion," *Commentary* (January 1994) p. 26.

165. Hadley Arkes, "Abortion Facts and Feelings," *First Things* (April 1994) p. 34–38 and James Q. Wilson and Hadley Arkes, "Abortion Facts and Feelings II: An Exchange," (May 1994) pp. 39–42.

166. Charles Krauthammer, "Abortion: The Debate Is Over," *Washington Post* (December 4, 1992) p. A31.

167. " 'Family Values'—Not a Political Issue," p. 14.

168. Editorial, "Redefining Abortion Politics," *First Things* (March 1990) p. 11.

169. Irving Kristol, "Old Truths and the New Conservatism," *The Yale Review* (May 1958) p. 371.

170. Gertrude Himmelfarb, quoted in *Does the West Still Exist?* p. 71.

171. Gertrude Himmelfarb, quoted in *Does the West Still Exist?* p. 88.

172. Irving Kristol, "The Tragedy of Multiculturalism," *Wall Street Journal* (July 31, 1991) p. 10.

173. Midge Decter, "E Pluribus Nihil: Multiculturalism and Black Children," *Commentary* (September 1991) p. 29.

174. Daniel Patrick Moynihan, "Defining Deviancy Down." *The American Scholar* (Summer 1992) p. 17–30.

175. Charles Krauthammer, "Defining Deviancy Up," *The New Republic* (November 22, 1993) pp. 20–25.

176. *The Moral Sense*, p. xi.

177. " 'Family Values'—Not a Political Issue," p. 14.

178. See Owen Harries, "The Cold War and the Intellectuals," *Commentary* (October 1991) p. 13–20.

179. No one, except the scholar Bernard Levin, who predicted in the *London Times* in August 1977 that Communism in Eastern Europe would collapse on Bastille Day, 1989. His remarkable prediction is reprinted in *The National Interest* (Spring 1993) pp. 64–65.

7

Neoconservatism, Ideas, and Consequences

There are such things as truth and reality and there is a connection between them, as there is also a connection between the aesthetic sensibility and the moral imagination, between culture and society. We all pay lip service to the adage "Ideas have consequences," but it is only in extremes that we take it seriously, when the ideas of Stalin or Hitler issue in the realities of gulags and death camps. . . . Well short of dire situations there is an intimate, pervasive relationship between what happens in our schools and universities, in the intellectual and artistic communities, and what happens in society and the polity.—Gertrude Himmelfarb, 1994

Let me just say that a hundred years from now historians will be writing about Bea and Irving Kristol as one of the great intellectual partnerships, and one of the great love stories, of our time.—Charles Krauthammer, 1995

"No Newt," George Will has declared, "without *The Public Interest*."[1] There is not, of course, a direct link between a neoconservative journal and the smashing Republican victory in 1994. Furthermore, only time will tell whether the 1994 election signaled a major party realignment. Whatever the long-term political situation turns out to be, the results of the election and the terms in which the issues were argued on both sides point to a remarkable long-term sea change in American political discourse. The fact that conservatives beat liberals in this one election is not nearly as important as the fact that the conservative problematic—the way in which social and political questions are posed—was victorious. The tone of the ideas, rhetoric, and language used by both parties is drastically different from what it was only ten or fifteen years ago. Consider, for instance, Daniel Patrick Moynihan. His politics have not changed much in the past thirty years; in fact, his views on social policy have been remarkably consistent. When the Moynihan Report was published in 1965, its author was reviled as a racist and worse. Now, that report is regarded as conventional wisdom by the vast majority of the political spectrum and Moynihan is regarded as one of the last unrepentant left-liberal Democrats.[2] And in the speeches of politicians such as Newt Gingrich, Bill Bradley, and even Bill Clinton, there is far more than an echo of old articles sitting in bound volumes of *Commentary* and *The Public Interest*.

This is not to say that philosophers rule or that policy makers and statesmen govern on the basis of an essay in the previous issue of their favorite journal, and certainly not on the basis of articles written long ago. Issues concerning the politics of ideology, the role of social institutions, and the limits of human nature are not often the fodder of modern American political campaigns. Moynihan, the rare American who is both a major intellectual and an important statesman, says, "I have served in the Cabinet or sub-Cabinet of four Presidents. I do not believe I have ever heard at a Cabinet meeting a serious discussion of political ideas—one concerned with how men, rather than markets, behave."[3] Nevertheless, what pass for the truisms of everyday political slogans, speeches, and advertisements change over time and are clearly influenced by something. They are not hand-delivered by the political gods who promptly retire to K Street or Madison Avenue. Instead, even the banalities of modern politics manifest a national mood shaped over time in which ideologies and intellectuals have played a major role.

Ideas are not always translated clearly in debate, discussion, and lifestyle; they are at least drained of their purity when confronted by real-life situations. Mangled, confused, or even inscrutable, ideas determine the criteria and set the goals toward which pragmatic men strive. And this applies not only to "practical" ideas in the narrow sense, but to moral ideals as well. The principal function of ideologies is to define what makes a society moral, and the job of politics is to translate moral ideals (however imperfectly) into reality. As John Maynard Keynes wrote in his classic book, *The General Theory of Employment, Interest and Money*,

> the ideas of economists and political philosophers, both when they are right and when they are wrong, are more powerful than is commonly understood. Indeed the world is ruled by little else. Practical men, who believe themselves to be quite exempt from any intellectual influences, are usually the slaves of some defunct economist. Madmen in authority, who hear voices in the air, are distilling their frenzy from some academic scribbler of a few years back. I am sure that the power of vested interests is vastly exaggerated compared with the gradual encroachment of ideas. . . . Soon or late, it is ideas, not vested interests, which are dangerous for good or evil.[4]

The neoconservatives have devoted their careers to shaping the ideas and the intellectual climate that will govern the lives of even the most self-consciously practical men. Deepening Keynes's insight, the neoconservatives have asked the crucial question: how is it that ideas are so crucially important, even to a population that does not directly engage ideas? The answer the neoconservatives provide is a simple one, but one that has guided their life work. Man is, regardless of other influences and distractions, a moral and cultural animal. This is not to say that self-interest or even the pursuit of material goods is unimportant. Of course they matter, but it is very easy to accord them too much importance. At one point, many neoconservatives succumbed to the incentive-centered reductionism of economists. Articles in the early issues of *The Public Interest* were based on the assumption that given enough of the right information, government could design incentives that could bring prosperity and even satisfaction to society.[5]

As the neoconservatives came to stress, seemingly rational imperatives like self-interest, economic incentives, and the pursuit of prosperity are not enough to solve problems of poverty, let alone those of human fulfillment. Even when kept in their proper sphere, such concerns reside in a moral environment that determines how they will be manifested. And what sustains this moral environment? Ideas. Not even a philistine can escape the impact of ideas; it is futile to deny the significance of ideas, and ultimately dangerous to try.

Nonetheless, many have tried. When the neoconservatives realized that there was no place for themselves within American liberalism, they did not immediately see the right as being much more hospitable. It is for this reason that Gertrude Himmelfarb, in 1980, called the neoconservatives politically homeless. Liberalism had clearly self-destructed, but the right seemed prisoner to a narrow economism tinged with a vulgar anti-intellectualism. Because of the efforts of William Buckley, these forces were considerably muted on the intellectual right, but they were still prominent in sectors of the Republican Party and its corporate constituency. There was, the neoconservatives came to believe, nothing wrong with capitalism—actually, there was a lot right with it. But, as Irving Kristol said in the title of his second book, it was worthy of only two cheers; a third cheer was not only idolatrous, but manifested a disregard for the moral and cultural climate upon which a healthy free market economy depends. The economy is only one part of any human system and both the left and the right have greatly erred in giving it more than its limited due. Productivity and efficiency are important, but they are not moral virtues and cannot sustain an economy. They are pleasant products of—not reasons for—a capitalist economy.

Moreover, giving capitalism that third cheer would ultimately and paradoxically undermine that climate. Capitalism, even for its own sake, is safer with only two cheers. Daniel Bell warned—as did Joseph Schumpeter before him—that capitalism can generate cultural contradictions that slowly undermine the bourgeois ethic upon which the free market depends. And that ethic needs constant defense and reinforcement.

It was with this idea in hand that the neoconservatives—especially Irving Kristol and Michael Novak—approached businessmen and the Republican Party. It is no good, as Kristol wrote in a *Wall Street Journal* column, being the "stupid party."[6] If businessmen reject ideas, ideas and their influence will not disappear. The war of ideas requires mandatory conscription; avoiding the draft will not make the war go away—it will merely make the side of the draft dodger lose. But, as in war, everyone has a distinct responsibility and should not try to do what they are not equipped to do. Thus, the neoconservatives told the businessmen: You are very good at what you do. You are extraordinarily talented people who run the most productive and socially beneficial economy the world has ever known, and you deserve extensive accolades for that. But, for God's sake (and capitalism's), don't think you can defend yourself against your cultural critics. They could not make an advanced economy run, and you don't understand the broader social, political, and institutional requirements that allow you to be so successful at what you do. And we understand your opponents, often better than they understand themselves. It takes a life's work to be able to know how to wage the war of ideas, and that is what we have done. And it takes journals, conferences, and institutions to develop those ideas, and you can help support those endeavors.

Gradually, the neoconservatives, businessmen, and the Republican Party have reached a mutual accommodation. Until around fifteen years ago, the philosophy of the Republican Party was "me-too" combined with "not so fast," basically saying that the Democratic welfare state was fine, if a bit excessive at times. These Republicans, whom Irving Kristol calls "those conservatives whose Good Book is the annual budget,"[7] offered no alternative vision and thus did not even attempt to capture the moral imagination of the American people. The only exceptions were the extremists, who called for all kinds of unreasonable things like the elimination of Social Security and the complete repeal of the New Deal. Between extremism and fawning accommodation, nothing.

Now, of course, the situation is completely different. The fact that the Republican Party is now the party of intellectual imagination and ideological excitement and the Democratic Party is scrambling for its very bearings is, historically speaking, striking. And it is surely no coincidence that the Republican Party started getting ideas when the neoconservatives joined or became fellow travelers. The connection has never been stronger than today, when a key figure—some would say *the* key figure—in the transformation of the modern Republican Party is William Kristol. For it has been the neoconservatives, informing the American right of the importance of the limits of what Irving Kristol is fond of calling "thinking economically," who have provided the theoretical and moral foundation for the emergence of a vibrant, energetic political and cultural conservatism.

Because ideas are critical—even inescapable—they can also be destructive. Societal arrangements are very delicate, the product of centuries of inarticulate accumulated wisdom. They must be approached respectfully and with the utmost prudence. Unfortunately, prudence is not a traditional intellectual value; it dictates caution, humility, and appreciation for the here and now. Prudence contradicts key components of the intellectual imagination, which encourages not only large visions, but equally broad-minded plans on how to realize those visions.

Without the restraining influence of prudence and the humility that informs it, intellectuals can delegitimize institutions and mores with surprising ease. This was the core of the neoconservative discussion of the counterculture—and the encouragement and acquiescence of intellectuals to the counterculture—which began in the 1960s. The "intentions" behind ideas are not the issue; more important is bad faith, which is what intellectuals operate from when they do not consider the consequences of their ideas. Or, more precisely, the unintended consequences of ideas—for these are often more important and more lasting than the intended consequences. A primary duty of the intellectual is to realize that ideas have to be filtered through a complicated culture, society, and polity from which an idea will never, under any circumstance, emerge in its pure form manifesting predicted consequences.

While large segments of the American right heaped scorn on the counterculture for its anti-Americanism, vulgar Marxism, and utter lack of appreciation, the neoconservatives agreed—but deepened this attack. The New Left was reacting not only to the Vietnam War, "impersonal" universities, or Jim Crow laws, but to the lack of spiritual nourishment in bourgeois America. And frankly, the neoconservatives conceded, there was something to the claim that bourgeois society fails to provide the sense of transcendent purpose that such a moral and cultural animal as man demands. That is why, after all, capitalism does not deserve three cheers and religion is so important. Renunciation of a worldly life void of identifiably transcendent meaning was a small price to pay for this moral satisfaction and ultimate comfort, this sense of contentment in a confused world. Idealism is a natural human sentiment, and people will sacrifice a lot for ideals, even seemingly irrational and ultimately unattainable ones.

Historically speaking, such sacrifice is rather common—so common, in fact, that for large parts of human history, giving of oneself completely to one's country, religion, or culture was considered the natural way of things. But the bourgeois, enmeshed in a web of private concerns and personal duties, does not understand such stirrings and is unable to evaluate another who seeks the transcendent. Indeed, he is likely to be impressed by the attendant sacrifice, perhaps not asking seriously what the goal of the sacrifice is and whether it is morally worthy. Thus, it was not surprising that the New Left was called "idealist," or "the best generation ever," as it did rather absurd things in the name of what the neoconservatives easily recognized as vulgar, infantile ideologies. The neoconservatives did not just denounce the New Left—though they did plenty of that—but they provided an alternative vision, an idealism for those who appreciate society as it stands but yearn to make it better.

This idealism does not denounce the world; it embraces it, at least when properly constituted in a bourgeois mold. It celebrates freedom, but only if freedom is defined properly—if it does not tolerate licentiousness, but rather stresses that man is free to live a virtuous life. There are a lot of ways to manifest virtue—through religious faith, by raising children, actively participating in mediating structures and in the arenas of public discourse and political life, or by making a productive career amidst the infinite possibilities available in a vibrant capitalist economy. The nexus of freedom and community need not be unpleasant—and legions of thinkers have taught us how to make it peaceful—but it can become as bloody a crossroads as the one that Lionel Trilling said is formed by the intersection of literature and politics. Those who are too intellectually timid, complacent, or shortsighted to take the hard stances necessary to defend this precious arrangement are, to the neoconservatives, morally culpable for the consequences of their ideas or lack of ideas. The neoconservatives directed this critique at liberalism, which, from the 1950s to the present day, never took its own principles seriously enough to stand for them. And for the neoconservatives, a group that considers ideas with the utmost seriousness, there can be no greater intellectual treason.

But the neoconservatives took their ideas seriously, and the consequences are evident. Current debates over a panoply of issues, from the welfare state to religion in the public square, are conducted with the ideas and sometimes the very language employed by contributors to *Commentary* and *The Public Interest* two and three decades ago. The Supreme Court may follow election returns, but American political debate follows the Kristols.

The neoconservatives have had such success because they have stuck to their principles, which are firmly anchored in the American democratic ethos. The neoconservative vision is both inclusive and restrained; it is based on virtues accessible to all—enterprise, appreciation, fortitude, and commitment to community. While chastening experience inoculated them from the simplistic liberal view of integration, the neoconservatives nonetheless sought a true pluralism, where all groups could coexist peacefully without sacrificing their valuable identities. People of any race, religion, or ethnicity could be welcome citizens of America so long as they shared a basic consensus of values, aspirations, and moral sentiments. This is why the neoconservatives were such passionate supporters of civil rights, and why they spoke with special authority when they vigorously opposed all efforts to classify and separate Americans on the basis of race—in the form of segregation or affirmative action. Nathan Glazer's classic *Affirmative Discrimination* and the many other neoconservative works on the subject might not have convinced their opponents immediately, but they laid the theoretical groundwork for a return to the meritocratic ideal.

Today, it is the neoconservative case against affirmative action that pervades the land. The neoconservatives never framed the issue in terms of white men being discriminated against; the same can be said for Newt Gingrich and his Republican legions. As neoconservatives from Thomas Sowell to Nathan Glazer to Irving Kristol have painstakingly demonstrated, the true tragedy of affirmative action is its devastating unintended consequences. The neoconservatives have successfully infused the debate with the idea that "affirmative action" is a capricious misnomer. Having once demanded that American institutions make a special effort to include members of historically disadvantaged groups, affirmative action rapidly disintegrated into a balkanizing nightmare where people scramble to attach themselves to racial and ethnic identities in order to receive naked preferences apportioned by quota. But the true tragedy, the neoconservatives have stressed, is that the intended beneficiaries are the ones who suffer the most. Successful blacks, women, Hispanics, and any other "minority" covered under an affirmative action plan are often confronted—usually silently—with the noxious question, "Is he or she a quota hire?"

Even more disturbing is the philosophical basis of affirmative action—that its "beneficiaries" need the special treatment. As the neoconservative social scientist Glenn Loury claims, when Rutgers President Francis Lawrence created an uproar in early 1995 by declaring that blacks needed special preference because of their genetic inferiority, he was merely articulating the basis for affirmative action implicitly shared by many white liberals.[8] Even to hardened supporters of affirmative action, these arguments make sense; who today offers a serious, moral defense of affirmative action, at least as presently constituted? Instead, supporters of affirmative action deny that they support quotas or just change the subject by calling their opponents racist.

A similar dynamic is at work with the welfare state. *National Review* conservatives opposed the welfare state from the beginning, on principle: they saw it as a fundamental usurpation of freedom and a dangerous concentration of power and money in the hands of a largely incompetent federal government. But as William Buckley indicated, the neoconservatives do not make so comprehensive a case against the welfare state. Neoconservatives have been able to delegitimize much of the welfare state by stressing how the unintended consequences of various programs have harmed its supposed beneficiaries. At the same time, neoconservatives and their sympathizers offer ways that an energetic government can help to strengthen families, reinforce the bourgeois ethic, provide security for the elderly and opportunities for the disadvantaged. And this case is not only much better, but far more effective than broad cases against "big government" or "the liberal welfare state" per se.

Prudent intellectuals aware of the limits of their craft, the neoconservatives do not propose a comprehensive, state-run program to replace the welfare state they have come to believe is so destructive. Instead, Irving Kristol offers a principle. "The essential purpose of politics, after all, is to transmit to our children a civilization and a nation that they can be proud of. This means we should figure out what we want before we calculate what we can afford, not the reverse, which is the normal conservative predisposition."[9] A conservative welfare state should express conservative principles; therefore, Kristol reasons, it is fine to provide generous assistance to mothers on welfare who, because of divorce, widowhood, or abandonment, need short-term help. But welfare mothers who have children when they are not married deserve neither our compassion nor our money—though a far smaller allowance should provide for their children. And able-bodied men should receive no government assistance whatsoever. They should visit the Salvation Army. A perfect arrangement? Of course not, Kristol concedes—but one that is politically possible and better than what we have now.[10]

Social problems like those in our cities are, according to the neoconservatives, far too complicated for any one solution to "work." What is good, Midge Decter asks, about sending mothers of three-year-olds to work? But what is the alternative?[11] James Q. Wilson summarizes the neoconservative case on welfare in one title to a *Wall Street Journal* column: "A New Approach to Welfare Reform: Humility."[12] Even William Kristol—the best example of how neoconservatism has defined what we now call conservatism—proposes no overhaul of specific programs or departments. Instead, in classic neoconservative style, he proposes a new problematic with which to consider the public services traditionally supplied by the government.

In his 1994 Bradley Lecture at the American Enterprise Institute, Kristol said that conservatives concerned with eliminating the Department of Education or bringing back school prayer may never accomplish their goals directly. But conservatives can win the battle for school choice, where the government would provide all parents with vouchers they can use to send their children to religious schools. Similarly, conservatives were never able to win even a battle in their effort to reform—let alone privatize—the U.S. Postal Service, despite popular support. But that fight is no longer so necessary. In the early 1970s, Fred Smith started Federal Express to compete with the Postal Service, and the Postal Service was not allowed to retain its absolute monopoly. William Kristol explains, "it is politically easier to defend a small business from the government than to break up a huge government monopoly." Complementary efforts to make communication more efficient are being executed by technological developments such as fax machines. Under the weight of this competition, even the Postal Service has become more competitive. Not inculcated with a blind animus against government, William Kristol is able to see the specific ways in which it fails—and propose to the Republicans policies that reflect his idea that "instead of changing government institutions, people will simply go around them."[13] And there is no shortage of neoconservative ideas or institutions helping them do so.

When asked, "What is the legacy of the French Revolution?" the Chinese Communist leader Chou En-lai replied that it is too soon to tell. The same can be said for the neoconservatives; we have just begun to see the intended consequences of their ideas and—in good neoconservative fashion—must await the unintended consequences as well. But it is safe to say that the neoconservatives have helped to bring about what Edmund Burke called "the most important of all revolutions . . . a revolution in sentiments, manners and moral opinions."[14] Their ideological development over the past fifty years has culminated in what we know identify as American conservatism; in that sense, they have been so successful that it is now appropriate to drop the prefix "neo" from their appellation. But the neoconservatives have not left behind a party platform or a set of position papers, but a set of principles that will be applied to social and political questions that have not even been conceived yet. And the guiding light behind their project is best articulated by George Will: "What Irving's career has affirmed is not only that slogans are no substitute for ideas, and not only that ideas have consequences, but that only ideas have large and lasting consequences."[15]

Notes

1. George Will in "Toasts and Remarks Delivered at a Dinner in Honor of Irving Kristol on his Seventy-fifth Birthday" (Washington: American Enterprise Institute, January 21, 1995) p. 5.

2. See Mickey Kaus, "Pat Answers," *The New Republic* (June 5, 1995) p. 4.

3. George Will, *Statecraft as Soulcraft* (New York: Simon and Schuster, 1986) p. 16.

4. John Maynard Keynes, *The General Theory of Employment, Interest and Money* (New York: Harcourt, Brace and World, 1936) pp. 383–84.

5. James Q. Wilson reflects on the early rationalism of the neoconservatives in his essay, "On the Rediscovery of Character," *The Public Interest* (Fall 1985) p. 3–16.

6. Irving Kristol, "The Stupid Party." *Wall Street Journal* (January 15, 1976).

7. Irving Kristol, "A Conservative Welfare State." *Wall Street Journal* (June 14, 1993) p. 14.

8. Juan Williams, "White Man's Burden." *Washington Post National Weekly Edition* (April 10–16) p. 24.

9. "A Conservative Welfare State," p. 14.

10. "A Conservative Welfare State," p. 14.

11. Midge Decter, response to question at forum at Temple Beth Shalom in Livingston, N.J., April 1, 1995.

12. James Q. Wilson, "A New Approach to Welfare Reform: Humility," *Wall Street Journal* (December 29, 1994) p. 10.

13. William Kristol, "The Future of Conservatism in the U.S.," *The American Enterprise* (July-August 1994) pp. 32–37.

14. Edmund Burke, *Reflections on the Revolution in France*. J. G. A. Pocock, ed. (Indianapolis: Hackett, 1987) p. 70.

15. "Toasts and Remarks," p. 5.

Index

Hughes, H. Stuart, 79
Hutchins, Robert, 57

About the Author

Mark Gerson's work has been published in *The New Republic, The Wall Street Journal, Commentary,* and many other publications. He is the editor of *The Essential Neoconservative Reader* (Addison Wesley, 1996) and author of *In the Classroom* (Free Press, 1996). A 1994 summa cum laude graduate of Williams College, Gerson is currently attending Yale Law School.